TABLE OF CONTENTS

DENNIS EISEN, Ph.D.

BUYING STOCKS

WITHOUT

M🛡NEY

HOW LONG-TERM EQUITY OPTIONS CAN BE
USED TO BUILD WEALTH AND ACQUIRE STOCK
WITH LITTLE RISK AND NO CAPITAL

Lakeside Publishers
Rockville, Maryland

1ST EDITION

Published by **Lakeside Publishers,** 13408 Glen Lea Way, Rockville, MD 20850-3638 • Phone: (301) 762-1441 • Fax: (301) 762-1206 • Toll free: (800) 304-1802 • E-mail: LakePubs@aol.com

Publisher's Cataloging in Publication Data
Eisen, Dennis.
  Buying stocks without money : how long-term equity options can be used to build wealth and aquire stocks with little risk and no capital / Dennis Eisen. – 1st ed.
  p. cm.
  Includes bibliographical references and index.
  ISBN 0-9653713-1-X

  1. Stock options. 2. Investments. I. Title

HG6042.E57 1998 332.63'228 QBI98-687

PREFACE

There comes a time in the life of every investor when he or she runs out of money to invest. The birth of a baby, the purchase of a home, a second child, braces, another baby (oops!), and, later on, tuition payments, wedding expenses, a second home—all of these can temporarily suspend regular investment plans. Permanent crimps in investing can arise when retirement plans are fully funded or retirement itself commences. Professionals and nonprofessionals alike are subject to the laws of supply and demand, and can find themselves at times between jobs, underemployed, or just plain out of work. These things happen to us all, and for most, the idea of maintaining regular investment plans during such tribulations seems impossible. Where would the money come from?

I myself had been a regular investor for over three decades, faithfully putting aside the dollars needed for retirement and stuffing them into stocks, bonds, and mutual funds. Imagine my surprise the day my financial advisor informed me that my retirement plan was now fully funded. This was a good-news/bad-news situation. The good news was that I would now be able to retire at sixty percent of my peak earnings for the rest of my life. The bad news was that as a compulsive saver and avid investor, I would no longer be able to contribute new capital with which to play the market, either for the purpose of buying new issues or for acquiring additional shares of my favorite companies. I could certainly sell existing equities to do such things, but as an inveterate "buy-and-hold" investor, I was loath to trade in any of my equity holdings.

My need to continue my investment program beyond what I was legally permitted to contribute to my retirement plan was driven by four concerns:

—What would happen if I outlived what the actuarial tables said were going to be my golden years?

—Would there be enough in my retirement plan that I could spoil my grandchildren while I was still alive, yet leave enough in my estate for my wife, my children, and (alas) the cut due the Internal Revenue Service?

—I knew I would miss the research, discussions, evaluations, and decision making that go into the selection and buying of stocks.

—And, hey, the difference between being an old man and an elderly gentleman is *money*.

The first strategy that occurred to me for continuing my investment program was to go on margin. Most brokers will lend you up to fifty percent of the value of your account to buy more stocks. The trouble with this method is that one has to repay these funds with interest. The interest rate is high—often higher than what can be safely earned on bonds, preferred stock, and even the appreciation on many "growth" stocks. Furthermore, the specter of a dreaded margin call because of a market slump, however temporary, certainly made me (as it does most investors) very leery.

It then occurred to me that there is a great way to acquire stocks without trading what you've got or using borrowed funds. Simply stated, the method involves the sale of long-term options on highly rated companies, using the premiums received to further your investment program. There is no interest paid on the funds received; the funds never have to be repaid (because they have not been borrowed); and the equity requirements needed to do this are much lower than those for regular margin buying. Although I adapted and perfected this technique to suit my own needs and situation, it can be used by any investor who has built up some measure of equity and would like to acquire additional stocks without contributing additional capital. As we shall see later, the potential benefits far outweigh any incremental risks, especially when appropriate hedges and proper safeguards are incorporated.

What makes this technique so effective is that it exploits the fact that option prices do not reflect the expected long-term growth rates of the underlying equities. The reason for this is that standard option pricing formulas, used by option traders everywhere, do not incorporate this variable. With short-term options, this doesn't matter. With long-term options, however, this oversight often leads the market to overvalue premiums. Taking advantage of this mispricing is the foundation of my strategy.

I have been using this technique for the past four years—very cautiously at first, because of the newness of these long-term options (they were only invented in 1990) and the almost complete lack of information regarding their safety and potential. It was this lack of analysis that led me to start my own research into the realm of long-term equity options. Having determined their relative risk/reward ratio, I am now very comfortable generating several thousand dollars a month in premiums which I use to add to my stock positions. I am often told that what I am doing is much akin to what a fire or hazard insurance company does, generating premiums and paying claims as they arise. A better analogy might be to a title insurance company, for with proper research, claims should rarely occur.

This book is divided into four sections: The first one consists of Chapters 1 through 5 and describes the basic approach in using long-term options to further investment programs. The second section, Chapters 6 through 12, refines this approach and shows how to institute controls to reduce risk. The potential reward and the long-term safety of the basic approach and refinements are established through extensive computer simulation and backtesting. This is accomplished by going back ten years and asking what would have been the outcome if the various techniques had been applied in as consistent a manner as possible during that time period.

The third section, Chapters 13 through 15, contains the analytic formulas for the rapid computation of volatility and option premiums for both European- and American-style options. The 1997 Nobel prize in economics was awarded to Myron Scholes and Robert Merton, who along with Fischer Black were the original developers of these formulas. With minor variations, they are still used today for calculating option premiums by market makers and option traders alike. Although college mathematics is needed to understand the formulas, the short, simple algorithms given for their numerical evaluation can be used by virtually anyone who knows BASIC or can set up a spreadsheet on a personal computer. For readers without access to computer tools, there are various appendices containing tables for looking up option premiums and assignment probabilities.

Finally, Chapters 16 and 17 contain suggested resources for additional information, including Internet websites and capsule reviews of introductory, intermediate, and advanced books on options.

The methods developed in this book are based on my three decades of investing in real estate and the equities market, plus the modeling experience gained through the development of analytic, decision-making tools for various agencies of the federal government and numerous trade associations, research institutes, and private-sector clients. My first book, ***Decision Making in Federal Real Estate: How the Government Decides Whether and with Whom to Buy, Build or Lease,*** remains the classic in its field.

I wish to thank the various investment analysts and members of the brokerage industry for their insightful comments and suggestions. These include Ed Elfenbein, publisher of the *Microcap Stock Digest,* who reviewed and edited the manuscript, and Charlie Meyers, senior vice president for investments at Legg Mason Wood Walker, Inc., who introduced me to the world of options. Thanks also to Susan Hough of S&H Graphics and Jack Price of Signature Book Printing for their superb efforts in cover design and book production. I am particularly grateful to the numerous investors like myself that I have met in investment chat rooms on America Online. I know them only by their internet screen names, but their collective insights into the stock and options markets added much to my own knowledge. More than that, I found the instant feedback of such interactions to be invaluable as I bounced new ideas off a jury of my peers and refined my own thoughts in the process. Finally, I owe special thanks to my wife, Doris, for the encouragement she provided and sacrifices she made to keep me at this task until the job was done.

PART I:
THE BASIC APPROACH

1

CHAPTER 1

INTRODUCTION

What is an Option?

Although options are typically bought and sold through security dealers and brokers, it is important to understand that options are not securities. Unlike stocks, warrants, or corporate bonds, options are not authorized or issued by any company on its behalf. Rather, an option is simply a contract between two parties, a buyer and a seller. The buyer is often referred to as the owner or option *holder*, and the seller is often referred to as the option *writer*. A call option gives the option holder the right to *buy* an asset at a set price within a certain time, while a put option gives the option holder the right to *sell* an asset at a set price within a certain time. In neither case is the option holder ever obligated to buy or sell.

For an example of an option contract, let us suppose that you're in the market for a new car. Sitting there in the dealer's showroom is that spectacular model you'd love to own. It being popular, there is little discount from the sticker price of $40,000. You tell the salesman that you get your bonus in three months. Anxious to make a deal, he says, "Okay, the price may well go up between now and then, but if you give us a nonrefundable check for $250 today, I'll guarantee that price for the next 90 days. Not only that, but if the price goes down, you can back out of the deal." This sounds good to you, so you write the dealer a check for $250. Congratulations! You have just entered into a bona fide option contract.

Why did this seem like a good idea to you? By the terms of the deal, no matter how high the sticker price goes in the next 90 days, your effective purchase price will be just $40,250, including the "premium" you paid of $250. If the sticker price were to increase by 10%, to $44,000, you would be $3,750 ahead of the game. On the other hand, if the sticker price dropped to $39,000 (and such things can happen), your effective price would be $39,250, including the $250 premium. This is because by the terms of the deal, you are not obligated to buy the car for $40,000, and are free to buy it from that dealership or anywhere else at the market price of $39,000. In that situation, you would still be $750 better off than if you had purchased the car for $40,000 today.

But that's not all. Having just written that check for $250, you are then asked by the salesman if you would like to buy "lemon" insurance. "What's that?" you ask. "Well," says the salesman, "for just $100 more, I will give you the privilege of selling the car back to me at whatever price you paid for it within 30 days of purchase, no questions asked." This too sounds good, and you write the dealer a check for another $100. Congratulations again: you have just entered into your second option contract of the day.

The first option contract is a classic example of a call option, because it gave you the right, but not the obligation, to buy the car. The second option contract is a classic example of a put option, because it gave you the right, but not the obligation, to sell (i.e., "put" back) the car to the dealership. Notice that, when used in this manner, both option contracts served to reduce risk. The first (the call option) protects you against an unanticipated price increase, and the second (the put option) protects you against buying a "lemon." You may not realize it at first, but the second one also protects you against a significant price decrease right after buying the car. For if the price did drop to $39,000 within 30 days of buying the car for $40,000, in principle you could return the car to the dealer, get your money back, and buy an equivalent new one for $39,000. (In practice, the dealership would likely refund the difference in cash—which is just as good as far as you're concerned.)

Whether it entailed a call or a put, the option involved was essentially characterized by three principal variables: the buy/sell price of the underlying asset (the car), the time period during which the option could be exercised (30 or 90 days), and the premium involved ($100 or $250). One other important feature of at least the call option in this case is that it likely is transferable. If you had decided not to buy the car within the 90-day time period, you could have sold the option to a friend for whatever price the two of you agreed upon. If the sticker price had indeed increased to $44,000, that right to buy the car for $40,000 would be worth more than the $250 you originally paid for it. On the other hand, if the price had gone down or remained the same, the value of the right to buy the car for $40,000 would have shrunk to zero by the time the 90-day period expired.

Option contracts in which the underlying assets are corporate stocks do not differ in principle from the ones described above and are also characterized by the buy/sell price of the underlying asset (the stock), the time period during which the option can be exercised, and the premium involved. The difference is that in the case of investment assets, option contracts are used for a much wider range of purposes, including not only risk reduction, but also profit enhancement and leveraged control.

People often use option contracts to decrease the risk associated with stock ownership. Suppose you own 100 shares of Intel and want to protect yourself against a significant drop in value. Wouldn't it be nice to have someone else contractually promise to buy those shares from you for a guaranteed amount no matter what, even if the price fell to zero? That person will want a reasonable fee for providing that assurance, of course. As with fire or auto insurance, you hope never to file a claim. But if loss did occur because a house collapsed (or stock plummeted), financial disaster can be averted or substantially mitigated, depending on the terms of the policy and extent of coverage elected. In this type of situation, an option contract is the exact analog of an insurance policy.

Another reason people use options is to enhance portfolio income. Those 100 shares of Intel you own are probably not paying a dividend worth writing home about. For a reasonable fee, you might grant someone else the right to purchase those 100 shares from you, within a specified time period, at a price pegged above today's market value. Real estate operators and land owners do this all the time, offering tenants or developers the right to purchase property at a specified price by some future date in return for an up-front cash payment. If the right to purchase is exercised, that's fine, because it means the owner got his or her price. If the right to purchase expires without exercise, that's okay too, because the extra cash augments whatever rental payments are being received—thereby increasing the effective yield rate. In either event, the up-front payment is retained by the property owner.

The third reason people use options is to control a large amount of stock without having to buy or own it. Suppose an investor feels that Intel (or any other stock) is about to rise significantly in price. Wouldn't it be nice to pay a current owner of that stock a reasonable fee for the right to purchase his or her shares at a mutually agreed upon price within a certain period of time? In this situation, the potential purchaser is the exact analog of the real estate developer in the example above, who seeks to control a potential project without committing valuable cash resources until market conditions warrant.

Investors who believe a stock is about to "tank" also enter into option contracts for the right to sell a stock within a specified period of time at a price reflecting its current value. Such a transaction is simpler and requires much less cash than taking on the potentially unlimited risk associated with "short selling." (A short sale is where the investor borrows shares of a stock and sells them in the hope that they can be subsequently purchased back at a lower price and the shares then returned to the original shareholder. Substantial collateral is required and numerous technical conditions must be met to conduct short sales.)

Features of Standardized Equity Options

If every component and clause had to be negotiated each time an option contract was set up, the options market would grind to a halt. To maintain a rapid but orderly options market, option contracts are assigned six standard parameters: *product, type, unit of trade, strike price, expiration date,* and *style.*

1. *Product.* Options are distinguished by the underlying *product* involved: if it is one of several market indexes, such as Standard & Poor's 100 (S&P 100), the option is called an *index* option. If the underlying product involves common stock, it is called an *equity* option. Besides index and equity options, options are now available

on interest rates, Treasury securities, commodities, and futures. We will deal exclusively with equity options in this book.

2. *Type.* Options are also classified by the type of privilege (either buying or selling) granted the option holder. As we have seen, a call option gives the option holder the right to purchase a specified number of shares, ordinarily 100, of the underlying security at a specified price at any time within a specified period. In contrast, a put option gives the option holder the right to sell a specified number of shares, ordinarily 100, of the underlying security at a specified price at any time within a specified period. The price specified in the option contract is referred to as the *exercise* or *strike* price, and the last day on which this right to purchase or sell can be exercised is called the *expiration* date. A typical call option (or simply, call) might be for the right to buy 100 shares of Intel at $120 per share at any time up to and including the third Friday in April. A typical put option (or simply, put) might be for the right to sell 100 shares of Intel at $120 per share during the same period.

Note that the holder of a call does not have to exercise his or her right to purchase. Similarly, the holder of a put does not have to exercise his or her right to sell. This lack of obligation on the part of option holders is one of the major differences between an option and a futures contract. On the other hand, option writers (sellers) are obligated to sell (in the case of call options) or buy (in the case of put options) the agreed-upon number of shares at the agreed-upon price if the option holder exercises his or her rights within the time period specified in the option contract.

3. *Unit of trade.* The number of shares specified in an option contract is called the *unit of trade.* As mentioned above, it is ordinarily 100 shares of the underlying equity. In the event of stock splits, mergers, and acquisitions, the unit of trade is adjusted accordingly. For example, when Travelers, Inc., split 4:3 in 1997, the unit of trade for existing option contracts became 133 shares. When 3Com Corporation merged with U.S. Robotics that same year, 1.75 shares of COMS were exchanged for each share of USRX; the unit of trade of the existing option contracts on USRX thus became 175 shares of 3Com (with corresponding adjustments in the exercise price). It is even possible for the unit of trade to be less than 100 shares, which

would be the case when there are reverse stock splits (wherein a greater number of shares is exchanged for a lesser number of shares of the underlying security).

4. *Strike price.* Strike price intervals for standard equity options are set in increments of $2.50 when the price of the underlying equity ("stock price") is between $5 and $25, $5.00 when the stock price is between $25 and $200, and $10.00 when the stock price is over $200. Options are ordinarily not available on stocks priced under $5. Strike prices are adjusted for splits, major stock dividends, recapitalizations, spin-offs, etc., when and if they occur during the life of the option.

5. *Expiration date.* At any given time there are four potential expiration dates available for standard option contracts. These are the *current* or *spot* month, the immediate *following* month, an *intermediate* month, and a *far* month, the last being not more than eight months away. Whichever expiration month is chosen, option contracts always expire at noon on the Saturday following the third Friday of that month. Because trading stops on the day prior to formal expiration (with Saturday morning activity reserved for broker corrections and clearing house operations), from the viewpoint of the investor, the effective expiration date for option contracts is the third Friday of the specified month. It is for this reason that investors usually speak in terms of "expiration Friday." See the section below on *option cycles* for further information on expiration dates.

6. *Style.* Option contracts are also classified by the basis of the window during which option holders may exercise their rights. American-style options give holders the right to buy or sell at any time prior to expiration of the option. Holders of European-style option contracts may exercise their rights during a very limited time period, ordinarily on the day of or day before expiration. At present, all exchange-traded equity options are American-style.

Puts Versus Short Sales

It is certainly cheaper and ordinarily far less risky to buy a put option than to effect a short sale of a stock. Say Intel is at $120 a share and an investor believes it to be overpriced. The margin or collateral requirement to effect a short sale of 100 shares of Intel at $120 is

150% of the stock price—$18,000 in this case. The first $12,000 of this are the proceeds received from the sale of the stock. These funds must be left on deposit to ensure the short seller will return those borrowed shares. The additional $6,000 that must be deposited in this case helps to guarantee that the short seller will be able to replace the borrowed shares in the event that the price of Intel stock rises rather than falls. This additional amount also serves as the source of funds for any dividends that the original shareholder is entitled to along the way.

On the other hand, suppose the Intel puts with a strike price of $120 command a premium of $8 a share. The margin requirement in this case will be the premium cost of $800 plus 20% of the stock value, or just $3,200 in all. Besides the much greater margin required, short selling can be particularly risky because of the potential for unlimited loss should the stock rise rather than fall. In addition to this, the short seller must arrange for the borrowing of shares (often difficult in the case of thinly traded issues) and wait for an uptick in price, whereas the put buyer can act immediately.

Option Class and Series

All option contracts on the same underlying security and having the same *type* (put versus call) and *style* (American versus European) are referred to as constituting an option *class*. Thus, TWA (Trans World Airlines) calls comprise an option class, as do Intel puts.

Further, all option contracts within the same class and having the same *unit of trade* (i.e., 100 shares), *strike* price, and *expiration* date are referred to as comprising an option *series*. Thus, the July 1999 Intel $100 calls constitute an option series, as do the April 2000 General Electric $85 puts.

Since we seem to have covered all the parameters, what else is left that might distinguish one option from another belonging to the same series? The answer is the particular *stock exchange* where the various options are traded. For example, TWA options are independently traded on the American, Chicago, and Philadelphia Stock Exchanges. Thus, an October 1998 TWA $10 call option contract purchased on the American Stock Exchange can be closed by a sale of the equivalent option contract on the Philadelphia Stock Exchange. The purchase and sale of these two option contracts will precisely offset each other because the contracts belong to the same option series.

Premiums

A common characteristic of all contracts, including options, is that they involve consideration. For option holders this refers to the right to exercise the option at the price and terms specified. For option writers, it is the *premium*, or amount of money paid to them by the option buyers for those exercise rights. Whether or not the option is ever exercised by the option holder, the option writer retains the premium. It is universally acknowledged that there are seven factors that determine the premium:

- Current stock price
- Exercise or strike price
- Time to expiration
- Current risk-free interest rate
- Cash dividends
- Option style (European vs. American)
- Volatility of the underlying equity

The first three parameters (stock price, strike price, and expiration date) are part of every option contract and are readily understood. The next three parameters (the risk-free interest rate,* dividends, and option style) certainly have an effect on premiums, but only in a relatively minor way. The final parameter, volatility, measures the degree to which the price of the stock fluctuates from day to day. What is important to understand is that the greater the volatility and the longer the time to expiration, the higher the premium. This is because the greater the daily fluctuation in stock price and the longer the duration of coverage, the greater the uncertainty as to where the stock price will be at any subsequent moment. Equally crucial is the fact that option premiums *do not ordinarily reflect the expected rate of growth* of the stock price. A

---

*The risk-free interest rate is regarded as the interest rate on U.S. Treasury bills of the same duration as the option.

demonstration of this remarkable fact is given in Chapter 13. It is this phenomenon that forms the basis of the investment approach developed in this book.

Exercise and Assignment

If and when an option holder decides to exercise his or her option to buy or sell, the brokerage firm sends a notice to exercise to the Options Clearing Corporation (OCC), which in turn assigns fulfillment of that option to a current option writer of the same series, on either a random or a first-in, first-out basis. The OCC, created in 1972, serves not only as a clearing house for option trades but also as the ultimate guarantor of contract performance. Upon receipt and verification of the terms of the option contract at the time it was made between buyer and seller (and checking that they match in all respects), the OCC steps in and severs the contractual relationship between the parties, thus becoming the "buyer" to every option writer and the "writer" to every option holder. Owing to this, it does not matter that the original option writer (or every writer for that particular series) may have disappeared from the face of the Earth.

Option Codes

To facilitate trading, options are symbolized by a three- to five-character trading symbol, made up of a root symbol designating the underlying equity, a single letter designating the expiration month, and a single letter designating the strike price. The tables below contain the expiration month codes and strike price codes for whole- and half-dollar amounts. I keep a copy of these tables pinned on the wall by my telephone.

Let's consider some examples. For most stocks listed on the New York and American Stock Exchanges, the root symbol for the option (no matter where the option itself is traded) is the same as its ordinary trading symbol. Thus, the March $145 Gillette calls are coded as G (for Gillette) + C (March call) + I ($145), or GCI. The November $90 Boeing calls are coded as BA (for Boeing) + K (November call) + R ($90), or BAKR. The June $67½

Table 1.1: Expiration Month Codes

	Jan	Feb	Mar	Apr	May	Jun	Jul	Aug	Sep	Oct	Nov	Dec
Calls	A	B	C	D	E	F	G	H	I	J	K	L
Puts	M	N	O	P	Q	R	S	T	U	V	W	X

Table 1.2: Strike Price Codes (Whole Dollars)

A	$5	$105	$205	$305	$405	$505	$605	$705
B	10	110	210	310	410	510	610	710
C	15	115	215	315	415	515	615	715
D	20	120	220	320	420	520	620	720
E	25	125	225	325	425	525	625	725
F	30	130	230	330	430	530	630	730
G	35	135	235	335	435	535	635	735
H	40	140	240	340	440	540	640	740
I	45	145	245	345	445	545	645	745
J	50	150	250	350	450	550	650	750
K	55	155	255	355	455	555	655	755
L	60	160	260	360	460	560	660	760
M	65	165	265	365	465	565	665	765
N	70	170	270	370	470	570	670	770
O	75	175	275	375	475	575	675	775
P	80	180	280	380	480	580	680	780
Q	85	185	285	385	485	585	685	785
R	90	190	290	390	490	590	690	790
S	95	195	295	395	495	595	695	795
T	100	200	300	400	500	600	700	800

Table 1.3: Strike Price Codes (Half Dollars)

U	7½	37½	67½	97½	127½	157½	187½	217½
V	12½	42½	72½	102½	132½	162½	192½	222½
W	17½	47½	77½	107½	137½	167½	197½	227½
X	22½	52½	82½	112½	142½	172½	202½	232½
Y	27½	57½	87½	117½	147½	177½	207½	237½
Z	32½	62½	92½	122½	152½	182½	212½	242½

America Online puts are coded as AOL (for America Online) + R (June put) + U ($67½), or AOLRU.

In the first example for Gillette, the option trading symbol GCI happens to coincide with the stock trading symbol that is used for the Gannett Company. In the second example for Boeing, the option trading symbol BAKR happens to coincide with the stock trading symbol for Baker Communications. Because of such potential conflicts, brokerage houses and options exchanges preface option trading symbols with some sort of character which unambiguously signals that what follows is an option, not a stock. Quotation requests submitted to the Chicago Board Options Exchange (CBOE) use a period, so that .GCI and .BAKR designate the particular options quotes on Gillette and Boeing, while GCI and BAKR are used for the stock quotes on Gannett and Baker. Because the decimal point is sometimes hard to see, some brokerage houses use the prefix "Q" in transmitting orders to their trading desks, thus coding the examples given as QGCI, QBAKR, and QAOLRU. (The letter Q can be safely used this way because no stock symbols on any of the exchanges where options are traded begin with that letter.)

Because the trading symbols for NASDAQ stocks have at least four characters in them, they are all assigned three-letter option symbols which often have no relation to the trading symbol. For example, Intel (INTC) has the option symbol INQ, Ascend Communications (ASND) has the option symbol QQA, and Madge Networks (MADGF) the option symbol MQE. Because very few stock symbols even contain the letter Q, this letter is often utilized in this manner so as to avoid conflict with already existing trading symbols. Thus, October $100 Intel calls are coded as INQ (for Intel) + J (October call) + T ($100), or INQJT, and March $30 Ascend puts are coded as QQA (for Ascend) +O (March put) + F ($30), or QQAOF.

The system described seems pretty simple at first blush. A difficulty, however, arises when a stock is so volatile that the spread in strike prices would require more than one occurrence of the same price code for the same expiration month. In those circumstances, the various exchanges that set up trading symbols are sometimes forced to adopt an alternative option symbol for the underlying stock, or even to assign price code symbols that bear little relation to the above tables for strike price. Thus, the January 1998 Intel $45 puts were coded by the American Stock Exchange as NQMI (rather than INQMI), the August 1997 Intel $67.50 calls were coded as INQHW (rather than INQHU), and the July 1997 Intel $87.50 puts were coded as INQSB (rather than INQSY).

Half-dollar amounts typically arise as a result of 2:1 stock splits. For stock splits other than 2:1 (for example, 3:1 or 4:3), the resulting trading symbols can often be even more arbitrary.

In view of this, utmost care must be given to determining the proper option codes before transacting trades or submitting such requests to brokers. Because of the large number of options available and the fact that new strike positions and expiration months are continually being created, no printed list of symbol tables could possibly be kept timely enough. One of the best on-line sources for obtaining accurate trading symbols (and with them, bid and ask quotations on a 20-minute delayed basis) is from the Chicago Board Options Exchange (CBOE). Their internet address is *http://www.cboe.com*, and many internet providers expedite the process of connecting to them through the use of an embedded keyword such as "CBOE" or "OPTIONS" (both used by America Online, for example). Access to CBOE is free, and a wealth of material is available from them in addition to delayed quotes and the trading symbols for the calls or puts you are interested in.

Option Cycles

When listed options began trading for the first time, they were each assigned four quarterly expiration dates throughout the year. Cycle 1 options expired in the months of January, April, July, and October. Cycle 2 options expired in the months of February, May, August, and November. And cycle 3 options expired in the months of March, June, September, and December.

The system was subsequently modified so that every equity option has four expiration dates consisting of the nearest two months and two additional months taken from one of the original quarterly cycles. The table below illustrates the system, with the added month shown in bold italics.

The spot month in Table 1.4 refers to the month in which the next expiration date occurs. The spot month begins the Monday after expiration Friday and ends on the following expiration Friday, thus spanning parts of two calendar months. As the spot month opens, options for that month and two other months will have already been trading. If options for the next nearest month do not exist, options for that month will be opened for trading. If options for the two nearest months have already been trading, the fourth option opened for trading will be the next one in sequence from the respective quarterly cycle.

Table 1.4: Standard Options Available

Spot Month	Cycle 1 Options				Cycle 2 Options				Cycle 3 Options			
Jan	Jan	*Feb*	Apr	Jul	Jan	Feb	May	*Aug*	Jan	*Feb*	Mar	Jun
Feb	Feb	*Mar*	Apr	Jul	Feb	*Mar*	May	Aug	Feb	Mar	Jun	*Sep*
Mar	Mar	Apr	Jul	*Oct*	Mar	*Apr*	May	Aug	Mar	*Apr*	Jun	Sep
Apr	Apr	*May*	Jul	Oct	Apr	May	Aug	*Nov*	Apr	*May*	Jun	Sep
May	May	*Jun*	Jul	Oct	May	*Jun*	Aug	Nov	May	Jun	Sep	*Dec*
Jun	Jun	Jul	Oct	*Jan*	Jun	*Jul*	Aug	Nov	Jun	*Jul*	Sep	Dec
Jul	Jul	*Aug*	Oct	Jan	Jul	Aug	Nov	*Feb*	Jul	*Aug*	Sep	Dec
Aug	Aug	*Sep*	Oct	Jan	Aug	*Sep*	Nov	Feb	Aug	Sep	Dec	*Mar*
Sep	Sep	Oct	Jan	*Apr*	Sep	*Oct*	Nov	Feb	Sep	*Oct*	Dec	Mar
Oct	Oct	*Nov*	Jan	Apr	Oct	Nov	Feb	*May*	Oct	*Nov*	Dec	Mar
Nov	Nov	*Dec*	Jan	Apr	Nov	*Dec*	Feb	May	Nov	Dec	Mar	*Jun*
Dec	Dec	Jan	Apr	*Jul*	Dec	*Jan*	Feb	May	Dec	*Jan*	Mar	Jun

A handbook that is particularly useful in dealing with options is the *Directory of Exchange Listed Options,* available without charge from the Options Clearing Corporation (1-800-OPTIONS). The *Directory* contains much useful information, including a list of option trading symbols, option cycles, and the exchange(s) where each option trades.

2

CHAPTER 2

LONG-TERM OPTIONS

Introduction

An incredible number of books have been written on the subject of options and options trading. A search using the keyword "options" on the on-line bookstore Amazon.com yielded over 300 titles, ranging from academic treatises to texts on elementary, intermediate, and advanced trading techniques. There is no particular need for yet another book on how to construct and utilize spreads, straddles, and other option combinations. Instead, the purpose of this book is to highlight the fact that option premiums in general do not reflect the expected long-term growth rate of the underlying equities, and to explain an investment strategy that can be used to take maximum advantage of this phenomenon.

As I mentioned before, my own interest in this subject stems from the fact that I could no longer contribute additional funds to my retirement plan. As a long-term investor in the market, I had assembled a stock portfolio over many years, and I simply did not wish to raise cash by selling any of my winners. My few losers and laggards had long since been disposed of and the proceeds used to buy more shares of my better-performing stocks. I'm not a short-term, in-and-out investor, but I wanted to keep buying.

Options seemed the way to go, but as with stocks, purchasing calls requires money. What's more, options can only be paid for in cash, so going on margin and borrowing the funds from my broker was out of the question. My next thought was, well, if I'm going to raise cash, why not sell covered calls on my portfolio? I tried this a few times and promptly had some of my stocks called away from me when their share prices sharply increased as a result of takeover rumors or (positive) earnings surprises. I wasn't too happy about having to buy back shares using the little cash I had remaining to cover the gap between the exercise price received and the higher repurchase price. So much for covered calls.

By process of elimination, the only strategy remaining was selling puts. This method, you will recall, generates up-front money through the premiums received. Option premiums must be paid on the next business day and so are available for reinvestment even faster than proceeds from the sale of stock (which settle within three business days). And because these funds represent premiums paid, not dollars borrowed, they are yours to keep.

However, as the fine print in most travel ads states, "certain restrictions apply." Premiums have to stay in your account in case they are needed later, in the event of assignment. But because they are in your account, you can use them to acquire additional equities. The problem with this approach, I soon discovered, is that applying it to standard options does not bring in much money, especially in relation to the risk assumed in potentially having the underlying stock assigned to you. You can certainly sell a put whose exercise price is well below the current stock price, thereby minimizing the risk of assignment, but doing this brings in a very small premium.

A larger premium can be generated by selling a put with an exercise price much closer to or just below the current price, but this can entail significant risk of assignment. Substantial premiums seen on out-of-the-money* puts typically indicate highly volatile stocks or instances where the market (probably correctly) anticipates a sharp drop in the value of the underlying equity—situations that had no appeal for me whatsoever.

And if all that isn't enough, there is also the fact that dealing in standard options, with their quickly changing market values, typically requires substantial if not full-time commitment to the task. Most option traders I've met have had little time for anything else during

---

*A put is said to be *out of the money* if the strike price of the put is less than the current stock price. It is *at the money* if the two are essentially equal, and it is *in the money* if the strike price is greater than the stock price.

their working days and have often spent a good deal of their evenings and weekends conducting research into what trades to enter and when to cover and get out. This kind of nerve-wracking, nail-biting, glued-to-the-console environment is not what I wanted either.

It then occurred to me that there was a solution to this dilemma. There does exist a class of options whose premiums are relatively large, which bear less risk than standard options, and which, because the underlying equities are comparatively stable, do not have to be monitored with anywhere near the same intensity as standard options. What distinguishes this class of options is their long-term expiration date, which permits the market price of the underlying equity plenty of time to recover should the overall market, industry sector, or the company itself encounter temporary downturn or adverse conditions. It occurred to me that by selling puts on stronger, well-endowed firms whose intermediate- and long-term prospects are above average, it might be possible to achieve high returns without incurring undue risk.

LEAPS

The class of options that fits this description was actually created by the Chicago Board Options Exchange (CBOE) in 1990. Because standard options expire at most eight months after their inception, the CBOE introduced a new product for investors wishing to hedge common stock positions over a much longer time horizon. Those options, called LEAPS (Long-term Equity AnticiPation Securities), are long-term options on common stocks of companies that are listed on securities exchanges or that trade over the counter. LEAP options expire on the Saturday following the third Friday in the month of January approximately two and a half years from the date of the initial listing. They roll into and become standard options after the May, June, or July expiration date corresponding to the expiration cycle of the underlying security.

In most other ways, LEAPS are identical to standard options. Strike price intervals for LEAPS follow the same rules as standard options; i.e., they are $2.50 when the price of the underlying equity ("stock price") is between $5 and $25, $5.00 when the stock price is between $25 and $200, and $10.00 when the stock price is over $200. As for standard options, strike prices for LEAPS are adjusted for splits, major stock dividends, recapitalizations, spin-offs, etc., when and if they occur during the life of the option. Like standard options, equity LEAPS generally may be exercised on any business day before the expiration date.

Margin requirements for LEAPS follow the same rules as standard options. Uncovered put or call writers must deposit 100% of the option proceeds plus 20% of the aggregate contract value (the current price of the underlying equity multiplied by $100) minus the amount, if any, by which the LEAP option is out of the money. The minimum margin is 100% of the option proceeds plus 10% of the aggregate contract value. We will have a lot to say about margin requirements in Chapter 4.

LEAP Premiums

Option premiums in general vary directly with the remaining time to expiration. As a result of their longer lives, LEAPS have premiums that can be considerably greater than that of their standard-option counterparts. Table 2.1 shows the premiums per share for an at-the-money put option where the stock price and strike price are both $100, the risk-free interest rate is 6%, and the effect of dividends is ignored. As outlined in Chapter 1, the only other parameters are expiration time, stock volatility, and option style. Each entry in the table is the theoretical premium corresponding to the expiration time in months shown in column 1 and the stock volatility, ranging from a fairly low level of 0.15 to a fairly high level of 0.65. The premiums shown were calculated using the simple *Black-Scholes* pricing formula for European-style options that is described in Chapter 14. A more detailed set of premium tables for European-style options appears in Appendix A. For comparison and reference purposes, the analog at-the-money call premiums are shown in Table 2.2.

Intel's stock, for example, has a volatility of about 0.35, so when the stock price is $100, an at-the-money put option should command a premium of $829.60 ($8.296 x 100 shares) with six months to expiration and a premium of $1,313.40 ($13.314 x 100 shares) with 24 months to expiration. Chapter 13 shows how volatility is calculated from historical stock prices.

The at-the-money premiums shown in Table 2.1 for puts and in Table 2.2 for calls scale directly with the price level involved. That is, if the stock price and strike price are both $50, the corresponding per share premiums is exactly half the amounts shown.

The first question people often ask is why the at-the-money call premiums are so much greater than the corresponding put premiums for the same time horizon and volatility level. Note, for example, that for a stock with a volatility of 0.35 and an expiration date 30 months away, the put premium is $14.035 per share, versus $27.964 for the call premium. Isn't this difference due to general inflation and/or the expected growth rate in the underlying equity?

The answer is no. The reason the call premiums are greater is that option pricing models assume that stock prices are just as likely to increase by, say, 10%, as they are to decrease by 10% on any given day. On a cumulative basis, there is therefore no limit to how high prices can go up over time, but there is a definite lower limit (zero) to how low prices can go. It is this possibility of unrestricted price movement upward versus restricted price movement downward that explains why calls are more expensive than puts.

Commissions

There is another major advantage associated with LEAP options. Because of the inherently greater premium levels involved, the brokerage commission charged is going to be a smaller percentage of the proceeds received. At a full-service firm, the brokerage commission to buy or sell a single option might be $45. In percentage terms, this amount is almost 12% of the premium for the one- month Intel option, but just 3.2% of the premium for the 30-month LEAP option. Commission costs per contract rapidly decrease at a full-service firm if more than one contract is involved and might range from $25 to $35 each for three contracts down to just $15 to $20 each for ten contracts.

At a discount broker, the commission might be $20 each, but it is typically subject to a minimum fee of $40 and a maximum fee of $70 on transactions involving one to ten contracts. For on-line, deep-discount, and option-specialized brokers, the commission might be

Table 2.1: European-Style At-the-Money Put Premiums
as a Function of Time and Volatility
Stock Price = $100
Strike Price = $100

Mo	Volatility										
	0.15	0.20	0.25	0.30	0.35	0.40	0.45	0.50	0.55	0.60	0.65
1	1.485	2.057	2.629	3.202	3.776	4.349	4.922	5.495	6.067	6.639	7.211
2	1.965	2.767	3.572	4.378	5.185	5.991	6.797	7.603	8.408	9.212	10.015
3	2.283	3.258	4.237	5.220	6.202	7.185	8.167	9.149	10.128	11.107	12.083
4	2.520	3.636	4.760	5.888	7.018	8.147	9.275	10.401	11.526	12.649	13.769
5	2.705	3.943	5.192	6.447	7.703	8.959	10.214	11.466	12.716	13.963	15.207
6	2.854	4.199	5.560	6.927	8.296	9.665	11.032	12.397	13.758	15.115	16.468
7	2.976	4.419	5.879	7.348	8.819	10.290	11.760	13.225	14.687	16.143	17.594
8	3.079	4.608	6.160	7.722	9.287	10.852	12.414	13.973	15.526	17.073	18.613
9	3.164	4.774	6.410	8.058	9.709	11.361	13.009	14.653	16.291	17.921	19.544
10	3.237	4.920	6.634	8.362	10.094	11.826	13.555	15.278	16.994	18.702	20.400
11	3.298	5.049	6.836	8.639	10.446	12.254	14.057	15.855	17.644	19.423	21.192
12	3.349	5.165	7.020	8.892	10.771	12.649	14.523	16.390	18.248	20.095	21.929
13	3.393	5.267	7.187	9.125	11.071	13.016	14.956	16.889	18.811	20.721	22.617
14	3.429	5.360	7.339	9.340	11.349	13.358	15.361	17.355	19.338	21.307	23.262
15	3.460	5.442	7.479	9.539	11.608	13.677	15.739	17.792	19.832	21.858	23.867
16	3.485	5.516	7.607	9.724	11.850	13.975	16.094	18.203	20.298	22.377	24.437
17	3.505	5.583	7.725	9.895	12.076	14.256	16.429	18.590	20.737	22.866	24.975
18	3.521	5.642	7.834	10.055	12.287	14.519	16.743	18.955	21.151	23.328	25.483
19	3.533	5.696	7.934	10.204	12.486	14.767	17.041	19.300	21.543	23.765	25.964
20	3.542	5.744	8.026	10.343	12.672	15.001	17.321	19.627	21.915	24.180	26.420
21	3.548	5.787	8.111	10.472	12.847	15.222	17.587	19.937	22.267	24.573	26.853
22	3.552	5.825	8.189	10.594	13.012	15.431	17.839	20.231	22.601	24.947	27.264
23	3.553	5.859	8.262	10.707	13.168	15.628	18.077	20.509	22.919	25.302	27.655
24	3.551	5.889	8.329	10.813	13.314	15.815	18.304	20.774	23.222	25.640	28.027
25	3.548	5.915	8.390	10.913	13.452	15.992	18.519	21.026	23.509	25.962	28.382
26	3.543	5.938	8.447	11.006	13.583	16.159	18.723	21.266	23.783	26.269	28.719
27	3.536	5.957	8.499	11.093	13.706	16.318	18.917	21.495	24.044	26.561	29.041
28	3.527	5.974	8.547	11.174	13.822	16.469	19.102	21.712	24.293	26.840	29.348
29	3.517	5.988	8.591	11.251	13.932	16.612	19.277	21.919	24.531	27.106	29.640
30	3.506	6.000	8.631	11.322	14.035	16.747	19.444	22.117	24.757	27.360	29.920

Table 2.2: European-Style At-the-Money Call Premiums as a Function of Time and Volatility
Stock Price = $100
Strike Price = $100

Mo	0.15	0.20	0.25	0.30	0.35	0.40	0.45	0.50	0.55	0.60	0.65
					Volatility						
1	1.984	2.555	3.128	3.701	4.274	4.848	5.421	5.993	6.566	7.138	7.710
2	2.960	3.762	4.567	5.373	6.180	6.986	7.792	8.598	9.403	10.207	11.010
3	3.772	4.746	5.726	6.708	7.691	8.674	9.656	10.637	11.617	12.596	13.572
4	4.500	5.616	6.740	7.868	8.998	10.127	11.255	12.382	13.506	14.629	15.749
5	5.174	6.412	7.661	8.916	10.172	11.428	12.683	13.935	15.185	16.432	17.676
6	5.809	7.155	8.515	9.882	11.252	12.621	13.988	15.352	16.714	18.071	19.423
7	6.416	7.858	9.319	10.787	12.259	13.730	15.199	16.665	18.126	19.583	21.034
8	7.000	8.529	10.081	11.643	13.208	14.773	16.335	17.894	19.447	20.994	22.534
9	7.565	9.174	10.810	12.458	14.110	15.761	17.410	19.053	20.691	22.322	23.944
10	8.114	9.797	11.511	13.239	14.971	16.703	18.432	20.155	21.871	23.579	25.277
11	8.649	10.401	12.188	13.990	15.798	17.605	19.409	21.206	22.995	24.775	26.544
12	9.173	10.988	12.843	14.716	16.594	18.473	20.347	22.213	24.071	25.918	27.753
13	9.686	11.561	13.480	15.419	17.364	19.309	21.250	23.182	25.104	27.014	28.910
14	10.190	12.120	14.100	16.101	18.110	20.118	22.121	24.115	26.098	28.068	30.022
15	10.685	12.668	14.705	16.765	18.834	20.902	22.965	25.018	27.058	29.084	31.093
16	11.173	13.205	15.296	17.412	19.538	21.664	23.783	25.891	27.986	30.065	32.125
17	11.654	13.731	15.874	18.044	20.225	22.405	24.577	26.739	28.885	31.014	33.123
18	12.128	14.249	16.441	18.662	20.894	23.126	25.350	27.562	29.758	31.935	34.090
19	12.596	14.759	16.996	19.266	21.549	23.830	26.103	28.363	30.606	32.828	35.027
20	13.059	15.260	17.542	19.859	22.188	24.517	26.838	29.143	31.431	33.696	35.937
21	13.516	15.754	18.079	20.440	22.815	25.190	27.555	29.904	32.234	34.541	36.821
22	13.968	16.241	18.606	21.010	23.429	25.847	28.255	30.647	33.018	35.364	37.681
23	14.416	16.722	19.125	21.570	24.031	26.491	28.941	31.373	33.783	36.166	38.519
24	14.859	17.197	19.637	22.121	24.622	27.123	29.612	32.082	34.529	36.948	39.335
25	15.298	17.665	20.141	22.663	25.203	27.742	30.269	32.777	35.260	37.713	40.132
26	15.733	18.128	20.637	23.196	25.773	28.350	30.913	33.457	35.974	38.459	40.910
27	16.164	18.586	21.128	23.721	26.334	28.947	31.545	34.123	36.673	39.190	41.669
28	16.591	19.039	21.611	24.239	26.886	29.533	32.166	34.776	37.358	39.904	42.412
29	17.015	19.486	22.089	24.748	27.429	30.110	32.775	35.417	38.029	40.604	43.138
30	17.436	19.929	22.560	25.251	27.964	30.677	33.374	36.046	38.686	41.289	43.849

$15 each, but typically subject to a minimum fee of $35 and a maximum fee of $50 to $60 on transactions of one to ten contracts.

Although there can be significant differences in total commission costs between full-service brokers and other firms, I prefer to work with options-knowledgeable people at a full-service firm. I can readily do this because I am not a short-term investor, and the relatively small number of trades I do per year does not result in significant commissions in terms of absolute dollars. This is particularly true when one remembers that in selling options that subsequently expire worthless, only one commission is involved, not two.

LEAPS Available

LEAPS are currently traded on over 250 widely followed equities (as well as on numerous industry sector, domestic, and international indices). Table 2.3 lists the equity LEAPS available in May, 1998 and shows the name of the underlying security, its stock symbol, the standard option symbol, the exchange code(s) showing where the option is traded, the options cycle governing when the LEAP rolls over into a standard option, position limits, and the option symbol for the LEAPS expiring in the years 1999 and 2000.

Exchange codes. LEAPS are traded on one or more of four major exchanges*, as indicated by the following symbols:

A   American Stock Exchange
C   Chicago Board Options Exchange
P   Pacific Stock Exchange
X   Philadelphia Stock Exchange

Expiration cycles. These are the January, February, and March cycles that control how and when each LEAP rolls over into a standard option. It is important to note that the trading symbol for a LEAP option will change when it does roll over and become a standard option, and quote requests, statements, trades, close-outs and

---

*The New York Stock Exchange no longer trades options and transferred any options that had been traded exclusively there to the Chicago Board Options Exchange in 1997.

exercise instructions should reflect this. In the table that follows, the numerical codes used for the expiration cycles are:

1 January Sequential
2 February Sequential
3 March Sequential

The expiration cycle of a given class of options also tells you the specific month that the corresponding LEAP is due to open for trading. For example, Intel is cycle 1, so the next set of Intel LEAPS is supposed to open right after the May expiration. Boeing is cycle 2, so the next set of Boeing LEAPS is supposed to open right after the June expiration. And Pfizer is cycle 2, so the next set of Pfizer LEAPS is supposed to open right after the July expiration.

Position limits. The maximum number of open option contracts (including both LEAPS and standard options) permitted on the underlying equity appears in the next column. These limits are set in accordance with the number of outstanding shares and the trading volume. The largest, most frequently traded stocks are assigned initial position limits of 25,000 contracts, while smaller, less-active issues have position limits of 20,000 on down to 4,500 contracts. As a result of stock splits, mergers, acquisitions, and other factors, these limits are periodically adjusted. Position limits are imposed so as to prevent any person or entity from controlling the market on a given issue. Because every option contract has both a buyer and a seller, the open contract count is the sum of the number of opening calls bought and the number of opening puts sold.

LEAP symbols. To facilitate trading, LEAP options are symbolized by a four- to six-character trading symbol made up of a root symbol designating the underlying equity, a single character designating the expiration month, and a single letter designating the strike price involved. Because LEAPS expire only in January, the code letter for the expiration month is always "A" for calls and "M" for puts. The root symbols for the underlying equity began with the letter "Z" for January 1997 LEAPS, the letter "W" for January 1998 LEAPS, the letter "V" for January 1999 LEAPS, and the letter "L" for January 2000 LEAPS. This Z/W/V/L sequence of initial letters will likely be repeated every four years, the letter "Z" having already been assigned as the starting letter for the January 2001 LEAPS. As each LEAP rolls over into a standard option approximately a half year prior to expiration, the root symbol portion of the trading code is changed to that of the standard option. Because of conflicts that frequently arise with existing trading symbols of stocks and standard options, there is often no consistency in the designations of LEAP root symbols. In the case of Columbia Gas Systems, for example, the root symbols for the years 1998, 1999, and 2000 are, respectively, WC, VCS, and LCG. A dash indicates that there was no LEAP option offered for that year on a particular security.

A final word of caution: it is frequently the case that as a result of mergers, acquisitions, and stock splits, there is more than one LEAP root symbol for a given stock and expiration year. Table 2.3 shows in each case the principal root symbol. For example, the LEAP 2000 symbol shown for Campbell Soup is LLL; this has since been changed to ULL to reflect the adjustment for the spin-off and distribution of Vlasic Foods International on March 30, 1998. The only sure way to determine the correct root symbol for a given LEAP series is to consult an on-line table showing the specific LEAP options available, such as the one maintained by the Chicago Board Options Exchange (CBOE) at *http://www.cboe.com.* Or you can call CBOE directly at 1-800-OPTIONS.

Buying Stocks Without Money

This section heading (and for that matter, the name of this book) is not be taken literally. Obviously, buying stocks takes money. But by now you've guessed where the money for those stocks comes from: not out of your pocket, but from the premiums accumulated from the sales of the LEAP puts. As described in the preface, the purpose of my selling LEAP puts was not just to enhance the cash flow and dividend yield of my stock portfolio. Rather, it was to furnish the funds with which to continue stock acquisition.

The appropriate strategies for generating option premiums consistent with a high rate of premium retention and low rate of financial exposure are the subject of the next several chapters.

Table 2.3: LEAPS Available May, 1998

Underlying Equity	Stock	Option	Exch	Cyc	Pos'ns	1999	2000
Abbott Labs	ABT	ABT	X	2	25,000	VBT	LBT
Acuson	ACN	ACN	P	1	4,500	VAU	LAU
Adaptec	ADPT	APQ	A	1	25,000	—	LYA
Adobe Systems	ADBE	AEQ	P	1	10,500	VAE	LAE
Advanced Micro	AMD	AMD	P	1	10,500	VVV	LVV
Aetna	AET	AET	A	1	25,000	VLC	LLC
AirTouch Comm.	ATI	ATI	ACP	1	25,000	VRH	LRH
Allied Signal	ALD	ALD	X	3	20,000	VAD	LAL
Allstate	ALL	ALL	ACP	1	25,000	VLS	LZL
Altera	ALTR	LTQ	P	3	25,000	VZT	LZT
ALZA	AZA	AZA	P	1	10,500	VZA	LZA
Amerada Hess	AHC	AHC	X	2	7,500	VHS	LHS
America Online	AOL	AOL	ACP	1	25,000	VAN	LOL
American Express	AXP	AXP	AC	1	25,000	VAX	LAX
American Home	AHP	AHP	A	1	25,000	VAH	LAH
American Intern'l	AIG	AIG	C	2	25,000	VAF	LAJ
Ameritech	AIT	AIT	C	1	25,000	VHO	LHT
Amgen	AMGN	AMQ	A	1	25,000	VAM	LMN
Amoco	AN	AN	C	2	25,000	VAO	LAO
AMR	AMR	AMR	A	2	25,000	VMR	LAR
Andrew	ANDW	AQN	C	1	10,500	VNA	LNA
Anheuser-Busch	BUD	BUD	X	3	20,000	VBD	LBD
Apple Computer	AAPL	AAQ	A	1	25,000	VAA	LAA
Applied Materials	AMAT	ANQ	P	1	10,500	VPJ	LPJ
ASA Holdings	ASAI	ASA	A	2	4,500	VSL	LSL
Ascend Comm.	ASND	QQA	ACPX	3	25,000	VSD	LZC
Associates First	AFS	AFS	AC	3	20,000	—	LLA
AT&T	T	T	C	1	25,000	VT	LT
At Home	ATHM	AHQ	P	1	20,000	VAY	LAY
Atlantic Richfield	ARC	ARC	C	1	10,500	VFR	LFR
Atmel	ATML	AQT	C	2	25,000	VLH	LMG
Avon Products	AVP	AVP	C	1	7,500	VVP	LVP

Table 2.3 (cont.): LEAPS Available May, 1998

Underlying Equity	Stock	Option	Exch	Cyc	Pos'ns	1999	2000
Baker Hughes	BHI	BHI	P	1	10,500	VBH	LBH
BancOne	ONE	ONE	P	2	25,000	VBE	LBE
BankBoston	BKB	BKB	X	2	20,000	VKB	LKB
BankAmerica	BAC	BAC	C	1	25,000	VBA	LBA
Bankers Trust NY	BT	BT	P	1	10,500	VET	LET
Bank of NY	BK	BK	C	1	25,000	—	LKJ
Barrick Gold	ABX	ABX	A	1	25,000	VBX	LBX
Bay Networks	BAY	BAY	C	3	25,000	VLB	LBN
Bell Atlantic	BEL	BEL	C	1	25,000	VBU	LEU
BellSouth	BLS	BLS	A	1	25,000	VBL	LBL
Best Buy Co.	BBY	BBY	C	3	20,000	VBY	LBS
Biogen	BGEN	BGQ	ACP	1	25,000	VNG	LGB
Boeing	BA	BA	C	2	25,000	VBO	LBO
Borland Intern'l	BORL	BLQ	C	1	25,000	VOB	LOB
Boston Chicken	BOST	BQN	AC	1	25,000	VPN	LPN
Boston Scientific	BSX	BSX	C	2	10,500	VSB	LIS
Bristol-Myers	BMY	BMY	C	3	25,000	VBM	LBM
Burlington Nor'n	BNI	BNI	C	1	10,500	VNI	LNI
C-Cube Micro	CUBE	UQB	AC	2	25,000	VCE	LCX
Cabletron Systems	CS	CS	AX	1	20,000	VCJ	LCJ
Campbell Soup	CPB	CPB	C	2	10,500	VXL	LLL
Caterpillar	CAT	CAT	A	2	25,000	VKT	LKT
CBS Corp.*	CBS	CBS	A	1	25,000	—	—
Cendant	CD	CD	ACX	2	10,500	VUC	LUL
Centocor	CNTO	COQ	C	1	25,000	VCT	LCO
Chase Manhattan	CMB	CMB	A	3	25,000	VCX	LCK
Chevron	CHV	CHV	A	3	25,000	VCH	LCH
Chiron	CHIR	CIQ	AC	1	10,500	VHR	LHR
Chrysler	C	C	C	1	25,000	VCY	LCR
Chubb	CB	CB	C	1	10,500	VCU	LCU
Cirrus Logic	CRUS	CUQ	CP	3	25,000	VUR	LRL
Cisco Systems	CSCO	CYZ	CP	1	25,000	VYV	LYL

Table 2.3 (cont.): LEAPS Available May, 1998

Underlying Equity	Stock	Option	Exch	Cyc	Pos'ns	1999	2000
Citicorp	CCI	CCI	C	1	25,000	VCP	LCC
Clarify	CLFY	QCY	C	2	7,500	VFY	LYU
Clear Channel	CCU	CCU	C	1	4,500	VYU	LWU
Coca-Cola	KO	KO	C	2	25,000	VKO	LKO
Coeur d'Alene	CDE	CDE	C	2	7,500	—	LCV
Colgate-Palmolive	CL	CL	C	2	10,500	VGO	LGO
Columbia Gas	CG	CG	A	2	4,500	VCS	LCG
Columbia/HCA	COL	COL	AC	2	25,000	VOM	LZO
Comp. Tele Chile	CTC	CTC	AC	2	7,500	VDT	LDT
Compaq	CPQ	CPQ	P	1	10,500	VKP	LKP
CompUSA	CPU	CPU	AC	2	20,000	VZP	LZP
Computer Assoc.	CA	CA	C	2	25,000	VCA	LCA
Conseco	CNC	CNC	AC	2	10,500	VEC	LEC
Corning	GLW	GLW	C	2	20,000	VGC	LWO
Cracker Barrel	CBRL	CBQ	P	3	10,500	VBR	LBR
Cypress Semi	CY	CY	C	3	25,000	VSY	LYR
Data General	DGN	DGN	P	3	10,500	VCW	LCW
Dayton Hudson	DH	DH	P	1	7,500	VDH	LDH
Dell Computer	DELL	DLQ	X	2	25,000	VDQ	LDE
Delta Air Lines	DAL	DAL	C	1	20,000	VDA	LDA
Diamond Offshore	DO	DO	C	3	25,000	VDC	LXE
Digital Equip't	DEC	DEC	AC	1	25,000	VDE	LDC
Disney (Walt)	DIS	DIS	AC	1	25,000	VDS	LWD
Dow Chemical	DOW	DOW	C	3	25,000	VDO	LDO
DSC Comm.	DIGI	DIQ	A	1	25,000	VD	LID
Dun & Bradstreet	DNB	DNB	A	2	10,500	VDB	LDB
DuPont (E.I.)	DD	DD	AC	1	25,000	VDD	LDD
Eastman Kodak	EK	EK	C	1	25,000	VEK	LEK
EFII	EFII	EFQ	C	1	10,500	VEF	LEF
Electronic Arts	ERTS	EZQ	C	3	25,000	VZW	LVY
Electronic Data	EDS	EDS	X	3	25,000	VEU	LED
EMC	EMC	EMC	C	1	25,000	VUE	LUE

Table 2.3 (cont.): LEAPS Available May, 1998

Underlying Equity	Stock	Option	Exch	Cyc	Pos'ns	1999	2000
Equifax	EFX	EFX	P	1	7,500	VQF	LQF
Ericsson Tel.	ERICY	RQC	ACX	1	25,000	VYD	LYD
ESS Tech.	ESST	SEQ	C	1	10,500	VWU	LAG
Exxon	XON	XON	C	1	25,000	VXO	LXO
Fannie Mae	FNM	FNM	X	3	25,000	VFN	LFN
FDX	FDX	FDX	C	1	7,500	VFX	LFX
Federated Stores	FD	FD	C	2	25,000	VFD	LFD
First Chicago	FCN	FCN	CX	1	25,000	VNC	LCD
First Union	FTU	FTU	P	1	20,000	VVD	LVD
Fleet Financial	FLT	FLT	A	1	25,000	—	LLN
Ford Motor	F	F	C	3	25,000	VFO	LFV
Forest Labs	FRX	FRX	C	2	7,500	—	LRS
FORE Systems	FORE	FQO	ACPX	1	20,000	VFY	LFY
Freddie Mac	FRE	FRE	A	1	25,000	—	LFM
Fruit of the Loom	FTL	FTL	C	2	7,500	VTL	LTL
Gannett	GCI	GCI	P	1	10,500	—	LHJ
Gap	GPS	GPS	C	3	25,000	VGS	LGS
Gateway 2000	GTW	GTW	ACP	3	25,000	VGB	LWB
General Electric	GE	GE	C	3	25,000	VGE	LGR
General Mills	GIS	GIS	P	1	10,500	VGI	LGI
General Motors	GM	GM	C	3	25,000	VGN	LGM
General Semi	SEM	SEM	X	3	25,000	VIY	LIY
Georgia-Pacific	GP	GP	X	1	10,500	VGP	LGP
Gillette	G	G	A	3	25,000	VZG	LZG
Glaxo Wellcome	GLX	GLX	A	2	25,000	VGX	LGX
Goodyear Tire	GT	GT	A	1	10,500	VYR	LYE
Green Tree Fin.	GNT	GNT	CX	3	25,000	VSJ	LGN
Grupo Televisa	TV	TV	AC	1	25,000	VVT	LVT
GTE	GTE	GTE	A	3	25,000	VGT	LGT
Gucci	GUC	GUC	ACX	1	7,500	VGU	LGU
Guidant	GDT	GDT	A	1	25,000	—	LYX
Halliburton	HAL	HAL	C	1	10,500	VHW	LYR

Table 2.3 (cont.): LEAPS Available May, 1998

Underlying Equity	Stock	Option	Exch	Cyc	Pos'ns	1999	2000
HealthSouth	HRC	HRC	C	3	10,500	VHC	LHH
Heinz (H.J.)	HNZ	HNZ	C	3	20,000	VHN	LHN
Hewlett-Packard	HWP	HWP	C	2	25,000	VHP	LWP
HFS Inc.	HFS	HFZ	AC	1	20,000	VFZ	LFZ
Hilton Hotels	HLT	HLT	P	1	7,500	VHL	LHL
Home Depot	HD	HD	X	2	25,000	VHD	LHD
Homestake Mining	HM	HM	C	1	25,000	VHM	LHM
Household Intern'l	HI	HI	A	1	10,500	VOH	LIH
IBM	IBM	IBM	C	1	25,000	VIB	LIB
Ikon Office Sol'ns	IKN	IKN	C	3	10,500	VKN	LLT
Informix	IFMX	IFQ	AC	2	25,000	VIF	LXF
Intel	INTC	INQ	A	1	25,000	VNL	LNL
Intern'l Game	IGT	IGT	A	1	25,000	VGG	LGG
Intern'l Paper	IP	IP	C	1	25,000	VNP	LNP
ITT	ITT	ITT	C	3	10,500	VLA	LIP
Johnson & John.	JNJ	JNJ	C	1	25,000	VJN	LJN
Kimberly Clark	KMB	KMB	A	1	25,000	VYK	LKL
KLA Tencor	KLAC	KCQ	CP	3	25,000	VXG	LXG
Kmart	KM	KM	C	3	25,000	VK	LKM
Kroger	KR	KR	A	1	10,500	VKK	LKK
Lam Research	LRCX	LMQ	P	3	25,000	VPC	LPC
Lehman Bros	LEH	LEH	AC	1	10,500	VHE	LHE
Lilly (Eli)	LLY	LLY	A	1	25,000	VIL	LZE
Limited	LTD	LTD	C	2	25,000	VLD	LLD
Liposome	LIPO	LPQ	C	2	25,000	VPB	LOF
Loral Space	LOR	LOR	C	1	25,000	VRO	LOO
Lowe's	LOW	LOW	X	1	25,000	VOY	LOY
LSI Logic	LSI	LSI	C	1	25,000	VBS	LHX
Lucent Tech.	LU	LU	ACX	1	25,000	VEU	LUN
Madge Net.	MADGF	MQE	AC	2	20,000	VDM	LLM
Magna Intern'l	MGA	MGA	C	2	7,500	VAG	LGA
Marriott Intern'l	MAR	MAR	X	1	7,500	VRR	LRR

Table 2.3 (cont.): LEAPS Available May, 1998

Underlying Equity	Stock	Option	Exch	Cyc	Pos'ns	1999	2000
Maytag	MYG	MYG	C	1	7,500	VMY	LMY
MBNA	KRB	KRB	AC	3	20,000	VZK	LZK
McDonald's	MCD	MCD	C	3	25,000	VMD	LMC
McGraw-Hill	MHP	MHP	X	2	4,500	VMP	LMP
MCI Comm.	MCIC	MCQ	C	1	25,000	VTU	LTU
MEMC Elec.	WFR	WFR	AC	1	10,500	—	LRF
Merck	MRK	MRK	C	1	25,000	VMK	LMK
Merrill Lynch	MER	MER	AC	1	25,000	VME	LME
Micron Tech.	MU	MU	CP	1	25,000	VGY	LGY
Microsoft	MSFT	MSQ	P	1	10,500	VMF	LMF
Minn. Mining	MMM	MMM	C	1	25,000	VMU	LMU
Mobil	MOB	MOB	C	2	25,000	VML	LML
Monsanto	MTC	MTC	C	1	10,500	VM	LCT
Morgan (J.P.)	JPM	JPM	X	3	20,000	VJP	LJP
Morgan Stanley	MWD	MWD	ACPX	1	10,500	VWD	LWW
Motorola	MOT	MOT	A	1	25,000	VMA	LMA
National Semi	NSM	NSM	C	2	25,000	VSN	LBV
NationsBank	NB	NB	X	2	25,000	VNB	LNB
Newbridge Net.	NN	NN	P	3	10,500	VNW	LNW
NEXTEL	NXTL	FQC	C	2	25,000	VFU	LFU
NIKE	NKE	NKE	P	1	7,500	VNK	LNK
Nokia	NOKA	NKA	AC	1	25,000	VOK	LOK
Norwest	NOB	NOB	P	1	20,000	VOE	LOE
Novell	NOVL	NKQ	A	2	25,000	VNN	LNO
Occidental Pet.	OXY	OXY	C	2	25,000	VXY	LXY
Office Depot	ODP	ODP	A	1	25,000	VDP	—
Oracle	ORCL	ORQ	C	3	25,000	VOR	LRO
Paine Webber	PWJ	PWJ	C	1	7,500	VWJ	—
PairGain Tech.	PAIR	PQG	C	1	10,500	VGF	LGC
PepsiCo	PEP	PEP	C	1	25,000	VP	LPP
Pfizer	PFE	PFE	A	3	25,000	VPE	LPE
Pharmacia&Upjohn	PNU	PNU	C	1	25,000	VUP	LUP
Phelps Dodge	PD	PD	A	1	10,500	VZD	LZD

Table 2.3 (cont.): LEAPS Available May, 1998

Underlying Equity	Stock	Option	Exch	Cyc	Pos'ns	1999	2000
Philip Morris	MO	MO	A	3	25,000	VPM	LMO
PHP Healthcare	PPH	PPH	C	2	4,500	VPH	LPH
Pitney Bowes	PBI	PBI	A	1	10,500	VBW	LPI
Placer Dome	PDG	PDG	X	3	25,000	VDG	LPD
Platinum Software	PSQL	PQS	C	1	10,500	VPO	LPO
PMI Group	PMA	PMA	ACP	3	4,500	—	LVS
Polaroid	PRD	PRD	C	1	7,500	VRD	LRD
Potash Saskat'n	POT	POT	C	3	10,500	VPT	LPT
PPG Industries	PPG	PPG	X	2	10,500	VPP	LP
Procter & Gamble	PG	PG	A	1	25,000	VPG	LPR
Quaker Oats	OAT	OAT	X	1	10,500	VQO	LQO
Qualcomm	QCOM	QAQ	C	1	25,000	VLM	LLU
Rambus	RMBS	BNQ	ACP	2	10,500	—	LIX
Read-Rite	RDRT	RDQ	CP	1	25,000	VJW	LJW
Reebok Intern'l	RBK	RBK	A	1	10,500	VRK	LRK
Republic Ind's	RWIN	WQR	AC	1	25,000	VRW	LPU
RJR Nabisco	RN	RN	ACX	3	25,000	VRJ	LRJ
Safeway	SWY	SWY	AC	3	10,500	VYW	LYW
Saks Holdings	SKS	SKS	AC	1	7,500	VVK	LLK
Santa Fe	SDC	SDC	ACPX	1	10,500	VEJ	LEJ
Sara Lee	SLE	SLE	A	1	25,000	VZS	LZS
SBC Comm.	SBC	SBC	P	1	10,500	VFE	LFE
Schering-Plough	SGP	SGP	P	2	10,500	VSG	LSG
Schlumberger	SLB	SLB	C	2	25,000	VWY	LYS
Schwab	SCH	SCH	C	3	10,500	VYS	LWS
Seagate Tech.	SEG	SEG	A	3	25,000	VTT	LTZ
Sears, Roebuck	S	S	C	1	25,000	VRS	LS
SkyTel	MTEL	MMQ	C	3	25,000	VEM	LEM
SLM Holdings	SLM	SLM	C	1	10,500	VZL	LYM
SmithKline B'm	SBH	SBH	P	2	4,500	VPF	LPF
Solutia	SOI	SOI	C	1	20,000	VOA	LOA
Southwest Air	LUV	LUV	C	3	20,000	VUV	LOV

Table 2.3 (cont.): LEAPS Available May, 1998

Underlying Equity	Stock	Option	Exch	Cyc	Pos'ns	1999	2000
Sprint	FON	FON	X	2	25,000	VN	LON
Storage Tech.	STK	STK	C	3	20,000	VSK	LSK
Sun Micro	SUNW	SUQ	P	1	7,500	VSU	LSU
SunAmerica	SAI	SAI	X	3	7,500	VSA	LSE
SunTrust Bank	STI	STI	P	1	10,500	—	LNJ
Sybase	SYBS	SBQ	P	3	25,000	VYB	LYB
TCI	TCOMA	TCQ	A	1	25,000	VTM	LTE
Tele. Argentina	TAR	TAR	ACP	1	25,000	VTD	LRA
Tele. Brasileiras	TBR	TBR	ACX	1	25,000	VZB	LZR
Tele. Mexico	TMX	TMX	ACX	2	25,000	VTE	LMX
Tenneco	TEN	TEN	A	2	10,500	VTG	LNG
Terex	TEX	TEX	AX	1	7,500	VYX	LXL
Texaco	TX	TX	A	1	20,000	VXC	LTO
Texas Instru.	TXN	TXN	C	1	25,000	VXT	LTN
3Com	COMS	THQ	P	1	10,500	VTH	LTH
Tiffany	TIF	TIF	X	2	4,500	—	LFF
Time Warner	TWX	TWX	X	3	25,000	VTW	LTW
Tommy Hilfiger	TOM	TOM	C	2	10,500	VIH	LSD
Toys "R" Us	TOY	TOY	C	3	25,000	VTY	LYT
Travelers	TRV	TRV	X	3	25,000	VRV	LRV
Triton Energy	OIL	OIL	ACX	2	7,500	VOI	LOI
Tyco International	TYC	TYC	X	1	25,000	VPA	LPA
TWA	TWA	TWA	ACX	1	25,000	VWA	LWA
UAL	UAL	UAL	C	2	4,500	VUA	LUA
Unilever	UN	UN	A	2	25,000	VVN	LVN
Union Carbide	UK	UK	A	1	20,000	VCB	LCB
Union Pacific	UNP	UNP	X	2	20,000	VUJ	LUJ
Unisys	UIS	UIS	A	1	25,000	VUI	LUI
United HealthCare	UNH	UNH	AC	3	25,000	VUH	LUH
United Tech.	UTX	UTX	C	2	10,500	VXU	LXT
Unocal	UCL	UCL	P	1	10,500	VCL	LCL
US Filter	USF	USF	C	1	4,500	VVS	LSF

Table 2.3 (cont.): LEAPS Available May, 1998

Underlying Equity	Stock	Option	Exch	Cyc	Pos'ns	1999	2000
US Surgical	USS	USS	A	1	10,500	VSS	LUS
US WEST Comm.	USW	USW	A	1	25,000	VSW	LUW
US WEST Media	UMG	UMG	A	1	25,000	VUG	LUG
USA Waste Serv.	UW	UW	AC	1	10,500	VUW	LUY
USAirways	U	U	P	3	25,000	VUU	LUU
USX-Marathon	MRO	MRO	A	1	20,000	VXM	LXM
USX-U.S. Steel	X	X	A	1	10,500	VXS	LXS
Wal-Mart	WMT	WMT	C	3	25,000	VWT	LWT
Warner-Lambert	WLA	WLA	A	1	20,000	VWL	LWL
Wells Fargo	WFC	WFC	A	1	7,500	VWF	LWF
Wendy's Intern'l	WEN	WEN	P	3	10,500	VVE	LVE
Westinghouse	WX	WX	A	1	25,000	VWX	LWX
Williams	WMB	WMB	C	2	7,500	VBB	LMB
Winstar Comm.	WCII	WQS	AC	1	25,000	VMQ	LQG
WMX Technologies	WMX	WMX	X	2	25,000	VWM	LWM
Woolworth	Z	Z	X	2	25,000	VFW	LFW
WorldCom	WCOM	LDQ	P	3	10,500	VQM	LQM
Xerox	XRX	XRX	CP	1	10,500	VXR	LXX
Xilinx	XLNX	XLQ	CP	3	25,000	VXJ	LXJ
Yahoo	YHOO	YHQ	ACPX	1	25,000	—	LYH
YPF Anonima	YPF	YPF	AC	1	25,000	VYP	LYF

*LEAPS for the CBS Corporation opened for trading on May 18, 1998 commencing with the January 2001 series.

3

CHAPTER 3

BASIC STRATEGY

The Underlying Premise

As stated earlier, option premiums do not reflect inflation or the growth prospects of the underlying issue. This does not matter much for standard options because of the relatively short time to expiration—eight months at the most. It does matter, however, for LEAP options, which can expire as many as 30 months later. By not taking inflation or the growth prospects of the underlying issue into account, the level of risk of a put option winding up in the money and being exercised against the writer appears to be larger than it really is. As a result, premiums for long-term put options are often overpriced with respect to the true level of risk involved. A quick glance at the tables in Appendix C shows why the chances of a LEAP put winding up in the money are that much smaller when inflation and growth prospects are taken into account.

As an example, suppose you were considering the sale of an at-the-money put on a stock priced at $100 a share whose volatility was 0.40 and which paid no dividend. The risk-free interest rate is currently 6%. You are considering the sale of a standard put expiring in three months or a LEAP put expiring in two years. From Table A.5 in Appendix A we see that the premium for the three-month European-style put is $7.185 a share, and for the 24-month LEAP put it is $15.815 a share. Neither premium reflects the earnings growth rate of 15% a year forecast for the company. From Table C.5 in Appendix C we see that without growth in earnings or the stock price, the probability of the three-month put winding up in the money is 0.431, while for the 24-month LEAP put it is 0.310.

For a 15% growth in earnings, however, Table C.32 shows that the probability of winding up in the money falls to 0.358 for the three-month put and to just 0.153 for the 24-month LEAP put. (These probabilities hold independently of whether a European- or an American-style pricing formula was used to determine the premiums.) Thus, the effect of earnings growth was to lower the relative chances of financial exposure by only about one sixth (0.358/0.431 = 0.831) for the three-month put but by over one half (0.153/0.310 = 0.494) for the 24-month LEAP put.

The analogy isn't quite exact, but I think of this as being akin to selling earthquake insurance based on the claim rate in California to homeowners on the East Coast, or health insurance based on the claim rate for smokers to nonsmokers. Yes, there will be claims—earthquakes happen everywhere given enough time, and even nonsmokers get sick—but on a statistical basis there will be far fewer such claims from East Coast homeowners and nonsmokers. Or, in the case of LEAPS, from the put holders on growing companies.

The Fundamental Approach

From the foregoing premise, it seemed to me that a good investment strategy was to sell LEAP puts on companies whose long-term prospects were so good, and balance sheets so strong, that the possibility of being assigned the stock or otherwise incurring a loss was remote. The premiums received could then be used to purchase more of my favorite stocks. At the time I started doing this, in 1993, the number of long-term LEAP options available was much smaller than it is today. When the CBOE introduced LEAPS in October 1990, it started with calls on just 14 stocks. LEAP puts were first instituted about a year later. By 1993, equity LEAPS were available on only a hundred or so issues, about half the number that were available by 1997.

In the beginning, I approached LEAP selection very conservatively. The underlying stocks had to have Standard & Poor's ratings of B+ or better, the exercise prices had to be at least two price intervals out of the money, the expiration date had to be at least 15 months away, and sales were limited to a single contract. In each instance, the underlying issue also had to be a large-cap, blue-chip company which, if assigned to me, would fit right into my portfolio of conservative stocks. As time progressed, I relaxed several of these restrictions, selling LEAP puts on stocks with S&P ratings of B or better, and expiration dates as close as eight months away, and sales were expanded to multiple contracts. Exercise prices were set at the money if I relished the thought of being assigned the stock and set one strike interval below that if I was more or less indifferent to having to purchase that issue for my equity portfolio.

As a rule, I also try to avoid stocks with volatilities that are extremely low or extremely high. I often calculate the volatility of a stock using one or both of two different methods. The first is by a direct calculation based on the daily price history over the past twelve months. This history is available without charge from many internet providers (I use America Online), and the calculation is readily performed using the method described in Chapter 13. The second method is to calculate the implied volatility level that is derivable from quoted option premiums by means of the approach described in Chapter 14.

Stocks with extremely low volatilities will typically have premiums too low to justify the commission and margin requirement involved. Stocks with extremely high volatilities (say 0.75 and above) typically represent issues that are so unstable that the prospects of doubling or nothing (bankruptcy) may be commensurately equal. This is not to say that you should avoid stocks with moderately high volatilities. Tables C.1 though C4, for example, show that the chances of in-the-money puts expiring in the money decrease significantly with increasing volatility, while Table C.5 shows that the chances of at-the-money puts expiring in the money are roughly independent of volatility. In any event, I try to write LEAP puts of such combinations of strike price, expiration date, and volatility that they will generate premiums of $500 or more per contract. I don't always get that, but that is the standard figure I shoot for. By the way, the largest premium I have generated to date for an out-of-the money LEAP put was $3,600 per contract (for the January 2000 LEAP puts, strike $160, at the time Dell Computers was at $180 in July 1997).

Because of the relatively large premiums involved, I estimated that the net cost (strike price less premium received) of any stock assigned to me would be in most instances less than the market price at the time the option was exercised. That is, suppose a stock is trading for $102 a share and a LEAP put with strike price $100 is written for a premium of $12. At expiration, suppose the stock has fallen ten points to $92 and is therefore assigned. My effective purchase price is thus $90 ($102 less $12), $2 a share below market value. This ignores commissions, but the effects of the latter are not as great as you might think. Whatever commissions are charged for purchase of the stock are going to be offset in good measure by the interest earned on the $1,200 premium (or imputed interest if the premium was used to buy stock) over a period of as long as 30 months.

Margin and Collateral

Although put writers are not going on margin (they are not borrowing money from their brokers to buy securities), they do have to be approved to open a margin account. There is no minimum dollar requirement to open a margin account as such, but brokers will typically require equity (securities and cash) of at least $25,000 and evidence of stock market experience before permitting customers to sell puts.

The collateral requirement for writers of at-the-money puts is 20% of the value of the underlying stock plus the premium received. (For deep out-of-the-money puts this percentage drops to just 10%.) In the example above, 100 shares of the underlying equity was worth $10,200 at the time the LEAP put was sold. To enter this transaction, you would have to have at least $2,000 in collateral (the exact formula is a complex one and is discussed in Chapter 4). The $25,000 in your margin account would in principle be sufficient to collateralize a dozen such contracts. You would not want to do this, of course, because collateral requirements are calculated on a daily basis, and any downturn in the market, no matter how temporary, would result in a margin call.

My comfort level if I were a relatively small investor with $25,000 in stock market assets would be the sale of two such put contracts. In the event that the option was unexpectedly exercised, the $25,000 in the account plus $2,400 in premiums would be more than enough to cover the acquisition cost of the 200 shares of stock at $100 a share that would have to be purchased under the terms of the option contract. As my stock market account grew to an intermediate size of

$250,000, my comfort level would expand to a limit of 20 contracts at any one time. With enough time, a large account with $2.5 million would be sufficient to handle 200 contracts comfortably. I hope you succeed in achieving this level.

Selection and Timing

Over the years, I have found that which long-term option contract to enter is much more important than when to enter it. In this sense, dealing in long-term LEAP options employs much the same buy-and-hold philosophy that I have used to purchase stocks. This approach differs markedly from that taken by short-term equity and options traders, who may buy an issue at 10:00 a.m. and sell it by 2:00 p.m., hoping for eighth- and quarter-point increases (or decreases). To adequately describe the intensity of a trading environment is difficult. Suffice it to say that for a trader, news that the kitchen is on fire is an unpardonable distraction.

My approach to the selection of a LEAP put to sell is the same as my approach to choosing a stock. In a certain sense, it is easier to pick a good LEAP than to pick a good stock, because the universe of stocks contains thousands of issues and the screening needed to separate the potentially good ones from the rest can occupy a substantial amount of time. On the other hand, there are just 250 or so stocks with LEAPS, and it is easy enough to track their historical performances by creating a hypothetical portfolio and using almost any internet provider to update it automatically on a daily basis. Although the number of stocks in any one portfolio may be restricted to say, 100 issues, most providers will permit multiple portfolios.

The purpose of this book is not to tell you how to select good stocks—there are plenty of books and other informational resources for that. I personally use a number of free, internet-accessible information sources to narrow down the field of eligible stocks, among them the websites described in detail in Chapter 16. These include First Call, Hoover's StockScreener, Wall Street Research Net, Yahoo!Finance, StockSmart, Daily Stocks, Zacks Investment Service, FinancialWeb, and the broad-based services provided through America Online. (America Online is not free, of course, but you have to pay somebody to access the internet.) The various criteria I bring to bear can be summed up in two questions: would I buy this stock in its own right for my long-term stock portfolio, and would I mind having it unexpectedly "put to me" at the net acquisition cost (strike price less premium received) as a result of temporary market conditions and a panicky put holder?

As far as timing is concerned, I follow the same sort of "dollar-cost averaging" procedure used by millions of conservative, long-term equity investors. To minimize the impact of fluctuating prices, dollar-cost averaging adherents invest the same amount of money in stocks on a consistent, nonvarying periodic schedule. I follow an analogous procedure by selling the same dollar value of LEAP puts almost every month throughout the year. This procedure means that I do not have to guess whether stock prices are high or low, or whether they are going to go higher or lower over the short run.

Tactical Decision Making

If selecting underlying equities by means of the above methods is thought of as strategic decision making, choosing the appropriate parameters of the individual LEAP contracts can be though of as tactical decision making. The three independent parameters are the strike price, expiration date, and number of contracts written. Which to select will depend on how much you are willing to risk (i.e., the chance of exercise and assignment) to obtain a given reward (i.e., the LEAP premium offered).

Strike prices can range from deep out of the money to deep in the money. In addition, there will typically be two or three expiration dates available, such as January 1999, January 2000, and (when opened) January 2001. The number of contracts will depend on the risk/reward ratio, of course, but will more likely be a function of the margin, collateral, and assets needed to comfortably handle the transaction(s) involved. Whether to select a conservative, aggressive, or neutral at-the-money approach to strike prices depends on a number of factors that will be discussed in detail in the chapters to come. In situations where more than one contract for a given equity is being considered, the best position may turn out to be a mix of strike prices and expiration dates.

Selling Puts Versus Good-to-Canceled Orders

As I've said, my main objective in selling LEAP puts is to pocket the option premium and let the option expire worthless. In addition to this, I frequently sell LEAP puts where my specific goal is to have the option exercised against me as a way of acquiring stock at a net price significantly below the current market value. In this situation, I select a strike price a few steps higher than the one I would normally use for the pure premium retention play. Naturally, the higher the strike price, the greater the premium received and the higher the chances that the LEAP put will be assigned to me. The strike price so selected is typically one or two steps into the money—but rarely more than this. If too deep an into-the-money put is sold, the net acquisition cost (strike price less option premium) may not be significantly below the current market value.

Although some would say that selling in-the-money puts is a high-risk tactic, it is not very different from acquiring stock using a good-to-canceled (GTC) order at a price pegged that much below the current market value. That is, suppose a stock with a volatility of 0.40 and that is paying no dividend sells for $100 today. Assume the risk-free interest rate is 6%. Suppose investor A places a one-year GTC order to buy the stock at $92 a share, and suppose investor B sells a LEAP with strike price $110, expiring in 12 months.

Table A.3 in Appendix A shows that for a risk-free interest rate of 6% and for a stock paying no dividends, the corresponding put premium is almost exactly $18 per share. If the stock closes above $110 (without an intermediate dip), investor B is the clear winner, because the $18 premium is retained. If the stock closes between $92.01 and $110 (again without an intermediate dip to $92 or below), investor B is again the winner, as his or her effective price will be $92 for a stock worth somewhere between that figure and $110. And if the stock closes at or below $92, then the cost basis for both investors will have been $92 a share and their (unrealized) losses will be close to identical.

In actual practice, investor B will be ahead even in the latter situation because (i) the option premium of $1,800 will have been earning interest over the one-year period, and (ii) the GTC order will more likely than not have been triggered earlier than the assignment, thereby incurring a larger opportunity (or borrowing) cost on the

$9,200 needed to purchase the stock. About the only circumstances in which investor A would come out ahead is if the stock were to temporarily fall to $92 (or below), triggering the GTC order, and then closes above $110 without the LEAP option ever having been exercised. Almost everyone agrees that the use of GTC orders at prices pegged below market is a sound and conservative approach to stock acquisition. Selling puts to achieve the same ends can be even more cost effective.

Sometimes Life Deals You Lemons

Over the years there have been few instances where a LEAP option proved unprofitable to me. I do not mean to imply by this that the numerous LEAP puts I sold almost always expired out of the money and were therefore worthless to the option holder. On the contrary, on a certain number of occasions I did have to utilize mitigation procedures in order to preserve my profits and eliminate the potential for exercise and assignment against me. It was often the case that an out-of-the-money LEAP went into the money along the way because of subsequent price dips in the underlying issue.

On only four occasions (out of more than four hundred transactions) was I ever required to purchase the underlying issue because an option was exercised against me with months to go before the expiration date. The reason for this is simple: option holders of LEAP puts in most instances have bought them for insurance purposes and hope for recovery and a rise of the stock price to the same extent as the option writer. Under normal circumstances, they will not exercise the right to put the stock to the option writer until close to the end of the insurance period, as the expiration date approaches.

Risk Reduction Using Spreads

One way of reducing risk is to set up a hedging strategy. This is particularly useful if you are going to sell LEAP puts on lower-rated companies or those known to be highly volatile. One strategy I have occasionally used is to simultaneously purchase a LEAP put with a strike price well below the strike price of the LEAP put I was selling.

If the same expiration date is selected, this is referred to as a *bull put spread*. It may not always be possible to do this, however, because of the narrow set of strike prices that may be available (each 30-month LEAP series is ordinarily introduced for just three strike prices: one at the money, one in the money, and one out of the money). If that is the case, the LEAP put purchased with a lower strike price will have an expiration date one year prior to that of the LEAP put sold, a hedging strategy usually referred to as a *diagonal put spread*. This short leg of the spread can be subsequently rolled out to match the expiration date of the longer LEAP whenever that strike price opens up.

What this hedging technique does is to reduce potential profit and potential loss. Profit is reduced because the net premium received is going to be the difference between the premium received from the sale of the higher-strike LEAP put and the premium paid for the purchase of the lower-strike LEAP put. On the other hand, the maximum amount of financial exposure is reduced from that of the strike price of the LEAP put sold to that of the difference between the two strike prices involved.

To estimate the costs of lower-strike LEAP puts, the set of tables in Appendix A has been prepared, showing the theoretical values for European-style LEAP put premiums. Like the figures in Table 1.2, they are based on a stock price of $100, a risk-free interest rate of 6%, and no dividend. The premiums shown were calculated using the simple Black-Scholes pricing formula for European-style options that is described in Chapter 14. In Table 2.2, we noted that the theoretical premium for a 30-month, at-the money LEAP put for a stock priced at $100 with volatility 0.35 was $14.035 per share ($1,403.50 per contract). If we lower the strike price in steps of $5, the corresponding premiums, as extracted from the tables in Appendix A, are shown in Table 3.1.

Suppose, for example, we hedged the 30-month, at-the-money LEAP by purchasing the corresponding 30-month LEAP put with a strike price of $80 (assuming it was available) for $6.708 per share. The net profit per contract would be $1,403.50 less $670.80, or $732.70, still a sizable amount. The maximum potential exposure, however, drops from $100 (without an offsetting LEAP) to just $20 per share (the difference between the two strike prices involved).

**Table 3.1: European-Style 30-Month Put Premiums
as a Function of Strike Price
Stock Price = $100
Volatility = 0.35**

Strike Price	LEAP Premium
$100	$14.035
95	11.952
90	10.032
85	8.283
80	6.708
75	5.312
70	4.096
65	3.061
60	2.201

If the 30-month LEAP with the $80 strike was not available, you could set up a partial hedge by purchasing an 18-month LEAP with strike price $80 for just $4.908 a share, as indicated in Table A.9. The net premium this way would be $1,403.50 less $490.80, or $912.70 per contract. As the expiration date of the shorter LEAP approached, you could close out both LEAPS, replace the expiring one with a 12-month LEAP whose expiration date matched that of the original 30-month LEAP, or let it expire without replacement because the price of the underlying stock was now significantly higher (say 15% or more) than its original market value, thus transforming the original at-the-money put into one that was considerably out of the money.

Using Rollouts to Recover

Let's consider again the example where at the time the stock price is $102 a share, a LEAP put with strike price $100 is sold for a premium of $12 a share. Suppose further that as the expiration date had approached, the stock had fallen ten points to $92. Rather than accept assignment, the idea now is to *roll the option* out and down. The first step in doing this is to buy back the put, thereby closing out your position in the original option. Since expiration is relatively close (presumably a month or less away), closing out the option will cost not much more than its intrinsic value of $8 a share ($100 less $92). To be conservative, suppose this is $9 a share, or $900 to close the contract of 100 shares. At the same time, you sell a LEAP put whose expiration date is two years away (the "roll out") and with a strike price of $90 (the "roll down").

Suppose the premium generated from the sale of this replacement LEAP put is again $1,200. The overall effect of this maneuver is to net another $300 ($1,200 received less the $900 outlay) for an overall profit of $1,500. Doing this also gives the underlying stock an additional two years to recover. Note that recovery no longer means coming back to the original $100 level. As far as you, the option writer, are concerned, being at or above $90 in two years is going to be good enough. This process can be continued indefinitely in most instances, until such time as the stock price stabilizes.

Suppose the premium on the replacement LEAP happened to be less than the close-out price of the prior LEAP and is, say, $700. In that situation, the net out-of-pocket cost would be $200 ($700 received less the $900 outlay). This offsets the original $1,200 premium by $200 but still results in an overall profit of $1,000.

In rare instances a replacement LEAP may not be available, a situation indicated by the occasional dashes in Table 2.3. (The primary reason this occurs is because of announced or pending mergers and acquisitions that never materialize.) Depending how you feel about the company and its prospects, the simplest thing to do under these circumstances is to close out the option or accept assignment. This situation has never happened to me.

It is possible of course to incur a loss as a result of writing a naked put. The worst-case situation theoretically is where the stock price falls to zero as a result of bankruptcy or total financial catastrophe. It would be a truly unusual circumstance if one of the big-cap firms underlying almost all LEAP options went out of business, however. For a big-cap stock, a more credible worst-case situation might be a 25% decline in stock price as a result of a general market correction (in the unusually sharp correction of October 19,

1987, the market fell 22.6%). If the price of the stock in our example thereby fell from $102 to $76.50 and the stock was assigned to you at the strike price of $100, the immediate financial exposure would be the strike price of $100 less the market value of $76.50 plus the premium of $12, or $11.50 per share. From Table A.5, we see that by immediately writing a near-the-money LEAP put with strike $75, we would expect to receive a premium of about $10 for an expiration date 24 months away (0.75 x $13.314 = $9.99). If this were done and the stock went down no further, the overall loss would be $11.50 less $10, or just $1.50 a share. This potential loss of $150 per contract under the circumstances described is small in comparison to the potential benefits.

A Double-Glove Approach

Medical or rescue workers facing uncertain situations often put on an extra pair of gloves for added protection. Analogously, it is possible for you to do the same when future prospects or other market conditions are not as strong as you would like. To ensure double protection in selling LEAP puts, you can sell a put that is at least one strike interval below the at-the-money level and then additionally hedge by purchasing a LEAP put that is several strike intervals below that one. The premiums can still be significant.

Suppose the stock price is $100 a share. Looking at Table 3.1, if you were to sell a LEAP put with strike price $95 and buy one with strike price $80, your net premium would be $1,192.50 less $670.80, or $521.70 per contract. Your maximum financial exposure would now be $95 less $80, or $15 per share. This double-glove approach is my favorite one in those marginal situations involving stocks with higher volatilities and/or lower ratings that might have otherwise been eliminated from consideration.

Protective Stops

There is yet another method of protecting option positions that is theoretically available, namely the use of *stop* and *stop-limit* orders. For call or put option owners, a *stop sell* order is an instruction to the broker to sell (thereby closing) a position at a specified price or at the best price *below* it if it is unavailable. A *stop-limit sell* order is an instruction to sell (thereby closing) a position at a specified price and no other. For call or put writers, a *stop buy* order is an instruction to the broker to buy (thereby closing) a position at a specified price or at the best price *above* it if it is unavailable. A *stop-limit buy* order is an instruction to buy (thereby closing) a position at a specified price and no other.

As an example of a stop buy order, suppose you had written a LEAP put for a $10 premium and would like to buy it back and close your position if it went to $12. If you entered a stop-limit buy order for $12 and the price jumped from anywhere below $12 to $12.25, say, your transaction would not be executed. If you had entered a stop buy order for $12, under the same circumstances your position would be closed out for $12.25.

The use of stop buy or stop-limit buy orders seems at first blush like an ideal way to hedge against an unanticipated move in the wrong direction (downward) for LEAP put writers. The difficulty is in the execution. Although all four stock exchanges that handle listed options (CBOE, American, Philadelphia, and Pacific) permit the use of stop and stop-limit orders, as a matter of course most brokerage firms will not accept option stop orders or stop limit orders from individual customers. The reasons commonly cited by brokerage houses for this are the fact that the rules for option stop orders and option stop-limits vary from exchange to exchange,* and the inability of in-place computer software and communication systems to reliably handle the complex instructions that must be wired to the trading floor. Stop buy and stop-limit buy orders are everyday occurrences on the stock exchanges but are typically done on behalf of institutional investors or those having direct links to the floor traders.

There is a second reason why I prefer not to use stop orders or stop-limit orders (even if I could readily do so). Over a multiyear period, the steady earnings growth of a solid company will result in a stock price movement up and away from the specified strike price. However, it is quite possible to experience a short-term price decrease in the underlying stock because of normal volatility in the

---

*The Philadelphia Stock Exchange, for example, does not permit GTC orders at prices set above the market. Any stop buy or stop-limit buy requests must be done on a daily basis.

equity markets. Once stop and stop limit orders are triggered because of a temporary downturn in stock price, it is not possible to capitalize on the eventual recovery in stock price and the associated erosion in the LEAP put that was in all likelihood going to expire worthless.

Another reason I don't like to use stop orders is because they are executed in a different manner for options than for stocks. Suppose you owned a stock whose bid price is $10.00 and whose ask price is $10.25 and you submit a stop loss order at $9.00 to protect your position. If the bid/ask falls to $9.00/$9.25, your trade will be executed because the price you want to sell at matches the bid price offered by buyers.

This would not be the case if the same situation involved an option, however. By the rules of the game, your $9.00 stop loss order would not go off until the either the *ask* price reached $9.00 (in which case the bid might be $8.75) or a trade went off at $9.00, whichever occurred first. The analogous situation holds with respect to stop buy orders. Difficulties in trying to explain all this to customers may be the real reason brokerage houses will not accept stop orders on options.

Timing the Market

There may be individual investors who are good at timing the market, but I am not one of them. It is for this reason that I adopted a long-term, buy-and-hold approach to stocks, and a regular, almost dollar-cost averaging approach to acquiring stocks over 30 years of investing. I have tried to adopt this philosophy with regard to options activity, selling just a few LEAP puts per month throughout the year rather than attempting to jump in and do it all during the three-month window in June, July, and August when the new round of LEAPS is being established.

On the other hand, I do not ignore market conditions. When the market is especially volatile, I will often hedge by selling LEAP puts that are further out of the money than I would otherwise. Doing this is especially useful when the market appears overbought and a market correction appears possible. Of course, if such a market correction appears likely, I usually suspend selling LEAP puts and adopt a wait-and-see approach.

4

CHAPTER 4

MARGIN

Introduction

Writers of naked puts and uncovered calls are considered to be short the stock because of the obligation of the option writer to purchase the underlying equity should the option holder exercise his or her rights. As a result, writers of naked puts and uncovered calls must maintain margin accounts in much the same way that any short seller does. Because of the potential need to purchase stock or close out positions, investors must have sufficient collateral in their accounts (in the form of capital and/or equities) to ensure that such obligations can be met. For writers of naked puts and uncovered calls, the collateral required is the greater of:

$$0.20 \times Stock\ Price\ - OTM\ Amount + \ Current\ Premium\ [1]$$
$$0.10 \times Stock\ Price\ + \ Current\ Premium\ [2]$$

The *OTM Amount* in the first formula is the amount by which the option is out of the money. For puts this is defined as the amount by which the stock price exceeds the strike price. For calls this is defined as the amount by which the strike price exceeds the stock price. By regulation, this collateral must be maintained in a margin account, and for that reason, it is often referred to as the *margin* required.

Examples

In late May 1998, XYZ Corporation is at $53.375, and you write a January 2000 LEAP put with strike price $55. The stock pays no dividend and has a volatility of 0.35. The risk-free interest rate is 6%. From the tables in Appendix B, or using the computer algorithm in Chapter 15, the premium for an American-style put with 20 months to expiration comes to $8.28. Based on this, the initial margin requirement for this slightly in-the-money option is calculated as 0.20 x $53.375 x 100 + $8.28 x 100, or $1,895.50. (Note that 10% of the stock price plus the premium would only be $533.75 + $828, or $1,361.75.)

Suppose, six months later, that XYZ's stock has moved up to $58.50 a share. With 14 months to expiration, the premium for that option will have fallen to $5.46. The current margin requirement for this option is 0.20 x $58.50 x 100 - ($58.50 - $55) x 100 + $5.46 x 100, or $1,366 (10% of the stock price plus premium would only be $585 + $546, or $1,131).

Further suppose, six months later, that XYZ's stock has moved up to $62.75 a share. With just eight months to expiration, the premium for that option will now have fallen to just $2.87. The margin requirement for this option is now 0.10 x $62.75 x 100 + $2.87 x 100, or $914.50 (the regular formula gives 0.20 x $62.75 x 100 - ($62.75 - $55) x 100 + $2.87 x 100, or $767.00).

Now suppose that, some time after, XYZ's stock zooms to $150.00 a share (perhaps due to a buyout offer) and that the premium for that option falls essentially to zero. The margin requirement for this option is now 0.10 x $150.00 x 100, or $1,500. This amount is greater than the $914.50 margin required when the stock was at $62.75 and even more than the $1,320 margin required when the stock was only at $58.50 a share. The put is getting safer and safer, yet the margin requirement is getting larger and larger!

The reason this paradox occurs is simply that the margin formulas shown above were originally developed for uncovered (naked) call options: as the stock price increases, the greater the exposure to the call writer, and the greater the margin has to be to ensure the writer's ability to meet his or her obligation (either to purchase the stock or buy back the call). Rather than develop alternative formulas for put options, the regulators simply adopted the same rules for use with puts. If the margin requirement becomes too high because of this quirk, the solution for investors is rather easy: simply buy back the option and close the position. A full-service brokerage firm that wants your business will often charge just a nominal amount to close out an essentially worthless option under such circumstances. It is in their best interest to do so, for it permits investors to write additional puts and generate further commissions on an immediate basis rather than waiting for the original option to expire. If your broker does not wish to discount the commission under these circumstances, you should consider finding one who does.

Collateral Requirements

The amount of collateral that must be maintained in your account is determined not only by the naked puts and uncovered calls you have written, but by the extent to which you have purchased stocks, bonds, and other securities on margin using funds borrowed from the broker to finance some portion of their acquisition. Collateral (margin) requirements for these other types of securities can range from 50% for stocks and mutual funds all the way down to just 10% for U.S. Treasury obligations. Because the combined value of these assets may decrease, the net equity (market value less borrowings) must meet certain minimum maintenance requirements established by the Federal Reserve Board, the New York Stock Exchange, and the brokerage house itself.

The minimum required maintenance equity on marginable securities is 25% of asset value under Rule 431 of the New York Stock Exchange but is usually set at a higher level, such as 30%, by most brokerage firms. The net equity in your account must be greater than the sum of the minimum maintenance equity on the marginable securities and the required margin on the naked puts, uncovered calls, and any other margined transactions (such as short sales, with their margin of 150% of the short sale value—a figure set high enough to guarantee replacement of the borrowed securities and payment of interim dividends). For example, suppose your account has $100,000 in marginable stocks and mutual funds and that the required margin for the puts you wrote is $25,000. How much can you borrow against your equity if the house rules require a minimum maintenance of 30%?

If B is the amount borrowed, the remaining equity will be $100,000 - B. This figure must not fall below the sum of the $25,000 option margin plus 30% of the $100,000 market value; that is:

$$\$100,000 - B \geq \$25,000 + 0.30 \times \$100,000 = \$55,000$$

This shows that the maximum value that can be borrowed is $45,000. It would be dangerous to borrow that much (or anywhere near that amount), because any decrease in equity value or increase in required option margin would instantly invoke a margin call, requiring the investor either to sell securities or to deposit enough cash or securities into his or her account to bring the account into balance. This is unfortunately exactly what happened to Victor Niederhoffer, who had bet the wrong way on an unbelievable number of currency and index options on the fateful day in October 1997 when the Dow Jones Industrial Average fell 554 points in a single session and he received an additional collateral call of $45 million or so (which he did not have). His autobiography, *Education of a Speculator*, published in early 1997 by John Wiley & Sons, is worthwhile reading.

All brokers produce a daily margin report for each client maintaining a margin account, showing security by security and option by option the margin requirement for each item and how the combined amounts stand in relation to overall limits independently imposed by the brokerage house and Rule 431 of the New York Stock Exchange. Most such reports will also show when the net equity falls below the internal warning level of 50% specified by Regulation T of the Federal Reserve Board.

Who Can Deal in Options?

There is much confusion as to which investors can utilize options as parts of their investment programs. Fiduciaries (those administrating funds on behalf of others) are bound by the prudent-man rules of common law as well as by those of ERISA (Employees Retirement Income Security Act) for retirement accounts. Selling puts seems to meet the standard of the prudent-man rule in that the use of such a mechanism does not in and of itself violate the prudent-man rule. There are no legal restrictions on the use of options by persons investing for themselves in nonretirement accounts; in this situation, limitations placed on options activity are matters between the investor and the broker(s) involved.

The prudent-man restrictions of ERISA do not apply to self-administered pension, retirement, and profit-sharing plans covering a single employee (or the employee and his or her spouse). The reasoning behind this exemption is that as long as the individual is making his or her own investment decisions, it is not the government's place to restrict the level of risk or the investment activities involved, however speculative they may be.

The reason there is confusion about this is because such a laissez-faire philosophy was not always the case. Prior to the enactment of ERISA in 1974, the Internal Revenue Service took the position that no security in a pension plan could be purchased at a price that exceeded the market price at the time of purchase. That would certainly seem to inhibit the writing of naked puts, because any assignment that took place would by definition involve the purchase of stock at (strike) prices greater than the market value whenever exercised. The word "inhibit" rather than "prohibit" is used here because, in theory, if the investor was nimble enough, an in-the-money put could be bought back and the position closed prior to the option being exercised, thereby circumventing such an occurrence.

In addition, Section 4975 of the Internal Revenue Code prohibits certain account holders from borrowing funds or using their funds as security for loans. This has been interpreted by some to mean that pension, retirement, and profit-sharing accounts cannot be margined or have the contingent liability of a stock purchase imposed by a naked put or uncovered call. This is not the case, however.

What it all comes down to is the fact that it is the brokerage houses which serve as custodians for IRA's, SEP's, Keogh's, 401(k)'s and the like that determine the extent to which options may be utilized as part of an individual's investment strategy. Some firms are so conservative as to discourage purchasing calls or protective puts, or even the sale of covered calls—even though a margin account is not needed to conduct any of these option activities. Some brokerage houses will not permit retirement accounts to purchase calls or protective puts, limiting option transactions to the selling of covered calls alone. Even if option activities are permitted by the house rules, bear in mind that individual brokers may discourage such activities simply because of their unfamiliarity with and lack of experience in doing options.

Many brokerage firms do, however, extend margin privileges to pension, retirement, and profit-sharing plans so that they can participate in a wider range of option activities, including the sale of naked puts. In such instances, the range and scope of option activities that brokerage houses permit depends on the experience, account balance, and investment objectives of the account holder.

Establish Your Comfort Zone

To allow for day-to-day fluctuations in the market, and even modest corrections in stock prices along the way, you will want to maintain enough collateral in your brokerage account to avoid virtually any threat of a margin call. How much more collateral to have on hand in relation to the maintenance requirements depends on the premium yield rate desired and the corresponding comfort zone. By the premium yield rate, we mean the dollars received in premiums from the sale of LEAP puts each year as a fraction of your overall portfolio account.

Premium yield is maximized when collateral is equal to the minimum margin requirement. To get some idea of what this might be, let's determine the margin requirements associated with the receipt of each $10,000 worth of LEAP put premiums. From Table 2.1, we see that for a stock price of $100 a share, premiums for a European-style at-the-money LEAP put for a stock with a mid-level volatility of 0.30 range from $8.892 to $11.322 per share ($889 to $1,132 per contract) for times to expiration ranging from 12 to 30 months, respectively. For American-style at-the money LEAP puts, Table B.5 shows the premiums ranging from $9.547 to $13.276 ($955 to $1,328 per contract).

On this basis, we can adopt a conservative figure of $1,000 in premiums per contract for every $100 in stock price. Thus $10,000 in premiums would be the amount received if we sold at-the-money LEAP puts on 10 contracts of a $100 stock. The aggregate stock price on these ten 100-share lots is 10 x 100 x $100, or $100,000.

Since the margin requirement on at-the-money options is 20% of the stock price (plus option premium), you would need $20,000 in cash and equities in your account to generate the $10,000 in premiums. The premiums so received would have to be retained in your account as additional margin (but of course could be used to acquire more stock). If the average time to expiration was 18 months, the annualized premium yield would be $10,000 / ($20,000 x 1.5), or 33.3% per year.

It would be foolish, of course, to sell anywhere near the number of options permitted by the margin requirements. As a practical matter, I would want to have at least three or four times the equity called for under the margin requirements in my account, or perhaps $60,000 to $80,000 in the situation described. Under these circumstances, the annualized premium yield would thus be $10,000 / ($70,000 x 1.5), or roughly 10% per year. I have found that generating premiums equal to 10% of one's portfolio value is a readily achievable, conservative policy. When combined with dividends and capital appreciation, it can mean a substantial difference in the overall growth of an investor's portfolio.

Earthquakes Happen

Historically, there have been days when the bottom seemed to drop out of the market. Whether triggered by a sudden collapse of a foreign stock market, an unexpected increase in interest rates, or other causes, these crashes can result in domestic stock markets falling 10 or 15% during the course of a day or week. On October 19, 1987, the market fell a record 22.6% in a single trading session, and a substantial number of investors who were short puts with expiration dates not far away were impacted significantly. Since the market recovered within 18 months, had the same investors been short LEAP puts with expiration dates up to 30 months away, the financial impact would have been significantly lessened. (Of course, LEAPS did not come into being until 1990, so this was not a possibility at the time.)

Events such as these, when they do occur, have a threefold impact on your portfolio. To start with, the value of your equity portfolio will likely decrease in the same proportion as the overall market. In addition to this, a great many of your short put positions may move from being out of the money to being in the money. And because of the manner in which margin is computed, the collateral requirements to maintain those short put positions may increase significantly (as they did for trader Niederhoffer).

In a worst case scenario, your required margin could move from the minimum level of 10% to the maximum level of 20% of the value of the underlying equities. Such an occurrence could in principle trigger a margin call for additional collateral for very aggressive investors overpositioned with far too many short puts.

When this happens, I have always used the opportunity to make additional money while reducing the risk of eventual assignment. In most instances, market drops reflect oversold situations which are temporary in nature. When this happens, I immediately take advantage of the situation not only by rolling the puts that have gone into the money out and down, but also by increasing the number of contracts.

Let's go back to our previous example in which, in May of 1998, XYZ Corporation is at $53.375 and you write a January 2000 LEAP put with strike price $55 and receive a premium of $8.28. The reason you confidently entered this transaction was because the company earned $2.50 a share and earnings were projected to increase to between $2.90 and $3.00 in one year. As calculated earlier, the initial margin requirement for this option (based on 20% of the stock price plus the premium) is $1,895.50. One year later, earnings are $2.94 and XYZ moves up to $62.75 a share. The premium for that option has fallen to $2.87, for which the margin requirement for this option (based on 10% plus premium) falls to just $914.50. Earnings are projected to go to $3.40 to $3.50 one year after that.

Now suppose that shortly after that, the market falls a whopping 15%, with the stock price dropping to $53.375, thus wiping out an entire year's gain overnight. With eight months to expiration, the premium jumps to $6.03, with a corresponding margin requirement of 0.20 x $53.375 x 100 + $603, or $1,670.50, more than 1.8 times what it was the day before. Although you have taken a conservative approach to put writing, the aggregate impact on your overall margin requirements (because the market break has affected all your put positions in the same way) can be disconcerting. To compound matters, this option, like many of your other options, is now in the money, and early exercise at $55 a share is a potential threat.

In situations such as this, the idea is to take advantage of the temporary slump and not only roll out the option, but also consider increasing the number of contracts involved. You therefore buy back the option for $603 a contract and sell one or more LEAP puts on XYZ with expiration dates 20 months away (since the current LEAP expires in eight months, there will be one that expires in 20 months; two months must pass before LEAP options with 30-month expiration dates will open). You can be aggressive and write a LEAP put with the same strike price of $55, write a slightly out-of-the-money LEAP put with strike $50, or be conservative and write a LEAP put with strike $45.

For a strike price of $55, the premium will be $8.28, for which the margin requirement will be $1,895.50. For a strike price of $50, the premium will be $5.83, for which the margin requirement will be 0.20 x $53.375 x 100 - ($53.375 - $50.00) x 100 + $583, or $1,313. For a strike price of $45, the premium will be $3.84, for which the margin requirement will be 0.10 x $53.375 x 100 + $384, or $917.75.

The appropriate decision here depends very much on how critical it is to maintain your margin requirements. If you are still well within your margin limit, you could keep the $55 strike price, thus pocketing a net premium of $828 less $603, or $225 per contract, with overall margin increasing from $1,670 to $1,895. If margin maintenance is of some concern, you could sell five contracts with a strike price of $50 for every four you buy back, thus essentially breaking even on the transaction after paying commissions while slightly decreasing margin requirements ($1,670 margin on each of four contracts is $6,680, and $1,313 margin on each of five contracts is $6,565). If margin requirements are of great concern, you might sell three contracts with a strike price of $45 for every two you buy back, thus incurring a very small premium shortfall while significantly decreasing margin requirements ($1,670 margin on each of two contracts is $3,340, and $918 margin on each of three contracts is $2,754).

Another thing you should consider doing, if reducing margin becomes important, is to close out positions whose premiums have become relatively small. Even in a general market pull-back or serious contraction, there will likely be issues still so far out of the money that the associated premiums are negligible. Consider the example of the XYZ Corporation stock that went from $53.375 to $150 in a little over a year and that has now perhaps backed off to $100. With a strike price of $55, the premium is essentially zero, yet the margin required to carry maintain this position is $1,000 per contract (i.e., 10% of $10,000). As previously indicated, many brokers will gladly work with their customers in such circumstances and charge a minimum commission to close out such positions.

Covered Put Writing

As stated before, margin is required for writing naked puts and uncovered calls. Investors seeking to increase portfolio income routinely use covered calls to do so. A covered call is where the investor writes a call while also owning the stock. This is sometimes referred to as a *buy-write* if the investor writes the call while simultaneously purchasing the stock. In practice, there is no difference between a buy-write and a selling a covered call. In either instance, there is no margin requirement, and the potential for unlimited exposure should there be a sharp rise in the price of the underlying equity is thereby eliminated. Does the same sort of thing happen if an investor resorts to covered put writing?

First of all, exactly what does it mean to write a covered put? Incredibly enough, there is no universal agreement as to what is meant by this expression. The latest (April 1996) edition of *Understanding Stock Options*, published by the Options Industry Council (a trade organization comprised of the various options exchanges and the Options Clearing Corporation), states that a "put writer is considered to be uncovered if he does not have a corresponding short stock position or has not deposited cash equal to the exercise value of the put." The latest (February 1994) edition of *Characteristics and Risks of Standardized Options*, published by the Options Clearing Corporation, does not use the term covered put as such but refers only to writers of cash-secured puts. In the latest (ninth edition) and earlier editions of the Pass Trak® *Series 7, General Securities Representative*, published by Dearborn Financial Publishing, Inc., a naked (or uncovered) option is defined as "the position of an options investor who writes a call or a put on a security he does not own." An insert in the ninth edition expanded this definition, stating that "in a cash account, a put is covered and the writer is not required to meet option margin requirements if she deposits into the account or presents: cash equal to the aggregate exercise price of the put; an escrow agreement in which a bank certifies that it holds on deposit for the writer funds equal to the aggregate exercise price of the put; or money market securities with a current market value equal to or greater than the aggregate exercise price of the put."

As a result, there are people who believe a covered put writer is one who: (a) is long (owns) the stock; (b) is short the stock; or (c) has cash or cash-equivalent funds in an amount equal to the aggregate exercise price of the put. The correct answer, however, is (b) or (c) in a margin account and (c) in a cash account.

Since we are going to be selling puts in a margin account, let's compare the relative risks and rewards of writing uncovered puts versus covered ones, wherein the investor is short the stock. Interestingly, writing a put while simultaneously short the stock can be more risky than writing a naked put. To understand why, remember that when you write a naked put, the theoretical worst-case situation is where the stock plummets to zero, for a net loss equal to the exercise price less the premium received. Should the price of the stock increase, the gain is the premium received.

Now suppose you write a put and are simultaneously short the stock. In this situation, the investor is completely protected if the price collapses, because any loss on the option as the price of the stock moves below the exercise price is matched dollar for dollar by the gain incurred on the shorted stock. On the other hand, should the price of the stock increase, the potential for loss increases without limit. This is because the unlimited liability on the upside of the short position is mitigated only by the premium received from the sale of the put.

5

CHAPTER 5

DISPOSITION AND TAXES

Introduction

The tax consequences arising out of option transactions are extremely complex. Options, like stocks, are classified as capital assets, and the disposition of such assets is a taxable event. As with stocks, how long the position has been held determines whether the gain or loss is classified as short- or long-term. Furthermore, how the gain or loss is treated also depends on whether the option contract has been terminated through trade, expiration, or exercise and assignment. Because of this sensitivity to how an option contract is terminated, the first part of this chapter describes all three terminating actions and the corresponding times by which they must be initiated and accomplished. These are especially important in nip-and-tuck situations where the exercise price of an option is very close to the market price as the expiration day approaches.

Trading

Until June 23, 1997, trading in all equity options, including LEAP options, stopped at 4:10 p.m.* Today, however, in order to minimize disruptions in the options market as a result of news announcements and earnings reports made after the regular markets close at 4:00 p.m., trading in equity options now ceases at 4:02 p.m. Customers are typically required by brokerage firms to submit requests for

---

* All times in this chapter unless otherwise specified are Eastern time.

option trades by 3:55 p.m. at the latest because of the time needed for them to process the trade. This entails looking up trading symbols, verifying account numbers, and filling out trading slips and submitting them to trading desks, which must in turn transmit the orders to the trading floor of the appropriate stock exchange in time for verification and confirmation. Requests for option trades submitted by customers between 3:55 p.m. and the 4:02 p.m. absolute cutoff time are often accepted and submitted in hopes of beating the deadline, but the customer assumes all risk in such instances. These times apply to expiration Friday* as well.

Although there are no exceptions to the 4:02 p.m. trading cutoff on expiration Friday, the CBOE now extends this closing time on the final trading day of each quarter so as to accommodate the particularly large number of transactions submitted by institutional and mutual fund managers on those days. (The other three exchanges that handle options do not do this, however.) For future reference, note that trading in broad-based and international indexes stops at 4:15 p.m.

Exercise

Option exercise ordinarily begins with the option holder notifying his or her brokerage firm that exercise is to take place.** Through a sequence of steps, notification in turn is given to the appropriate clearinghouse member of the Option Clearing Corporation, the relevant options exchange and, ultimately, the Options Clearing Corporation itself. Predictably, there are different cutoff times at different points in this chain and they vary from brokerage firm to brokerage firm. At the various option exchanges, the cutoff time for notification is typically 4:30 p.m. on all days except expiration Friday, when it is 5:30 p.m.

---

*Options expire on the Saturday following the third Friday of the month, but trading stops on the prior business day. If that Friday is a (stock exchange) holiday, trading ends on Thursday.

**As a matter of course, brokerage firms will automatically exercise options expiring in the money by a certain amount unless instructions to the contrary have been received from the customer. This threshold amount is typically one-half or three-quarters of a point.

The 5:30 p.m. deadline has been known to be extended up to half an hour by options exchanges on the rare occasion when there is a backlog of exercise orders awaiting execution because of jammed communication lines or networking glitches. In any event, the Option Clearing Corporation must receive its notification by 8:00 p.m. (7:00 p.m. in Chicago, where the OCC is located) on all days, including expiration Friday.

To meet all deadlines and allow enough time for confirmation, brokerage firms typically require customers to submit exercise requests by 4:00 p.m. on regular days and by 4:30 p.m. or soon thereafter on expiration Friday. Brokerage firms will rarely, if ever, take on the risk of attempting to submit exercise notices after the cutoff time imposed by clearinghouse members or options exchanges. Although options do not formally expire until noon the next day, Saturday morning is used for reconciliation between open and closed orders and the selection of which option writers get assigned.

Assignment

The assignment of options for which notification has been received in a timely fashion by the Options Clearing Corporation is performed by noon on Saturday. After that time, option rights become absolutely extinguished. However, option writers who did not close their positions will not find out whether the options were exercised against them until some time on the following Monday when they are notified by their brokerage firms. Surprises do happen in this regard.

Holders of slightly in-the-money options frequently elect not to exercise their rights to buy or sell the underlying equity, and holders of at-the-money or slightly out-of-the-money options will sometimes exercise their options during the last trading day because they do not know where the final closing price will be relative to the strike price. Holders of at-the-money or slightly out-of-the money options have been known to exercise their options simply because they want to put stock to or call away stock from the other fellow.

Another surprise that often happens in the final days or hours of trading is that an option writer will instruct his or her broker to buy back the option and close the position only to receive a notice of assignment a business day or so later. If the exercise preceded closing, the option writer is a candidate for assignment notwithstanding the fact that the writer did not receive notification until after the closing transaction took place.

The real surprise to option writers that occurs from time to time is that options are exercised against them that are significantly out of the money. This typically happens as a result of major news (bad or good) announced immediately after regular trading hours on expiration Friday. Suppose you are the writer of a put on XYZ Corporation with strike price $40. You have been monitoring the price of the underlying stock all day long on expiration Friday and are happy to see it close at 4:00 p.m. at $40 5/8. Two minutes later, you see the last trades for $40 puts on XYZ close out at 1/16th. Great, you figure, the premium you collected all those months ago was pure profit, and you can go home and relax for the weekend. At 4:20 p.m., however, XYZ Corporation issues an earnings warning, or announces that it has lost its largest client, or issues a press release stating that its latest wonder drug seems to have harmed more people that it helped. The consensus among analysts is that XYZ will open 3 or more points down when trading commences Monday morning. For the next hour, holders of the $40 put option who stuck around after trading stopped are submitting exercise notices to their brokers. On Monday morning, XYZ opens at $36 a share, and numerous put writers of the $40 strike option who did not close out their positions on Friday wake up to find they are the owners of a $36 stock that has just cost them $40 plus commission.

In situations like this, only a certain fraction of the out-of-the-money options will have been exercised, for the reason that many of the option holders will have considered their option worthless and gone home for the weekend by 4:00 p.m. Suppose the open interest in the $40 put options totaled 1,000 contracts, of which 200 were so exercised at the last minute. Who gets assigned and who does not is determined by a two-step procedure: The Options Clearing Corporation first allocates the 200 assignments among the various brokerage firms in proportion to the open interest each firm represents. That is, if clients of the ABC Securities Corporation had written 120 of the 1,000 open put options, then 20% of 120, or 24 assignments (120 x 200/1,000) would be allocated to ABC. That firm will in turn select 24 option contracts at random from among the 120 open interest put writers and notify them accordingly. It is thus luck of the draw that determines who gets stuck and who does not in such situations.

To avoid such situations, it is therefore recommended that investors make arrangements with their brokers to close out all option contracts that might have any possibility of taking the option writer by surprise owing to bad news announced after trading ends on expiration Friday. If you had pocketed $1,000 in premiums many months before (and earned interest on that amount since then), buying back the option for 1/8th ($12.50) is a relatively small price to pay, and doing this will permit you to leave for the weekend on expiration Friday with complete peace of mind. As stated before, for active participants, many brokers will forgo the usual commission on such deals and charge a nominal amount under the circumstances.

Trading Halts

A frequently asked question on the CBOE bulletin board is exactly what happens to option writers and option holders when trading in the underlying equity is halted. In general, halting the trading in the underlying equity automatically halts the trading of associated options. This restriction applies strictly to trading, so under ordinary situations (order imbalance, news pending, etc.), option holders are still able to exercise their option rights. Much more tricky is what happens on those occasional instances when the OCC suspends option exercise as well. This situation is particularly worrisome near expiration Friday.

As stated in *Characteristics and Risks of Standard Options*, the "OCC or an options market may restrict the exercise of an option while trading in an option has been halted, and the restriction may remain in effect until shortly before expiration." So relax—this means that the OCC must lift the exercise restrictions in sufficient time for option holders to exercise their options before such rights are permanently extinguished.

The Taxpayers Relief Act of 1997

The Tax Act of 1997 introduced substantial changes in the ways in which gains and losses on capital assets are recognized, treated, and taxed. Gains and losses, previously classified as short-term or long-term, are now classified as being short-term, mid-term, or long-term. As before, assets held for under 12 months are short-term; assets held between 12 and 18 months are mid-term, and assets held for 18 months and longer are long-term. Short-term assets are taxed at ordinary income rates, which for individuals can be as high as 39.6%. Mid-term assets are taxed at the flat rate of 28%, and long-term assets are taxed at the flat rate of 20%. A flat rate of 10% is also applicable to individuals in a 15% tax bracket. These rates apply to both the regular and alternative minimum taxes as well. The tax rate on long-term gain on collectibles remains at 28%, and the long-term rate on real estate investments is 25%.

Starting in the year 2001, the capital gains tax rates of 20% and 10% for assets held for five years or more will be 18% and 8%, respectively. Note, however, that the 18% rate (but not the 8% rate) will be restricted to assets acquired on or after January 1, 2001. Individuals in a 15% tax bracket will have their long-term capital gains taxed at just 8% starting in 2001, even on assets acquired before then. These rates are summarized in the table below. As can be seen, the tax on $1,000 of capital gains can range from a maximum of $396 down to as little as $80, depending on the holding period and tax bracket involved.

Table 5.1: Effective Tax Rates on Capital Gains Under the Taxpayers Relief Act of 1997

Prior to Jan 1, 2001		On and After Jan 1, 2001	
Classification of Gain	Applicable Rate	Classification of Gain	Applicable Rate
Short-term (<12 months)	39.6%*	Short-term (<12 months)	39.6%*
Mid-term (12-18 months)	28%	Mid-term (12-18 months)	28%
Long-term (>18 months)	20%	Long-term (>18 months)	18%
Long-term (15% taxpayer)	10%	Long-term (15% taxpayer)	8%
Long-term (collectibles)	28%	Long-term (collectibles)	28%
Long-term (real estate)	25%	Long-term (real estate)	25%

* Maximum tax bracket applicable

Since LEAPS typically have life spans of at most 30 months (although they can by regulation be issued for up to 39 months), the special five-year tax rates of 18% and 8% are of little relevance to option contracts (unless super-long LEAPS are introduced).

Tax Implications for Option Holders

For call and put buyers who sell their options, the gain or loss is the difference between the net sales price (sales price less commission) and the adjusted cost basis (purchase price plus commission). The gain or loss will be classified as short-, mid-, or long-term, depending upon whether the position was held for less than 12 months, between 12 and 18 months, or 18 months or longer. By extension, the capital loss for call and put buyers whose options expire worthless is the adjusted cost basis, and the loss is classified as being short-, mid- or long-term based on the time period between acquisition and expiration.

For call buyers who exercise their options, the adjusted cost basis of acquiring the stock (strike price plus commission) is increased by the adjusted cost basis of the call. Whether the gain or loss upon ultimate sale of the stock is short-, mid-, or long-term will depend on the subsequent holding period of the stock alone, without regard to how long the call was held. For put buyers who exercise their options, the net sales proceeds are reduced by the adjusted cost basis of the put. Whether the gain or loss upon delivery is classified as short-, mid-, or long-term depends solely on how long the stock alone was held, without regard to how long the put was held.

As an example, suppose you purchase a LEAP put for $10 a share plus a $30 commission to protect your position on XYZ, a $50 stock that you've owned for six months:

Cost Basis	$1,000
Plus: Commission	$30
Adjusted Cost Basis	$1,030

Fifteen months later you sell the LEAP put on XYZ for $2 a share less a $25 commission:

Sales Proceeds	$200
Less: Commission	$25
Net Sales Proceeds	$175

The capital gain and corresponding tax for this transaction is therefore:

Adjusted Cost Basis	$1,030
Less: Net Sales Proceeds	$175
Mid-Term Capital Loss	$855
Income Tax @ 28%	$239.40-

The dash indicates a credit that can offset the taxpayer's other tax liability.

Tax Implications for Option Writers

For call and put writers, premiums received are not treated as immediate income. How and when option writers pay taxes on such premiums depends on the disposition of the option involved. For call and put writers who close out their positions by buying back the options involved, the gain or loss is the difference between the adjusted close-out cost (close-out cost plus commission) and the net premium (premium less commission) originally received. In general, the resultant capital gain or loss is treated as a short-term gain or loss, irrespective of the time period involved.* By extension, if the option expires without exercise, the net premium (premium less commission) is treated as a short-term capital gain, irrespective of the time period involved.

---

*The one exception to this occurs when an in-the-money call is written on stock already owned for more than 12 months and the call is purchased back at a loss. In this situation the capital loss is treated as a long-term loss.

As an example, suppose you write a LEAP put on XYZ for $10 a share less a $30 commission:

Premium Generated	$1,000
Less: Commission	$30
Net Premium	$970

Fifteen months later, you buy back that LEAP put for $2 a share plus a $25 commission:

Close-Out Cost	$200
Plus: Commission	$25
Adjusted Close-Out Cost	$225

The short-term capital gain and maximum corresponding tax for this transaction is therefore:

Net Premium	$970
Less: Adjusted Close-Out Cost	$225
Short-Term Capital Gain	$745
Income Tax @ 39.6%	$295.02 (maximum)

Notice that the gain is treated as short-term, irrespective of the holding period.

For call writers whose options were exercised against them, the adjusted sales price (strike price plus commission) of the delivered stock is increased by the net premium (premium less commission) originally received. Whether the gain or loss upon delivery of the stock is classified as short-, mid-, or long-term depends two things: how long the stock was held, and whether the call at the time it was written was out of the money, in but near the money, or deep out of the money.

In general, writing out-of-the-money calls or calls on stock already qualifying for mid- or long-term treatment has no effect on holding period. On the other hand, writing in-but-near-the-money calls on stock held less than 12 months can suspend the prior holding period of the stock, while writing deep-out-of-the-money calls on stock held less than 12 months can eliminate the prior holding period of the stock altogether. Whether a call is classified as in but near the money or deep out of the money depends not only on the relative strike and stock prices involved, but also on the remaining time to expiration. There is no simple formula for all of this, and readers should consult the appropriate tables published by the Internal Revenue Service to determine whether a specific in-the-money call written on stock already owned qualifies for mere suspension versus elimination of the prior holding period.

Covered call writers can elect to use stock they already own or stock they immediately purchase in the open market to deliver, so to that extent they can influence or control the holding period and cost basis of the delivered stock. Such complexities are another reason why I prefer not to utilize covered call writing as part of my investment program.

For put writers whose options were exercised against them, the adjusted purchase price (strike price plus commission) of the acquired stock is decreased by the net premium (premium less commission) originally received. Whether the gain or loss upon delivery of the stock is short-, mid-, or long-term will depend on the subsequent holding period of the stock alone, without regard to when the option was written. As an example, suppose you write a LEAP put with a strike price of $50 on XYZ for $10 a share less a $30 commission:

Premium Generated	$1,000
Less: Commission	$30
Net Premium	$970

Fifteen months later the option is exercised against you (because the stock fell to $40) and you purchase the delivered stock for $50 a share plus a $75 commission:

Strike Price of Stock	$5,000
Plus: Commission	$75
Adjusted Purchase Price	$5,075
Less: Net Premium	$970
Adjusted Cost Basis	$4,105

Six months later, you sell your XYZ shares for $48 a share less a $75 commission:

Sales Proceeds	$4,800
Less: Commission	$75
Net Sales Proceeds	$4,725

The capital gain and maximum corresponding tax for this transaction is therefore:

Net Sales Proceeds	$4,725
Less: Adjusted Cost Basis	$4,105
Short-Term Capital Gain	$620
Income Tax @ 39.6%	$245.52 (maximum)

Notice that the gain is treated as short-term because the holding period is that of the stock, without regard to the length of time the option position was held. Further note that there was a capital gain on ultimate disposition, even though you sold the stock at a price ($48) lower than what you paid for it ($50), a consequence of the premium received 21 months before.

Other Tax Implications

The tax consequences in the case of spreads, strangles, straddles and other combinations are much more complicated and are beyond the scope of this book. Indeed, I think an entire book could be written about the tax implications of puts and calls. There are many traps that await the unwary in the options arena. As a simple instance, suppose you purchased a put to protect a stock in your portfolio that was acquired less than one year before that. The tax implications regarding the put itself are as described above. What is not so apparent is that the holding period of the stock being protected is completely eliminated in that instance and will not begin again until the put is disposed of.

As an example, let's go back to our very first example where you purchased a LEAP put on XYZ to protect your position on this $50 stock that you had purchased for $45 plus a $75 commission and had owned for six months. Fifteen months later, you sold the LEAP put for a loss of $855 and tax credit of $239.40. And suppose you then sold the XYZ stock itself 10 months after that for $80 a share less a $85 commission.

Sales Proceeds	$8,000
Less: Commission	$85
Net Sales Proceeds	$7,915
Cost Basis	$4,500
Plus: Commission	$75
Adjusted Cost Basis	$4,575

The capital gain and maximum corresponding tax for this transaction after having held this stock for 31 months is therefore:

Net Sales Proceeds	$7,915
Less: Adjusted Cost Basis	$4,575
Short-Term Capital Gain	$3,340
Income Tax @ 39.6%	$1,322.64 (maximum)

This is considerably more than the 20% long-term capital gain tax of $668 you were expecting to pay, because as far as tax law is concerned, you had only held the stock for 10 months. There are ways to avoid this, such as by waiting the requisite 12 months before buying the protective put or by "marrying" the put and the stock; that is, by buying both the stock and the put at the same time with the announced intention of selling the stock by exercising the put. In any case, none of this is to scare you away from the use of protective puts as part of your overall asset management program. Rather, it is just to show you that tax law is complex, that as it is applied to options it is even more complex, and that a tax advisor should be consulted before embarking on any extensive options program.

By the way, it is possible to use some of these quirks in the tax law to your advantage in certain situations. For example, suppose you own a stock for close to one year that has tanked badly, but which for one reason or another you do not wish to dispose of immediately. If you do delay the sale, the short-term capital loss will become a long-term loss (and therefore no longer available to offset short-term gains). On the other hand, if you purchase a put or a deep-in-the-money call on that stock, the holding period on the stock is immediately set back to zero, preserving its short-term status. This is true whether you hold the option one minute or one year.

PART II:
RISK, REWARD, AND SAFETY

6

CHAPTER 6

BASELINE ANALYSIS

Reaction and Challenge

As I perfected the basic strategy described in the previous chapters, I began to describe the method to friends and fellow investors. Many of them were horrified to hear that I was dealing with uncovered puts. "Too risky," they said; "It's doomed to failure"; "The gains you make on successful deals will be overwhelmed by gigantic losses on your losers," etc., etc. Listening to them would have you convinced I was playing the ponies or gambling at Las Vegas. It's not hard to understand these initial reactions; after all, *Characteristics and Risks of Standard Options*, a joint publication of the various option exchanges, emphatically states that "As with writing uncovered calls, the risk of writing put options is substantial." This warning is repeated in their companion pamphlet, *Understanding Stock Options*. Few seemed to recall the statement made in the former publication that "The risk of being an option writer may be reduced by the purchase of other options on the same underlying interest—and thereby assuming a spread position—or by acquiring other types of hedging positions in the options markets or other markets."

How could I convince other investors (and myself as well) that what I was doing had the potential to increase the rate of return on my investment portfolio without unnecessary risk? After all, people do invest their funds in uninsured money market funds paying 5% a year rather than federally-insured passbook savings accounts paying just 3% a year. The added return must bring with it a certain degree of added risk, yet almost everyone is willing to accept the risk/reward ratio in this situation.

Methodology

To address this issue, suppose we ask what would have happened if each and every month for the past 10 years or so, starting in January 1987, one had sold an at-the-money (ATM) LEAP put on virtually every single issue listed in Table 2.3 and pocketed the premium. LEAP puts did come into being until 1990, and even then they only appeared on just a handful of stocks, so we will have to imagine for the moment that such puts had been in existence for those equities over the time period in question.

First of all, recall that by "at-the-money" is meant the strike price equal to or immediately below the market price of the underlying issue that accords with standard option rules: if the price of the stock was $23, the option sold was the one at $22.50; if the price was $44, the option sold was the one at $40; and if the price was $247, the option sold was the one at $240.

In most instances, there would have been not just one but two such LEAP puts available for sale each month: the one that expired in the January about a year to a year and a half away, and the one that expired in the January about two to two and a half years away. We will call these the "near" and "far" LEAPS, for the lack of better terms. If the expiration date of the near LEAP was less than eight months away, it was not sold, as we want to restrict the study to an analysis of long-term options.

Since the LEAPS did not exist for most of these issues over the time period in question, no historical information is available on the premiums that such options would have commanded. What was done instead was to use the daily history of closing stock prices over the past decade to compute historical volatility, and from this to use the standard Black-Scholes formula for computing the LEAP put premium on a month-to-month basis. So as not to make the modeling process too complex, the risk-free rate of return was kept at 6% per year throughout, and all volatility calculations were based on the prior one-year (typically 253 trading days) price history.

A data base containing the ten-year history of daily high, low, and closing prices of the 217 common stocks that had LEAPS on March

31, 1997 was downloaded from the America Online historical price files. The list of stocks is shown in Table 6.1, along with their respective ratings by First Call (F/C) and Standard & Poor's (S&P) as of March 31, 1997. Also shown are the volatilities calculated for March 31, 1997. The figures range from a low of 0.150 for Amoco Corporation to an unusually high 1.456 for Compania Tele de Chile. Only 10 of the 217 stocks had volatilities greater than 0.65.

The First Call rating system generates a numerical average determined from the ratings supplied by the industry analysts who follow the stock. An individual analyst's ratings range from 1 (strongest recommendation) to 5 (strong sell). Because of the averaging technique involved, it is rare to see First Call ratings worse than 3.5. The S&P ratings range from A+ (strongest possible) downward. Just one stock (Pitney Bowes) was not rated by First Call, while 37 stocks were not rated by Standard & Poor's. Most of the issues not rated by S&P represented American Depositary Receipts (ADRs) of foreign stocks.

For the 216 issues with First Call ratings, the average is 2.1, which is slightly better than the average rating of about 2.2 for the universe of stocks rated by First Call. Among the 180 issues with S&P ratings, the average is just under B+. (The S&P average was calculated by letting A+ = 5.0, A = 4.5, A- = 4.0, B+ = 3.5, B= 3.0, B- = 2.5, C+ = 2.0, and C = 1.5. The numerical average calculated on this basis was 3.4.) The average volatility for all 217 issues in Table 6.1 is 0.346.

Because of mergers, acquisitions, and spin-offs, LEAPS are no longer issued on seven of the companies appearing in Table 6.1: ENSERCH Corporation merged with Texas Utilities on August 5, 1997; General Instrument spun off into General Semiconductor (and two other firms) on July 25, 1997; Tambrands merged with Procter & Gamble on July 21, 1997; Pacific Telesis Group merged with SBC Communications on April 1, 1997; U.S. Robotics Corporation merged with 3Com on June 13, 1997; Signet Bank was acquired by First Union on November 28, 1997; Salomon was acquired by Travelers on November 28, 1997; and CUC International became Cendant Corporation on December 31, 1997. By the time you read this, other reorganizations will have undoubtedly taken place.

Table 6.1: LEAPS Available in March, 1997

Name of Underlying Equity	Stock	F/C	S&P	Vol.
Abbott Labs	ABT	2.2	A+	0.230
Acuson	ACN	2.2	B-	0.449
Adobe Systems	ADBE	1.7	B+	0.504
Advanced Micro	AMD	2.5	B-	0.537
AirTouch Comm.	ATI	1.6	NR	0.298
Allied Signal	ALD	1.9	B+	0.203
Allstate	ALL	1.9	NR	0.261
Altera	ALTR	1.5	B	0.616
ALZA	AZA	2.4	B	0.246
Amerada Hess	AHC	2.5	B-	0.214
America Online	AOL	1.9	C	0.748
American Express	AXP	2.4	B+	0.252
American Home	AHP	2.0	A+	0.262
American International	AIG	1.6	A+	0.195
Amgen	AMGN	1.8	B	0.311
Amoco	AN	2.7	B+	0.150
AMR	AMR	2.0	B-	0.264
Anheuser-Busch	BUD	2.4	A	0.217
Apple Computer	AAPL	3.1	B	0.536
Applied Materials	AMAT	1.5	B	0.536
ASA Holdings	ASAI	2.6	A	0.341
AT&T	T	2.5	B+	0.271
Atlantic Richfield	ARC	2.7	B+	0.173
Atmel	ATML	1.7	B	0.644
Avon Products	AVP	1.8	B+	0.237
Baker Hughes	BHI	2.0	B	0.315
BankBoston	BKB	1.8	B	0.229
BankAmerica	BAC	1.7	B+	0.270
Bankers Trust NY	BT	2.8	B	0.220
Barrick Gold	ABX	2.4	A	0.302
Bay Networks	BAY	2.6	B	0.510
Bell Atlantic	BEL	2.1	A-	0.226
BellSouth	BLS	2.3	B+	0.291
Best Buy Co.	BBY	3.1	B	0.576
Biogen	BGEN	1.7	B-	0.433
Boeing	BA	1.5	B+	0.246
Borland International	BORL	2.7	C	0.718
Boston Scientific	BSX	1.4	NR	0.354
Bristol-Myers Squibb	BMY	2.6	A	0.255
Burlington Northern	BNI	1.6	NR	0.208
Cabletron Systems	CS	2.0	B+	0.497
Campbell Soup	CPB	2.3	B+	0.209
Caterpillar	CAT	2.7	B	0.247
Centocor	CNTO	1.8	C	0.607

Table 6.1 (cont.): LEAPS Available in March, 1997

Name of Underlying Equity	Stock	F/C	S&P	Vol.
Chase Manhattan	CMB	1.5	B	0.245
Chevron	CHV	2.7	B	0.205
Chiron	CHIR	2.6	C	0.441
Chrysler	C	2.3	B	0.262
Chubb	CB	2.3	A	0.257
Cirrus Logic	CRUS	2.4	B-	0.652
Cisco Systems	CSCO	1.5	B	0.430
Citicorp	CCI	1.9	B	0.237
Coca-Cola	KO	2.0	A+	0.221
Columbia Gas	CG	2.5	NR	0.203
Compania Tele de Chile	CTC	2.4	NR	1.456
Compaq	CPQ	1.5	B	0.405
Conseco	CNC	1.0	B+	0.331
Corning	GLW	1.4	B+	0.301
Cracker Barrel	CBRL	1.8	A	0.325
CUC International	CU	1.5	B	0.348
Cypress Semi	CY	2.5	B	0.530
Dayton Hudson	DH	1.9	A	0.314
Dell Computer	DELL	1.9	B	0.508
Delta Air Lines	DAL	1.8	B-	0.247
Digital Equipment	DEC	3.0	C	0.504
Disney (Walt)	DIS	2.0	A	0.221
Dow Chemical	DOW	2.9	B	0.157
DSC Communications	DIGI	2.2	B	0.628
Dun & Bradstreet	DNB	2.6	B+	0.990
DuPont (E.I.) de Nemours	DD	2.1	B+	0.231
Eastman Kodak	EK	2.0	B	0.273
EFII	EFII	1.3	NR	0.529
EMC	EMC	1.9	B	0.436
ENSERCH	ENS	2.8	B	0.317
Equifax	EFX	2.0	A-	0.324
Ericsson Telephone	ERICY	2.2	NR	0.332
Exxon	XON	2.6	A-	0.192
Fannie Mae	FNM	1.5	A	0.340
Federal Express	FDX	2.4	B-	0.249
Federated Stores	FD	1.7	NR	0.287
First Chicago	FCN	2.3	NR	0.274
Ford Motor	F	1.9	B-	0.224
Fruit of the Loom	FTL	2.3	B-	0.268
Gap	GPS	1.8	A	0.393
General Electric	GE	1.6	A+	0.209
General Instrument	GIC	2.4	NR	0.419
General Mills	GIS	2.6	A	0.179
General Motors	GM	2.0	B	0.236

Table 6.1 (cont.): LEAPS Available in March, 1997

Name of Underlying Equity	Stock	F/C	S&P	Vol.
Georgia-Pacific	GP	2.5	B-	0.193
Gillette	G	1.6	A+	0.242
Glaxo Wellcome	GLX	2.4	NR	0.231
Goodyear Tire	GT	2.3	B	0.189
Grupo Televisa	TV	2.2	NR	0.373
GTE	GTE	1.9	B+	0.259
HealthSouth	HRC	1.6	B+	0.346
Heinz (H.J.)	HNZ	2.6	A+	0.211
Hewlett-Packard	HWP	2.2	A	0.378
HFS Inc.	HFS	1.1	NR	0.423
Hilton Hotels	HLT	1.5	B+	0.291
Home Depot	HD	1.4	A+	0.293
Homestake Mining	HM	2.7	B-	0.330
Household International	HI	2.1	B+	0.236
IBM	IBM	1.9	B-	0.316
Informix	IFMX	2.5	B	0.810
Intel	INTC	1.6	B+	0.331
International Game	IGT	1.5	B+	0.351
International Paper	IP	2.5	B	0.228
ITT	ITT	2.3	NR	0.403
Johnson & Johnson	JNJ	1.9	A+	0.242
KMart	KM	2.5	B+	0.418
Kroger	KR	1.8	B+	0.245
Limited	LTD	2.5	A	0.298
Liposome	LIPO	1.7	C	0.662
Lowe's	LOW	1.8	A-	0.383
Lucent Technologies	LU	2.0	NR	0.354
Madge Networks	MADGF	2.7	NR	0.877
Magna International	MGA	1.4	B	0.185
Marriott International	MAR	1.6	NR	0.218
Maytag	MYG	2.2	B-	0.266
MBNA	KRB	1.9	A-	0.671
McDonald's	MCD	2.4	A+	0.210
McGraw-Hill	MHP	2.5	NR	0.192
MCI Communications	MCIC	2.0	B	0.333
MEMC Electronic	WFR	2.2	NR	0.635
Merck	MRK	2.2	A+	0.253
Merrill Lynch	MER	2.7	B+	0.290
Micron Technology	MU	2.4	B	0.644
Microsoft	MSFT	1.6	B+	0.285
Minn. Mining	MMM	2.9	A+	0.214
Mobil	MOB	2.3	B+	0.175
Mobile Telecomm.	MTEL	2.8	NR	0.587
Monsanto	MTC	1.7	B+	0.314

Table 6.1 (cont.): LEAPS Available in March, 1997

Name of Underlying Equity	Stock	F/C	S&P	Vol.
Morgan (J.P.)	JPM	2.5	B+	0.199
Motorola	MOT	2.2	A+	0.354
National Semiconductor	NSM	2.1	B-	0.478
NationsBank	NB	2.0	A-	0.247
Newbridge Networks	NN	1.7	B	0.509
NEXTEL	NXTL	1.5	NR	0.461
NIKE	NKE	1.9	A	0.334
Novell	NOVL	2.7	B	0.546
NYNEX	NYN	2.4	B+	0.234
Occidental Petroleum	OXY	2.6	B-	0.213
Office Depot	ODP	2.6	B+	0.614
Oracle	ORCL	1.5	B	0.428
Pacific Telesis	PAC	2.6	B	0.279
PepsiCo	PEP	2.0	A	0.264
Pfizer	PFE	2.0	A-	0.258
Pharmacia & Upjohn	PNU	2.7	NR	0.284
Phelps Dodge	PD	2.5	B+	0.231
Philip Morris	MO	1.5	A+	0.289
PHP Healthcare	PPH	3.0	B-	0.662
Pitney Bowes	PBI	NR	A+	0.223
Placer Dome	PDG	2.3	B-	0.308
Polaroid	PRD	2.9	B+	0.217
Potash Saskatchewan	POT	2.3	NR	0.277
PPG Industries	PPG	2.7	A-	0.177
Procter & Gamble	PG	1.7	A	0.210
Quaker Oats	OAT	2.9	B+	0.241
Qualcomm	QCOM	1.6	B-	0.549
Reebok International	RBK	2.4	B+	0.311
RJR Nabisco	RN	1.7	NR	0.300
Safeway	SWY	1.9	B	0.295
Salomon Bros.	SB	2.3	B+	0.270
Sara Lee	SLE	2.3	A	0.214
SBC Communications	SBC	2.2	A	0.209
Schering-Plough	SGP	2.3	A+	0.258
Schlumberger	SLB	2.0	B+	0.261
Schwab	SCH	2.5	B+	0.402
Seagate Technology	SEG	1.7	B	0.477
Sears, Roebuck	S	2.0	B	0.296
Signet Banking	SBK	2.4	B	0.264
SmithKline Beecham	SBH	1.9	NR	0.215
Southwest Air	LUV	2.2	A-	0.350
Sprint	FON	2.2	B+	0.267
Storage Technology	STK	2.0	B-	0.479
Sun Microsystems	SUNW	1.6	B	0.464

Table 6.1 (cont.): LEAPS Available in March, 1997

Name of Underlying Equity	Stock	F/C	S&P	Vol.
SunAmerica	SAI	1.5	A	0.369
Sybase	SYBS	2.7	C	0.562
Tambrands	TMB	2.8	B	0.237
TCI	TCOMA	1.6	NR	0.403
Tele. Argentina	TAR	2.1	NR	0.329
Tele. Brasileiras	TBR	1.3	NR	0.304
Tele. Mexico	TMX	2.3	NR	0.256
Tenneco	TEN	2.5	B	0.224
Texaco	TX	2.5	B	0.204
Texas Instruments	TXN	2.1	B	0.425
3Com	COMS	2.0	B-	0.603
Tiffany &	TIF	1.9	B	0.377
Time Warner	TWX	2.0	B-	0.266
Toys "R" Us	TOY	2.2	B+	0.325
TWA	TWA	2.0	NR	0.682
Travelers	TRV	1.8	A	0.320
Triton Energy	OIL	2.0	B-	0.297
U.S. Robotics	USRX	2.3	B+	0.655
UAL	UAL	1.9	B-	0.356
Union Carbide	UK	2.5	NR	0.230
Unisys	UIS	3.0	C	0.498
United HealthCare	UNH	1.8	B+	0.513
United Technologies	UTX	2.0	B	0.214
Unocal	UCL	2.6	B+	0.257
US Surgical	USS	1.9	B+	0.417
US WEST Comm.	USW	2.4	B+	0.229
US WEST Media	UMG	1.5	NR	0.283
USAir Group	U	2.4	B-	0.431
USX-Marathon	MRO	2.4	NR	0.283
USX-U.S. Steel	X	2.2	NR	0.239
Viacom	VIA.B	1.8	NR	0.304
Wal-Mart	WMT	2.1	A+	0.285
Warner-Lambert	WLA	1.8	A-	0.271
Wells Fargo	WFC	2.2	B+	0.191
Wendy's International	WEN	1.9	A-	0.286
Westinghouse	WX	2.6	B-	0.304
WMX Technologies	WMX	2.3	B	0.255
Woolworth	Z	1.7	C	0.318
WorldCom	WCOM	1.8	B	0.431
Xerox	XRX	1.6	B-	0.310
YPF Anonima	YPF	1.9	NR	0.219

The Simulation Model

After downloading the historical data, I constructed a detailed simulation model which could calculate the effects on each of the 217 issues listed above of having sold a put each month for the period from January, 1987 (or whenever the company came into being) through March 31, 1997. I started the analysis with 1987 because I wanted to include one of the worst days ever from the viewpoint of put sellers—the market decline of 22.6% on October 19, 1987.

Each data history file contained the daily high, low, and closing prices for the stock from January 1, 1987, onward. It is possible to distort the results if the LEAP puts were consistently taken as being sold at that point each month when the underlying issue achieved its low price (and hence commanded its highest put premium). So as not to bias the results, the assumption was made that all LEAP puts were sold at the closing price on the last day of the month.

It is also possible to distort the results if the LEAP puts were consistently taken as being sold only in that month or months where the underlying issue achieved its low price (and hence commanded its highest put premium). It was for this reason that the assumption was made that LEAP puts were sold on each stock each and every month during the calendar year (subject only to a minimum expiration date of eight months).

Yet another way to distort the results is to select a cutoff date ending on a sharp upbeat in market prices. To minimize this possibility, a cutoff date of March 31, 1997 (rather than year-end 1996, or some point later in 1997) was selected for the financial simulation. The reason for this was that the Dow Jones Industrial Average of 6583 and the NASDAQ Composite index of 1222 on March 31, 1997 were well below their closing values for 1996 and were at near their lows for 1997, just prior to their rapid climb to current levels.

Finally, there is the selection of the option pricing formula. As I describe in Chapters 14 and 15, the effect of dividends and the early exercise provisions of American-style options is to increase the price of puts. To adopt as conservative an approach as possible, all premiums were calculated by ignoring dividends and early exercise (i.e., European-style options).

Adopting the procedures outlined above effectively eliminated any attempt to maximum LEAP premiums by "timing the market" or influence the results by selecting a good year to start or a market peak at which to evaluate the final outcomes. All other baseline assumptions and specific output results are summarized in the sequence of tables that follows.

The Results

Table 6.2 shows that by the end of March, 1997, a total of 21,976 near-term and 23,914 far-term LEAP puts would have been written, or 45,890 in all. The number of near-term puts sold is less than the number of far-term puts because of the minimum eight-month expiration period that was imposed on the process. Of the 21,976 near-term puts sold, 20,022 of them would have reached their expiration dates prior to the end of the simulation on March 31, 1997. Of the 23,914 far-term puts sold, 19,383 of them would have reached their expiration dates. The remaining 1,954 near-term active LEAP puts and 4,531 far-term active LEAP puts represent open interest and are investigated as well.

Of the 20,022 near-term LEAP puts that expired, 15,178, or 75.8%, expired out-of-the money (OTM), with no financial exposure to the put writer.* This left 4,844, or 24.2%, of the near-term LEAP puts to expire in the money (ITM). In a similar manner, of the 19,383 far-term LEAP puts that expired, 15,457, or 79.7%, expired out of the money, and 3,926, or 20.3%, expired in the money. The percentage of the far-term puts which expired in the money is thus smaller than that of the near-term puts (20.3% versus 24.2%). This is a result of the additional year that the underlying stock had to recover from any financial difficulties encountered along the way, as well as of the natural growth of earnings during that time frame.

Table 6.3 shows the premiums collected and the corresponding financial exposure incurred during the study period for the LEAP puts which expired prior to March 31, 1997. The premiums collected

---

*This ignores the possibility of early exercise when the option might have been in the money; however, as many if not most puts are purchased as insurance against market decline, in-the-money puts are ordinarily not exercised until close to expiration.

were $3.8 million on the near-term LEAP puts and $4.5 million on the far-term LEAP puts. The total of almost $8.4 million in premiums shown is just for the 39,405 LEAP puts that expired, not for the total number of 45,890 written.

So as to establish a baseline of the premiums received and financial exposure encountered, no hedging strategies whatsoever were adopted on this initial run. The premiums received in this baseline run were presumed to be immediately invested in money market funds earning a risk-free rate of return of 6%. Such funds, if left on deposit and compounded to the end of the simulation run on March 31, 1997, would be substantial. To focus on the underlying mechanics of the LEAP process, Table 6.3 considers the effects of interest earned on the premiums only between the time the premium was received and the expiration date of the corresponding LEAP. The combined total amount of the LEAP premium and the interest earned through expiration is called the *forward value* of the premium, and is seen to be $4.1 million for the near-term LEAPS and $5.1 million for the far-term LEAPS. It is the forward value of the premiums that are then used to cover the financial exposure incurred by various LEAP puts which expired in the money.

Financial exposure is the difference between the stock price and the strike price at expiration, if the latter is greater. For the 4,844 near-term LEAP puts expiring in the money, the financial exposure is $2.7 million, which is equivalent to an average potential loss of $558 per contract. For the 3,926 far-term LEAP puts expiring in the money it is $2.9 million, for an average potential loss of $743 per contract. Why is the average loss on the far-term ITM LEAP puts greater than the average loss on the near-term ITM LEAP puts? The reason is that the universe of 217 stocks includes several lower-rated issues that fared very poorly over the 10-year period investigated. Because of the virtually downhill price histories of these particular issues, the longer the term of the LEAP put, the greater the financial exposure encountered.

On the other hand, the higher premium associated with far-term LEAPS often more than offsets the higher level of financial risk involved. To see this, note that the realized gain on the near-term LEAP puts is calculated as the $4,081,004 forward value of the premiums less the $2,701,176 in financial exposure involved, or $1,379,828. This realized gain as a percentage of the $3,828,194 in premiums collected on the near-term LEAP puts is 36.0%, and is referred to as the *retention rate* in Table 6.3. For the far-term LEAP puts, the retention rate is 48.1%. So while the average loss on the far-term ITM LEAP puts is higher, so is their retention rate. The overall retention rate is 42.6%.

Table 6.4 shows what's happening with the 6,485 active LEAP puts that had not yet expired by the cutoff date of the simulation. The premiums collected on the 1,954 active near-term LEAP puts totaled $698,972. When invested at 6% per year (compounded monthly), they were worth $712,791 on March 31, 1997. These active near-term LEAP puts had a residual value of $652,565 on that date, for an unrealized gain of $60,226. In a similar manner, the unrealized gain on the 4,531 active far-term LEAP puts was $266,175. The total unrealized gain was thus $326,401 on March 31, 1997. The number of active far-term LEAP puts is going to be much larger than the number of near-term LEAP puts because there are that many more of them whose expiration date is later than March 31, 1997.

Table 6.5 brings together the financial results on the 39,405 expired and 6,485 active LEAP puts. This table shows the effect of leaving the net realized gains on deposit to compound at 6% interest from expiration through the end of the study period on March 31, 1997. A total of $10,836,330 in premiums would have been received over the 10-year study period on the 45,890 LEAP puts written, including both expired and still-active LEAPS. By March 31, 1997, the total realized gain and interest earned from the sale of the expired LEAP puts would have been $4,471,186. Combining this with the unrealized gain of $326,401 on the active puts yields an overall account value on March 31, 1997 of $4,797,587.

As a final, overall figure of merit, we note that the account value of close to $4.8 million on March 31, 1997 is 44.3% of the $10,836,330 in premiums generated over the course of the run. It is to be emphasized that it is not the account value of $4.8 million nor the $10.8 million in premiums that is important here, but rather the ratio of the two. Obviously, no one is going to sell one or more LEAP contracts each month on every one of the possible stocks for which LEAPS are available. What we have established is that if you had sold a *random* number of at-the-money LEAP puts on a *random* number of stocks on a *random* schedule throughout each year over the past ten years, and invested the net premiums in money market funds, the expected value of your account balance at the end would be about 44% of the total premiums ever collected.

The realized and unrealized gains determined above ignore the effect of taxation and all transaction costs, fees, and commissions. These can be significant because irrespective of the holding period involved, the gains on puts that expire worthless are treated as short-term capital gains. On this basis, after-tax results on a net-commission basis would be somewhat smaller than those shown in the tables.

Of course, this isn't the real problem associated with the above results. The real problem is that the high level of financial exposure relative to the premiums collected. Although only 22.3% of the LEAPS will expire in the money, their effect is to force the return of 58.4% of the forward values of the premiums received (the complement of the 42.6% retention rate in Table 6.3).

In view of this, maybe my friends were correct in saying that "the gains you make on successful deals will be overwhelmed by gigantic losses on your losers." On the other hand, surely one could decrease one's financial exposure by being more discriminating about what stocks to select for selling LEAP puts on, as well as by adopting appropriate hedging strategies, such as the use of spreads and roll-outs and the selling of out-of-the money puts. Each of these techniques will be considered in the chapters that follow.

Run No. 1:

ATM Strike Price is the High, Low, or Closing Stock Price: C
No. of Steps LEAP Put is below the ATM Strike Price: 0
Minimum No. of Months till Expiration: 8
Premium Reinvestment Rate: 6.0%
Minimum First Call Rating: 5.0
Minimum Standard & Poor's Rating: None
No. of Stocks Meeting Either Criterion: 217

Table 6.2: LEAP OTM and ITM Rates

	LEAPS Written	LEAPS Expired	Expired OTM	OTM Rate	Expired ITM	ITM Rate	LEAPS Active
Near:	21,976	20,022	15,178	75.8%	4,844	24.2%	1,954
Far:	23,914	19,383	15,457	79.7%	3,926	20.3%	4,531
Total:	45,890	39,405	30,635	77.7%	8,770	22.3%	6,485

Table 6.3: Premiums Collected and Realized Gain for Expired LEAPS

	LEAPS Expired	Premiums Collected	Forward Value	ITM Exposure	Realized Gain	Retent'n Rate
Near:	20,022	$3,828,194	$4,081,004	$2,701,176	$1,379,828	36.0%
Far:	19,383	$4,526,083	$5,097,433	$2,918,755	$2,178,678	48.1%
Total:	39,405	$8,354,277	$9,178,437	$5,619,931	$3,558,506	42.6%

Table 6.4: Premiums Collected and Unrealized Gain on Active LEAPS

	LEAPS Active	Premiums Collected	Forward Value	Residual Value	Unrealized Gain
Near:	1,954	$698,972	$712,791	$652,565	$60,226
Far:	4,531	$1,783,085	$1,865,301	$1,599,126	$266,175
Total:	6,485	$2,482,057	$2,578,092	$2,251,691	$326,401

Table 6.5: Premiums Collected and Account Values

	Original Cont'cts	Premiums Collected	Compound Gain	Unrealized Gain	Account Value	Value Ratio
Near:	21,976	$4,527,167	$1,727,337	$60,226	$1,787,564	39.5%
Far:	23,914	$6,309,168	$2,743,849	$266,175	$3,010,023	47.7%
Total:	45,890	$10,836,330	$4,471,186	$326,401	$4,797,587	44.3%

CHAPTER 7

ELIMINATING DOGS

Introduction

So far, we have considered the effect of selling at-the-money puts on the entire universe of 217 stocks that had LEAP options on March 31, 1997. We saw that 77.7% of the time, the stock closed out of the money, and for every $8,354 received in premiums and interest on expired LEAPS, the net amount retained was $3,559. The remaining portion of the premiums and interest, $5,620, was needed to close out losing positions. Because of the longer expiration time involved, the net amount retained on the far-term LEAPS averaged out to 48.1%, while on the near-term LEAPS the net amount retained averaged out to just 36.0%. Finally, the account balance at the end of the ten-year period was 44.3% of the total premiums ever collected.

Such results are hardly worth boasting about. One way to improve them might be to restrict the sale of LEAP puts to better-quality issues. In this chapter, we'll investigate what would have happened if we had sold LEAP puts only on those issues whose underlying stocks were rated 2.0 or better by First Call *or* were rated B or better by Standard & Poor's. We use "or" rather than "and" because the 37 stocks appearing in Table 6.1 that were not rated by Standard & Poor's would automatically have been eliminated on that account alone. We will conduct this investigation in three phases.

In the first phase, the universe will consist of those issues whose underlying stocks were rated 2.0 or better by First Call *or* were rated B or better by Standard & Poor's. In the second phase, the universe will be restricted even further to those issues whose underlying stocks were rated 1.6 or better by First Call *or* B+ or better by Standard & Poor's. And in the third phase, the universe will be restricted to those issues whose underlying stocks were rated 1.2 or better by First Call *or* A- or better by Standard & Poor's. For lack of better nomenclature, we will refer to these populations as the "B minimum," "B+ minimum," and "A- minimum" universes.

The B Minimum Universe

The method used in the previous chapter was first applied to those LEAPS whose underlying stocks were rated 2.0 or better by First Call *or* B or better by Standard & Poor's. To be precise, the above criteria ought to be applied on a month-by-month basis to each stock over the ten-year history studied. But since there is no readily available history file of First Call ratings, what was done instead was to include or exclude issues on the basis of their First Call and S&P ratings of March 31, 1997. On that basis, LEAP puts would have been sold on 178 of the 217 stocks listed in Table 6.1. As is discussed below, the elimination of the lowest-rated 39 issues substantially improved the results.

As shown in Table 7.1, the number of LEAP contracts written over the ten-year simulation decreases to 38,637. Of these, 33,312 expired and 5,325 were still active on the cutoff date of March 31, 1997. The percentage of options expiring out of the money is now 80.0%. Although this represents an increase of just 2.4 percentage points in the OTM rate from the base level of 77.7% in Run No. 1, the impact on overall retention rates is significant. Table 7.2 shows that the overall retention rate grows from 42.6% in Run No. 1 to 54.3%, an increase of 11.7 percentage points. This premium retention rate is now 46.6% on the near-term LEAPS and 60.9% on the far-term LEAPS.

From Table 7.4, we see that the account value on March 31, 1997 resulting from the net premiums, accrued interest, and unrealized gains will be $5,117,983. This figure is 57.5% of the $8,895,368 in premiums ever generated.

The B+ Minimum Universe

Suppose we had discriminated even further and restricted the sale of LEAP puts to stocks that had a First Call rating of 1.6 or better *or* an S&P rating of B+ or better on March 31, 1997. The number of issues qualifying would now be just 115, with dramatically improved results.

As shown in Table 7.5, the number of LEAP contracts written decreases to 25,302, with 21,858 having expired and 3,444 still active on March 31, 1997. The percentage of options expiring out of the money would have increased even further to 84.0%. Table 7.6 shows that the overall retention rate is now 66.2%, an increase of 23.6 percentage points from the baseline level of 42.6% in Run No. 1. The premium retention rate is now 57.8% on the near-term LEAPS and 73.4% on the far-term LEAPS.

From Table 7.8, we see that the account value on March 31, 1997 resulting from the net premiums, accrued interest, and unrealized gains will be $3,697,495. This figure is 69.7% of the $5,303,771 in premiums ever generated.

The A- Minimum Universe

Now suppose we further restricted the sale of LEAP puts to stocks that had a First Call rating of 1.2 or better *or* an S&P rating of A- or better on March 31, 1997. The number of issues qualifying would have fallen to just 50, representing the highest-quality issues having LEAP options.

As shown in Table 7.9, the number of LEAP contracts written decreases to 11,520, with 10,018 having expired and 1,502 still active on March 31, 1997. The percentage of options expiring out of the money would have increased further still to 87.1%. Table 7.10 shows that the overall retention rate is now 79.9%, an increase of 37.3 percentage points from the base level of 42.6% in Run No. 1. The premium retention rate is now 71.8% on the near-term LEAPS and 86.8% on the far-term LEAPS.

From Table 7.12, we see that account value on March 31, 1997 resulting from the net premiums, accrued interest, and unrealized gains will be $1,611,512. This figure is 84.9% of the $1,898,748 in premiums ever generated.

Run No. 2:

ATM Strike Price is the High, Low, or Closing Stock Price: C
No. of Steps LEAP Put is below ATM Strike Price: 0
Minimum No. of Months till Expiration: 8
Premium Reinvestment Rate: 6.0%
Minimum First Call Rating: 2.0
Minimum Standard & Poor's Rating: B
No. of Stocks Meeting Either Criterion: 178

Table 7.1: LEAP OTM and ITM Rates

	LEAPS Written	LEAPS Expired	Expired OTM	OTM Rate	Expired ITM	ITM Rate	LEAPS Active
Near:	18,501	16,898	13,180	78.0%	3,718	22.0%	1,603
Far:	20,136	16,414	13,465	82.0%	2,949	18.0%	3,722
Total:	38,637	33,312	26,645	80.0%	6,667	20.0%	5,325

Table 7.2: Premiums Collected and Realized Gain for Expired LEAPS

	LEAPS Expired	Premiums Collected	Forward Value	ITM Exposure	Realized Gain	Retent'n Rate
Near:	16,898	$3,117,588	$3,323,413	$1,871,962	$1,451,451	46.6%
Far:	16,414	$3,686,137	$4,151,508	$1,907,776	$2,243,732	60.9%
Total:	33,312	$6,803,725	$7,474,921	$3,779,739	$3,695,183	54.3%

Table 7.3: Premiums Collected and Unrealized Gain on Active LEAPS

	LEAPS Active	Premiums Collected	Forward Value	Residual Value	Unrealized Gain
Near:	1,603	$602,343	$614,183	$524,708	$89,474
Far:	3,722	$1,489,300	$1,556,507	$1,184,486	$372,020
Total:	5,325	$2,091,643	$2,170,689	$1,709,195	$461,495

Table 7.4: Premiums Collected and Account Values

	Original Cont'cts	Premiums Collected	Compound Gain	Unrealized Gain	Account Value	Value Ratio
Near:	18,501	$3,719,931	$1,817,314	$89,474	$1,906,788	51.3%
Far:	20,136	$5,175,437	$2,839,175	$372,020	$3,211,195	62.0%
Total:	38,637	$8,895,368	$4,656,489	$461,495	$5,117,983	57.5%

Run No. 3:

ATM Strike Price is the High, Low, or Closing Stock Price: C
No. of Steps LEAP Put is below ATM Strike Price: 0
Minimum No. of Months till Expiration: 8
Premium Reinvestment Rate: 6.0%
Minimum First Call Rating: 1.6
Minimum Standard & Poor's Rating: B+
No. of Stocks Meeting Either Criterion: 115

Table 7.5: LEAP OTM and ITM Rates

	LEAPS Written	LEAPS Expired	Expired OTM	OTM Rate	Expired ITM	ITM Rate	LEAPS Active
Near:	12,116	11,080	9,055	81.7%	2,025	18.3%	1,036
Far:	13,186	10,778	9,299	86.3%	1,479	13.7%	2,408
Total:	25,302	21,858	18,354	84.0%	3,504	16.0%	3,444

Table 7.6: Premiums Collected and Realized Gain for Expired LEAPS

	LEAPS Expired	Premiums Collected	Forward Value	ITM Exposure	Realized Gain	Retent'n Rate
Near:	11,080	$1,835,915	$1,957,072	$895,583	$1,061,489	57.8%
Far:	10,778	$2,156,467	$2,428,733	$846,840	$1,581,893	73.4%
Total:	21,858	$3,992,382	$4,385,805	$1,742,423	$2,643,382	66.2%

Table 7.7: Premiums Collected and Unrealized Gain on Active LEAPS

	LEAPS Active	Premiums Collected	Forward Value	Residual Value	Unrealized Gain
Near:	1,036	$386,048	$393,551	$330,773	$62,778
Far:	2,408	$925,341	$966,239	$689,007	$277,233
Total:	3,444	$1,311,389	$1,359,790	$1,019,779	$340,010

Table 7.8: Premiums Collected and Account Values

	Original Cont'cts	Premiums Collected	Compound Gain	Unrealized Gain	Account Value	Value Ratio
Near:	12,116	$2,221,964	$1,340,532	$62,778	$1,403,309	63.2%
Far:	13,186	$3,081,807	$2,016,953	$277,233	$2,294,186	74.4%
Total:	25,302	$5,303,771	$3,357,485	$340,010	$3,697,495	69.7%

Run No. 4:

ATM Strike Price is the High, Low, or Closing Stock Price: C
No. of Steps LEAP Put is below ATM Strike Price: 0
Minimum No. of Months till Expiration: 8
Premium Reinvestment Rate: 6.0%
Minimum First Call Rating: 1.2
Minimum Standard & Poor's Rating: A-
No. of Stocks Meeting Either Criterion: 50

Table 7.9: LEAP OTM and ITM Rates

	LEAPS Written	LEAPS Expired	Expired OTM	OTM Rate	Expired ITM	ITM Rate	LEAPS Active
Near:	5,516	5,065	4,292	84.7%	773	15.3%	451
Far:	6,004	4,953	4,435	89.5%	518	10.5%	1,051
Total:	11,520	10,018	8,727	87.1%	1,291	12.9%	1,502

Table 7.10: Premiums Collected and Realized Gain for Expired LEAPS

	LEAPS Expired	Premiums Collected	Forward Value	ITM Exposure	Realized Gain	Retent'n Rate
Near:	5,065	$656,632	$700,038	$228,728	$471,310	71.8%
Far:	4,953	$783,524	$882,534	$202,719	$679,815	86.8%
Total:	10,018	$1,440,155	$1,582,571	$431,447	$1,151,125	79.9%

Table 7.11: Premiums Collected and Unrealized Gain on Active LEAPS

	LEAPS Active	Premiums Collected	Forward Value	Residual Value	Unrealized Gain
Near:	451	$138,639	$141,294	$116,837	$24,457
Far:	1,051	$319,954	$333,714	$218,707	$115,007
Total:	1,502	$458,593	$475,008	$335,544	$139,464

Table 7.12: Premiums Collected and Account Values

	Original Cont'cts	Premiums Collected	Compound Gain	Unrealized Gain	Account Value	Value Ratio
Near:	5,516	$795,270	$603,605	$24,457	$628,062	79.0%
Far:	6,004	$1,103,477	$868,443	$115,007	$983,450	89.1%
Total:	11,520	$1,898,748	$1,472,048	$139,464	$1,611,512	84.9%

Summary of Results

As a way of comparing the results obtained so far, let's tabulate the OTM rates, retention rates, and overall ten-year value ratios for the four cases investigated.

Table 7.13: Figures of Merit as a Function of Stock Rating

Run No.	Uni-verse	No. of Issues	Steady-State OTM Rate	Steady-State Retent'n Rate	Ten-Year Value Ratio
1.	All	217	77.7%	42.6%	44.3%
2.	B min	178	80.0%	54.3%	57.5%
3.	B+ min	115	84.0%	66.2%	69.7%
4.	A- min	50	87.1%	79.9%	84.9%

As Table 7.13 clearly shows, as the quality of the underlying stocks increases, the greater the chance that the options will expire out of the money, the greater the percentage of premiums retained, and the greater the account balance as a percentage of premiums collected.

We do not mean to imply that investors should limit the sale of LEAP puts strictly to high-quality B+, A-, or A rated companies. Situations will arise from time to time where it is financially advantageous to sell options on companies with lesser-quality issues, especially in those instances involving reorganizations, turnarounds, takeovers, and mergers.

8

CHAPTER 8

OUT-OF-THE-MONEY LEAPS

Introduction

We saw in the previous chapter that restricting the sale of at-the-money LEAP puts to better stocks could significantly increase the proportion of LEAPS that would expire worthless, thereby reducing financial risk and increasing retention rates and ultimate profitability. Another way to reduce risk while maintaining adequate retention rates is to sell LEAP puts that are one or more steps below the at-the-money exercise price. However, although writing out-of-the-money puts is certainly safer than writing at-the-money puts, the premiums will be correspondingly smaller because of the reduced level of risk involved. Whether such a strategy is cost effective is the subject of this chapter.

Our study employs two series of computer runs. In the first series, we repeat the simulations performed in Runs No. 3 and 4, but this time all of the strike prices are set one step below the at-the-money exercise prices used earlier. Recall that strike price intervals for LEAP (and standard) options are set in increments of $2.50 when the stock price is between $5 and $25, in increments of $5.00 when the stock price is between $25 and $200, and in increments of $10.00 when the strike price is over $200. The one-step out-of-the-money strike price for a stock at $21 is therefore $17.50; for a stock at $34, it is $25; and for a stock at $205, it is $190.

In the second series, we repeat the simulations, but this time with all of the strike prices set two steps below the at-the-money exercise prices used before.

One-Step OTM LEAPS on the B+ Minimum Universe

Run No. 5 is the analog of Run No. 3, in which the sale of LEAP puts was restricted to the 115 stocks in the B+ minimum universe, but this time the strike prices are set one step out of the money. As shown in Table 8.1, the number of LEAP contracts written is again 25,302, with 21,858 contracts expired and 3,444 still active on March 31, 1997. The percentage of options expiring out of the money increases from 84.0% in Run No. 3 to 92.5%.

Setting the exercise price one step below the ATM strike price reduces risk significantly but heavily impacts the premiums received. This can be readily observed by comparing the $2,066,174 in premiums collected for the expired LEAP puts in Table 8.2 against the $3,992,382 in premiums shown in Table 7.6. On the other hand, the overall retention increases from 66.2% in Table 7.6 to 70.4% in Table 8.2. Account value as a percentage of total premiums collected is up from 69.7% in Table 7.8 to 72.6% in Table 8.4.

One-Step OTM LEAPS on the A- Minimum Universe

Run No. 6 is the analog of Run No. 4, in which the sale of LEAP puts was restricted to the 50 stocks in the A- minimum universe, but this time with the strike prices set at one step out of the money. As shown in Table 8.5, the number of LEAP contracts written is again 11,520, with 10,018 contracts expired and 1,502 still active on March 31, 1997. The percentage of options expiring out of the money increases from 87.1% in Run No. 4 to 95.1%.

Setting the exercise price one step below the ATM strike price again reduces risk significantly, and again heavily impacts the premiums received: compare the $649,621 in premiums collected for the expired LEAP puts in Table 8.6 against the $1,440,155 in premiums in Table 7.10. And again, the overall retention rate increases from 79.9% in Table 7.10 to 90.0% in Table 8.6. Account value as a percentage of total premiums collected is now 91.6% (Table 8.8), well ahead of the 84.9% figure seen in Table 7.12.

Two-Step OTM LEAPS on the B+ Minimum Universe

Run No. 7 is the analog of Run No. 3, in which the sale of LEAP puts was restricted to the 115 stocks in the B+ minimum universe, but this time with the strike prices set at two steps out of the money. As shown in Table 8.9, the number of LEAP contracts written is again 25,302, with 21,858 contracts expired and 3,444 still active on March 31, 1997. The percentage of options expiring out of the money increases from 84.0% in Run No. 3 to 95.6%.

As you might predict, setting the exercise price two steps below the ATM strike price greatly reduces risk, but also impacts the premiums received even more dramatically. Compare the $1,136,869 in premiums collected for expired LEAP puts in Table 8.10 against the $3,992,382 shown in Table 7.6. Overall retention rate in Table 8.10 increases to 71.1% from the 66.2% figure seen in Table 7.6. Account value as a percentage of total premiums collected in Table 8.12 is now 73.6%, up from 69.7% in Table 7.8.

Two-Step OTM LEAPS on the A- Minimum Universe

Run No. 8 is the analog of Run No. 4, in which the sale of LEAP puts was restricted to the 50 stocks in the A- minimum universe, but now with the strike prices set at two steps out of the money. As shown in Table 8.13, the number of LEAP contracts written is again 11,520, with 10,018 contracts expired and 1,502 still active on March 31, 1997. The percentage of options expiring out of the money increases from 87.1% in Run No. 4 to 97.1%.

The other results are entirely predictable. Premiums collected for the expired LEAP puts total $330,155 in Table 8.14 compared with the $1,440,155 in Table 7.10. The overall retention rate increases from 79.9% in Table 7.10 to 95.7%, and account value as a percentage of total premiums collected is now 98.3%, well ahead of the 84.9% seen in Table 7.12.

Run No. 5:

ATM Strike Price is the High, Low, or Closing Stock Price: C
No. of Steps LEAP Put is below ATM Strike Price: 1
Minimum No. of Months till Expiration: 8
Premium Reinvestment Rate: 6.0%
Minimum First Call Rating: 1.6
Minimum Standard & Poor's Rating: B+
No. of Stocks Meeting Either Criterion: 115

Table 8.1: LEAP OTM and ITM Rates

	LEAPS Written	LEAPS Expired	Expired OTM	OTM Rate	Expired ITM	ITM Rate	LEAPS Active
Near:	12,116	11,080	10,177	91.9%	903	8.1%	1,036
Far:	13,186	10,778	10,040	93.2%	738	6.8%	2,408
Total:	25,302	21,858	20,217	92.5%	1,641	7.5%	3,444

Table 8.2: Premiums Collected and Realized Gain for Expired LEAPS

	LEAPS Expired	Premiums Collected	Forward Value	ITM Exposure	Realized Gain	Retent'n Rate
Near:	11,080	$870,704	$929,123	$393,369	$535,754	61.5%
Far:	10,778	$1,195,471	$1,347,097	$429,109	$917,989	76.8%
Total:	21,858	$2,066,174	$2,276,221	$822,478	$1,453,743	70.4%

Table 8.3: Premiums Collected and Unrealized Gain on Active LEAPS

	LEAPS Active	Premiums Collected	Forward Value	Residual Value	Unrealized Gain
Near:	1,036	$232,269	$236,786	$194,803	$41,982
Far:	2,408	$593,555	$618,822	$444,505	$174,317
Total:	3,444	$825,824	$855,608	$639,308	$216,300

Table 8.4: Premiums Collected and Account Values

	Original Cont'cts	Premiums Collected	Compound Gain	Unrealized Gain	Account Value	Value Ratio
Near:	12,116	$1,102,973	$690,495	$41,982	$732,477	66.4%
Far:	13,186	$1,789,026	$1,191,361	$174,317	$1,365,678	76.3%
Total:	25,302	$2,891,998	$1,881,855	$216,300	$2,098,155	72.6%

Run No. 6:

ATM Strike Price is the High, Low, or Closing Stock Price: C
No. of Steps LEAP Put is below ATM Strike Price: 1
Minimum No. of Months till Expiration: 8
Premium Reinvestment Rate: 6.0%
Minimum First Call Rating: 1.2
Minimum Standard & Poor's Rating: A-
No. of Stocks Meeting Either Criterion: 50

Table 8.5: LEAP OTM and ITM Rates

	LEAPS Written	LEAPS Expired	Expired OTM	OTM Rate	Expired ITM	ITM Rate	LEAPS Active
Near:	5,516	5,065	4,800	94.8%	265	5.2%	451
Far:	6,004	4,953	4,729	95.5%	224	4.5%	1,051
Total:	11,520	10,018	9,529	95.1%	489	4.9%	1,502

Table 8.6: Premiums Collected and Realized Gain for Expired LEAPS

	LEAPS Expired	Premiums Collected	Forward Value	ITM Exposure	Realized Gain	Retent'n Rate
Near:	5,065	$264,349	$282,199	$65,498	$216,701	82.0%
Far:	4,953	$385,272	$434,226	$66,443	$367,784	95.5%
Total:	10,018	$649,621	$716,426	$131,940	$584,485	90.0%

Table 8.7: Premiums Collected and Unrealized Gain on Active LEAPS

	LEAPS Active	Premiums Collected	Forward Value	Residual Value	Unrealized Gain
Near:	451	$76,630	$78,093	$63,358	$14,735
Far:	1,051	$189,212	$196,907	$128,283	$68,623
Total:	1,502	$265,842	$275,000	$191,641	$83,359

Table 8.8: Premiums Collected and Account Values

	Original Cont'cts	Premiums Collected	Compound Gain	Unrealized Gain	Account Value	Value Ratio
Near:	5,516	$340,979	$280,707	$14,735	$295,443	86.6%
Far:	6,004	$574,484	$474,186	$68,623	$542,809	94.5%
Total:	11,520	$915,463	$754,893	$83,359	$838,252	91.6%

Run No. 7:

ATM Strike Price is the High, Low, or Closing Stock Price:	C
No. of Steps LEAP Put is below ATM Strike Price:	2
Minimum No. of Months till Expiration:	8
Premium Reinvestment Rate:	6.0%
Minimum First Call Rating:	1.6
Minimum Standard & Poor's Rating:	B+
No. of Stocks Meeting Either Criterion:	115

Table 8.9: LEAP OTM and ITM Rates

	LEAPS Written	LEAPS Expired	Expired OTM	OTM Rate	Expired ITM	ITM Rate	LEAPS Active
Near:	12,116	11,080	10,547	95.2%	533	4.8%	1,036
Far:	13,186	10,778	10,343	96.0%	435	4.0%	2,408
Total:	25,302	21,858	20,890	95.6%	968	4.4%	3,444

Table 8.10: Premiums Collected and Realized Gain for Expired LEAPS

	LEAPS Expired	Premiums Collected	Forward Value	ITM Exposure	Realized Gain	Retent'n Rate
Near:	11,080	$447,303	$477,653	$208,363	$269,291	60.2%
Far:	10,778	$689,566	$777,415	$237,967	$539,448	78.2%
Total:	21,858	$1,136,869	$1,255,068	$446,329	$808,739	71.1%

Table 8.11: Premiums Collected and Unrealized Gain on Active LEAPS

	LEAPS Active	Premiums Collected	Forward Value	Residual Value	Unrealized Gain
Near:	1,036	$133,071	$135,651	$111,068	$24,583
Far:	2,408	$364,184	$379,020	$280,836	$98,184
Total:	3,444	$497,255	$514,671	$391,904	$122,767

Table 8.12: Premiums Collected and Account Values

	Original Cont'cts	Premiums Collected	Compound Gain	Unrealized Gain	Account Value	Value Ratio
Near:	12,116	$580,374	$360,255	$24,583	$384,837	66.3%
Far:	13,186	$1,053,750	$720,099	$98,184	$818,283	77.7%
Total:	25,302	$1,634,124	$1,080,354	$122,767	$1,203,120	73.6%

Run No. 8:

ATM Strike Price is the High, Low, or Closing Stock Price: C
No. of Steps LEAP Put is below ATM Strike Price: 2
Minimum No. of Months till Expiration: 8
Premium Reinvestment Rate: 6.0%
Minimum First Call Rating: 1.2
Minimum Standard & Poor's Rating: A-
No. of Stocks Meeting Either Criterion: 50

Table 8.13: LEAP OTM and ITM Rates

	LEAPS Written	LEAPS Expired	Expired OTM	OTM Rate	Expired ITM	ITM Rate	LEAPS Active
Near:	5,516	5,065	4,880	96.3%	185	3.7%	451
Far:	6,004	4,953	4,847	97.9%	106	2.1%	1,051
Total:	11,520	10,018	9,727	97.1%	291	2.9%	1,502

Table 8.14: Premiums Collected and Realized Gain for Expired LEAPS

	LEAPS Expired	Premiums Collected	Forward Value	ITM Exposure	Realized Gain	Retent'n Rate
Near:	5,065	$123,882	$132,344	$28,160	$104,184	84.1%
Far:	4,953	$206,272	$232,609	$20,686	$211,922	102.7%
Total:	10,018	$330,155	$364,952	$48,846	$316,106	95.7%

Table 8.15: Premiums Collected and Unrealized Gain on Active LEAPS

	LEAPS Active	Premiums Collected	Forward Value	Residual Value	Unrealized Gain
Near:	451	$39,263	$40,008	$32,289	$7,719
Far:	1,051	$104,640	$108,597	$72,106	$36,491
Total:	1,502	$143,903	$148,605	$104,395	$44,210

Table 8.16: Premiums Collected and Account Values

	Original Cont'cts	Premiums Collected	Compound Gain	Unrealized Gain	Account Value	Value Ratio
Near:	5,516	$163,146	$140,287	$7,719	$148,006	90.7%
Far:	6,004	$310,912	$281,540	$36,491	$318,031	102.3%
Total:	11,520	$474,058	$421,826	$44,210	$466,037	98.3%

Summary of Results

To compare the results obtained, let's again tabulate the OTM rate, the retention rate, and the overall ten-year value ratio for the runs done so far.

Table 8.17: Figure of Merit Comparisons

Run No.	Uni- verse	No. of Issues	Steps Below ATM	Steady-State OTM Rate	Steady-State Retention Rate	Ten-Year Account Ratio
1.	All	217	0	77.7%	42.6%	44.3%
2.	B min	178	0	80.0%	54.3%	57.5%
3.	B+ min	115	0	84.0%	66.2%	69.7%
4.	A- min	50	0	87.1%	79.9%	84.9%
5.	B+ min	115	1	92.5%	70.4%	72.6%
6.	A- min	50	1	95.1%	90.0%	91.6%
7.	B+ min	115	2	95.6%	71.1%	73.6%
8.	A- min	50	2	97.1%	95.7%	98.3%

For the B+ minimum universe of 115 stocks, the proportion of LEAPS expiring worthless is seen to rise from a low of 84.0% to 92.5% to 95.6% as exercise prices are moved further out of the money. The corresponding retention rates and account ratios improve somewhat: retention rates move from 66.2% to 70.4% to 71.1%, and account ratios move from 69.7% to 72.6% to 73.6%.

For the A- minimum universe of 50 stocks, the proportion of LEAPS expiring worthless is seen to rise from a low of 87.1% to 99.1% to 97.1% as exercise prices are moved further out of the money. This time, however, the corresponding retention rates and account ratios improve significantly, the former going from 79.9% to 90.0% to 95.7%, the latter moving from 84.9% to 91.6% to 98.3%.

What all this tells us is that by writing out-of-the-money LEAP puts on better-quality stocks, it is possible to bring up the proportion of LEAPS expiring worthless to levels well over 95% and achieve premium retention rates of 90% or more, with account ratios as high as 98% of the total premiums collected. Mind you, these results are calculated from having sold a *random* number of out-of-the-money LEAP puts on a *random* number of these better quality stocks on a *random* schedule throughout each year over a ten-year period. As such, they do not reflect any tactical decision making or any involvement on the part of the investor other than his or her investing the net premiums in money market funds.

The next chapter investigates the extent to which the above results can be improved by using a simple recovery-and-repair strategy in those situations where LEAP options appear to be expiring in the money as their expiration dates approach.

9

CHAPTER 9

ROLL 'EM OUT

Introduction

The previous chapter demonstrated that by writing LEAP puts on higher-quality issues one or two steps below the at-the-money market price, it is possible to increase the rate at which the options expire out of the money to levels ranging from 92% to 97%. An impressive result, to be sure, but more impressive results can be achieved by rolling out any LEAP puts that appear to be winding up in the money as expiration approaches. This entails a two-step process of (i) buying back the LEAP puts shortly before the expiration date (thus closing out those positions), and (ii) writing an equivalent number of LEAP puts with expiration dates either one or two years away.

We saw in Chapter 3 that there are numerous ways to carry out this type of mitigation strategy: besides selecting the expiration date, we can also choose an appropriate strike price. Suppose an at-the-money LEAP put had been sold on a stock with a volatility of 0.40 and the price was $100 a share with 25 months to expiration. From Table 2.1, we see that the (European-style) option premium is very close to $1,600 per contract. Now suppose that some two years later, the stock is, unfortunately, down to $90. To close out the position, we buy back the option for close to its intrinsic value* of $1,000, a

---

*The intrinsic value of an in-the-money (put or call) option is the difference between the strike price and stock price.

strategy which by itself would ensure an overall profit of $600 per contract, even after commissions (remember that the premium has been earning interest for a year and a half).

What happens next is that we roll out the option. Since the month is January (that's when all LEAPS expire), there will be two replacement LEAPS available: the near-term LEAP expiring the following January, and the far-term LEAP expiring the January two years away. There will, of course, be a range of strike prices available to us—$95, $90, $85, and so on; most likely, the original $100 price will be available and perhaps an $80 strike as well. With two expiration dates (near and far) and, say, five strike prices at or near the money, there are as many as ten viable alternatives open to you. Which of these to select will depend on how long a time you feel will be required before the company resumes its earnings growth, regains market share lost, or otherwise recovers its former price levels. The more rapid and certain the recovery, the higher the strike price and shorter the term you can afford to select. The weaker the prospects of recovery, the lower the strike price and longer the term you should select. If the company has really faltered, your best course of action may well be to limit further financial exposure and not perform the second leg of the procedure.

Procedure

To investigate the extent to which the use of rollovers can mitigate financial exposure and thereby enhance overall performance, the following assumptions were made in all instances where a LEAP put wound up in the money as expiration approached: (i) the in-the-money LEAP put was purchased for its intrinsic value (the difference between stock and exercise prices at expiration), and (ii) a single LEAP put was then sold at a strike price and expiration date which reflected the same philosophy as that governing the original LEAP put. That is, if the original LEAP put was a near-term LEAP, the replacement LEAP sold was also near term (with an expiration date one year away); if the original LEAP put was a far-term LEAP, the replacement LEAP sold was also far term (with an expiration date two years away).

Similarly, if the original LEAP put was out of the money, at the money, or in the money at the time it was sold, a correspondingly conservative, neutral, or aggressive stance was adopted for the replacement LEAP put sold. That is, LEAP puts originally one step out of the money were replaced by one-step out-of-the-money puts. These strike prices are relative to the stock price at the time, so in the example cited above, the at-the-money LEAP put of $100 would be replaced by an at-the-money $90 LEAP put with an expiration date two years away.

With this approach in mind, six computer simulations were conducted in order to determine the impact of rollovers on the bottom line. These simulations were run for the at-the-money LEAPS, one-step out-of-the-money LEAPS, and two-step out-of-the-money LEAPS, in each case for both the B+ minimum and A- minimum stock universes.

Rolling At-the-Money LEAPS

Run No. 9 is the analog of Run No. 3 and shows the effect of adopting a rollover strategy for any issues winding up in the money from among the 115 stocks in the B+ minimum universe. As a result of rollovers, the total number of LEAP contracts written increases from 25,302 to 29,292. The net effect of rollovers is to reduce the ITM exposure of $3,174,423 in Run No. 3 to $1,249,983 (using the premiums received from the additional LEAP contracts for that purpose). As a result, the retention rate on the premiums received from the sale of the expired LEAP contracts increases from 66.2% in Run No. 3 to the 78.5% shown in Table 9.2. From Table 9.4 we see that the account value on March 31, 1997 will have grown to $4,360,099. This sum is 80.3% of the total premiums collected over the ten-year period and is significantly higher than the 69.7% without rollovers seen in Run No. 3.

Run No. 10 is the analog of Run No. 4 and shows the effect of adopting a rollover strategy for any stocks winding up in the money from among the 50 issues in the A- minimum universe. As a result of rollovers, the total number of LEAP contracts written increases from 11,520 to 12,932. The net effect of rollovers is to reduce the ITM exposure of $431,447 in Run No. 4 to $247,180 (again using the premiums received from the additional LEAP contracts for that purpose). As a result, the retention rate on the premiums received from the sale of the expired LEAP contracts increases from 79.9% in Run No. 4 to 92.7%, as shown in Table 9.6. From Table 9.8, we see that the account value on March 31, 1997 will have grown to $1,849,570. This sum is 95.9% of the total premiums collected over the ten-year period, and is significantly higher than the 84.9% without rollovers seen in Run No. 4

Rolling One-Step Out-of-the-Money LEAPS

Run No. 11 is the analog of Run No. 5 and shows the effect of adopting a rollover strategy for any stocks winding up in the money from among the 115 issues in the B+ minimum universe. As a result of rollovers, the total number of LEAP contracts written increases from 25,302 to 27,074. Yet again, the net effect of rollovers is to reduce the ITM exposure of $822,478 in Run No. 5 to $686,414. The retention rate on the premiums received from the sale of the expired LEAP contracts increases from 70.4% in Run No. 5 to 76.9%, as shown in Table 9.10. From Table 9.12, we see that the account value on March 31, 1997 will have grown to $2,284,359. This sum is 77.9% of the total premiums collected over the ten-year period and is significantly higher than the 72.6% without rollovers seen in Run No. 5.

Run No. 12 is the analog of Run No. 6 and shows the effect of adopting a rollover strategy for any stocks winding up in the money from among the 50 issues in the A- minimum universe. As a result of rollovers, the total number of LEAP contracts written increases from 11,520 to 12,010. The net effect of rollovers is to reduce the ITM exposure of $131,940 in Run No. 6 to $91,637. The retention rate on the premiums received from the sale of the expired LEAP contracts increases from 90.0% to 96.2%, as shown in Table 9.14, and from Table 9.16 we see that the account value on March 31, 1997 will have grown to $891,361. This is 96.8% of the total premiums collected over the ten-year period, and is significantly higher than the 91.6% without rollovers seen in Run No. 6.

Note that the retention rate for the far-term LEAPS is 101.8%. Retention rates greater than 100% can be achieved as a result of the interest earned between the sale of options and their corresponding expiration dates.

Rolling Two-Step Out-of-the-Money LEAPS

Run No. 13 is the analog of Run No. 7 and shows the effect of adopting a rollover strategy for the 115 issues in the B+ minimum universe. As a result of rollovers, the total number of LEAP contracts written increases from 25,302 to 26,306. The rollovers reduce the ITM exposure from $446,329 in Run No. 7 to $390,194. The retention rate on the premiums received increases from 71.1% to 76.1%, as shown in Table 9.18. From Table 9.20, we see that the account value on March 31, 1997 will have grown to $1,281,850, which is 77.5% of the total premiums collected over the ten-year period and which is significantly higher than the 73.6% without rollovers seen in Run No. 7.

Run No. 14 is the analog of Run No. 8 and shows the effect of adopting a rollover strategy for any stocks winding up in the money for the 50 issues in the A- minimum universe. As a result of rollovers, the total number of LEAP contracts written goes from 11,520 to 11,815. The rollovers reduce the ITM exposure from $48,846 in Run No. 8 to $32,351, and the retention rate on the premiums received increases from 95.7% to 100.7%, as shown in Table 9.22. From Table 9.24, we see that the account value on March 31, 1997 will have grown to $490,331, which is 103.2% of the total premiums collected over the ten-year period, and is higher than the 98.3% without rollovers seen in Run No. 8. As we saw in Run No. 12, retention rates greater than 100% can be achieved as a result of the interest earned between the sale of options and their corresponding expiration dates.

Run No. 9:

ATM Strike Price is the High, Low, or Closing Stock Price: C
No. of Steps LEAP Put is below ATM Strike Price: 0
Minimum No. of Months till Expiration: 8
ITM Near-Term LEAPS are Rolled Over: Y
ITM Far-Term LEAPS are Rolled Over: Y
Premium Reinvestment Rate: 6.0%
Minimum First Call Rating: 1.6
Minimum Standard & Poor's Rating: B+
No. of Stocks Meeting Either Criterion: 115

Table 9.1: LEAP OTM and Rollout Rates

	LEAPS Written	LEAPS Expired	Expired OTM	OTM Rate	LEAPS Rolled	Rollout Rate	LEAPS Active
Near:	14,496	13,321	10,941	82.1%	2,380	17.9%	1,175
Far:	14,796	12,076	10,466	86.7%	1,610	13.3%	2,720
Total:	29,292	25,397	21,407	84.3%	3,990	15.7%	3,895

Table 9.2: Premiums Collected and Realized Gain for Expired LEAPS

	LEAPS Expired	Premiums Collected	Forward Value	ITM Exposure	Realized Gain	Retent'n Rate
Near:	13,321	$1,835,915	$1,957,072	$654,353	$1,302,719	71.0%
Far:	12,076	$2,156,467	$2,428,733	$595,630	$1,833,103	85.0%
Total:	25,397	$3,992,382	$4,385,805	$1,249,983	$3,135,821	78.5%

Table 9.3: Premiums Collected and Unrealized Gain on Active LEAPS

	LEAPS Active	Premiums Collected	Forward Value	Residual Value	Unrealized Gain
Near:	1,175	$427,669	$435,578	$376,392	$59,186
Far:	2,720	$1,010,901	$1,054,817	$750,400	$304,417
Total:	3,895	$1,438,571	$1,490,395	$1,126,792	$363,603

Table 9.4: Premiums Collected and Account Values

	Original Cont'cts	Premiums Collected	Compound Gain	Unrealized Gain	Account Value	Value Ratio
Near:	12,116	$2,263,585	$1,661,559	$59,186	$1,720,745	76.0%
Far:	13,186	$3,167,368	$2,334,938	$304,417	$2,639,354	83.3%
Total:	25,302	$5,430,953	$3,996,497	$363,603	$4,360,099	80.3%

Run No. 10:

ATM Strike Price is the High, Low, or Closing Stock Price:	C
No. of Steps LEAP Put is below ATM Strike Price:	0
Minimum No. of Months till Expiration:	8
ITM Near-Term LEAPS are Rolled Over:	Y
ITM Far-Term LEAPS are Rolled Over:	Y
Premium Reinvestment Rate:	6.0%
Minimum First Call Rating:	1.2
Minimum Standard & Poor's Rating:	A-
No. of Stocks Meeting Either Criterion:	50

Table 9.5: LEAP OTM and Rollout Rates

	LEAPS Written	LEAPS Expired	Expired OTM	OTM Rate	LEAPS Rolled	Rollout Rate	LEAPS Active
Near:	6,396	5,899	5,019	85.1%	880	14.9%	497
Far:	6,536	5,383	4,851	90.1%	532	9.9%	1,153
Total:	12,932	11,282	9,870	87.5%	1,412	12.5%	1,650

Table 9.6: Premiums Collected and Realized Gain for Expired LEAPS

	LEAPS Expired	Premiums Collected	Forward Value	ITM Exposure	Realized Gain	Retent'n Rate
Near:	5,899	$656,632	$700,038	$134,574	$565,464	86.1%
Far:	5,383	$783,524	$882,534	$112,606	$769,927	98.3%
Total:	11,282	$1,440,155	$1,582,571	$247,180	$1,335,392	92.7%

Table 9.7: Premiums Collected and Unrealized Gain on Active LEAPS

	LEAPS Active	Premiums Collected	Forward Value	Residual Value	Unrealized Gain
Near:	497	$147,675	$150,418	$126,012	$24,407
Far:	1,153	$341,495	$356,386	$299,944	$126,443
Total:	1,650	$489,170	$506,805	$355,955	$150,849

Table 9.8: Premiums Collected and Account Values

	Original Cont'cts	Premiums Collected	Compound Gain	Unrealized Gain	Account Value	Value Ratio
Near:	5,516	$804,306	$722,905	$24,407	$747,312	92.9%
Far:	6,004	$1,125,019	$975,816	$126,443	$1,102,259	98.0%
Total:	11,520	$1,929,325	$1,698,721	$150,849	$1,849,570	95.9%

Run No. 11:

ATM Strike Price is the High, Low, or Closing Stock Price: C
No. of Steps LEAP Put is below ATM Strike Price: 1
Minimum No. of Months till Expiration: 8
ITM Near-Term LEAPS are Rolled Over: Y
ITM Far-Term LEAPS are Rolled Over: Y
Premium Reinvestment Rate: 6.0%
Minimum First Call Rating: 1.6
Minimum Standard & Poor's Rating: B+
No. of Stocks Meeting Either Criterion: 115

Table 9.9: LEAP OTM and Rollout Rates

	LEAPS Written	LEAPS Expired	Expired OTM	OTM Rate	LEAPS Rolled	Rollout Rate	LEAPS Active
Near:	13,109	12,017	11,024	91.7%	993	8.3%	1,092
Far:	13,965	11,400	10,621	93.2%	779	6.8%	2,565
Total:	27,074	23,417	21,645	92.4%	1,772	7.6%	3,657

Table 9.10: Premiums Collected and Realized Gain for Expired LEAPS

	LEAPS Expired	Premiums Collected	Forward Value	ITM Exposure	Realized Gain	Retent'n Rate
Near:	12,017	$870,704	$929,123	$340,533	$588,590	67.6%
Far:	11,400	$1,195,471	$1,347,097	$345,880	$1,001,217	83.8%
Total:	23,417	$2,066,174	$2,276,221	$686,414	$1,589,807	76.9%

Table 9.11: Premiums Collected and Unrealized Gain on Active LEAPS

	LEAPS Active	Premiums Collected	Forward Value	Residual Value	Unrealized Gain
Near:	1,092	$247,335	$251,999	$210,567	$41,432
Far:	2,565	$619,244	$645,502	$459,968	$185,535
Total:	3,657	$866,579	$897,502	$670,535	$226,967

Table 9.12: Premiums Collected and Account Values

	Original Cont'cts	Premiums Collected	Compound Gain	Unrealized Gain	Account Value	Value Ratio
Near:	12,116	$1,118,039	$763,604	$41,432	$805,036	72.0%
Far:	13,186	$1,814,714	$1,293,789	$185,535	$1,479,323	81.5%
Total:	25,302	$2,932,753	$2,057,392	$226,967	$2,284,359	77.9%

Run No. 12:

ATM Strike Price is the High, Low, or Closing Stock Price: C
No. of Steps LEAP Put is below ATM Strike Price: 1
Minimum No. of Months till Expiration: 8
ITM Near-Term LEAPS are Rolled Over: Y
ITM Far-Term LEAPS are Rolled Over: Y
Premium Reinvestment Rate: 6.0%
Minimum First Call Rating: 1.2
Minimum Standard & Poor's Rating: A-
No. of Stocks Meeting Either Criterion: 50

Table 9.13: LEAP OTM and Rollout Rates

	LEAPS Written	LEAPS Expired	Expired OTM	OTM Rate	LEAPS Rolled	Rollout Rate	LEAPS Active
Near:	5,782	5,325	5,059	95.0%	266	5.0%	457
Far:	6,228	5,139	4,915	95.6%	224	4.4%	1,089
Total:	12,010	10,464	9,974	95.3%	490	4.7%	1,546

Table 9.14: Premiums Collected and Realized Gain for Expired LEAPS

	LEAPS Expired	Premiums Collected	Forward Value	ITM Exposure	Realized Gain	Retent'n Rate
Near:	5,325	$264,349	$282,199	$49,438	$232,761	88.1%
Far:	5,139	$385,272	$434,226	$42,199	$392,027	101.8%
Total:	10,464	$649,621	$716,426	$91,637	$624,789	96.2%

Table 9.15: Premiums Collected and Unrealized Gain on Active LEAPS

	LEAPS Active	Premiums Collected	Forward Value	Residual Value	Unrealized Gain
Near:	457	$77,516	$78,989	$64,648	$14,341
Far:	1,089	$194,114	$202,127	$129,501	$72,626
Total:	1,546	$271,630	$281,116	$194,149	$86,967

Table 9.16: Premiums Collected and Account Values

	Original Cont'cts	Premiums Collected	Compound Gain	Unrealized Gain	Account Value	Value Ratio
Near:	5,516	$341,865	$301,311	$14,341	$315,652	92.3%
Far:	6,004	$579,386	$503,083	$72,626	$575,709	99.4%
Total:	11,520	$921,251	$804,394	$86,967	$891,361	96.8%

Run No. 13:

ATM Strike Price is the High, Low, or Closing Stock Price: C
No. of Steps LEAP Put is below ATM Strike Price: 2
Minimum No. of Months till Expiration: 8
ITM Near-Term LEAPS are Rolled Over: Y
ITM Far-Term LEAPS are Rolled Over: Y
Premium Reinvestment Rate: 6.0%
Minimum First Call Rating: 1.6
Minimum Standard & Poor's Rating: B+
No. of Stocks Meeting Either Criterion: 115

Table 9.17: LEAP OTM and Rollout Rates

	LEAPS Written	LEAPS Expired	Expired OTM	OTM Rate	LEAPS Rolled	Rollout Rate	LEAPS Active
Near:	12,678	11,616	11,054	95.2%	562	4.8%	1,062
Far:	13,628	11,144	10,702	96.0%	442	4.0%	2,484
Total:	26,306	22,760	21,756	95.6%	1,004	4.4%	3,546

Table 9.18: Premiums Collected and Realized Gain for Expired LEAPS

	LEAPS Expired	Premiums Collected	Forward Value	ITM Exposure	Realized Gain	Retent'n Rate
Near:	11,616	$447,303	$477,653	$190,971	$286,682	64.1%
Far:	11,144	$689,566	$777,415	$199,223	$578,192	83.8%
Total:	22,760	$1,136,869	$1,255,068	$390,194	$864,874	76.1%

Table 9.19: Premiums Collected and Unrealized Gain on Active LEAPS

	LEAPS Active	Premiums Collected	Forward Value	Residual Value	Unrealized Gain
Near:	1,062	$140,761	$143,416	$117,980	$25,436
Far:	2,484	$376,759	$391,969	$288,840	$103,129
Total:	3,546	$517,520	$535,385	$406,820	$128,565

Table 9.20: Premiums Collected and Account Values

	Original Cont'cts	Premiums Collected	Compound Gain	Unrealized Gain	Account Value	Value Ratio
Near:	12,116	$588,065	$385,946	$25,436	$411,383	70.0%
Far:	13,186	$1,066,325	$767,338	$103,129	$870,467	81.6%
Total:	25,302	$1,654,389	$1,153,285	$128,565	$1,281,850	77.5%

Run No. 14:

ATM Strike Price is the High, Low, or Closing Stock Price: C
No. of Steps LEAP Put is below ATM Strike Price: 2
Minimum No. of Months till Expiration: 8
ITM Near-Term LEAPS are Rolled Over: Y
ITM Far-Term LEAPS are Rolled Over: Y
Premium Reinvestment Rate: 6.0%
Minimum First Call Rating: 1.2
Minimum Standard & Poor's Rating: A-
No. of Stocks Meeting Either Criterion: 50

Table 9.21: LEAP OTM and Rollout Rates

	LEAPS Written	LEAPS Expired	Expired OTM	OTM Rate	LEAPS Rolled	Rollout Rate	LEAPS Active
Near:	5,705	5,254	5,065	96.4%	189	3.6%	451
Far:	6,110	5,046	4,940	97.9%	106	2.1%	1,064
Total:	11,815	10,300	10,005	97.1%	295	2.9%	1,515

Table 9.22: Premiums Collected and Realized Gain for Expired LEAPS

	LEAPS Expired	Premiums Collected	Forward Value	ITM Exposure	Realized Gain	Retent'n Rate
Near:	5,254	$123,882	$132,344	$19,707	$112,636	90.9%
Far:	5,046	$206,272	$232,609	$12,643	$219,965	106.6%
Total:	10,300	$330,155	$364,952	$32,351	$332,602	100.7%

Table 9.23: Premiums Collected and Unrealized Gain on Active LEAPS

	LEAPS Active	Premiums Collected	Forward Value	Residual Value	Unrealized Gain
Near:	451	$39,263	$40,008	$32,289	$7,719
Far:	1,064	$105,885	$109,929	$72,180	$37,749
Total:	1,515	$145,148	$149,937	$104,469	$45,468

Table 9.24: Premiums Collected and Account Values

	Original Cont'cts	Premiums Collected	Compound Gain	Unrealized Gain	Account Value	Value Ratio
Near:	5,516	$163,146	$152,879	$7,719	$160,598	98.4%
Far:	6,004	$312,157	$291,985	$37,749	$329,733	105.6%
Total:	11,520	$475,303	$444,863	$45,468	$490,331	103.2%

Summary of Results

To compare the results obtained, let's again tabulate the OTM rate, the retention rate, and the overall ten-year value ratio for all runs done so far.

Table 9.25: Figure of Merit Comparisons

	Run No.	Uni-verse	No. of Issues	Steps Below ATM	Steady-State OTM Rate	Steady-State Retention Rate	Ten-Year Account Ratio
Without Rollover	1.	All	217	0	77.7%	42.6%	44.3%
	2.	B min	178	0	80.0%	54.3%	57.5%
	3.	B+ min	115	0	84.0%	66.2%	69.7%
	4.	A- min	50	0	87.1%	79.9%	84.9%
	5.	B+ min	115	1	92.5%	70.4%	72.6%
	6.	A- min	50	1	95.1%	90.0%	91.6%
	7.	B+ min	115	2	95.6%	71.1%	73.6%
	8.	A- min	50	2	97.1%	95.7%	98.3%
With Rollover	9.	B+ min	115	0	84.3%	78.5%	80.3%
	10.	A- min	50	0	87.5%	92.7%	95.9%
	11.	B+ min	115	1	92.4%	76.9%	77.9%
	12.	A- min	50	1	95.3%	96.2%	96.8%
	13.	B+ min	115	2	95.6%	76.1%	77.5%
	14.	A- min	50	2	97.1%	100.7%	103.2%

As we can readily see from the table, adopting a rollover strategy to mitigate potential financial exposure can substantially improve both retention rates and long-term account values.

At-the-Money Results

For the B+ minimum universe of 115 stocks, the retention rate progressively increases from 66.2% without rollovers in Run No. 3 to 78.5% with rollovers in Run No. 9, with a corresponding increase in account ratio from 69.7% to 80.3%. For the A- minimum universe of 50 stocks, the retention rate progressively increases from 79.9% without rollovers in Run No. 4 to 92.7% with rollovers in Run No. 10, with a corresponding increase in account ratio from 84.9% to 95.9%.

One-Step Out-of-the-Money Results

For the B+ minimum universe of 115 stocks, the retention rate progressively increases from 70.4% without rollovers in Run No. 5 to 76.9% with rollovers in Run No. 11, with a corresponding increase in account ratio from 72.6% to 77.9%. For the A- minimum universe of 50 stocks, the retention rate progressively increases from 90.0% without rollovers in Run No. 6 to 96.2% with rollovers in Run No. 12, with a corresponding increase in account ratio from 91.6% to 96.8%.

Two-Step Out-of-the-Money Results

For the B+ minimum universe of 115 stocks, the retention rate progressively increases from 71.1% without rollovers in Run No. 7 to 76.1% with rollovers in Run No. 13, with a corresponding increase in account ratio from 73.6% to 77.5%. For the A- minimum universe of 50 stocks, the retention rate progressively increases from 95.7% without rollovers in Run No. 8 to 100.7% with rollovers in Run No. 14, with a corresponding increase in account ratio from 98.3% to 103.2%.

10

CHAPTER 10

BUY 'EM OUT

Introduction

What we've hopefully established by now is that selling LEAP puts can be controlled for risk, thus reducing financial exposure to levels well within acceptable limits. So far, the only thing we've done with the premiums generated has been to invest them in money market funds and watch them grow at 6% a year. But as the title of this book suggests, I have had in mind a better use of the premiums received, which is to use them to acquire additional shares of stock in my favorite companies.

Your list of favorite companies is certainly not going to coincide with my list; in fact, it is safe to say that no two people reading this book will have the same set of pet stocks. In view of this, what I propose to do is to take the premiums generated and use them to cover the costs of any high-quality stocks from among the list of companies in Table 6.1 that were assigned because the LEAP puts wound up in the money by the expiration date.

Procedure

To be conservative, the premiums generated from the sale of LEAP puts are placed into a money market account until the puts expire out of the money and worthless. This approach has the twofold advantage of terminating any financial obligation associated with the expiring LEAP put and of eliminating the maintenance margin requirement (as described in Chapter 4). As the premiums build up in this manner, you can purchase stock and add it to your equity portfolio.

You can also use the accumulated premiums to purchase stock that was assigned to you because of option positions that expired in the money. The procedure detailed in this chapter consists of accepting the exercise and assignment of any stocks whose far-term LEAP puts expired in the money but rolling out any near-term LEAP puts that did so. The reason the far-term in-the-money LEAP puts are accepted for assignment and the near-term LEAP puts are rolled out (rather than the reverse) is to delay stock purchase long enough for the premiums received to build up ahead of the monetary requirements for stock acquisition.

In practice, you would be free to accept exercise and assignment of any stock you believed was worthwhile, assuming you had the dollars to acquire it. As we want to concentrate on the effects of stock acquisition, the computer runs in this chapter will be restricted to the universe of 115 stocks rated B+ or better and the universe of 50 stocks rated A- or better. For each universe, three runs will be made, ranging from the conservative sale of at-the-money LEAP puts to the very conservative sale of LEAP puts two steps out of the money.

In each instance, any near-term LEAPS that appear to be winding up in the money will be rolled in much the same manner as in the previous chapter. For any far-term LEAPS that expire in the money, the procedure followed is to purchase the assigned stock.

At-the-Money LEAPS on the B+ Minimum Universe

Run No. 15 is the analog of Run No. 3, but where the in-the-money near-term LEAPS are rolled out and the in-the-money far-term LEAPS are accepted for assignment from among the total universe of 115 stocks rated B+ or better and for which the original strike price was at the money.

All line items for the near-term LEAPS are identical to those in Run No. 9 (which is Run No. 3 with rollovers). On the other hand, the 1,479 far-term LEAPS in Table 10.1 that expired in the money are all accepted for assignment. The ITM exposure for the far-term

LEAPS in Table 10.2 is $3,899,612 and represents the funding required to finance the acquisition of the 147,900 shares so assigned.

The realized gain in Table 10.2 is again the difference between the forward value and ITM exposure. It is a negative $1,470,879 for the far-term LEAPS, because the cost basis of $3.9 million is greater than the $2.4 million available from the far-term premiums alone. However, when the near-term LEAP premiums are used to pay for the acquired stock, the additional capital needed from external sources over the ten-year period is just a little over $168,000, an almost breakeven situation. Table 10.3 shows the unrealized gain for the 3,583 active but unexpired LEAPS.

Table 10.4 shows the premiums collected and the account values resulting at the end of the ten-year study period. The account value for the far-term LEAPS includes the close to $7.9 million in the new column marked stock value. The overall investment account on March 31, 1997 is just shy of $8.0 million. This sum is close to 150% of the $5,345,392 in total premiums collected over the ten-year period and is substantially higher than the 69.7% account ratio (without rollovers) in Run No. 3 or the 80.3% account ratio (with rollovers) in Run No. 9. Table 10.5 details the portfolio of 147,900 shares of stock acquired in 93 different companies as a result of exercise and assignment. The names these companies were known by are those of March 31, 1997, and do not reflect any mergers, acquisitions or spin-offs that have occurred since then.

At-the-Money LEAPS on the A- Minimum Universe

Run No. 16 is the analog of Run No. 4, but where the in-the-money near-term LEAPS are rolled out and the in-the-money far-term LEAPS are accepted for assignment from among the total universe of 50, stocks rated A- or better and for which the original strike price was at the money.

The ITM exposure of $1,241,101 in Table 10.7 represents the funding required to finance the acquisition of the 51,800 shares of stock resulting from the 518 far-term option contracts that expired in the money and were assigned. The realized gain in Table 10.7 is $565,464 for the near-term LEAPS and a negative $358,568 for the far-term LEAPS. The combined realized gain is this time a relatively large positive amount, signifying that the total premiums received were more than enough to cover the ITM exposure of the near-term LEAPS as well as pay for the stock acquired through assignment of the far-term LEAPS that expired in the money. As a result, the account value of $2,941,554 at the end of ten-year period includes stock valued at close to $2.5 million. The account value is 154.2% of the premiums collected over the ten-year period and is substantially higher than the 95.9% account ratio (with rollovers) seen in Run No. 10. Table 10.10 details the portfolio of 51,800 shares of stock acquired in 40 different companies as a result of exercise and assignment.

One-Step OTM LEAPS on the B+ Minimum Universe

Run No. 17 is the analog of Run No. 5, but where the in-the-money near-term LEAPS are rolled out and the in-the-money far-term LEAPS are accepted for assignment from among the total universe of 115 stocks rated B+ or better and for which the original strike price was one step out of the money. The ITM exposure of $1,759,423 in Table 10.12 represents the funding required to finance the acquisition of the 73,800 shares of stock resulting from the 738 far-term option contracts that expired in the money and were assigned. The realized gain in Table 10.12 is $588,590 for the near-term LEAPS and a negative $412,326 for the far-term LEAPS. The combined realized gain of $176,264 is a positive amount, signifying that the total premiums received are enough to cover the ITM exposure of the near-term LEAPS as well as pay for the stock acquired through assignment of the far-term LEAPS that expired in the money. As a result, the account value of $4,334,794 at the end of the ten-year period includes stock valued at close to $3.9 million. The account value is 149.1% of the premiums collected over the ten-year period and is substantially higher than the 77.9% account ratio (with rollovers) seen in Run No. 11. Table 10.15 details the portfolio of 73,800 shares of stock acquired in 66 different companies as a result of exercise and assignment.

One-Step OTM LEAPS on the A- Minimum Universe

Run No. 18 is the analog of Run No. 6, but where the in-the-money near-term LEAPS are rolled out and the in-the-money far-term

LEAPS are accepted for assignment, from among the total universe of 50 stocks rated A- or better and for which the original strike price was one step out of the money.

The ITM exposure of $511,671 in Table 10.17 represents the funding required to finance the acquisition of the 22,400 shares of stock resulting from the 224 far-term option contracts that expired in the money and were assigned. The realized gain in Table 10.17 is $232,761 for the near-term LEAPS and a negative $77,444 for the far-term LEAPS. The combined realized gain is again positive, signifying that the total premiums received were enough to cover the ITM exposure of the near-term LEAPS as well as pay for the stock acquired stock through assignment of the far-term LEAPS that expired in the money. As a result, the account value of $1,326,217 at the end of the ten-year period includes stock valued at just over $1.0 million. The account value is 144.7% of the premiums collected over the ten-year period and is again substantially higher than the 96.8% account ratio (with rollovers) seen in Run No. 12. Table 10.20 details the portfolio of 22,400 shares of stock acquired in 24 different companies as a result of exercise and assignment.

Two-Step OTM LEAPS on the B+ Minimum Universe

Run No. 19 is the analog of Run No. 7, but where the in-the-money near-term LEAPS are rolled out and the in-the-money far-term LEAPS are accepted for assignment from among the total universe of 115 stocks rated B+ or better and for which the original strike price was two steps out of the money.

The ITM exposure of $768,734 in Table 10.22 represents the funding required to finance the acquisition of the 43,500 shares of stock resulting from the 435 far-term option contracts that expired in the money and were assigned. The realized gain in Table 10.22 is $286,682 for the near-term LEAPS and a positive $8,680 for the far-term LEAPS. In this situation, the premiums received from sale of the far-term LEAPS alone were enough to cover the cost of the stock acquired through assignment of the far-term LEAPS that expired in the money. As a result, the account value of $2,522,336 at the end of the ten-year period includes stock valued at close to $2.0 million. The account value is 153.6% of the premiums collected over the ten-year period and is substantially higher than the 77.5% account ratio (with rollovers) seen in Run No. 13. Table 10.25 details the portfolio of 43,500 shares of stock acquired in 49 different companies as a result of exercise and assignment.

Two-Step OTM LEAPS on the A- Minimum Universe

Run No. 20 is the analog of Run No. 8, but where the in-the-money near-term LEAPS are rolled out and the in-the-money far-term LEAPS are accepted for assignment from among the total universe of 50 stocks rated A- or better and for which the original strike price was two steps out of the money.

The ITM exposure of $190,502 in Table 10.27 represents the funding required to finance the acquisition of the 10,600 shares of stock resulting from the 106 far-term option contracts that expired in the money and were assigned. The realized gain in Table 10.27 is $112,636 for the near-term LEAPS and a positive $42,107 for the far-term LEAPS. In this situation, the premiums received from sale of the far-term LEAPS was more than enough to cover the cost of the stock acquired through assignment of the far-term LEAPS that expired in the money. As a result, the account value of $730,440 at the end of the ten-year period includes stock valued at $462,413. The account value is 154.1% of the premiums collected over the ten-year period and is substantially higher than the 103.2% account ratio (with rollovers) seen in Run No. 14. Table 10.30 details the portfolio of 10,600 shares of stock acquired in 16 different companies as a result of exercise and assignment.

Run No. 15:

ATM Strike Price is the High, Low, or Closing Stock Price: C
No. of Steps Near-Term LEAP Put is below ATM Strike Price: 0
No. of Steps Far-Term LEAP Put is below ATM Strike Price: 0
Minimum No. of Months till Expiration: 8
ITM Near-Term LEAPS are Rolled Over: Y
Stocks of ITM Far-Term LEAPS are Purchased: Y
Premium Reinvestment Rate: 6.0%
Minimum First Call Rating: 1.6
Minimum Standard & Poor's Rating: B+
No. of Stocks Meeting Either Criterion: 115

Table 10.1: LEAP OTM and ITM Rates

	LEAPS Written	LEAPS Expired	Expired OTM	OTM Rate	Expired ITM	ITM Rate	LEAPS Active
Near:	14,496	13,321	10,941	82.1%	2,380	17.9%	1,175
Far:	13,186	10,778	9,299	86.3%	1,479	13.7%	2,408
Total:	27,682	24,099	20,240	84.0%	3,859	16.0%	3,583

Table 10.2: Premiums Collected and Realized Gain for Expired LEAPS

	LEAPS Expired	Premiums Collected	Forward Value	ITM Exposure	Realized Gain	Retent'n Rate
Near:	13,321	$1,835,915	$1,957,072	$654,353	$1,302,719	71.0%
Far:	10,778	$2,156,467	$2,428,733	$3,899,612	-$1,470,879	-68.2%
Total:	24,099	$3,992,382	$4,385,805	$4,553,966	-$168,161	-4.2%

Table 10.3: Premiums Collected and Unrealized Gain on Active LEAPS

	LEAPS Active	Premiums Collected	Forward Value	Residual Value	Unrealized Gain
Near:	1,175	$427,669	$435,578	$376,392	$59,186
Far:	2,408	$925,341	$966,239	$689,007	$277,233
Total:	3,583	$1,353,010	$1,401,817	$1,065,399	$336,419

Table 10.4: Premiums Collected and Account Values

	Original Cont'cts	Premiums Collected	Compound Gain	Unrealized Gain	Stock Value	Account Value	Account Ratio
Near:	12,116	$2,263,585	$1,661,559	$59,186	$0	$1,720,745	76.0%
Far:	13,186	$3,081,807	-$1,858,621	$277,233	$7,857,106	$6,275,718	203.6%
Total:	25,302	$5,345,392	-$197,062	$336,419	$7,857,106	$7,996,463	149.6%

Table 10.5: List of Stocks Purchased

Name of Company	Trading Symbol	No. of Shares	Cost Basis	Stock Value
Abbott Labs	ABT	1,200	$25,050	$67,350
Adobe Systems	ADBE	1,000	$29,238	$40,125
Allied Signal	ALD	2,200	$34,625	$156,750
American Express	AXP	3,500	$73,565	$209,563
American Home	AHP	900	$28,575	$54,000
Amoco	AN	1,400	$64,925	$121,275
Anheuser-Busch	BUD	1,200	$29,400	$50,550
ASA Holdings	ASAI	2,300	$42,088	$47,725
AT&T	T	2,100	$66,937	$72,975
Atlantic Richfield	ARC	3,500	$383,275	$472,500
Avon Products	AVP	1,300	$20,470	$68,250
BankAmerica	BAC	800	$34,500	$80,700
Barrick Gold	ABX	300	$5,963	$7,125
Bell Atlantic	BEL	700	$34,725	$42,700
BellSouth	BLS	1,200	$29,549	$50,550
Boeing	BA	2,000	$77,663	$197,250
Boston Scientific	BSX	500	$8,925	$30,875
Bristol-Myers Squibb	BMY	2,400	$69,200	$141,600
Burlington Northern	BNI	400	$19,000	$29,600
Cabletron Systems	CS	200	$3,800	$5,900
Campbell Soup	CPB	200	$3,875	$9,275
Chase Manhattan	CMB	3,100	$75,150	$290,238
Chubb	CB	300	$9,615	$16,163
Compaq	CPQ	1,800	$22,167	$137,925
Conseco	CNC	1,300	$9,077	$46,313
Corning	GLW	1,600	$50,700	$71,000
Cracker Barrel	CBRL	2,200	$45,550	$57,475
CUC International	CU	1,700	$3,097	$38,250
Dayton Hudson	DH	1,700	$35,986	$70,975
Dun & Bradstreet	DNB	5,300	$227,925	$134,488
DuPont (E.I.) de Nemours	DD	600	$21,125	$63,600
Equifax	EFX	300	$2,259	$8,175
Exxon	XON	400	$25,000	$43,100
Fannie Mae	FNM	100	$1,788	$3,613
Gap	GPS	1,500	$17,757	$50,250
General Electric	GE	600	$14,519	$59,550
General Mills	GIS	2,400	$115,073	$149,100

Table 10.5 (cont.): List of Stocks Purchased

Name of Company	Trading Symbol	No. of Shares	Cost Basis	Stock Value
GTE	GTE	600	$20,088	$27,975
HealthSouth	HRC	900	$2,936	$17,213
Heinz (H.J.)	HNZ	1,000	$23,182	$39,500
Hewlett-Packard	HWP	2,500	$26,835	$133,125
Hilton Hotels	HLT	2,300	$22,700	$55,775
Home Depot	HD	100	$4,675	$5,350
Household International	HI	2,000	$41,750	$172,250
Intel	INTC	100	$650	$13,913
International Game	IGT	2,600	$34,325	$41,925
Johnson & Johnson	JNJ	1,300	$27,793	$68,738
KMart	KM	6,400	$86,172	$77,600
Kroger	KR	400	$7,000	$20,400
Limited	LTD	5,400	$90,811	$99,225
Lowe's	LOW	900	$24,126	$33,638
Magna International	MGA	3,300	$32,861	$163,763
Merck	MRK	1,500	$55,875	$126,375
Merrill Lynch	MER	2,300	$31,775	$197,513
Minn. Mining	MMM	400	$17,778	$33,800
Mobil	MOB	400	$23,925	$52,250
Monsanto	MTC	200	$2,131	$7,650
Morgan (J.P.)	JPM	1,500	$70,500	$147,375
Motorola	MOT	800	$11,067	$48,300
NationsBank	NB	1,700	$33,256	$94,350
NEXTEL	NXTL	2,900	$35,738	$38,788
NIKE	NKE	900	$12,825	$55,688
NYNEX	NYN	2,100	$80,939	$95,813
Office Depot	ODP	2,400	$44,457	$48,900
Oracle	ORCL	1,500	$4,060	$57,844
PepsiCo	PEP	400	$7,379	$13,050
Pfizer	PFE	1,500	$34,686	$126,188
Philip Morris	MO	2,100	$126,075	$240,188
Pitney Bowes	PBI	1,600	$43,914	$94,000
Polaroid	PRD	2,800	$76,875	$111,300
PPG Industries	PPG	600	$11,925	$32,400
Quaker Oats	OAT	900	$30,156	$32,850
Reebok International	RBK	1,700	$33,413	$76,288
Salomon	SB	3,000	$89,613	$149,625

Table 10.5 (cont.): List of Stocks Purchased

Name of Company	Trading Symbol	No. of Shares	Cost Basis	Stock Value
Sara Lee	SLE	1,100	$25,613	$44,550
Schlumberger	SLB	3,200	$171,800	$343,200
Schwab	SCH	100	$200	$3,188
Southwest Air	LUV	2,100	$49,138	$46,463
Sprint	FON	2,200	$45,621	$99,825
Sun Microsystems	SUNW	700	$4,263	$20,213
SunAmerica	SAI	400	$927	$15,050
TCI	TCOMA	2,400	$33,038	$28,800
Toys "R" Us	TOY	3,000	$76,500	$84,000
Travelers	TRV	200	$1,308	$9,575
United HealthCare	UNH	800	$15,266	$38,100
Unocal	UCL	1,700	$39,088	$64,813
US Surgical	USS	2,500	$68,525	$76,250
US WEST Comm.	USW	600	$13,893	$20,325
Warner-Lambert	WLA	1,000	$32,790	$86,500
Wells Fargo	WFC	2,100	$130,350	$596,663
Wendy's International	WEN	1,800	$8,475	$37,125
Xerox	XRX	2,100	$37,394	$119,438
Totals		147,900	$3,899,610	$7,857,106

Run No. 16:

ATM Strike Price is the High, Low, or Closing Stock Price: C
No. of Steps Near-Term LEAP Put is below ATM Strike Price: 0
No. of Steps Far-Term LEAP Put is below ATM Strike Price: 0
Minimum No. of Months till Expiration: 8
ITM Near-Term LEAPS are Rolled Over: Y
Stocks of ITM Far-Term LEAPS are Purchased: Y
Premium Reinvestment Rate: 6.0%
Minimum First Call Rating: 1.2
Minimum Standard & Poor's Rating: A-
No. of Stocks Meeting Either Criterion: 50

Table 10.6: LEAP OTM and ITM Rates

	LEAPS Written	LEAPS Expired	Expired OTM	OTM Rate	Expired ITM	ITM Rate	LEAPS Active
Near:	6,396	5,899	5,019	85.1%	880	14.9%	497
Far:	6,004	4,953	4,435	89.5%	518	10.5%	1,051
Total:	12,400	10,852	9,454	87.1%	1,398	12.9%	1,548

Table 10.7: Premiums Collected and Realized Gain for Expired LEAPS

	LEAPS Expired	Premiums Collected	Forward Value	ITM Exposure	Realized Gain	Retent'n Rate
Near:	5,899	$656,632	$700,038	$134,574	$565,464	86.1%
Far:	4,953	$783,524	$882,534	$1,241,101	-$358,568	-45.8%
Total:	10,852	$1,440,155	$1,582,571	$1,375,675	$206,896	14.4%

Table 10.8: Premiums Collected and Unrealized Gain on Active LEAPS

	LEAPS Active	Premiums Collected	Forward Value	Residual Value	Unrealized Gain
Near:	497	$147,675	$150,418	$126,012	$24,407
Far:	1,051	$319,954	$333,714	$218,707	$115,007
Total:	1,548	$467,629	$484,132	$344,719	$139,413

Table 10.9: Premiums Collected and Account Values

	Original Cont'cts	Premiums Collected	Compound Gain	Unrealized Gain	Stock Value	Account Value	Account Ratio
Near:	5,516	$804,306	$722,905	24,407	$0	$747,312	92.9%
Far:	6,004	$1,103,477	-$394,965	$115,007	$2,474,200	$2,194,242	198.8%
Total:	11,520	$1,907,784	$327,941	$139,413	$2,474,200	$2,941,554	154.2%

Table 10.10: List of Stocks Purchased

Name of Company	Trading Symbol	No. of Shares	Cost Basis	Stock Value
Abbott Labs	ABT	1,200	$25,050	$67,350
American Home	AHP	900	$28,575	$54,000
Anheuser-Busch	BUD	1,200	$29,400	$50,550
ASA Holdings	ASAI	2,300	$42,088	$47,725
Barrick Gold	ABX	300	$5,963	$7,125
Bell Atlantic	BEL	700	$34,725	$42,700
Bristol-Myers Squibb	BMY	2,400	$69,200	$141,600
Chubb	CB	300	$9,615	$16,163
Conseco	CNC	1,300	$9,077	$46,313
Cracker Barrel	CBRL	2,200	$45,550	$57,475
Dayton Hudson	DH	1,700	$35,986	$70,975
Equifax	EFX	300	$2,259	$8,175
Exxon	XON	400	$25,000	$43,100
Fannie Mae	FNM	100	$1,788	$3,613
Gap	GPS	1,500	$17,757	$50,250
General Electric	GE	600	$14,519	$59,550
General Mills	GIS	2,400	$115,073	$149,100
Heinz (H.J.)	HNZ	1,000	$23,182	$39,500
Hewlett-Packard	HWP	2,500	$26,835	$133,125
Home Depot	HD	100	$4,675	$5,350
Johnson & Johnson	JNJ	1,300	$27,793	$68,738
Limited	LTD	5,400	$90,811	$99,225
Lowe's	LOW	900	$24,126	$33,638
Merck	MRK	1,500	$55,875	$126,375
Minn. Mining	MMM	400	$17,778	$33,800
Motorola	MOT	800	$11,067	$48,300
NationsBank	NB	1,700	$33,256	$94,350
NIKE	NKE	900	$12,825	$55,688
PepsiCo	PEP	400	$7,379	$13,050
Pfizer	PFE	1,500	$34,686	$126,188
Philip Morris	MO	2,100	$126,075	$240,188
Pitney Bowes	PBI	1,600	$43,914	$94,000
PPG Industries	PPG	600	$11,925	$32,400
Sara Lee	SLE	1,100	$25,613	$44,550
Southwest Air	LUV	2,100	$49,138	$46,463
SunAmerica	SAI	400	$927	$15,050
Travelers	TRV	200	$1,308	$9,575
Wal-Mart	WMT	2,700	$59,025	$75,263
Warner-Lambert	WLA	1,000	$32,790	$86,500
Wendy's International	WEN	1,800	$8,475	$37,125
Totals		51,800	$1,241,100	$2,474,200

Run No. 17:

ATM Strike Price is the High, Low, or Closing Stock Price: C
No. of Steps Near-Term LEAP Put is below ATM Strike Price: 1
No. of Steps Far-Term LEAP Put is below ATM Strike Price: 1
Minimum No. of Months till Expiration: 8
ITM Near-Term LEAPS are Rolled Over: Y
Stocks of ITM Far-Term LEAPS are Purchased: Y
Premium Reinvestment Rate: 6.0%
Minimum First Call Rating: 1.6
Minimum Standard & Poor's Rating: B+
No. of Stocks Meeting Either Criterion: 115

Table 10.11: LEAP OTM and ITM Rates

	LEAPS Written	LEAPS Expired	Expired OTM	OTM Rate	Expired ITM	ITM Rate	LEAPS Active
Near:	13,109	12,017	11,024	91.7%	993	8.3%	1,092
Far:	13,186	10,778	10,040	93.2%	738	6.8%	2,408
Total:	26,295	22,795	21,064	92.4%	1,731	7.6%	3,500

Table 10.12: Premiums Collected and Realized Gain for Expired LEAPS

	LEAPS Expired	Premiums Collected	Forward Value	ITM Exposure	Realized Gain	Retent'n Rate
Near:	12,017	$870,704	$929,123	$340,533	$588,590	67.6%
Far:	10,778	$1,195,471	$1,347,097	$1,759,423	-$412,326	-34.5%
Total:	22,795	$2,066,174	$2,276,221	$2,099,956	$176,264	8.5%

Table 10.13: Premiums Collected and Unrealized Gain on Active LEAPS

	LEAPS Active	Premiums Collected	Forward Value	Residual Value	Unrealized Gain
Near:	1,092	$247,335	$251,999	$210,567	$41,432
Far:	2,408	$593,555	$618,822	$444,505	$174,317
Total:	3,500	$840,890	$870,821	$655,072	$215,750

Table 10.14: Premiums Collected and Account Values

	Original Cont'cts	Premiums Collected	Compound Gain	Unrealized Gain	Stock Value	Account Value	Account Ratio
Near:	12,116	$1,118,039	$763,604	$41,432	$0	$805,036	72.0%
Far:	13,186	$1,789,026	-$502,215	$174,317	$3,857,656	$3,529,758	197.3%
Total:	25,302	$2,907,065	$261,388	$215,750	$3,857,656	$4,334,794	149.1%

Table 10.15: List of Stocks Purchased

Name of Company	Trading Symbol	No. of Shares	Cost Basis	Stock Value
Abbott Labs	ABT	400	$4,900	$22,450
Adobe Systems	ADBE	400	$15,150	$16,050
Allied Signal	ALD	1,100	$18,425	$78,375
Altera	ALTR	500	$1,955	$21,500
American Express	AXP	1,200	$21,860	$71,850
American Home	AHP	100	$3,175	$6,000
Anheuser-Busch	BUD	100	$2,450	$4,213
Applied Materials	AMAT	700	$2,439	$32,463
ASA Holdings	ASAI	2,600	$37,946	$53,950
AT&T	T	200	$7,481	$6,950
Atlantic Richfield	ARC	2,200	$240,650	$297,000
Avon Products	AVP	500	$5,531	$26,250
BankAmerica	BAC	300	$12,938	$30,263
Barrick Gold	ABX	200	$3,975	$4,750
Bell Atlantic	BEL	100	$4,613	$6,100
Boeing	BA	1,100	$40,375	$108,488
Boston Scientific	BSX	100	$1,850	$6,175
Bristol-Myers Squibb	BMY	1,600	$46,769	$94,400
Burlington Northern	BNI	100	$4,750	$7,400
Chase Manhattan	CMB	2,400	$51,375	$224,700
Compaq	CPQ	1,500	$17,057	$114,938
Conseco	CNC	900	$3,967	$32,063
Cracker Barrel	CBRL	1,500	$30,150	$39,188
CUC International	CU	1,700	$3,097	$38,250
Dun & Bradstreet	DNB	2,200	$74,525	$55,825
Gap	GPS	200	$925	$6,700
General Mills	GIS	1,300	$61,762	$80,763
HealthSouth	HRC	700	$1,523	$13,388
Hewlett-Packard	HWP	1,500	$15,449	$79,875
Hilton Hotels	HLT	1,600	$15,850	$38,800
Household International	HI	1,200	$22,650	$103,350
International Game	IGT	2,500	$32,538	$40,313
KMart	KM	4,000	$50,500	$48,500
Kroger	KR	100	$1,750	$5,100
Limited	LTD	4,100	$68,704	$75,338
Magna International	MGA	2,500	$17,636	$124,063
Merck	MRK	1,000	$36,875	$84,250

Table 10.15 (cont.): List of Stocks Purchased

Name of Company	Trading Symbol	No. of Shares	Cost Basis	Stock Value
Merrill Lynch	MER	800	$10,570	$68,700
Morgan (J.P.)	JPM	600	$21,750	$58,950
NationsBank	NB	400	$5,625	$22,200
NEXTEL	NXTL	2,400	$30,350	$32,100
NIKE	NKE	300	$3,750	$18,563
NYNEX	NYN	400	$15,606	$18,250
Office Depot	ODP	600	$9,872	$12,225
Oracle	ORCL	1,500	$4,060	$57,844
Pfizer	PFE	500	$8,992	$42,063
Philip Morris	MO	1,800	$108,050	$205,875
Pitney Bowes	PBI	600	$18,525	$35,250
Polaroid	PRD	2,500	$67,800	$99,375
PPG Industries	PPG	400	$7,950	$21,600
Reebok International	RBK	700	$9,050	$31,413
Salomon	SB	1,700	$56,675	$84,788
Schlumberger	SLB	1,500	$81,275	$160,875
Schwab	SCH	100	$200	$3,188
Southwest Air	LUV	1,000	$18,468	$22,125
Sprint	FON	1,200	$23,700	$54,450
SunAmerica	SAI	400	$927	$15,050
TCI	TCOMA	400	$5,236	$4,800
Toys "R" Us	TOY	2,800	$71,500	$78,400
United HealthCare	UNH	500	$641	$23,813
Unocal	UCL	200	$4,350	$7,625
US Surgical	USS	2,400	$66,200	$73,200
Wal-Mart	WMT	600	$13,725	$16,725
Wells Fargo	WFC	1,500	$93,450	$426,188
Wendy's International	WEN	800	$4,000	$16,500
Xerox	XRX	800	$13,563	$45,500
Totals		73,800	$1,759,424	$3,857,656

Run No. 18:

ATM Strike Price is the High, Low, or Closing Stock Price: C
No. of Steps Near-Term LEAP Put is below ATM Strike Price: 1
No. of Steps Far-Term LEAP Put is below ATM Strike Price: 1
Minimum No. of Months till Expiration: 8
ITM Near-Term LEAPS are Rolled Over: Y
Stocks of ITM Far-Term LEAPS are Purchased: Y
Premium Reinvestment Rate: 6.0%
Minimum First Call Rating: 1.2
Minimum Standard & Poor's Rating: A-
No. of Stocks Meeting Either Criterion: 50

Table 10.16: LEAP OTM and ITM Rates

	LEAPS Written	LEAPS Expired	Expired OTM	OTM Rate	Expired ITM	ITM Rate	LEAPS Active
Near:	5,782	5,325	5,059	95.0%	266	5.0%	457
Far:	6,004	4,953	4,729	95.5%	224	4.5%	1,051
Total:	11,786	10,278	9,788	95.2%	490	4.8%	1,508

Table 10.17: Premiums Collected and Realized Gain for Expired LEAPS

	LEAPS Expired	Premiums Collected	Forward Value	ITM Exposure	Realized Gain	Retent'n Rate
Near:	5,325	$264,349	$282,199	$49,438	$232,761	88.1%
Far:	4,953	$385,272	$434,226	$511,671	-$77,444	-20.1%
Total:	10,278	$649,621	$716,426	$561,109	$155,317	23.9%

Table 10.18: Premiums Collected and Unrealized Gain on Active LEAPS

	LEAPS Active	Premiums Collected	Forward Value	Residual Value	Unrealized Gain
Near:	457	$77,516	$78,989	$64,648	$14,341
Far:	1,051	$189,212	$196,907	$128,283	$68,623
Total:	1,508	$266,728	$275,895	$192,931	$82,964

Table 10.19: Premiums Collected and Account Values

	Original Cont'cts	Premiums Collected	Compound Gain	Unrealized Gain	Stock Value	Account Value	Account Ratio
Near:	5,516	$341,865	$301,311	$14,341	$0	$315,652	92.3%
Far:	6,004	$574,484	-$64,046	$68,623	$1,005,988	$1,010,565	175.9%
Total:	11,520	$916,350	$237,266	$82,964	$1,005,988	$1,326,217	144.7%

Table 10.20: List of Stocks Purchased

Name of Company	Trading Symbol	No. of Shares	Cost Basis	Stock Value
Abbott Labs	ABT	400	$4,900	$22,450
American Home	AHP	100	$3,175	$6,000
Anheuser-Busch	BUD	100	$2,450	$4,213
ASA Holdings	ASAI	2,600	$37,946	$53,950
Barrick Gold	ABX	200	$3,975	$4,750
Bell Atlantic	BEL	100	$4,613	$6,100
Bristol-Myers Squibb	BMY	1,600	$46,769	$94,400
Conseco	CNC	900	$3,967	$32,063
Cracker Barrel	CBRL	1,500	$30,150	$39,188
Gap	GPS	200	$925	$6,700
General Mills	GIS	1,300	$61,762	$80,763
Hewlett-Packard	HWP	1,500	$15,449	$79,875
Limited	LTD	4,100	$68,704	$75,338
Merck	MRK	1,000	$36,875	$84,250
NationsBank	NB	400	$5,625	$22,200
NIKE	NKE	300	$3,750	$18,563
Pfizer	PFE	500	$8,992	$42,063
Philip Morris	MO	1,800	$108,050	$205,875
Pitney Bowes	PBI	600	$18,525	$35,250
PPG Industries	PPG	400	$7,950	$21,600
Southwest Air	LUV	1,000	$18,468	$22,125
SunAmerica	SAI	400	$927	$15,050
Wal-Mart	WMT	600	$13,725	$16,725
Wendy's International	WEN	800	$4,000	$16,500
Totals		22,400	$511,671	$1,005,988

Run No. 19:

ATM Strike Price is the High, Low, or Closing Stock Price: C
No. of Steps Near-Term LEAP Put is below ATM Strike Price: 2
No. of Steps Far-Term LEAP Put is below ATM Strike Price: 2
Minimum No. of Months till Expiration: 8
ITM Near-Term LEAPS are Rolled Over: Y
Stocks of ITM Far-Term LEAPS are Purchased: Y
Premium Reinvestment Rate: 6.0%
Minimum First Call Rating: 1.6
Minimum Standard & Poor's Rating: B+
No. of Stocks Meeting Either Criterion: 115

Table 10.21: LEAP OTM and ITM Rates

	LEAPS Written	LEAPS Expired	Expired OTM	OTM Rate	Expired ITM	ITM Rate	LEAPS Active
Near:	12,678	11,616	11,054	95.2%	562	4.8%	1,062
Far:	13,186	10,778	10,343	96.0%	435	4.0%	2,408
Total:	25,864	22,394	21,397	95.5%	997	4.5%	3,470

Table 10.22: Premiums Collected and Realized Gain for Expired LEAPS

	LEAPS Expired	Premiums Collected	Forward Value	ITM Exposure	Realized Gain	Retent'n Rate
Near:	11,616	$447,303	$477,653	$190,971	$286,682	64.1%
Far:	10,778	$689,566	$777,415	$768,734	$8,680	1.3%
Total:	22,394	$1,136,869	$1,255,068	$959,706	$295,362	26.0%

Table 10.23: Premiums Collected and Unrealized Gain on Active LEAPS

	LEAPS Active	Premiums Collected	Forward Value	Residual Value	Unrealized Gain
Near:	1,062	$140,761	$143,416	$117,980	$25,436
Far:	2,408	$364,184	$379,020	$280,836	$98,184
Total:	3,470	$504,945	$522,436	$398,816	$123,621

Table 10.24: Premiums Collected and Account Values

	Original Cont'cts	Premiums Collected	Compound Gain	Unrealized Gain	Stock Value	Account Value	Account Ratio
Near:	12,116	$588,065	$385,946	$25,436	$0	$411,383	70.0%
Far:	13,186	$1,053,750	$35,031	$98,184	$1,977,738	$2,110,953	200.3%
Total:	25,302	$1,641,814	$420,978	$123,621	$1,977,738	$2,522,336	153.6%

Table 10.25: List of Stocks Purchased

Name of Company	Trading Symbol	No. of Shares	Cost Basis	Stock Value
Adobe Systems	ADBE	300	$11,363	$12,038
Allied Signal	ALD	500	$8,613	$35,625
Altera	ALTR	500	$1,955	$21,500
American Express	AXP	600	$10,930	$35,925
Applied Materials	AMAT	700	$2,439	$32,463
ASA Holdings	ASAI	1,900	$25,212	$39,425
Atlantic Richfield	ARC	700	$78,750	$94,500
Boeing	BA	100	$3,525	$9,863
Bristol-Myers Squibb	BMY	700	$20,350	$41,300
Chase Manhattan	CMB	1,600	$27,625	$149,800
Compaq	CPQ	800	$9,380	$61,300
Conseco	CNC	600	$499	$21,375
CUC International	CU	1,700	$3,097	$38,250
Dun & Bradstreet	DNB	1,600	$46,550	$40,600
Equifax	EFX	200	$1,439	$5,450
Gap	GPS	400	$1,850	$13,400
General Mills	GIS	100	$4,909	$6,213
HealthSouth	HRC	1,100	$3,563	$21,038
Hewlett-Packard	HWP	100	$1,116	$5,325
Hilton Hotels	HLT	900	$9,169	$21,825
Household International	HI	400	$7,550	$34,450
Intel	INTC	300	$1,950	$41,738
International Game	IGT	2,200	$28,000	$35,475
KMart	KM	2,600	$26,175	$31,525
Limited	LTD	1,500	$24,147	$27,563
Lowe's	LOW	500	$2,960	$18,688
Magna International	MGA	2,100	$11,098	$104,213
Merck	MRK	400	$14,600	$33,700
Merrill Lynch	MER	600	$7,848	$51,525
NationsBank	NB	200	$2,813	$11,100
NEXTEL	NXTL	2,000	$24,200	$26,750
Office Depot	ODP	300	$1,304	$6,113
Oracle	ORCL	2,000	$6,121	$77,125
Philip Morris	MO	1,300	$77,975	$148,688
Polaroid	PRD	1,700	$47,013	$67,575
Reebok International	RBK	500	$5,875	$22,438

Table 10.25 (cont.): List of Stocks Purchased

Name of Company	Trading Symbol	No. of Shares	Cost Basis	Stock Value
Salomon	SB	300	$9,750	$14,963
Schlumberger	SLB	600	$32,975	$64,350
Schwab	SCH	100	$200	$3,188
Southwest Air	LUV	300	$1,433	$6,638
Sprint	FON	1,100	$21,725	$49,913
Sun Microsystems	SUNW	600	$3,600	$17,325
SunAmerica	SAI	400	$927	$15,050
Toys "R" Us	TOY	1,200	$28,575	$33,600
Travelers	TRV	1,000	$6,147	$47,875
United HealthCare	UNH	500	$641	$23,813
US Surgical	USS	2,100	$59,175	$64,050
Wells Fargo	WFC	600	$37,500	$170,475
Wendy's International	WEN	1,000	$4,125	$20,625
Totals		43,500	$768,734	$1,977,738

Run No. 20:

ATM Strike Price is the High, Low, or Closing Stock Price: C
No. of Steps Near-Term LEAP Put is below ATM Strike Price: 2
No. of Steps Far-Term LEAP Put is below ATM Strike Price: 2
Minimum No. of Months till Expiration: 8
ITM Near-Term LEAPS are Rolled Over: Y
Stocks of ITM Far-Term LEAPS are Purchased: Y
Premium Reinvestment Rate: ,   6.0%
Minimum First Call Rating: 1.2
Minimum Standard & Poor's Rating: A-
No. of Stocks Meeting Either Criterion: 50

Table 10.26: LEAP OTM and ITM Rates

	LEAPS Written	LEAPS Expired	Expired OTM	OTM Rate	Expired ITM	ITM Rate	LEAPS Active
Near:	5,705	5,254	5,065	96.4%	189	3.6%	451
Far:	6,004	4,953	4,847	97.9%	106	2.1%	1,051
Total:	11,709	10,207	9,912	97.1%	295	2.9%	1,502

Table 10.27: Premiums Collected and Realized Gain for Expired LEAPS

	LEAPS Expired	Premiums Collected	Forward Value	ITM Exposure	Realized Gain	Retent'n Rate
Near:	5,254	$123,882	$132,344	$19,707	$112,636	90.9%
Far:	4,953	$206,272	$232,609	$190,502	$42,107	20.4%
Total:	10,207	$330,155	$364,952	$210,209	$154,743	46.9%

Table 10.28: Premiums Collected and Unrealized Gain on Active LEAPS

	LEAPS Active	Premiums Collected	Forward Value	Residual Value	Unrealized Gain
Near:	451	$39,263	$40,008	$32,289	$7,719
Far:	1,051	$104,640	$108,597	$72,106	$36,491
Total:	1,502	$143,903	$148,605	$104,395	$44,210

Table 10.29: Premiums Collected and Account Values

	Original Cont'cts	Premiums Collected	Compound Gain	Unrealized Gain	Stock Value	Account Value	Account Ratio
Near:	5,516	$163,146	$152,879	$7,719	$0	$160,598	98.4%
Far:	6,004	$310,912	$70,938	$36,491	$462,413	$569,842	183.3%
Total:	11,520	$474,058	$223,817	$44,210	$462,413	$730,440	154.1%

Table 10.30: List of Stocks Purchased

Name of Company	Trading Symbol	No. of Shares	Cost Basis	Stock Value
ASA Holdings	ASAI	1,900	$25,212	$39,425
Bristol-Myers Squibb	BMY	700	$20,350	$41,300
Conseco	CNC	600	$499	$21,375
Equifax	EFX	200	$1,439	$5,450
Gap	GPS	400	$1,850	$13,400
General Mills	GIS	100	$4,909	$6,213
Hewlett-Packard	HWP	100	$1,116	$5,325
Limited	LTD	1,500	$24,147	$27,563
Lowe's	LOW	500	$2,960	$18,688
Merck	MRK	400	$14,600	$33,700
NationsBank	NB	200	$2,813	$11,100
Philip Morris	MO	1,300	$77,975	$148,688
Southwest Air	LUV	300	$1,433	$6,638
SunAmerica	SAI	400	$927	$15,050
Travelers	TRV	1,000	$6,147	$47,875
Wendy's International	WEN	1,000	$4,125	$20,625
Totals		10,600	$190,502	$462,413

Summary

The tables below compare the overall ten-year value ratios for the B+ and A- minimum universes for the three independent situations in which LEAPS winding up in the money (i) are not rolled out, (ii) are rolled out, and (iii) are both rolled out (near-term) and assigned (far-term).

Table 10.31: Figure of Merit Comparisons

	Run No.	Uni-verse	No. of Issues	Steps Below ATM	Steady-State OTM Rate	Steady-State Retention Rate	Ten-Year Account Ratio
Without Rollover	1.	All	217	0	77.7%	42.6%	44.3%
	2.	B min	178	0	80.0%	54.3%	57.5%
	3.	B+ min	115	0	84.0%	66.2%	69.7%
	4.	A- min	50	0	87.1%	79.9%	84.9%
	5.	B+ min	115	1	92.5%	70.4%	72.6%
	6.	A- min	50	1	95.1%	90.0%	91.6%
	7.	B+ min	115	2	95.6%	71.1%	73.6%
	8.	A- min	50	2	97.1%	95.7%	98.3%
With Rollover	9.	B+ min	115	0	84.3%	78.5%	80.3%
	10.	A- min	50	0	87.5%	92.7%	95.9%
	11.	B+ min	115	1	92.4%	76.9%	77.9%
	12.	A- min	50	1	95.3%	96.2%	96.8%
	13.	B+ min	115	2	95.6%	76.1%	77.5%
	14.	A- min	50	2	97.1%	100.7%	103.2%
With Assignment	15.	B+ min	115	0	84.0%	-4.2%	149.6%
	16.	A- min	50	0	87.1%	14.4%	154.2%
	17.	B+ min	115	1	92.4%	8.5%	149.1%
	18.	A- min	50	1	95.2%	23.9%	144.7%
	19.	B+ min	115	2	95.5%	26.0%	153.6%
	20.	A- min	50	2	97.1%	46.9%	154.1%

As we can see from the tables, adopting the combined rollover and stock acquisition strategy can substantially improve long-term account values.

At-the-Money Results

For the B+ minimum universe of 115 stocks with at-the-money LEAPS, the account ratio progressively increases from 66.7% without rollovers in Run No. 3, to 84.1% with rollovers in Run No. 9, to 149.6% with the combined rollover/acquisition strategy in Run No. 15.

For the A- minimum universe of 50 stocks, the account ratio progressively increases from 84.9% without rollovers in Run No. 4, to 95.9% with rollovers in Run No. 10, to 154.2% with the combined rollover/acquisition strategy in Run No. 16.

One-Step Out-of-the-Money Results

For the B+ minimum universe of 115 stocks with one-step out-of-the-money LEAPS, the account ratio progressively increases from 72.6% without rollovers in Run No. 5, to 77.9% with rollovers in Run No. 11, to 149.1% with the combined rollover/acquisition strategy in Run No. 17.

For the A- minimum universe of 50 stocks, the account ratio progressively increases from 91.6% without rollovers in Run No. 6, to 96.8% with rollovers in Run No. 12, to 144.7% with the combined rollover/acquisition strategy in Run No. 18.

Two-Step Out-of-the-Money Results

For the B+ minimum universe of 115 stocks with two-step out-of-the-money LEAPS, the account ratio progressively increases from 73.6% without rollovers in Run No. 7, to 77.5% with rollovers in Run No. 13, to 153.6% with the combined rollover/acquisition strategy in Run No. 19.

For the A- minimum universe of 50 stocks, the account ratio progressively increases from 98.3% without rollovers in Run No. 8, to 103.2% with rollovers in Run No. 14, to 154.1% with the combined rollover/acquisition strategy in Run No. 20.

CHAPTER 11

ADVANCED STRATEGIES

Introduction

The strategies thus far investigated barely begin to cover the many ways to acquire stock using the premiums received from the sale of LEAP puts. One method that I especially like is to divide the potential universe of higher-rated issues having LEAP options into three categories: (i) stocks that I favor highly, currently hold in portfolio, and want to acquire more of; (ii) stocks that I would like to acquire for my portfolio at below-market prices; and (iii) stocks that I am more or less neutral about, but would not mind acquiring for my portfolio at prices substantially below today's market prices. In keeping with this "triage" approach, I sell into-the-money LEAP puts on stocks in the first category, at-the-money LEAP puts on the second category, and out-of-the-money puts on the third category. I use the term "into-the-money" rather than "in-the-money" to signify the use of exercise prices not more than one or at most two strikes above the current market price.

As a variation on this theme, you could take the 50 or so stocks classified as A- or better and sell into-the-money LEAP puts on the ones rated A+, at-the-money puts on the ones rated A, and out-of-the-money puts on the ones rated A-. Once you acquire proficiency and experience, you could start including B+ rated stocks in this last group as well.

There are so many variations possible on this strategy, that as a practical matter, I decided to limit the analysis to just two variations, both of which are examined in this chapter. The first method considered is to restrict the sale of LEAP puts to far-term LEAPS and not deal with near-term LEAPS at all. The second method is a mix and match approach, in which puts are simultaneously sold on both higher-quality, far-term LEAPS and broader-quality, near-term LEAPS.

Far-Term LEAPS Alone Strategy

The computer simulations conducted thus far have clearly demonstrated that far-term LEAPS are consistently more profitable and safer than near-term LEAPS. The reasons for this include the fact that standard option pricing formulas do not take into account the long-term growth rates of the underlying issue, and the quite reasonable assumption that over the long term, stock prices of better-quality issues move inexorably upwards.

The effect of restricting the sale of puts to far-term LEAPS can be seen by extracting the relevant line items from the twenty computer simulations already performed. The combined rollover and acquisition strategy is the equivalent of selling two far-term LEAPS on each issue every month. Should any such pair of LEAP puts appear to be winding up in the money as expiration approaches, one of them is rolled out while the other is used to acquire stock as a result of exercise and assignment. When this strategy is employed, the summary chart for far-term LEAPS appears as shown in Table 11.1, below.

Comparing the results for the far-term LEAPS alone in Table 11.1 with those for the mixed near-term/far-term LEAPS in Table 10.31 clearly shows the improvement in the steady-state out-of-the-money and retention rates obtainable. Although the account value ratios are roughly the same, in terms of absolute dollars the ten-year account values for the far-term LEAPS alone are much larger because the base of premiums collected to which those percentages are applied is so much larger.

The list of stocks acquired is the same as shown for Runs 15 through 20 in the previous chapter.

Table 11.1: Figure of Merit Comparisons
Far-Term LEAPS Alone

	Run No.	Uni-verse	No. of Issues	Steps Below ATM	Steady-State OTM Rate	Steady-State Retention Rate	Ten-Year Account Ratio
Without Rollover	1.	All	217	0	79.7%	48.1%	47.7%
	2.	B min	178	0	82.0%	60.9%	62.0%
	3.	B+ min	115	0	86.3%	73.4%	74.4%
	4.	A- min	50	0	89.5%	86.8%	89.1%
	5.	B+ min	115	1	93.2%	76.8%	76.3%
	6.	A- min	50	1	95.5%	95.6%	94.5%
	7.	B+ min	115	2	96.0%	78.2%	77.7%
	8.	A- min	50	2	97.9%	102.7%	102.3%
With Rollover	9.	B+ min	115	0	86.7%	85.0%	83.3%
	10.	A- min	50	0	90.1%	98.3%	98.0%
	11.	B+ min	115	1	93.2%	83.8%	81.5%
	12.	A- min	50	1	95.6%	101.8%	99.4%
	13.	B+ min	115	2	96.0%	83.8%	81.6%
	14.	A- min	50	2	97.9%	106.6%	105.6%
With Assignment	9/15	B+ min	115	0	86.5%	8.4%	142.7%
	10/16	A- min	50	0	89.8%	26.3%	147.9%
	11/17	B+ min	115	1	93.2%	24.6%	139.0%
	12/18	A- min	50	1	95.6%	40.8%	137.5%
	13/19	B+ min	115	2	96.0%	42.6%	140.6%
	14/20	A- min	50	2	97.9%	63.5%	144.4%

Mix-and-Match Strategies

Another strategy is to sell far-term LEAP puts on the higher-quality, A- minimum universe of 50 stocks while at the same time selling near-term LEAP puts on the broader-quality B+ minimum universe of 115 stocks. The near-term B+ LEAP puts would be rolled over if they wind up in the money as expiration approaches, while the far-term A- LEAP puts would be used for stock acquisition. Because of the higher financial exposure and potential risk of assignment of the near-term B+ LEAPS, the strike prices selected for them will be one step below the level selected for the far-term A- LEAP puts. Two such mix-and-match combinations have been selected to illustrate the approach, ranging from the most conservative to the most aggressive.

Conservative Mix-and-Match Strategy

Run No. 21 shows the results of selling far-term LEAPS that are one step out of the money on the A- minimum universe of 50 stocks while simultaneously selling near-term LEAPS that are two steps out of the money on the B+ minimum universe of 115 stocks. The results shown are stronger than those obtained in Run No. 18, for which the far-term LEAP universe was also the A- minimum universe of 50 stocks. In particular, collecting premiums from the larger universe of 115 near-term LEAPS has the net effect of lowering overall risk with only a moderate reduction of overall benefits. Although the account value is 122.3% of the total premiums collected—down from the 144.7% figure seen in Run No. 18—it is applied to a larger base. The list of acquired stocks for this mix-and-match strategy is the same as the one for Run No. 18.

Moderate Mix-and-Match Strategy

Run No. 22 shows the results of selling far-term LEAPS that are at the money on the A- minimum universe of 50 stocks while simultaneously selling near-term LEAPS that are one step out of the money on the B+ minimum universe of 115 stocks. The results shown are stronger than those obtained in Run No. 16, for which the far-term LEAP universe was also the A- minimum universe of 50 stocks. In particular, collecting premiums from the larger universe of 115 near-term LEAPS has the net effect of lowering overall risk, again with only a moderate reduction of overall benefits. And as with the conservative strategy, although the account value is 135.0% of the total premiums collected—down from the 154.2% figure seen in Run No. 16—it is applied to a larger base. The list of acquired stocks for this mix and match strategy is the same as the one for Run No. 16.

Run No. 21:

ATM Strike Price is the High, Low, or Closing Stock Price: C
No. of Steps Near-Term LEAP Put is below ATM Strike Price: 2
No. of Steps Far-Term LEAP Put is below ATM Strike Price: 1
Minimum No. of Months till Expiration: 8
ITM Near-Term LEAPS are Rolled Over: Y
Stocks of ITM Far-Term LEAPS are Purchased: Y
Premium Reinvestment Rate: 6.0%
Minimum Near-Term First Call Rating: 1.6
Minimum Near-Term Standard & Poor's Rating: B+
No. of Stocks Meeting Either Criterion: 115
Minimum Far-Term First Call Rating: 1.2
Minimum Far-Term Standard & Poor's Rating: A-
No. of Stocks Meeting Either Criterion: 50

Table 11.2: LEAP OTM and ITM Rates

	LEAPS Written	LEAPS Expired	Expired OTM	OTM Rate	Expired ITM	ITM Rate	LEAPS Active
Near:	12,678	11,616	11,054	95.2%	562	4.8%	1,062
Far:	6,004	4,953	4,729	95.5%	224	4.5%	1,051
Total:	18,682	16,569	15,783	95.3%	786	4.7%	2,113

Table 11.3: Premiums Collected and Realized Gain for Expired LEAPS

	LEAPS Expired	Premiums Collected	Forward Value	ITM Exposure	Realized Gain	Retent'n Rate
Near:	11,616	$447,303	$477,653	$190,971	$286,682	64.1%
Far:	4,953	$385,272	$434,226	$511,671	-$77,444	-20.1%
Total:	16,569	$832,576	$911,880	$702,642	$209,238	25.1%

Table 11.4: Premiums Collected and Unrealized Gain on Active LEAPS

	LEAPS Active	Premiums Collected	Forward Value	Residual Value	Unrealized Gain
Near:	1,062	$140,761	$143,416	$117,980	$25,436
Far:	1,051	$189,212	$196,907	$128,283	$68,623
Total:	2,113	$329,973	$340,323	$246,263	$94,060

Table 11.5: Premiums Collected and Account Values

	Original Cont'cts	Premiums Collected	Compound Gain	Unrealized Gain	Stock Value	Account Value	Account Ratio
Near:	12,116	$588,065	$385,946	$25,436	$0	$411,383	70.0%
Far:	6,004	$574,484	-$64,046	$68,623	$1,005,988	$1,010,565	175.9%
Total:	18,120	$1,162,549	$321,901	$94,060	$1,005,988	$1,421,948	122.3%

Run No. 22:

ATM Strike Price is the High, Low, or Closing Stock Price: C
No. of Steps Near-Term LEAP Put is below ATM Strike Price: 1
No. of Steps Far-Term LEAP Put is below ATM Strike Price: 0
Minimum No. of Months till Expiration: 8
ITM Near-Term LEAPS are Rolled Over: Y
Stocks of ITM Far-Term LEAPS are Purchased: Y
Premium Reinvestment Rate: 6.0%
Minimum Near-Term First Call Rating: 1.6
Minimum Near-Term Standard & Poor's Rating: B+
No. of Stocks Meeting Either Criterion: 115
Minimum Far-Term First Call Rating: 1.2
Minimum Far-Term Standard & Poor's Rating: A-
No. of Stocks Meeting Either Criterion: 50

Table 11.6: LEAP OTM and ITM Rates

	LEAPS Written	LEAPS Expired	Expired OTM	OTM Rate	Expired ITM	ITM Rate	LEAPS Active
Near:	13,109	12,017	11,024	91.7%	993	8.3%	1,092
Far:	6,004	4,953	4,435	89.5%	518	10.5%	1,051
Total:	19,113	16,970	15,459	91.1%	1,511	8.9%	2,143

Table 11.7: Premiums Collected and Realized Gain for Expired LEAPS

	LEAPS Expired	Premiums Collected	Forward Value	ITM Exposure	Realized Gain	Retent'n Rate
Near:	12,017	$870,704	$929,123	$340,533	$588,590	67.6%
Far:	4,953	$783,524	$882,534	$1,241,101	-$358,568	-45.8%
Total:	16,970	$1,654,227	$1,811,657	$1,581,635	$230,023	13.9%

Table 11.8: Premiums Collected and Unrealized Gain on Active LEAPS

	LEAPS Active	Premiums Collected	Forward Value	Residual Value	Unrealized Gain
Near:	1,092	$247,335	$251,999	$210,567	$41,432
Far:	1,051	$319,954	$333,714	$218,707	$115,007
Total:	2,143	$567,289	$585,713	$429,274	$156,439

Table 11.9: Premiums Collected and Account Values

	Original Cont'cts	Premiums Collected	Compound Gain	Unrealized Gain	Stock Value	Account Value	Account Ratio
Near:	12,116	$1,118,039	$763,604	$41,432	$0	$805,036	72.0%
Far:	6,004	$1,103,477	-$394,965	$115,007	$2,474,200	$2,194,242	198.8%
Total:	18,120	$2,221,516	$368,639	$156,439	$2,474,200	$2,999,278	135.0%

A Word of Caution

With enough time and experience, some investors may feel inclined to take on higher levels of risk by selling far-term LEAP puts that are deeply into the money and/or near-term LEAP puts that are at the money. Fight the urge to do so, for adopting too aggressive an approach can leave oneself especially vulnerable to a sudden downturn in the market. How to protect oneself against such a downturn is the subject of the next chapter.

12

CHAPTER 12

HEDGING FOR DISASTER

Introduction

Each LEAP put in the previous chapters was sold as a "pure play," without any attempt to hedge against an unexpected downturn in the market. As described in Chapter 3, it is possible to lessen potential losses by buying a deep out-of-the-money LEAP put at the same time the primary, near-the-money LEAP put is sold. This type of hedging strategy is particularly useful if you are going to sell LEAP puts on lower-rated companies or on stocks known to be highly volatile. What this does is reduce reducing potential profits while simultaneously reducing potential loss. Profit is reduced because the net premium generated is the difference between the premium *received* from the sale of the higher-strike LEAP put and the premium *paid* for the purchase of the lower-strike LEAP put.* On the other hand, the maximum amount of financial exposure is reduced from that of the strike price of the LEAP put sold to that of the difference between the two strike prices involved. Should the stock price fall below the strike price of the insurance put, the incremental financial exposure on the primary put is exactly counterbalanced by the incremental increase in value of the insurance put.

For example, suppose you sold an at-the-money LEAP put on a $100 stock with a volatility 0.50 and with 24 months till expiration. From Table 2.1 (or Table A.5 in Appendix A), you would expect to

---

*For reference purposes, we'll call this lower-strike LEAP put the insurance put.

receive a contract premium of $2,077.40 for it. Suppose now that you had simultaneously purchased a LEAP put with strike price of $85 on the same stock with the same expiration date. As indicated in Table A.8, you would expect to pay $1,374.10 for it. Your net premium is therefore $2,077.40 less $1,374.10, or $703.30. On the other hand, the maximum financial exposure is limited to $15 a share, or $1,500 per contract, no matter how low the price of the underlying issue at expiration.

Procedure

For analysis purposes, let us suppose the strike price of the insurance put to be three steps below the strike price of the primary, at-the-money put. To what extent is the purchase of such disaster insurance worth it? To answer this question, we repeat Runs No. 1 through 4, but where, for each at-the-money LEAP put sold, a corresponding LEAP put three steps out-of-the money is simultaneously purchased for insurance purposes.

If the primary ATM LEAP put sold winds up out of the money at expiration, the net profit is the premium received on the ATM put less the price paid for the lower-strike insurance put. If the ATM LEAP put winds up in the money, but above the strike price of the insurance put, the net profit or loss is calculated as the net premium received on the ATM LEAP and insurance puts, less the financial exposure incurred at expiration on the ATM LEAP put. If the stock price at expiration is below the strike price of the insurance put, the overall financial exposure is the difference between the two strike prices involved offset by net premium received on the ATM LEAP and insurance puts.

The Full Universe

Run No. 23 shows the effect of taking the full universe of 217 stocks considered in Run No. 1 and combining the same set of LEAP puts sold with the purchase of insurance puts at a strike price three steps out of the money. By comparing Table 12.2 with Table 6.3, we see that the premiums collected on expired LEAPS have fallen from $8,354,277 to $6,494,411, with the difference of $1,859,866 being the cost of the insurance puts purchased. On the other hand, the financial exposure from puts expiring in the money falls from

$5,619,931 to $4,325,249, a reduction of $1,294,682. Of the 39,405 expired LEAP contracts, 8,770 expired in the money, and it turns out that in just 2,541 of these instances was the stock price at expiration below the strike price of the insurance put.

What the computer simulation thus revealed was that in only 2,541 instances out of 39,405 expired LEAPS (6.4%) was the insurance protection of any value. The retention rate barely increased from 42.6% in Run No. 1 to 43.1% in Run No. 23, while the account value at the end of the ten-year period barely increased from 44.3% in Run No. 1 to 44.9% in Run No. 23.

The B Minimum Universe

Run No. 24 shows the effect of taking the B minimum universe of 178 stocks considered in Run No. 2 and combining the same set of LEAP puts sold with the purchase of insurance puts at a strike price three steps out of the money. By comparing Table 12.6 with Table 7.2, we see that the premiums collected on expired LEAPS have fallen from $6,803,725 to $5,334,626, with the difference of $1,469,099 being the cost of the insurance puts purchased. On the other hand, the financial exposure from puts expiring in the money falls from $3,779,739 to $3,043,533, a reduction of $736,206. Of the 33,312 expired LEAP contracts, 6,667 expired in the money, and in just 1,851 of these instances was the stock price at expiration below the strike price of the insurance put.

Thus, in only 1,851 instances out of 33,312 expired LEAPS (5.6%) was the insurance protection of any value. The retention rate *decreased* from 54.3% in Run No. 2 to 52.7% in Run No. 24, while the account value at the end of the ten-year period decreased from 57.5% in Run No. 2 to 55.2% in Run No. 24.

The B+ Minimum Universe

Run No. 25 shows the effect of taking the B+ minimum universe of 115 stocks considered in Run No. 3 and combining the same set of LEAP puts sold puts with the purchase of insurance puts at a strike price three steps out of the money. By comparing Table 12.2 with Table 7.6, we see that the premiums collected on expired LEAPS have fallen from $3,992,382 to $3,205,536, with the difference of

$786,846 being the cost of the insurance puts purchased. On the other hand, the financial exposure from puts expiring in the money falls from $1,742,423 to $1,449,616, a reduction of $292,807. Of the 21,858 expired LEAP contracts, 3,504 expired in the money, and in just 798 of these instances was the stock price at expiration below the strike price of the insurance put.

Thus, in only 798 instances out of 21,858 expired LEAPS (3.7%) was the insurance protection of any value. The retention rate decreased from 66.2% in Run No. 3 to 64.5% in Run No. 25, while the account value at the end of the ten-year period decreased from 69.7% in Run No. 3 to 67.4% in Run No. 25.

The A- Minimum Universe

Run No. 26 shows the effect of taking the A- minimum universe of 50 stocks considered in Run No. 4 and combining the same set of LEAP puts sold with the purchase of insurance puts at a strike price three steps out of the money. By comparing Table 12.6 with Table 7.10, we see that the premiums collected on expired LEAPS have fallen from $1,440,155 to $1,201,730, with the difference of $238,425 being the cost of the insurance puts purchased. On the other hand, the financial exposure from puts expiring in the money falls from $431,447 to $400,194, a reduction of $31,252. Of the 10,018 expired LEAP contracts, 1,291 expired in the money, and in just 261 of these instances it turns out, was the stock price at expiration below the strike price of the insurance put.

Thus, in only 261 instances out of 10,018 expired LEAPS (2.6%) was the insurance protection of any value. The retention rate decreased from 79.9% in Run No. 4 to 76.5% in Run No. 26, while the account value at the end of the ten-year period decreased from 84.9% in Run No. 4 to 80.3% in Run No. 26.

Run No. 23:

ATM Strike Price is the High, Low, or Closing Stock Price: C
No. of Steps LEAP Written Put is below ATM Strike Price: 0
No. of Steps LEAP Offset Put is below ATM Strike Price: 3
Minimum No. of Months till Expiration: 8
Premium Reinvestment Rate: 6.0%
Minimum First Call Rating: 5.0
Minimum Standard & Poor's Rating: None
No. of Stocks Meeting Either Criterion: 217

Table 12.1: LEAP OTM and ITM Rates

	LEAPS Written	LEAPS Expired	Expired OTM	OTM Rate	Expired ITM	ITM Rate	LEAPS Active
Near:	21,976	20,022	15,178	75.8%	4,844	24.2%	1,954
Far:	23,914	19,383	15,457	79.7%	3,926	20.3%	4,531
Total:	45,890	39,405	30,635	77.7%	8,770	22.3%	6,485

Table 12.2: Premiums Collected and Realized Gain for Expired LEAPS

	LEAPS Expired	Premiums Collected	Forward Value	ITM Exposure	Realized Gain	Retent'n Rate
Near:	20,022	$3,104,413	$3,308,219	$2,155,055	$1,153,164	37.1%
Far:	19,383	$3,389,999	$3,816,625	$2,170,194	$1,646,431	48.6%
Total:	39,405	$6,494,411	$7,124,844	$4,325,249	$2,799,595	43.1%

Table 12.3: Premiums Collected and Unrealized Gain on Active LEAPS

	LEAPS Active	Premiums Collected	Forward Value	Residual Value	Unrealized Gain
Near:	1,954	$567,091	$578,315	$502,069	$76,246
Far:	4,531	$1,361,606	$1,425,978	$1,130,129	$295,850
Total:	6,485	$1,928,697	$2,004,293	$1,632,197	$372,096

Table 12.4: Premiums Collected and Account Values

	Original Cont'cts	Premiums Collected	Compound Gain	Unrealized Gain	Account Value	Account Ratio
Near:	21,976	$3,671,504	$1,391,834	$76,246	$1,468,080	40.0%
Far:	23,914	$4,751,604	$2,014,816	$295,850	$2,310,665	48.6%
Total:	45,890	$8,423,108	$3,406,649	$372,096	$3,778,745	44.9%

Run No. 24:

ATM Strike Price is the High, Low, or Closing Stock Price:	C
No. of Steps LEAP Written Put is below ATM Strike Price:	0
No. of Steps LEAP Offset Put is below ATM Strike Price:	3
Minimum No. of Months till Expiration:	8
Premium Reinvestment Rate:	6.0%
Minimum First Call Rating:	2.0
Minimum Standard & Poor's Rating:	B
No. of Stocks Meeting Either Criterion:	178

Table 12.5: LEAP OTM and ITM Rates

	LEAPS Written	LEAPS Expired	Expired OTM	OTM Rate	Expired ITM	ITM Rate	LEAPS Active
Near:	18,501	16,898	13,180	78.0%	3,718	22.0%	1,603
Far:	20,136	16,414	13,465	82.0%	2,949	18.0%	3,722
Total:	38,637	33,312	26,645	80.0%	6,667	20.0%	5,325

Table 12.6: Premiums Collected and Realized Gain for Expired LEAPS

	LEAPS Expired	Premiums Collected	Forward Value	ITM Exposure	Realized Gain	Retent'n Rate
Near:	16,898	$2,547,457	$2,714,666	$1,539,961	$1,174,705	46.1%
Far:	16,414	$2,787,169	$3,137,963	$1,503,572	$1,634,391	58.6%
Total:	33,312	$5,334,626	$5,852,629	$3,043,533	$2,809,096	52.7%

Table 12.7: Premiums Collected and Unrealized Gain on Active LEAPS

	LEAPS Active	Premiums Collected	Forward Value	Residual Value	Unrealized Gain
Near:	1,603	$486,381	$495,954	$421,270	$74,685
Far:	3,722	$1,135,391	$1,188,231	$882,713	$305,519
Total:	5,325	$1,621,772	$1,684,186	$1,303,983	$380,203

Table 12.8: Premiums Collected and Account Values

	Original Cont'cts	Premiums Collected	Compound Gain	Unrealized Gain	Account Value	Account Ratio
Near:	18,501	$3,033,838	$1,435,859	$74,685	$1,510,544	49.8%
Far:	20,136	$3,922,560	$2,020,553	$305,519	$2,326,071	59.3%
Total:	38,637	$6,956,398	$3,456,412	$380,203	$3,836,615	55.2%

Run No. 25:

ATM Strike Price is the High, Low, or Closing Stock Price: C
No. of Steps LEAP Written Put is below ATM Strike Price: 0
No. of Steps LEAP Offset Put is below ATM Strike Price: 3
Minimum No. of Months till Expiration: 8
Premium Reinvestment Rate: 6.0%
Minimum First Call Rating: 1.6
Minimum Standard & Poor's Rating: B+
No. of Stocks Meeting Either Criterion: 115

Table 12.9: LEAP OTM and ITM Rates

	LEAPS Written	LEAPS Expired	Expired OTM	OTM Rate	Expired ITM	ITM Rate	LEAPS Active
Near:	12,116	11,080	9,055	81.7%	2,025	18.3%	1,036
Far:	13,186	10,778	9,299	86.3%	1,479	13.7%	2,408
Total:	25,302	21,858	18,354	84.0%	3,504	16.0%	3,444

Table 12.10: Premiums Collected and Realized Gain for Expired LEAPS

	LEAPS Expired	Premiums Collected	Forward Value	ITM Exposure	Realized Gain	Retent'n Rate
Near:	11,080	$1,528,723	$1,629,084	$758,543	$870,541	56.9%
Far:	10,778	$1,676,813	$1,887,890	$691,073	$1,196,817	71.4%
Total:	21,858	$3,205,536	$3,516,975	$1,449,616	$2,067,358	64.5%

Table 12.11: Premiums Collected and Unrealized Gain on Active LEAPS

	LEAPS Active	Premiums Collected	Forward Value	Residual Value	Unrealized Gain
Near:	1,036	$311,806	$317,881	$267,573	$50,307
Far:	2,408	$708,403	$740,885	$511,335	$229,550
Total:	3,444	$1,020,209	$1,058,766	$778,909	$279,857

Table 12.12: Premiums Collected and Account Values

	Original Cont'cts	Premiums Collected	Compound Gain	Unrealized Gain	Account Value	Account Ratio
Near:	12,116	$1,840,529	$1,074,331	$50,307	$1,124,639	61.1%
Far:	13,186	$2,385,217	$1,492,354	$229,550	$1,721,903	72.2%
Total:	25,302	$4,225,745	$2,566,685	$279,857	$2,846,542	67.4%

Run No. 26:

ATM Strike Price is the High, Low, or Closing Stock Price: C
No. of Steps LEAP Written Put is below ATM Strike Price: 0
No. of Steps LEAP Offset Put is below ATM Strike Price: 3
Minimum No. of Months till Expiration: 8
Premium Reinvestment Rate: 6.0%
Minimum First Call Rating: 1.2
Minimum Standard & Poor's Rating: A-
No. of Stocks Meeting Either Criterion: 50

Table 12.13: LEAP OTM and ITM Rates

	LEAPS Written	LEAPS Expired	Expired OTM	OTM Rate	Expired ITM	ITM Rate	LEAPS Active
Near:	5,516	5,065	4,292	84.7%	773	15.3%	451
Far:	6,004	4,953	4,435	89.5%	518	10.5%	1,051
Total:	11,520	10,018	8,727	87.1%	1,291	12.9%	1,502

Table 12.14: Premiums Collected and Realized Gain for Expired LEAPS

	LEAPS Expired	Premiums Collected	Forward Value	ITM Exposure	Realized Gain	Retent'n Rate
Near:	5,065	$564,691	$601,888	$208,718	$393,170	69.6%
Far:	4,953	$637,039	$717,371	$191,477	$525,894	82.6%
Total:	10,018	$1,201,730	$1,319,259	$400,194	$919,064	76.5%

Table 12.15: Premiums Collected and Unrealized Gain on Active LEAPS

	LEAPS Active	Premiums Collected	Forward Value	Residual Value	Unrealized Gain
Near:	451	$119,564	$121,862	$100,945	$20,917
Far:	1,051	$264,843	$276,696	$178,769	$97,927
Total:	1,502	$384,407	$398,558	$279,714	$118,844

Table 12.16: Premiums Collected and Account Values

	Original Cont'cts	Premiums Collected	Compound Gain	Unrealized Gain	Account Value	Account Ratio
Near:	5,516	$684,254	$494,713	$20,917	$515,630	75.4%
Far:	6,004	$901,882	$659,791	$97,927	$757,718	84.0%
Total:	11,520	$1,586,137	$1,154,504	$118,844	$1,273,349	80.3%

Conclusions

Historically, it would appear that the use of insurance puts to hedge against market downturns is not a cost-effective strategy when dealing with highly rated stocks, and over the long run, it appears to be only marginally beneficial for lesser-quality issues. As a result of this analysis and my own experience, I have never bought protective puts as a hedge against LEAP puts written on high quality companies rated B+ and above. In the short run, it is entirely possible for market prices to drop below exercise prices (this has happened to me on numerous occasions), but in such instances, I prefer to use rollout techniques as my primary recovery-and-repair strategy.

I sidestep the issue of whether or not to buy insurance puts on stocks rated B and below by ordinarily not writing LEAP puts on such lesser quality issues in the first place. On those (few) occasions that I elect to sell LEAP puts on lesser-rated companies, I weigh the cost of the insurance put against the premium received from the LEAP put written and the perceived downside risk. If I feel there is little downside risk (because the market is particularly strong, or the stock is bottoming out after a pronounced retreat), I will not bother purchasing an insurance put. If the market seems weak and the stock is well above its lows, I am far more likely to consider the use of an insurance put—or not selling a LEAP put at all.

Having said this, I would recommend the use of insurance puts when doing your first few transactions. It will make you, your broker, and your broker's branch manager more comfortable as you learn the ropes and become more proficient in selling naked puts. As your asset base grows and your option experience builds up, you can begin relaxing this constraint by phasing out the use of insurance puts, first on A rated companies, then on A- rated companies, and finally on B+ rated companies.

PART III:
VOLATILITY AND PREMIUMS

13

CHAPTER 13

MEASURING VOLATILITY

Introduction

The volatility of the underlying stock is extremely important in the world of options, for among other things, it determines the likelihood that an option will wind up in or out of the money by the expiration date. This chapter describes the procedure by which volatility is numerically calculated and shows how to calculate the chances that a given LEAP option will wind up in or out of the money by its expiration date.

To begin, suppose that:

P is the price of the underlying issue

S is the strike (exercise price) of the option

r is the risk-free interest rate in decimal form

t is the time in years till expiration

v is the annualized volatility in decimal form

δ is the annualized dividend rate in decimal form

Further, let h be given by:

$$h = \frac{ln(P/S)+\left(r-\delta+v^2/2\right)\times t}{v\sqrt{t}} \qquad (13.1)$$

Then the probability of winding up in the money by the expiration date for a put option is given by:

$$\text{Prob}\,(\textit{in-the-money put}) = \int_{-\infty}^{-h+v\sqrt{t}} \frac{e^{-x^2/2}}{\sqrt{2\pi}}\,dx \quad (13.2)$$

The probability of winding up in the money by the expiration date for a call option is given by:

$$\text{Prob}\,(\textit{in-the-money call}) = 1 - \int_{-\infty}^{-h+v\sqrt{t}} \frac{e^{-x^2/2}}{\sqrt{2\pi}}\,dx \quad (13.3)$$

The integral in Equations 13.2 and 13.3 is the standard Normal distribution, where

$$\int_{-\infty}^{\infty} \frac{e^{-x^2/2}}{\sqrt{2\pi}}\,dx = 1 \quad (13.4)$$

Example

As an example, consider the case of an at-the money put where the stock price P is the same as the exercise price S. The log of 1 is zero, so the formula for $-h+v\sqrt{t}$ now becomes:

$$-h+v\sqrt{t} = \left(0.5 \times v^2 + \delta - r\right) \times \left(\frac{\sqrt{t}}{v}\right) \quad (13.5)$$

What Equation 13.5 shows is that other things being equal, the higher the annual dividend rate, the more likely it is that a LEAP put will wind up in the money. This is a natural consequence of the fact that the effect of dividends is to reduce the value of the underlying stock.

Consider a case in which the volatility v is 0.3, the risk-free interest rate r is 6%, and the annualized dividend rate δ is 1.5%. In this situation $-h+v\sqrt{t}$ is zero, and the integral in either Equation 13.2 or Equation 13.3 is 0.5. Thus, the chances of such an at-the-money put (or call) winding up in the money at expiration under those circumstances are precisely one half. Whenever $0.5 \times v^2 + \delta - r$ is greater than zero, the chances that at-the-money puts will wind up in the money are going to be greater than fifty-fifty; and whenever $0.5 \times v^2 + \delta - r$ is less than zero, the chances that at-the-money puts will wind up in the money are going to be less than fifty-fifty. Appendix C contains a list of tables showing the probability of LEAP puts winding up in the money for a wide range of parameters.

Volatility

Looking at the six inputs to Equations 13.1 and 13.3, the stock price, strike price, interest rate, expiration date, and dividend rate are all known variables. The unknown variable is the volatility and estimates of it must be prepared based on the recent price history of the underlying stock.

A major assumption underlying most option pricing models is that prices are lognormally distributed about the mean. In descriptive terms, this means that if a stock is currently at $20 a share, it is just as likely to double and go to $40 as it is to be cut in half and wind up at $10 a share. In keeping with this assumption, annual volatility is computed by taking a time series of closing prices p_i where i runs from 1 to N and then calculating the logarithmic change ratios $x_i = ln(p_i/p_{i-1})$. The mean ratio is calculated as:

$$\mu = \frac{1}{N}\sum_{i=1}^{N} x_i = \frac{1}{N}\sum_{i=1}^{N} ln\left(p_i / p_{i-1}\right) = \frac{1}{N}\sum_{i=1}^{N}\left(ln\, p_i - ln\, p_{i-1}\right)$$
$$= \frac{1}{N}\left(ln\, p_N - ln\, p_0\right) = \frac{1}{N} ln\left(p_N / p_0\right) \qquad (13.6)$$

Note that the mean logarithmic change ratio depends solely on the ratio of the last term to the first term in the series, p_N/p_0.

The variance and standard deviation about the mean are calculated as:

$$var = \sigma^2 = \frac{1}{N-1}\sum_{i=1}^{N}\left(x_i - \mu\right)^2 \quad (13.7)$$

If the prices p_i have been collected every d (trading) days, the annualized volatility is calculated as the adjusted standard deviation, as follows:

$$v = \sqrt{\frac{T}{d}} \times \sigma \quad (13.8)$$

where T is the number of trading days in the year (ordinarily 252 to 254). If monthly data are used, $d = 21$; if weekly data are used, $d = 5$; and if daily trading data are used, $d = 1$. The number of observations N is usually selected so as to yield a stabilized result and is often chosen so that N times d equals T.

The table below illustrates how each of the above variables is calculated from a specified price history. The example chosen employs the month-end closing prices for Intel Corporation for the year 1996.

Table 13.1: Volatility Using Monthly Data

No.	Date	Price	$x_i = ln(p_i/p_{i-1})$	$(x_i - \mu)^2$
0	12/29/95	56.7500	-	-
1	01/31/96	55.2380	-0.02700464	0.00934638
2	02/29/96	58.8170	0.06277973	0.00004750
3	03/29/96	56.8750	-0.03357512	0.01065997
4	04/30/96	67.7500	0.17496860	0.01108737
5	05/31/96	75.5000	0.10830800	0.00149274
6	06/28/96	73.4440	-0.02760950	0.00946370
7	07/31/96	75.1250	0.02263005	0.00221295
8	08/30/96	79.8125	0.06052675	0.00008364
9	09/30/96	95.4375	0.17879140	0.01190704
10	10/31/96	109.8750	0.14087180	0.00506941
11	11/29/96	126.8750	0.14385890	0.00550370
12	12/31/96	130.9375	0.03151786	0.00145574
	Totals		0.83606383	0.06833014

The mean value of the price ratios in Table 13.1 is:

$\mu = 0.83606383/12 = ln(130.9375/56.75)/12 = 0.069672$

The variance is: $var = 0.06833014/11 = 0.006212$

The standard deviation is: $\sigma = \sqrt{var} = 0.078815$

The annualized volatility is: $v = \sqrt{12} \times \sigma = 0.273023$

The above example illustrates the procedure. It is to be noted, however, that the use of monthly data for estimating the annualized volatility does not yield sufficiently accurate results for modeling purposes. If the procedure is repeated using daily data, a much different value for the annualized volatility is obtained, as shown in Table 13.2.

The mean value of the price ratios in Table 13.2 is:

$\mu = 0.83606383/254 = ln(130.9375/56.75)/254 = 0.003292$

The variance is: $var = 0.12709460/253 = 0.0050235$

The standard deviation is: $\sigma = \sqrt{var} = 0.0224132$

The annualized volatility is: $v = \sqrt{254} \times \sigma = 0.357207$

The difference in the estimated annualized volatility brought about by using daily versus monthly data is seen to be significant and is the result of an insufficient sample size when monthly data are used.

Table 13.2: Volatility Using Daily Data

No.	Date	Price	$x_i = ln(p_i/p_{i-1})$	$(x_i - \mu)^2$
0	12/29/95	56.7500	-	-
1	01/02/96	58.6250	0.03250553	0.00085345
2	01/03/96	57.7500	-0.01503783	0.00033597
3	01/04/96	57.5000	-0.00433847	0.00005822
4	01/05/96	57.5000	0.00000000	0.00001083
5	01/08/96	57.6250	0.00217155	0.00000125
6	01/09/96	55.0000	-0.04662335	0.00249150
7	01/10/96	54.1250	-0.01603705	0.00037360
8	01/11/96	56.8750	0.04955970	0.00214074
9	01/12/96	56.6250	-0.00440533	0.00005924
10	01/15/96	53.3750	-0.05910817	0.00389373
11	01/16/96	55.7500	0.04353501	0.00161953
12	01/17/96	50.0000	-0.10885440	0.01257673
13	01/18/96	51.0000	0.01980251	0.00027261
14	01/19/96	51.3750	0.00732594	0.00001628
15	01/22/96	52.0000	0.01209189	0.00007745
16	01/23/96	52.6980	0.01333369	0.00010084
17	01/24/96	54.7500	0.03819987	0.00121859
18	01/25/96	54.6250	-0.00228575	0.00003111
19	01/26/96	55.0000	0.00684148	0.00001260
20	01/29/96	54.4480	-0.01008702	0.00017899
21	01/30/96	54.1250	-0.00594993	0.00008541
22	01/31/96	55.2380	0.02035481	0.00029115
23	02/01/96	56.2500	0.01815488	0.00022092
24	02/02/96	56.7500	0.00884959	0.00003089
25	02/05/96	58.5000	0.03037108	0.00073330
26	02/06/96	59.5000	0.01694948	0.00018654
27	02/07/96	58.2500	-0.02123220	0.00060142
28	02/08/96	57.8750	-0.00645859	0.00009507
29	02/09/96	58.0000	0.00215746	0.00000129
30	02/12/96	58.2330	0.00400915	0.00000051
31	02/13/96	57.1250	-0.01921037	0.00050634
32	02/14/96	58.0000	0.01520124	0.00014184
33	02/15/96	57.5000	-0.00865809	0.00014279
34	02/16/96	57.5660	0.00114715	0.00000460
35	02/20/96	57.8750	0.00535328	0.00000425
36	02/21/96	59.2500	0.02348011	0.00040758
37	02/22/96	61.0000	0.02910813	0.00066649
38	02/23/96	60.8180	-0.00298806	0.00003943
39	02/26/96	60.3750	-0.00731072	0.00011241
40	02/27/96	60.2500	-0.00207250	0.00002877
41	02/28/96	60.7500	0.00826445	0.00002473
42	02/29/96	58.8170	-0.03233618	0.00126934

Table 13.2 (cont.): Volatility Using Daily Data

No.	Date	Price	$x_i = ln(p_i/p_{i-1})$	$(x_i - \mu)^2$
43	03/01/96	56.0620	-0.04797272	0.00262803
44	03/04/96	54.8750	-0.02140036	0.00060969
45	03/05/96	55.3750	0.00907029	0.00003339
46	03/06/96	53.2500	-0.03913045	0.00179963
47	03/07/96	53.1250	-0.00235019	0.00003183
48	03/08/96	53.5000	0.00703397	0.00001401
49	03/11/96	55.2500	0.03218666	0.00083493
50	03/12/96	54.8750	-0.00681049	0.00010205
51	03/13/96	56.1250	0.02252334	0.00036986
52	03/14/96	56.1250	0.00000000	0.00001083
53	03/15/96	58.8750	0.04783505	0.00198412
54	03/18/96	59.5000	0.01055973	0.00005283
55	03/19/96	58.7500	-0.01268521	0.00025526
56	03/20/96	55.5000	-0.05690816	0.00362401
57	03/21/96	55.8750	0.00673394	0.00001185
58	03/22/96	56.1250	0.00446427	0.00000138
59	03/25/96	54.8970	-0.02212261	0.00064588
60	03/26/96	56.1250	0.02212263	0.00035461
61	03/27/96	56.6250	0.00886917	0.00003111
62	03/28/96	56.3750	-0.00442487	0.00005954
63	03/29/96	56.8750	0.00883005	0.00003067
64	04/01/96	57.1250	0.00438585	0.00000120
65	04/02/96	56.8750	-0.00438592	0.00005894
66	04/03/96	57.6250	0.01310063	0.00009622
67	04/04/96	59.2500	0.02780907	0.00060111
68	04/08/96	60.6250	0.02294148	0.00038612
69	04/09/96	61.8750	0.02040881	0.00029300
70	04/10/96	61.7500	-0.00202225	0.00002824
71	04/11/96	60.4410	-0.02142628	0.00061097
72	04/12/96	59.6250	-0.01359277	0.00028508
73	04/15/96	60.5610	0.01557609	0.00015091
74	04/16/96	64.8750	0.06881123	0.00429282
75	04/17/96	64.1990	-0.01047476	0.00018951
76	04/18/96	65.7500	0.02387206	0.00042356
77	04/19/96	65.2500	-0.00763363	0.00011936
78	04/22/96	67.7500	0.03759836	0.00117695
79	04/23/96	68.1160	0.00538757	0.00000439
80	04/24/96	70.2500	0.03084814	0.00075936
81	04/25/96	69.6250	-0.00893661	0.00014953
82	04/26/96	69.2500	-0.00540056	0.00007555
83	04/29/96	68.1250	-0.01637886	0.00038693
84	04/30/96	67.7500	-0.00551984	0.00007764
85	05/01/96	67.8750	0.00184326	0.00000210

Table 13.2 (cont.): Volatility Using Daily Data

No.	Date	Price	$x_i = ln(p_i/p_{i-1})$	$(x_i - \mu)^2$
86	05/02/96	68.0000	0.00183987	0.00000211
87	05/03/96	68.6990	0.01022698	0.00004810
88	05/06/96	68.7500	0.00074210	0.00000650
89	05/07/96	67.8750	-0.01280893	0.00025923
90	05/08/96	68.7500	0.01280883	0.00009058
91	05/09/96	68.6250	-0.00181983	0.00002613
92	05/10/96	69.1250	0.00725946	0.00001574
93	05/13/96	71.7500	0.03727144	0.00115463
94	05/14/96	72.8750	0.01555783	0.00015046
95	05/15/96	72.3750	-0.00688472	0.00010356
96	05/16/96	71.8750	-0.00693248	0.00010453
97	05/17/96	71.1250	-0.01048963	0.00018992
98	05/20/96	71.0000	-0.00175902	0.00002551
99	05/21/96	70.2500	-0.01061962	0.00019352
100	05/22/96	69.8750	-0.00535237	0.00007472
101	05/23/96	70.8750	0.01420985	0.00011921
102	05/24/96	71.0000	0.00176208	0.00000234
103	05/28/96	72.5000	0.02090661	0.00031029
104	05/29/96	71.3750	-0.01563887	0.00035836
105	05/30/96	71.5000	0.00174968	0.00000238
106	05/31/96	75.5000	0.05443530	0.00261568
107	06/03/96	76.6250	0.01479070	0.00013223
108	06/04/96	76.3180	-0.00401453	0.00005338
109	06/05/96	76.8750	0.00727182	0.00001584
110	06/06/96	75.2500	-0.02136484	0.00060794
111	06/07/96	75.2500	0.00000000	0.00001083
112	06/10/96	74.1250	-0.01506305	0.00033689
113	06/11/96	75.2500	0.01506296	0.00013857
114	06/12/96	76.7500	0.01973740	0.00027046
115	06/13/96	75.0000	-0.02306526	0.00069468
116	06/14/96	73.0000	-0.02702871	0.00091932
117	06/17/96	72.0000	-0.01379335	0.00029190
118	06/18/96	70.3750	-0.02282802	0.00068223
119	06/19/96	71.3750	0.01410962	0.00011703
120	06/20/96	71.1250	-0.00350876	0.00004624
121	06/21/96	71.3750	0.00350866	0.00000005
122	06/24/96	73.6150	0.03090107	0.00076228
123	06/25/96	72.8750	-0.01010310	0.00017942
124	06/26/96	72.5000	-0.00515908	0.00007141
125	06/27/96	73.8750	0.01878786	0.00024013
126	06/28/96	73.4440	-0.00585131	0.00008359
127	07/01/96	75.1250	0.02263005	0.00037398
128	07/02/96	74.7500	-0.00500424	0.00006882

Table 13.2 (cont.): Volatility Using Daily Data

No.	Date	Price	$x_i = ln(p_i/p_{i-1})$	$(x_i - \mu)^2$
129	07/03/96	74.8750	0.00167085	0.00000263
130	07/05/96	72.1250	-0.03741931	0.00165738
131	07/08/96	73.0000	0.01205855	0.00007686
132	07/09/96	73.3750	0.00512378	0.00000336
133	07/10/96	72.8750	-0.00683764	0.00010260
134	07/11/96	69.5000	-0.04741887	0.00257155
135	07/12/96	71.2500	0.02486799	0.00046554
136	07/15/96	69.3125	-0.02756957	0.00095241
137	07/16/96	70.0000	0.00986982	0.00004327
138	07/17/96	71.6250	0.02294896	0.00038641
139	07/18/96	72.5000	0.01214242	0.00007834
140	07/19/96	72.8750	0.00515902	0.00000349
141	07/22/96	72.1875	-0.00947882	0.00016308
142	07/23/96	69.5000	-0.03794018	0.00170006
143	07/24/96	69.0000	-0.00722029	0.00011050
144	07/25/96	72.1250	0.04429425	0.00168122
145	07/26/96	74.2500	0.02903695	0.00066282
146	07/29/96	72.8750	-0.01869210	0.00048328
147	07/30/96	74.3750	0.02037414	0.00029181
148	07/31/96	75.1250	0.01003346	0.00004545
149	08/01/96	77.0000	0.02465196	0.00045627
150	08/02/96	78.8125	0.02326614	0.00039898
151	08/05/96	78.1250	-0.00876157	0.00014528
152	08/06/96	79.8750	0.02215279	0.00035574
153	08/07/96	82.3750	0.03081898	0.00075776
154	08/08/96	80.7500	-0.01992406	0.00053897
155	08/09/96	82.3750	0.01992394	0.00027663
156	08/12/96	82.1250	-0.00303949	0.00004008
157	08/13/96	80.2500	-0.02309571	0.00069629
158	08/14/96	81.7500	0.01851890	0.00023187
159	08/15/96	81.7500	0.00000000	0.00001083
160	08/16/96	81.0000	-0.00921662	0.00015646
161	08/19/96	80.7500	-0.00309128	0.00004074
162	08/20/96	79.5000	-0.01560093	0.00035693
163	08/21/96	80.2500	0.00938974	0.00003719
164	08/22/96	83.0000	0.03369383	0.00092430
165	08/23/96	81.6250	-0.01670502	0.00039986
166	08/26/96	81.2500	-0.00460480	0.00006235
167	08/27/96	81.5000	0.00307200	0.00000005
168	08/28/96	81.2500	-0.00307221	0.00004050
169	08/29/96	81.3750	0.00153736	0.00000308
170	08/30/96	79.8125	-0.01938798	0.00051436

Table 13.2 (cont.): Volatility Using Daily Data

No.	Date	Price	$x_i = ln(p_i/p_{i-1})$	$(x_i - \mu)^2$
171	09/03/96	81.6250	0.02245546	0.00036725
172	09/04/96	82.2500	0.00762774	0.00001880
173	09/05/96	80.6250	-0.01995462	0.00054039
174	09/06/96	81.2500	0.00772198	0.00001963
175	09/09/96	83.5000	0.02731577	0.00057716
176	09/10/96	84.2500	0.00894193	0.00003193
177	09/11/96	85.0000	0.00886264	0.00003104
178	09/12/96	85.3750	0.00440213	0.00000123
179	09/13/96	88.1250	0.03170283	0.00080720
180	09/16/96	88.6250	0.00565773	0.00000560
181	09/17/96	94.2500	0.06153677	0.00339250
182	09/18/96	95.6250	0.01448344	0.00012526
183	09/19/96	97.0000	0.01427670	0.00012067
184	09/20/96	97.3750	0.00385843	0.00000032
185	09/23/96	95.7500	-0.01682891	0.00040483
186	09/24/96	96.5000	0.00780230	0.00002035
187	09/25/96	97.2500	0.00774186	0.00001980
188	09/26/96	97.3750	0.00128448	0.00000403
189	09/27/96	96.8750	-0.00514801	0.00007123
190	09/30/96	95.4375	-0.01494988	0.00033275
191	10/01/96	95.7500	0.00326899	0.00000000
192	10/02/96	99.0000	0.03337913	0.00090526
193	10/03/96	99.5000	0.00503784	0.00000305
194	10/04/96	101.6875	0.02174674	0.00034059
195	10/07/96	104.6250	0.02847808	0.00063436
196	10/08/96	101.6250	-0.02909297	0.00104876
197	10/09/96	100.7500	-0.00864733	0.00014254
198	10/10/96	99.8750	-0.00872283	0.00014435
199	10/11/96	105.3750	0.05360598	0.00253154
200	10/14/96	107.6250	0.02112752	0.00031812
201	10/15/96	111.1250	0.03200273	0.00082433
202	10/16/96	112.6250	0.01340797	0.00010234
203	10/17/96	110.7500	-0.01678830	0.00040320
204	10/18/96	110.0000	-0.00679503	0.00010174
205	10/21/96	107.7500	-0.02066660	0.00057399
206	10/22/96	105.5000	-0.02110277	0.00059509
207	10/23/96	109.3750	0.03607128	0.00107451
208	10/24/96	107.5000	-0.01729146	0.00042366
209	10/25/96	105.3750	-0.01996551	0.00054089
210	10/28/96	106.0000	0.00591351	0.00000687
211	10/29/96	104.3750	-0.01544894	0.00035121
212	10/30/96	106.7500	0.02249946	0.00036894
213	10/31/96	109.8750	0.02885363	0.00065342

Table 13.2 (cont.): Volatility Using Daily Data

No.	Date	Price	$x_i = ln(p_i/p_{i-1})$	$(x_i - \mu)^2$
214	11/01/96	108.7500	-0.01029165	0.00018450
215	11/04/96	110.2500	0.01369871	0.00010831
216	11/05/96	114.0000	0.03344792	0.00090940
217	11/06/96	118.8750	0.04187399	0.00148860
218	11/07/96	122.1250	0.02697261	0.00056079
219	11/08/96	122.2500	0.00102295	0.00000515
220	11/11/96	123.8750	0.01320474	0.00009827
221	11/12/96	121.0000	-0.02348241	0.00071685
222	11/13/96	119.5000	-0.01247422	0.00024856
223	11/14/96	119.8750	0.00313298	0.00000003
224	11/15/96	115.8750	-0.03393756	0.00138601
225	11/18/96	115.3750	-0.00432437	0.00005800
226	11/19/96	120.7500	0.04553452	0.00178446
227	11/20/96	120.8750	0.00103460	0.00000509
228	11/21/96	118.8750	-0.01668446	0.00039904
229	11/22/96	122.3750	0.02901749	0.00066182
230	11/25/96	121.5000	-0.00717588	0.00010957
231	11/26/96	123.7500	0.01834914	0.00022673
232	11/27/96	126.6250	0.02296656	0.00038710
233	11/29/96	126.8750	0.00197237	0.00000174
234	12/02/96	127.1250	0.00196844	0.00000175
235	12/03/96	125.8750	-0.00988153	0.00017353
236	12/04/96	129.5000	0.02839157	0.00063001
237	12/05/96	128.2500	-0.00969939	0.00016877
238	12/06/96	125.6875	-0.02018281	0.00055105
239	12/09/96	130.1250	0.03469686	0.00098629
240	12/10/96	129.1250	-0.00771466	0.00012114
241	12/11/96	136.8750	0.05828716	0.00302451
242	12/12/96	136.8750	0.00000000	0.00001083
243	12/13/96	132.3750	-0.03342930	0.00134842
244	12/16/96	127.2500	-0.03948517	0.00182985
245	12/17/96	130.0000	0.02138065	0.00032721
246	12/18/96	135.7500	0.04328051	0.00159911
247	12/19/96	137.5000	0.01280883	0.00009058
248	12/20/96	134.6250	-0.02113080	0.00059645
249	12/23/96	132.2500	-0.01779908	0.00044482
250	12/24/96	135.5000	0.02427748	0.00044041
251	12/26/96	136.6250	0.00826816	0.00002477
252	12/27/96	135.3750	-0.00919126	0.00015582
253	12/30/96	133.2500	-0.01582163	0.00036532
254	12/31/96	130.9375	<u>-0.01750696</u>	<u>0.00043258</u>
	Totals		0.83605590	0.12709460

The next step in the procedure is to calculate the value of the Normal distribution. Although it is possible to use tables and interpolation to arrive at values of N(x), it is often easier to use some sort of curve-fitting formula. There are many such formulas to choose from, depending on whether the fit between the approximation and the exact distribution is to be more precise in the central or the outlying portions (the tails) of the Normal distribution. A commonly used approximation for the Normal distribution is given by Equations 13.9 through 13.11, below.

If $z \geq 0$, then

$$\text{let } f(z) = \frac{e^{-z^2/2}}{\sqrt{2\pi}} \quad (13.9)$$

$$\text{let } g(z) = \frac{1}{(1 + 0.33267z)} \quad (13.10)$$

Then:

$$N(z) = \int_{-\infty}^{z} \frac{e^{-x^2/2}dx}{\sqrt{2\pi}} \quad (13.11)$$

$$\approx 1 - f(z) \times \left[0.4361836g(z) - 0.1201676g^2(z) + 0.9372980g^3(z)\right]$$

If z < 0, then N(z) = 1 - N(-z).

Stock Growth and Volatility

As mentioned earlier, long-term growth prospects in the earnings and in the corresponding stock price ordinarily have no effect on the price of a put or call option. This remarkable fact was noted by Cox and Rubenstein in their monumental book on option markets. Little emphasis was placed on this phenomenon, however, because of the relatively short expiration dates that existed on options at the time. To see why this must be the case, let's first consider a numerical example. Let it be the first one examined in this chapter, but where we will allow prices to rise at an additional 1% a month. The corresponding tableau appears below.

Table 13.3: Volatility Using Monthly Data as Inflated

No.	Date	Original Price	Adjusted Price	$x_i = ln(p_i/p_{i-1})$	$(x_i - \mu)^2$
0	12/29/95	56.7500	56.7500	-	-
1	01/31/96	55.2380	55.7904	-0.01705427	0.0093464
2	02/29/96	58.8170	59.9992	0.07273010	0.0000475
3	03/29/96	56.8750	58.5984	-0.02362479	0.0106600
4	04/30/96	67.7500	70.5009	0.18491890	0.0110874
5	05/31/96	75.5000	79.3513	0.11825850	0.0014928
6	06/28/96	73.4440	77.9623	-0.01765920	0.0094637
7	07/31/96	75.1250	80.5442	0.03258051	0.0022129
8	08/30/96	79.8125	86.4255	0.07047696	0.0000836
9	09/30/96	95.4375	104.3786	0.18874160	0.0119070
10	10/31/96	109.8750	121.3704	0.15082210	0.0050694
11	11/29/96	126.8750	141.5504	0.15380920	0.0055037
12	12/31/96	130.9375	147.5436	0.04146811	0.0014557
	Totals			0.95546772	0.0683301

The mean value of the price ratios in Table 13.3 is:

μ = 0.95546772/12 = ln(147.5436/56.75)/12 = 0.07962231

The variance is: var = 0.06833014/11 = 0.006212

The standard deviation is: $\sigma = \sqrt{var}$ = 0.078815

The annualized volatility is: $v = \sqrt{12} \times \sigma$ = 0.273023

Since the volatility is the same before, the put and call premiums for the same stock and exercise prices, expiration date, and risk-free interest rate must therefore be identical.

In general, suppose the growth-adjusted prices are given by $q_i = p_i \times (1+f)^i$, where f is the daily, monthly or annual inflation rate. The adjusted logarithmic change ratios are $x'_i = ln(q_i/q_{i-1}) = ln(1+f) + ln(p_i/p_{i-1}) = ln(1+f) + x_i$, where x_i are the unadjusted ratios. The growth adjusted mean ratio μ' is therefore equal to $\mu + ln(1+f)$, where μ is the unadjusted mean. As a result, each of the differences $x'_i - \mu'$ are equal to $x_i - \mu$, from which it follows that the variance, standard deviation, and volatility for the growth adjusted situation are the same as for the unadjusted case.

Stock Growth and In-the-Money Probabilities

As has just been demonstrated, the effect of earnings growth on stock price is ordinarily not reflected in option premiums. Earnings growth must, however, affect the chances that a given put or call will wind up in or out of the money. This effect was ignored in the past because of the relatively short durations of standard options. When it comes to LEAPS, the effect of earnings growth can be significant because of expiration up to two and a half years away. If we denote the annual growth rate in the stock price by α, the expected stock price at expiration is going to be $Pe^{\alpha t}$. If this term is used instead of the stock price at the inception of the option, the formula for h in Equation 13.1 becomes:

$$h = \frac{ln(P/S) + \left(r - \delta + \alpha + v^2/2\right) \times t}{v\sqrt{t}} \qquad (13.12)$$

So let's go back to the original example of an at-the-money LEAP put for which this time the formula for $-h + v\sqrt{t}$ is given by:

$$-h + v\sqrt{t} = \left(0.5 \times v^2 + \delta - r - \alpha\right) \times \left(\frac{\sqrt{t}}{v}\right) \qquad (13.13)$$

Equation 13.13 shows is that other things being equal, the higher the growth rate, the less likely it is that a LEAP put will wind up in the money. For the specific case where the volatility v is 0.3, the risk-free interest rate r is 6%, and the annualized dividend rate δ is 1.5%, the expression for $-h + v\sqrt{t}$ becomes $-\alpha \times \sqrt{t}/0.30$. For a growth rate of a modest 10% per year, and an expiration date 2.5 years away, $-h + v\sqrt{t}$ is -0.527, for which the integral in either Equation 13.2 or Equation 13.3 is almost exactly 0.300. Thus, the chances of such an at-the-money put (or call) winding up in the money at expiration under these circumstances are just 30%, substantially less than the 50% probability of winding up in the money had the growth rate not been taken into account.

As mentioned earlier, Appendix C contains a list of tables showing the probability of LEAP puts winding up in the money for a wide range of parameters. Of particular interest is the fact that the tables illustrate these probabilities for the five independent growth rates of zero, 5%, 10%, 15%, and 20%. It is thus possible to see the effect that earnings growth will have on LEAP puts that were initially out of the money, at the money, or even in the money.

14

CHAPTER 14

OPTION PREMIUMS

Introduction

As important as knowing the chances of a LEAP put winding up in the money is knowing whether the option in question is over- or underpriced. When it comes to long-term options, market makers use one of several analytic formulas to calculate option prices. This is because the computational complexity associated with multiperiod binomial models increases dramatically with the number of steps involved, thus restricting their applicability to standard, short-term option pricing.

Depending on the sophistication of the market maker, option pricing is typically determined either by straight-forward use of the original pricing formula developed by Fischer Black and Myron Scholes in 1973 or by the use of later extensions of this formula by Robert Merton, Giovanni Barone-Adesi, and Robert Whaley. In a nutshell, the Black-Scholes model determines option prices for European-style options (which can be exercised only at expiration and not before), ignoring the effects of dividends. The Merton model adjusts the Black-Scholes formula to take dividends into account (again for European-style options), the Barone-Adesi and Whaley model adjusts the Black-Scholes-Merton formula for the early exercise potential present in American-style options. This chapter shows how to use the basic Black-Scholes and Merton models to determine option prices.

The Black-Scholes Formula for Puts

The Black-Scholes formula for the put premium for European-style options with a zero dividend rate is given by:

$$Put = -P \times \int_{-\infty}^{-h} \frac{e^{-x^2/2}}{\sqrt{2\pi}} dx + S \times e^{-rt} \times \int_{-\infty}^{-h+v\sqrt{t}} \frac{e^{-x^2/2}}{\sqrt{2\pi}} dx \quad (14.1)$$

where:

P is the price of the underlying issue

S is the strike (exercise price) of the option

r is the risk-free interest rate in decimal form

t is the time in years till expiration

v is the annualized volatility in decimal form

and h is given by the formula:

$$h = \frac{ln(P/S) + \left(r + v^2/2\right) \times t}{v\sqrt{t}} \quad (14.2)$$

When t approaches zero in Equation 14.2, h takes on one of two values:

(i) $h \to +\infty$ if the stock price P equals or is greater than the strike price S

(ii) $h \to -\infty$ if P is less than S,

the result of which shows that the value of the put goes to zero if P equals or is greater than S, or it approaches S - P if P is less than S.

The integrals in Equation 14.1 are the standard Normal distribution, and the same curve-fitting formula can be used for their evaluation as was used in the previous chapter. Note that the right-hand integral is the probability that the put will wind up in the money.

The Black-Scholes Formula for Calls

For completeness, the corresponding Black-Scholes formula for the call premium is given by:

$$Call = P \times \int_{-\infty}^{h} \frac{e^{-x^2/2}}{\sqrt{2\pi}}\,dx - S \times e^{-rt} \times \int_{-\infty}^{h-v\sqrt{t}} \frac{e^{-x^2/2}}{\sqrt{2\pi}}\,dx \quad (14.3)$$

where *P, S, r, t,* v, and *h* are as defined earlier for the put formula. If the put price has already been calculated, one can use the shortcut formula (called the put-call parity formula) for the call, as follows:

$$Call = Put + P - S \times e^{-rt} \quad (14.4)$$

The Effect of Dividends on Option Premiums

To keep things simple and conservative, all put premiums used in conducting the ten-year economic simulations were calculated using a zero dividend rate. The effect of dividends is to lower the price of calls and to increase the price of puts. If we were to assume that dividends were paid continuously through the year (rather than in the usual quarterly distribution), the Merton variation of the Black-Scholes pricing formula can be used. This formula takes the following form for puts:

$$Put = -P \times e^{-\delta t} \times \int_{-\infty}^{-h} \frac{e^{-x^2/2}}{\sqrt{2\pi}}\,dx + S \times e^{-rt} \times \int_{-\infty}^{-h+v\sqrt{t}} \frac{e^{-x^2/2}}{\sqrt{2\pi}}\,dx \quad (14.5)$$

where

δ is the annual dividend rate, and *h* is modified as follows:

$$h = \frac{ln(P/S) + \left(r - \delta + v^2/2\right) \times t}{v\sqrt{t}} \quad (14.6)$$

The right-hand integral is again the probability that the put will wind up in the money and is the one adopted for that purpose in the previous chapter.

Numerical Example

To illustrate the effect that dividends have on option premiums, consider the case where the strike price and stock price are both

$100, the volatility is 0.35, the risk-free interest rate is 6.0%, there are 24 months till expiration, and the annual dividend rate is 2.0%. Applying the basic Black-Scholes formula yields a put premium for the zero-dividend case of $13.314. This was the figure shown in Table 1.2 back in Chapter 1. For the Merton variation, do the following:

Since $S = P = \$100$, the parameter h in Equation 14.6 is calculated as

$$h = \frac{[0.06 - 0.02 + 0.5 \times 0.35 \times 0.35] \times \left(\frac{24}{12}\right)}{0.35 \times \sqrt{\left(\frac{24}{12}\right)}} = \frac{0.2025}{0.4949748} = 0.409112$$

Therefore, $-h$ is -0.409112, and $-h + v\sqrt{t}$ is -0.409112 + 0.4949748, or 0.0858628. From tables of the Normal distribution or through the use of the curve-fitting formulas in Equations 13.9 through 13.11, we have N(-0.409112) = 1 - N(0.409112) = 0.341238 and N(0.0858628) = 0.534223. When the time to expiration is 2 years, $e^{-0.02t}$ is 0.960790 and $e^{-0.06t}$ is 0.886920. So, from Equation 14.5, the European put with its 2% annual dividend rate is calculated as

$$\begin{aligned}
\textit{European Put} = &-\$100 \times 0.960790 \times 0.341238 \\
&+ \$100 \times 0.886920 \times 0.534223 \\
= &-\$32.785 + \$47.381 = \$14.596
\end{aligned}$$

Thus, the annual 2% dividend has increased the price of the put by about $1.28 over the two-year period involved, thus showing that the effect of dividends on option pricing can indeed be significant.

The pricing of American options is so complex that market makers often restrict their pricing formulas to that of Black-Scholes or one of its more simple variations. Appendix A contains tables for the prices of European-style LEAP puts with zero dividend rates. The pricing of American-style options is examined in the next chapter.

Implied Volatility

Now that we've seen how to calculate the LEAP put premium for European-style options using the Black-Scholes-Merton formulas, the question arising as to whether one can work the process backwards and determine volatility if the premium is supplied. The answer to this question is both yes and no.

To begin, we first note that it is not possible to invert Equation 14.1 or Equation 14.5 to solve for the volatility directly. However, the volatility can be determined on a trial-and-error basis using a Newton-Raphson iterative search technique. A relatively short BASIC program for doing this is shown below, followed by two numerical examples.

```
10 'SOLVE FOR IMPLIED VOLATILITY
20 INPUT "Enter Stock Price:   ";P
30 INPUT "Enter Strike Price: ";S
40 INPUT "Enter Risk-Free Interest Rate (e.g., .06): ";R
50 INPUT "Enter Annual Dividend Rate (e.g., .02): ";DIV
60 INPUT "Enter Time to Expiration in Months (0 for days):
";TIMEX
70 INPUT "Enter Put Premium: ";PREMIUM
80 IF TIMEX>0 THEN T=TIMEX/12: GOTO 120
90 INPUT "Enter Time to Expiration in Days: ";TIMEXX
100 T=TIMEXX/365
110 '**************************************************
120 PRINT "Where do you want to send results: "
130 PRINT "   1 = Screen"
140 PRINT "   2 = Printer"
150 PRINT "   3 = Save to disk"
160 INPUT "Enter your selection: ";SELECT
170 IF SELECT=0 THEN SELECT =1
180 IF SELECT=1 THEN SAVEFILE$="SCRN:"
190 IF SELECT=2 THEN SAVEFILE$="LPT1:"
200 IF SELECT=3 THEN INPUT "Enter name of savefile:
";SAVEFILE$
210 OPEN SAVEFILE$ FOR OUTPUT AS 1
220 PRINT#1, "Stock Price: ";P
230 PRINT#1, "Strike Price: ";S
240 PRINT#1, "Risk-Free Interest Rate (e.g., .06): ";R
```

```
250 PRINT#1, "Annual Dividend Rate (e.g., .02): ";DIV
260 IF TIMEX>0 THEN PRINT#1, "Time to Expiration in Months:
";TIMEX
270 IF TIMEXX>0 THEN PRINT#1, "Time to Expiration in Days:
";TIMEXX
280 PRINT#1, "Put Premium: ";PREMIUM
290 '*************************************************
300 'COMPUTE BASIC PARAMETERS
310 ERT=EXP(-R*T)
320 EDT=EXP(-DIV*T)
330 PI2=SQR(2*3.14159265#)
340 SQT=SQR(T)
350 '*************************************************
360 'START TRIAL AND ERROR SEARCH FOR VOLATILITY
370 'USING NEWTON-RAPHSON ITERATION PROCESS
380 VOLD=.5 'first guess is .5
390 KOUNT=1 'set iteration counter
400 H=(LOG(P/S)+(R-DIV+VOLD*VOLD/2)*T)/(VOLD*SQT)
410 H1=-H 'negative h
420 PH=EXP(-H1*H1/2!)/PI2
430 KH=1/(1+.33267*ABS(H1))
440 CUMH=1-PH*(.4361836*KH-.1201676*KH*KH+.937298*KH*KH*KH)
450 IF H1<0 THEN CUMH=1-CUMH 'this is Normal(-h)
460 G1=-H+VOLD*SQT
470 GH=EXP(-G1*G1/2!)/PI2
480 KG=1/(1+.33267*ABS(G1))
490 CUMG=1-GH*(.4361836*KG-.1201676*KG*KG+.937298*KG*KG*KG)
500 IF G1<0 THEN CUMG=1-CUMG 'this is Normal(-h+beta)
510 PUTVAL=-P*EDT*CUMH+S*ERT*CUMG 'put Value at V=VOLD
520 F=-PREMIUM+PUTVAL 'function F at V=VOLD
530 DERIVH=(H/VOLD)-SQT 'derivative of Normal(-h) at V=VOLD
540 DERIVG=H/VOLD 'derivative of Normal(-h+v*sqrt) at V=VOLD
550 DERIVF=-P*EDT*CUMH*DERIVH+S*ERT*CUMG*DERIVG 'deriv. of F
560 VNEW=VOLD-F/DERIVF 'new estimate for volatility
570 '*************************************************
580 'DISPLAY CONVERGENCE DETAILS (optional)
590 IF KOUNT=1 THEN 600 ELSE 620
600 PRINT#1, " "
610 PRINT#1, USING "\ \ \ \      \ \
!";"No.","VOLD","VNEW","F"
620 PRINT#1, USING "## #.##### #.#####
###.####";KOUNT,VOLD,VNEW,F
```

```
630 '***************************************************
640 IF ABS(VNEW-VOLD)<.0001 THEN 680 'convergence test
650 VOLD=VNEW
660 KOUNT=KOUNT+1 'increase counter
670 IF KOUNT < 11 THEN 400 'cut-off limit on iterations
680 VOL=(VNEW+VOLD)/2 'final value for the critical stock
price
690 '***************************************************
700 PRINT#1, " "
710 PRINT#1, USING "Implied Volatility:  ##.#####";VOL
720 PRINT#1, " "
730 INPUT "Another Case (y/n): ";CASE$
740 IF CASE$="y" OR CASE$="Y" THEN CLOSE 1: GOTO 20
750 CLOSE 1
760 END
```

Numerical Examples

As examples of the results obtainable using the computer program, consider the two cases investigated earlier:

```
Stock Price:   100
Strike Price:  100
Risk-Free Interest Rate (e.g., .06):  .06
Annual Dividend Rate (e.g., .02):  0
Time to Expiration in Months:  24
Put Premium:  13.314
```

No.	VOLD	VNEW	F
1	0.50000	0.38384	7.4605
2	0.38384	0.35707	1.6934
3	0.35707	0.35144	0.3544
4	0.35144	0.35029	0.0723
5	0.35029	0.35005	0.0147
6	0.35005	0.35001	0.0030

```
Implied Volatility:   0.35003
```

```
Stock Price:   100
Strike Price:  100
Risk-Free Interest Rate (e.g., .06):  .06
Annual Dividend Rate (e.g., .02):  .02
Time to Expiration in Months:  24
Put Premium:  14.596
```

No.	VOLD	VNEW	F
1	0.50000	0.38456	7.3947
2	0.38456	0.35755	1.7191
3	0.35755	0.35163	0.3758
4	0.35163	0.35036	0.0808
5	0.35036	0.35008	0.0173
6	0.35008	0.35003	0.0037

Implied Volatility: 0.35005

At first blush, this numerical method for determining volatilities from premiums looks like a great shortcut to the laborious process of calculating them from historical price information. All one has to do is to obtain the premium quoted, say, for a LEAP put and then use the computer program to determine the volatility. The trouble with this is that it is not ordinarily possible to determine what pricing model the market maker used in the first place to arrive at the option premium quoted. The market maker may have used Black-Scholes (thereby ignoring dividends), or the Merton variation (thereby including dividends), or a multiperiod binomial model, or even a more sophisticated model for the pricing of American-style options.

15

CHAPTER 15

AMERICAN-STYLE OPTIONS

The Effect of American-Style Options

The ability to exercise early has no effect on the price of calls in the absence of dividends and only a moderate impact if dividends are taken into account. The principal difference between European- and American-style options occurs for put premiums. For American-style options, there is a significant upward effect on put premiums, whether or not dividends are present.

Unfortunately, there is no neat, concise, and exact formula for American-style put premiums. A good analytic approximation for these premiums is given by a formula developed by Giovanni Barone-Adesi and Robert Whaley, as follows:

$$American\ Put = European\ Put + Early\ Exercise\ Premium, \quad if\ P > P^*$$

$$= S - P, \qquad\qquad\qquad\qquad if\ P \le P^*$$

$$(15.1)$$

where the European put premium is the one calculated using the Merton variation presented in the previous chapter, and P^* is the critical stock price determined from the procedure outlined below.

The early exercise premium in Equation 15.1 is given by:

$$Early\ Exercise\ Premium = A \times \left(\frac{P}{P^*}\right)^Q \quad (15.2)$$

where:

$$A = -\frac{P^* \times \left[1 - e^{-\delta t} \times N\left(-h^*\right)\right]}{Q} \quad (15.3)$$

$$Q = \frac{1 - n - \sqrt{(n-1)^2 + 4k}}{2} \quad (15.4)$$

$$n = \frac{2(r - \delta)}{v^2} \quad (15.5)$$

$$k = \frac{2r}{v^2 \left(1 - e^{-rt}\right)} \quad (15.6)$$

$N(-h^*)$ again denotes the cumulative Normal distribution function, where h^* is the dividend adjusted parameter specified in the Merton variation, as evaluated at the critical stock price P^*:

$$h^* = \frac{ln\left(P^*/S\right) + \left(r - \delta + v^2/2\right) \times t}{v\sqrt{t}} \quad (15.7)$$

The critical stock price P^* is the iterative solution to the following equation:

$$S - P^* = European\ Put\left(P^*\right) - \left[1 - e^{-\delta t} \times N\left(-h^*\right)\right] \times \left(\frac{P^*}{Q}\right) \quad (15.8)$$

where the European put premium in Equation 15.8 is evaluated at the Critical Stock Price P^*.

Numerical Example

We illustrate the use of the methodology with the same example used for the Merton variation in the previous chapter, in which the strike price and stock price are $100, the volatility is 0.35, the risk-free interest rate is 6%, there are 24 months till expiration, and the annual dividend rate is 2%. By trial and error, Equation 15.8 is satisfied when $P*$ is \$58.1844 (a computer program showing how this is efficiently determined is included at the end of this chapter).

We then compute in order:

$$n = \frac{2(r-\delta)}{v^2} = \frac{2 \times (0.06 - 0.02)}{0.35^2} = 0.6530612$$

$$k = \frac{2r}{v^2\left(1 - e^{-rt}\right)} = \frac{2 \times 0.06}{0.35^2 \times \left(1 - e^{-0.12}\right)} = 8.662856$$

$$Q = \frac{1 - n - \sqrt{(n-1)^2 + 4k}}{2}$$

$$= \frac{0.3469388 - \sqrt{0.3469388^2 + 4 \times 8.662856}}{2} = -2.774911$$

$$h^* = \frac{\ln(P^*/S) + \left(r - \delta + v^2/2\right) \times t}{v\sqrt{t}}$$

$$= \frac{\ln(58.1844/100) + \left(0.06 - 0.02 + 0.5 \times 0.35^2\right) \times 2}{0.35\sqrt{2}}$$

$$= -0.6849906$$

$$N\left(-h^*\right) = N(0.6849906) = 0.7533173$$

$$A = -\frac{P^* \times \left[1 - e^{-\delta t} \times N\left(-h^*\right)\right]}{Q}$$

$$= -\frac{58.1844 \times \left(1 - e^{-0.04} \times 0.7533173\right)}{-2.774911} = 5.791803$$

$$\text{Early Exercise Premium} = A \times \left(\frac{P}{P^*}\right)^Q$$

$$= 5.791803 \times \left(\frac{100}{58.1844}\right)^{-2.774911}$$

$$= 1.288$$

The American put premium with a 2% dividend rate is therefore its European put value of $14.596 plus $1.288, or $15.884

As mentioned earlier, the critical stock price $P* = 58.1844$ is determined by trial and error so as to satisfy Equation 15.8. To verify that this is the case, we calculate the value of the European put premium using the Merton variation at that particular stock price, as follows:

$$
\begin{aligned}
Put(P^*) &= -58.1844 \times e^{-0.04} \times N(0.6849906) \\
&\quad + 100 \times e^{-0.12} \times N(0.6849906 + 0.35\sqrt{2}) \\
&= -58.1844 \times 0.9607894 \times 0.753317 \\
&\quad + 100 \times 0.8869204 \times 0.881003 \\
&= -42.1127 + 78.1380 = 36.0253
\end{aligned}
$$

The left-hand side of Equation 15.8 is given by:

$$
S - P^* = 100 - 58.1844 = 41.816,
$$

while the right-hand side of Equation 15.8 is calculated as:

$$
S - P^* = 36.0253 - (1 - 0.9607894 \times 0.753317) \times \left(\frac{58.1844}{-2.774911} \right)
$$

$$
= 36.0253 + 5.7918 = 41.817
$$

Because the two value are identical (within computational round-off), the critical stock price of 58.1844 is confirmed.

Comparison Table

The table below compares European- and American-style put premiums where the strike price and stock price are $100, the volatility is 0.35, the risk-free interest rate is 6%, there are 24 months till expiration, and the annual dividend rate ranges from 0% to 3%.

As is clearly apparent, the premiums in all cases are greater than the one utilized for the zero-dividend, European-style case. Because of this, the premiums, retention rates, and account values shown in each run throughout this book would have been somewhat higher if actual dividends and early exercise rights were taken into account.

Table 15.1: European vs. American Put Premiums

Dividend Rate	European Put	American Put
0%	13.314	14.880
1%	13.948	15.373
2%	14.596	15.884
3%	15.259	16.417

Appendix B contains detailed tables for the prices of American-style puts for a wide range of parameters.

Computer Program for American Put Premiums

A relatively short BASIC program for calculating American put premiums is shown below. By using a Newton-Raphson iterative search technique, the critical stock price can usually be obtained to within three decimal places in just four or five iterations, as shown in the example that follows.

```
10 'AMERICAN PUT PREMIUMS USING BARONE-ADESI AND WHALEY
APPROACH
20 INPUT "Enter Stock Price:   ";P
30 INPUT "Enter Strike Price: ";S
40 INPUT "Enter Risk-Free Interest Rate (e.g., .06): ";R
50 INPUT "Enter Volatility (e.g., 0.35): ";SD
60 INPUT "Enter Annual Dividend Rate (e.g., .02): ";DIV
70 INPUT "Enter Time to Expiration in Months (0 for days):
";TIMEX
80 IF TIMEX>0 THEN T=TIMEX/12: GOTO 120
90 INPUT "Enter Time to Expiration in Days: ";TIMEXX
100 T=TIMEXX/365
110 '*****************************************************
120 PRINT "Where do you want to send results: "
130 PRINT "   1 = Screen"
140 PRINT "   2 = Printer"
150 PRINT "   3 = Save to disk"
```

```
160 INPUT "Enter your selection: ";SELECT
170 IF SELECT=0 THEN SELECT =1
180 IF SELECT=1 THEN SAVEFILE$="SCRN:"
190 IF SELECT=2 THEN SAVEFILE$="LPT1:"
200 IF SELECT=3 THEN INPUT "Enter name of savefile:
";SAVEFILE$
210 OPEN SAVEFILE$ FOR OUTPUT AS 1
220 PRINT#1, "Stock Price: ";P
230 PRINT#1, "Strike Price: ";S
240 PRINT#1, "Risk-Free Interest Rate (e.g., .06): ";R
250 PRINT#1, "Volatility (e.g., 0.35): ";SD
260 PRINT#1, "Annual Dividend Rate (e.g., .02): ";DIV
270 IF TIMEX>0 THEN PRINT#1, "Time to Expiration in Months:
";TIMEX
280 IF TIMEXX>0 THEN PRINT#1, "Time to Expiration in Days:
";TIMEXX
290 '****************************************************
300 'COMPUTE BASIC PARAMETERS
310 SD2=SD*SD
320 N=2*(R-DIV)/SD2
330 ERT=EXP(-R*T)
340 EDT=EXP(-DIV*T)
350 K=2*R/(SD2*(1-ERT))
360 Q=(1-N-SQR((N-1)*(N-1)+4*K))/2
370 ALPHA=(R-DIV+.5*SD2)*T
380 BETA=SD*SQR(T)
390 PI2=SQR(2*3.14159265#)
400 H=(LOG(P/S)+ALPHA)/BETA
410 H1=-H 'negative h
420 PH=EXP(-H1*H1/2!)/PI2
430 KH=1/(1+.33267*ABS(H1))
440 CUMH=1-PH*(.4361836*KH-.1201676*KH*KH+.937298*KH*KH*KH)
450 IF H1<0 THEN CUMH=1-CUMH
460 G1=-H+BETA
470 GH=EXP(-G1*G1/2!)/PI2
480 KH=1/(1+.33267*ABS(G1))
490 CUMG=1-GH*(.4361836*KH-.1201676*KH*KH+.937298*KH*KH*KH)
500 IF G1<0 THEN CUMG=1-CUMG
510 EUROPEAN=-P*EDT*CUMH+S*ERT*CUMG 'EUROPEAN PUT
520 '****************************************************
530 'START TRIAL AND ERROR SEARCH FOR CRITICAL STOCK PRICE
540 'USING NEWTON-RAPHSON ITERATION PROCESS
550 POLD=P 'first guess is current stock price
560 KOUNT=1 'set iteration counter
570 H=(LOG(POLD/S)+ALPHA)/BETA
```

```
580 H1=-H 'negative h
590 PH=EXP(-H1*H1/2!)/PI2
600 KH=1/(1+.33267*ABS(H1))
610 CUMH=1-PH*(.4361836*KH-.1201676*KH*KH+.937298*KH*KH*KH)
620 IF H1<0 THEN CUMH=1-CUMH 'this is Normal(-h)
630 G1=-H+BETA
640 GH=EXP(-G1*G1/2!)/PI2
650 KG=1/(1+.33267*ABS(G1))
660 CUMG=1-GH*(.4361836*KG-.1201676*KG*KG+.937298*KG*KG*KG)
670 IF G1<0 THEN CUMG=1-CUMG 'this is Normal(-h+beta)
680 PUTVAL=-POLD*EDT*CUMH+S*ERT*CUMG 'put Value at P=POLD
690 F=-S+POLD+PUTVAL-(1-EDT*CUMH)*(POLD/Q) 'function F at
P=POLD
700 DERIVH=-PH/(POLD*BETA) 'derivative of Normal(-h) at
P=POLD
710 DERIVG=-GH/(POLD*BETA) 'derivative of Normal(-h+beta) at
P=POLD
720 DERIVP=-EDT*CUMH-POLD*EDT*DERIVH+S*ERT*DERIVG 'deriv. of
Put
730 DERIVF=1+DERIVP-(1-EDT*CUMH)/Q+EDT*DERIVH*(POLD/Q)
'deriv. of F
740 PNEW=POLD-F/DERIVF 'new estimate for critical stock
price
750 '***************************************************
760 'DISPLAY CONVERGENCE DETAILS (optional)
770 IF KOUNT=1 THEN 780 ELSE 800
780 PRINT#1, " "
790 PRINT#1, USING "\ \   \   \      \  \
!";"No.","POLD","PNEW","F"
800 PRINT#1, USING "##   ###.####   ###.####
###.####";KOUNT,POLD,PNEW,F
810 '***************************************************
820 IF ABS(PNEW-POLD)<.001 THEN 860 'convergence test
830 POLD=PNEW
840 KOUNT=KOUNT+1 'increase counter
850 IF KOUNT < 11 THEN 570 'cut-off limit on iterations
860 CSP=(PNEW+POLD)/2 'final value for the critical stock
price
870 '***************************************************
880 'COMPUTE EARLY EXERCISE PREMIUM
890 A=-CSP*(1-EDT*CUMH)/Q 'note minus sign
900 EARLY=A*(P/CSP)^Q 'early exercise premium
910 AMERICAN=EUROPEAN+EARLY 'candidate American put premium
920 IF P<=CSP THEN AMERICAN=S-P 'premium when put is deep in
the money
```

```
930 PRINT#1, " "
940 PRINT#1, USING "Critical Stock Price:  $###.####";CSP
950 PRINT#1, " "
960 PRINT#1, USING "European Put Premium:
$###.####";EUROPEAN
970 PRINT#1, USING "Early Exercise Premium: $##.####";EARLY
980 PRINT#1, USING "                        \      \";"-----
--"
990 PRINT#1, USING "American Put Premium:
$###.####";AMERICAN
1000 PRINT#1, " "
1010 '*****************************************************
1020 'COMPUTE MARGIN REQUIREMENTS
1030 IF P>S THEN OTM=100*(P-S) ELSE OTM=0
1040 AMER100=100*AMERICAN
1050 MARGIN1=20*P-OTM+AMER100
1060 MARGIN2=10*P+AMER100
1070 MARGIN=MARGIN1
1080 IF MARGIN2>MARGIN1 THEN MARGIN=MARGIN2
1090 PRINT#1, USING "20% of Price:  $#,###.##   @10%:
$#,###.##";20*P,10*P
1100 PRINT#1, USING "Less OTM:      $#,###.##
-  ";OTM
1110 PRINT#1, USING "Plus Premium:  $#,###.##
$#,###.##";AMER100;AMER100
1120 PRINT#1, USING "              \      \            \
\";"-------";"-------"
1130 PRINT#1, USING "  Total:       $#,###.##
$#,###.##";MARGIN1;MARGIN2
1140 PRINT#1, USING "  Margin Requirement:   $#,###.## (per
contract)";MARGIN
1150 PRINT#1, " "
1160 INPUT "Another Case (y/n): ";CASE$
1170 IF CASE$="y" OR CASE$="Y" THEN CLOSE 1: GOTO 20
1180 CLOSE 1
1190 END
```

Numerical Examples

As examples of the kind of results obtainable using the computer program, let's look at both at-the-money and out-of-the money situations. The first is the same one that was done by hand earlier.

```
Stock Price:   100
Strike Price:  100
Risk-Free Interest Rate (e.g., .06):   .06
Volatility (e.g., 0.35):   .35
Annual Dividend Rate (e.g., .02):   .02
Time to Expiration in Months:   24
 No.  POLD       PNEW        F
  1  100.0000   66.8516   38.8177
  2   66.8516   59.0941    5.8858
  3   59.0941   58.1949    0.5523
  4   58.1949   58.1819    0.0078
  5   58.1819   58.1819    0.0000

Critical Stock Price:  $ 58.1819
European Put Premium:  $ 14.5955
Early Exercise Premium: $ 1.2884
                        - - - - - - -
American Put Premium:  $ 15.8840

20% of Price:  $2,000.00  @10%:  $1,000.00
Less OTM:      $     0.00                -
Plus Premium:  $1,588.40            $1,588.40
               - - - - - - -        - - - - - - -
   Total:      $3,588.40            $2,588.40
   Margin Requirement:   $3,588.40 (per contract)
```

```
Stock Price:   100
Strike Price:  85
Risk-Free Interest Rate (e.g., .06):   .06
Volatility (e.g., 0.35):   .35
Annual Dividend Rate (e.g., .02):   .02
Time to Expiration in Months:   24

 No.  POLD       PNEW        F
  1  100.0000   59.5921   51.3915
  2   59.5921   50.7781    7.1807
  3   50.7781   49.4864    0.8096
  4   49.4864   49.4546    0.0190
  5   49.4546   49.4546    0.0000

Critical Stock Price:  $ 49.4546
European Put Premium:  $  8.3327
Early Exercise Premium: $ 0.6976
                        - - - - - - -
American Put Premium:  $  9.0303

20% of Price:  $2,000.00  @10%:  $1,000.00
Less OTM:      $1,500.00                 -
Plus Premium:  $  903.03            $  903.03
               - - - - - - -        - - - - - - -
   Total:      $1,403.03            $1,903.03
   Margin Requirement:   $1,903.03 (per contract)
```

Computer Program for American Call Premiums

For completeness, I've also developed a short BASIC program for calculating American call premiums. By using a Newton-Raphson iterative search technique, the critical stock price can usually be obtained to within three decimal places in a half dozen or so iterations, as shown in the example that follows. The reason more iterations are needed to arrive at American call premiums is because in the absence of dividends, there is no early exercise premium for calls. As a result, the smaller the dividend rate, the higher the critical stock price and the longer it takes to converge to it.

```
10 'AMERICAN CALL PREMIUMS USING BARONE-ADESI AND
WHALEY APPROACH
20 INPUT "Enter Stock Price:   ";P
30 INPUT "Enter Strike Price: ";S
40 INPUT "Enter Risk-Free Interest Rate (e.g., .06):
";R
50 INPUT "Enter Volatility (e.g., 0.35): ";SD
60 INPUT "Enter Annual Dividend Rate (e.g., .02):
";DIV
70 INPUT "Enter Time to Expiration in Months (0 for
days): ";TIMEX
80 IF TIMEX>0 THEN T=TIMEX/12: GOTO 120
90 INPUT "Enter Time to Expiration in Days: ";TIMEXX
100 T=TIMEXX/365
110 '***********************************************
120 PRINT "Where do you want to send results: "
130 PRINT "   1 = Screen"
140 PRINT "   2 = Printer"
150 PRINT "   3 = Save to disk"
160 INPUT "Enter your selection: ";SELECT
170 IF SELECT=0 THEN SELECT =1
180 IF SELECT=1 THEN SAVEFILE$="SCRN:"
190 IF SELECT=2 THEN SAVEFILE$="LPT1:"
200 IF SELECT=3 THEN INPUT "Enter name of savefile:
";SAVEFILE$
210 OPEN SAVEFILE$ FOR OUTPUT AS 1
220 PRINT#1, "Stock Price: ";P
230 PRINT#1, "Strike Price: ";S
240 PRINT#1, "Risk-Free Interest Rate (e.g., .06): ";R
250 PRINT#1, "Volatility (e.g., 0.35): ";SD
260 PRINT#1, "Annual Dividend Rate (e.g., .02): ";DIV
270 IF TIMEX>0 THEN PRINT#1, "Time to Expiration in
Months: ";TIMEX
280 IF TIMEXX>0 THEN PRINT#1, "Time to Expiration in
Days: ";TIMEXX
290 '***********************************************
300 'COMPUTE BASIC PARAMETERS
310 SD2=SD*SD
```

```
320 N=2*(R-DIV)/SD2
330 ERT=EXP(-R*T)
340 EDT=EXP(-DIV*T)
350 K=2*R/(SD2*(1-ERT))
360 Q=(1-N+SQR((N-1)*(N-1)+4*K))/2
370 ALPHA=(R-DIV+.5*SD2)*T
380 BETA=SD*SQR(T)
390 PI2=SQR(2*3.14159265#)
400 H1=(LOG(P/S)+ALPHA)/BETA
410 PH=EXP(-H1*H1/2!)/PI2
420 KH=1/(1+.33267*ABS(H1))
430 CUMH=1-PH*(.4361836*KH-
.1201676*KH*KH+.937298*KH*KH*KH)
440 IF H1<0 THEN CUMH=1-CUMH
450 G1=H1-BETA
460 GH=EXP(-G1*G1/2!)/PI2
470 KH=1/(1+.33267*ABS(G1))
480 CUMG=1-GH*(.4361836*KH-
.1201676*KH*KH+.937298*KH*KH*KH)
490 IF G1<0 THEN CUMG=1-CUMG
500 EUROPEAN=P*EDT*CUMH-S*ERT*CUMG 'EUROPEAN PUT
510 '************************************************
520 'START TRIAL AND ERROR SEARCH FOR CRITICAL STOCK
PRICE
530 'USING NEWTON-RAPHSON ITERATION PROCESS
540 POLD=P 'first guess is current stock price
550 KOUNT=1 'set iteration counter
560 H1=(LOG(POLD/S)+ALPHA)/BETA
570 PH=EXP(-H1*H1/2!)/PI2
580 KH=1/(1+.33267*ABS(H1))
590 CUMH=1-PH*(.4361836*KH-
.1201676*KH*KH+.937298*KH*KH*KH)
600 IF H1<0 THEN CUMH=1-CUMH 'this is Normal(h)
610 G1=H1-BETA
620 GH=EXP(-G1*G1/2!)/PI2
630 KG=1/(1+.33267*ABS(G1))
640 CUMG=1-GH*(.4361836*KG-
.1201676*KG*KG+.937298*KG*KG*KG)
650 IF G1<0 THEN CUMG=1-CUMG 'this is Normal(h-beta)
660 CALLVAL=POLD*EDT*CUMH-S*ERT*CUMG 'call Value at
P=POLD
670 F=S-POLD+CALLVAL+(1-EDT*CUMH)*(POLD/Q) 'function F
at P=POLD
680 DERIVH=PH/(POLD*BETA) 'derivative of Normal(h) at
P=POLD
690 DERIVG=GH/(POLD*BETA) 'derivative of Normal(h-
beta) at P=POLD
700 DERIVC=EDT*CUMH+POLD*EDT*DERIVH-S*ERT*DERIVG
'deriv. of Call
710 DERIVF=-1+DERIVC+(1-EDT*CUMH)/Q-
EDT*DERIVH*(POLD/Q) 'deriv. of F
720 PNEW=POLD-F/DERIVF 'new estimate for critical
stock price
730 '************************************************
```

```
740 'DISPLAY CONVERGENCE DETAILS (optional)
750 IF KOUNT=1 THEN 770 ELSE 790
760 PRINT#1, " "
770 PRINT#1, USING "\ \   \   \       \  \
!";"No.","POLD","PNEW","F"
780 PRINT#1, USING "##   ###.####  ###.####
###.####";KOUNT,POLD,PNEW,F
790 '************************************************
800 IF ABS(PNEW-POLD)<.001 THEN 840 'convergence test
810 POLD=PNEW
820 KOUNT=KOUNT+1 'increase counter
830 IF KOUNT < 11 THEN 570 'cut-off limit on
iterations
840 CSP=(PNEW+POLD)/2 'final value for the critical
stock price
850 '************************************************
860 'COMPUTE EARLY EXERCISE PREMIUM
870 A=CSP*(1-EDT*CUMH)/Q
880 EARLY=A*(P/CSP)^Q 'early exercise premium
890 AMERICAN=EUROPEAN+EARLY 'candidate American call
premium
900 IF P=>CSP THEN AMERICAN=P-S 'premium when call is
deep in the money
910 PRINT#1, " "
920 PRINT#1, USING "Critical Stock Price:
$###.####";CSP
930 PRINT#1, " "
940 PRINT#1, USING "European Call Premium:
$###.####";EUROPEAN
950 PRINT#1, USING "Early Exercise Premium:
$##.####";EARLY
960 PRINT#1, USING "                              \
\";"-------"
970 PRINT#1, USING "American Call Premium:
$###.####";AMERICAN
980 PRINT#1, " "
990 '************************************************
1000 'COMPUTE MARGIN REQUIREMENTS
1010 IF S>P THEN OTM=100*(S-P) ELSE OTM=0
1020 AMER100=100*AMERICAN
1030 MARGIN1=20*P-OTM+AMER100
1040 MARGIN2=10*P+AMER100
1050 MARGIN=MARGIN1
1060 IF MARGIN2>MARGIN1 THEN MARGIN=MARGIN2
1070 PRINT#1, USING "20% of Price:  $#,###.##   @10%:
$#,###.##";20*P,10*P
1080 PRINT#1, USING "Less OTM:      $#,###.##
-  ";OTM
1090 PRINT#1, USING "Plus Premium:  $#,###.##
$#,###.##";AMER100;AMER100
1100 PRINT#1, USING "                     \      \
\     \";"-------";"-------"
1110 PRINT#1, USING " Total:        $#,###.##
$#,###.##";MARGIN1;MARGIN2
```

```
1120 PRINT#1, USING "  Margin Requirement:
$#,###.## (per contract)";MARGIN
1130 PRINT#1, " "
1140 INPUT "Another Case (y/n): ";CASE$
1150 IF CASE$="y" OR CASE$="Y" THEN CLOSE 1: GOTO 20
1160 CLOSE 1
1170 END
```

Numerical Examples

As examples of the results obtainable with this program, we again consider both at-the-money and out-of-the money situations. The first is the same one that was done by hand, earlier. Note that the computation of call premiums typically takes longer to converge than does the computation of put premiums.

```
Stock Price:    100
Strike Price:   100
Risk-Free Interest Rate (e.g., .06):  .06
Volatility (e.g., 0.35):  .35
Annual Dividend Rate (e.g., .02):  .02
Time to Expiration in Months:  24

No.  POLD       PNEW         F
 1  100.0000  170.6420   33.7405
 2  170.6420  257.8725   13.3574
 3  257.8725  372.5958    5.7306
 4  372.5958  425.3898    1.5634
 5  425.3898  427.2815    0.0528
 6  427.2815  427.2836    0.0001
 7  427.2836  427.2833   -0.0000

Critical Stock Price:  $427.2834
European Call Premium:  $ 21.9824
Early Exercise Premium:  $ 0.0582
                         -------
American Call Premium:  $ 22.0407

20% of Price:  $2,000.00   @10%:  $1,000.00
Less OTM:      $    0.00                  -
Plus Premium:  $2,204.07           $2,204.07
               -------             -------
    Total:     $4,204.07           $3,204.07
    Margin Requirement:  $4,204.07 (per contract)
```

```
Stock Price:    100
Strike Price:   115
Risk-Free Interest Rate (e.g., .06):  .06
Volatility (e.g., 0.35):  .35
Annual Dividend Rate (e.g., .02):  .02
Time to Expiration in Months:  24

No.   POLD       PNEW         F
 1   100.0000   182.3433   46.6304
 2   182.3433   277.3311   17.7129
 3   277.3311   407.3093    7.6294
 4   407.3093   486.6183    2.4358
 5   486.6183   491.3691    0.1327
 6   491.3691   491.3751    0.0002
 7   491.3751   491.3751   -0.0000

Critical Stock Price:  $491.3751
European Call Premium: $ 16.5386
Early Exercise Premium: $ 0.0433
                        -------
American Call Premium: $ 16.5819

20% of Price:  $2,000.00    @10%:  $1,000.00
Less OTM:      $1,500.00               -
Plus Premium:  $1,658.19           $1,658.19
               -------             -------
   Total:      $2,158.19           $2,658.19
   Margin Requirement:  $2,658.19 (per contract)
```

PART IV:
ADDITIONAL RESOURCES

16

CHAPTER 16

MY FAVORITE WEBSITES

Introduction

Almost all on-line brokerage organizations maintain systems for obtaining real-time quotes on listed options. There are also numerous independent information providers that offer real-time or delayed quotes under various pricing plans. I subscribe to none of these because I think there are enough free resources available on the internet to allow an investor to make intelligent decisions without paying more than the basic monthly internet access charges. Bear in mind that the features described for the sites listed are constantly being modified and expanded—so much so that any detailed description that I could offer is quickly outdated.

Chicago Board Options Exchange (CBOE)

The Chicago Board Options Exchange (CBOE) offers bid and asked quotations on both standard and LEAP options on a 20-minute delayed basis. Their internet address is *http://www.cboe.com*, and many internet providers allow you to expedite the process of connecting to them through the use of an embedded keyword such as "CBOE" or "OPTIONS" (both words are used by American Online, for example). You can request a quote for a specific call or put option, a short list of near-term at-the-money options, or the full list of all standard and LEAP options available for the underlying issue.

The advantage of accessing this website though American Online is that the latter gives you access to the message boards of CBOE, where anyone can post an inquiry to other option investors or to the

CBOE itself. The CBOE's staff sweeps the message board several times a week and within a few days will respond to any question concerning rules, regulations and other technical matters having to do with options. This is the first place to learn of new LEAPS or standard options that are being introduced and to obtain the trading symbol(s) for the option(s) you are interested in.

In addition to quotations and message boards, this website also offers a free automated mailing service. To get there, click on Site Index and select E-mail from the list provided. You will then be presented with ten automated mailing lists, any number of which you may then subscribe to. For me, the most important one is the daily letter showing contract adjustments (including stock splits, mergers, and acquisitions) to existing options as well as announcements of newly established options and LEAPS. Other mailing lists include event calendars for seminars and classes given by the Options Institute, general announcements, and updated LEAP symbol directories. You can also receive daily market statistics and new series information in Excel (.xls) spreadsheet format. Additional information about options can also be found at various related or associated websites, including those of the major exchanges and clearing organization at *www.amex.com, www.pacificex.com, www.phlx.com,* and *www.optionsclearing.com.* A single website that links to all of these can be found at *www.optionscentral.com.*

Hoover's StockScreener

This is my favorite website for screening stocks on the basis of performance criteria. StockScreener permits searches by using up to 20 performance criteria, including six independent financial ratios, six independent growth rates, and several size, margin, return, and volatility (beta) criteria. StockScreener is easy to use. The only downside is that one cannot download the search results into a spreadsheet. The searches can be limited by exchange and/or industry group. The search results can be presented and printed out alphabetically or in ascending or descending numerical order. Clicking on a company's name will bring up a capsule description. Detailed financial information and news articles of the kind needed by industry analysts, financial advisors, and portfolio managers are also available by paid subscription. Their website address is *http://www.stockscreener.com,* and like most well designed sites, it can connect you to a plethora of related addresses for additional company and economic information.

Wall Street Research Net

This is another of my favorite websites for screening stocks on the basis of performance criteria. WSRN permits searches by using up to 13 performance criteria, including several independent financial ratios, growth rates, and size categories. The searches can be limited within various index groups, including the Dow Jones and the S&P 500, as well as by exchange and/or industry group. Although the WSRN reporting mechanism is not as flexible as StockScreener's, a great advantage of this service is the great number of links (they claim over 500,000) available to scores of primary government agencies, the Federal Reserve, and other sites that provide detailed statistical indicators and associated economic reports. The website address of Wall Street Research Net is *http://www.wsrn.com/index.html,* and just like StockScreener, financial information and news articles of the kind needed by industry analysts, financial advisors, and portfolio managers are available by subscription.

Yahoo!Finance

This is the place to go for breaking market news, a concise list of upgrades, downgrades, coverage initiated recommendations, and earnings surprises. You can use this site to monitor the market value of your portfolio. Their website address is *http://quote.yahoo.com,* and there are a vast number of links to other websites of potential interest to small investors. I like to link to *http://quote.yahoo.com/intlmarkets* to view in one concise table the market indexes of some 42 foreign stock markets around the world.

StockSmart

A great place to go for delayed market quotes on up to 12 stocks at the same time. StockSmart shows winners and losers within an industry group, upcoming splits, distributions, and dividends, recent splits and symbol changes, stock and index options, and a host of other information. You can use this site to maintain the market value of your portfolio. Their website address is *http://www.stocksmart.com,* and there are a large number of links to other websites of potential interest to small investors.

Zacks Investment Research

This fee-based website does offer a couple of free goodies, including the day's ten best and ten worst earnings surprises, company profiles, and annual income and balance sheets. What I really like, however, is the Wall Street Recommendations, which shows consensus estimates in earnings and the number and distribution of brokers rating a given stock as a strong buy, a moderate buy, a hold, a moderate sell, and a strong sell, along with its average score and its change from the previous week. Their site address is *http://www.zacks.com/docs/yahoo/,* and there are a large number of advanced features available by paid subscription if desired.

FinancialWeb

This is a completely free, fun-filled website offering several novel features for the individual investor. Among these are seamless links to Quote Central, Rapid Research, Stocktools, Wall Street Guru, SmallCap Investor, Stock Detective, and Bear Tracker sites. Like many other sites, the features offered are changing and evolving so rapidly that any detailed description is quickly dated. Their website address is *http://www.financialweb.com,* and there is an interesting on-line, small-cap investor newsletter you can register for as well.

Roberts Online Pricer

This website offers a tutorial on options which is well worth reading for both beginning- and intermediate-level options investors. The approximation method used by the Online Pricer to calculate American-style option premiums differs from the one presented in this book, and as a result the premiums obtained are not identical. For example, for an at-the-money LEAP of $100, with a volatility of 0.40, a dividend of 3%, a risk-free rate of 6%, and 24 months to expiration, the Online Pricer gives an American put value of $18.695. The value calculated using the standard Barone-Adesi and Whaley approach described earlier in this book is $18.978. Their website address is *http://www.intrepid.com/*, and from there you can move on to the subdomains *~robertl/option-text.html* (for the tutorial) or *~robertl/option-pricer.html* (for the pricer). In addition to the option pricer, this website offers a commission pricer which shows how much it would cost in brokerage commissions to purchase a given number of shares at a given price from over 40 discount brokers. The commission pricer can be found at subdomain *~robertl/index.html.*

First Call

This website makes its living from the sale of real-time earnings estimates and real time buy/hold/sell recommendations to corporate and institutional clients. Much of this information, however, is available without charge to individual investors on a daily or weekly recap basis. Earnings surprises, upcoming splits and dividend announcements, consensus estimates, upcoming earnings reports, estimate revisions, and numerous other reports can all be accessed free of charge. At one time First Call could be using the keyword FIRSTCALL on American Online, but this was discontinued in 1998. Their website address is *http://www.firstcall.com/individual.*

America Online

To access any of the above websites, one needs an internet provider, and America Online is the provider of choice for millions of individual investors. The main investment menu, accessed using the keyword QUOTES, is organized into seven sections, labeled Portfolio, Market News Center, News by Ticker, Historical Quotes, Company Research, Brokerage Center, and Mutual Fund Center. Each section will send you to or pick up information from numerous financial websites in a completely seamless manner. I particularly like Historical Quotes, as historical stock prices and volume activities can be downloaded for analysis or charting purposes in a matter of seconds on a daily, weekly or monthly basis as far back as January 1, 1987. The quotation service provides 15-minute delayed quotes on almost all listed securities, but not on options or LEAPS. On the other hand, the keyword CBOE sends you seamlessly to the Chicago Board Options Exchange, where one can get information on options on a delayed-quote basis.

On-Line Brokerage Services

As fine a source as the Chicago Board Options Exchange is, there are times when it is inaccessible because of internet traffic, file maintenance, or computer downtime. (This is often not a fault of the CBOE, because they depend on outside sources at the present time for market quotes.) To ensure coverage, I suggest opening and maintaining a no-cost/low-cost type account from one of the many on-line brokerage services that are readily available through the internet. Although there are numerous on-line brokerage establishments which will provide option quotes, many of them do not provide LEAP quotations along with them.

After examining several such on-line services, I selected Dreyfus Brokerage Services. They are one of the few websites that provide complete option chains, including LEAPS, and they do a magnificent job. As opposed to CBOE, you may restrict the option chain to that of calls or puts. The format of the displayed results is impressive and shows the last trade, bid and ask price, change (if any), daily high and low, trading volume, open interest, and the option symbol. Clicking on the option description will take you right to the option order entry for subscribers authorized to trade options. Access to option and LEAP quotes is completely free after hours and on weekends, when the markets are closed.

If you wish to access the same type of information during trading hours, you can do so by establishing an account with them. An opening and maintenance balance of just $1,000 is required. The funds so deposited can be invested in an interest-bearing money market account (or can be used to purchase equities), which is about as low-cost an arrangement as you will find. A higher balance of $2,000 or so is required to do options. Real-time quotes are available by subscription for those who want them. Their website address is *http://www.trackpbs.com*, and there are a large number of links (66 when I last counted) to other websites that can provide business news and other data.

Real-Time Quotes

Real-time quotes are costly and are ordinarily not required by buy-and-hold investors. Nonetheless, they can be instructive to watch during periods of high volatility in the markets. Such services cost from around $25 a month for a limited number of monthly quotations to as much as $75 a month for unlimited quotations. There are, however, websites that provide real-time quotes without charge. Some of them restrict users to 50 quotations per day, while others permit an unlimited number of quotations. An example of the former is Thomson RTQ Service, whose website address is *http://www.thomsonrtq.com*. An example of the latter is First International Financial Corporation's real-time stock quote and news service, whose website address is *http://www.freerealtime.com*.

In accordance with stock exchange rules, you must register for any site providing real-time quotations, which means supplying your name, address, telephone number and e-mail address (providing such information is the "price" you pay for the service). Thomson RTQ provides you with last price, the change, the bid and ask price, bidsize, asksize, the high trade, the low trade and trading volume, current rating by First Call and two other rating services, and a few other market statistics on the company. For most issues, intra-day and annual charts are available. First International provides somewhat more detailed information, including ex-dividend dates, stock split history, and greater charting capabilities. Many financial websites are in the process of adding real-time quote capabilities to their websites, so by the time you read this some of the websites mentioned here will already have this capability.

Daily Stocks

This relatively new website is a tremendous resource for investors. Besides giving you 50 free real-time stock quotes per day (from the same provider as the Thomson RTQ Service), it has an options pricer for calculating European- and American-style option premiums. It also shows a list of the ten most active options on the day, along with the top gainers and losers. There are a large number of links to other information providers, including charting services, news sources, magazine articles, earnings estimates, research reports, and a lot more. Their website address is *http://www.dailystocks.com.*

Discount Broker Evaluation

Before signing on with any on-line broker, Readers should visit *http://www.astro.lsa.umich.edu:80/users/philf/www/home.html,* where a substantial amount of information on well over five dozen discount and on-line stock and option brokers has been compiled and evaluated. The discount brokers are divided into three classes: deep-discount, middle-cost, and higher-cost discount brokers. At a minimum, the information provided includes the commission structure, account setup and maintenance charges, account minimums, broker call rates, and the fee and/or credit schedule for real-time quotes. The commission structure is ordinarily quite complete and includes per-contract and minimum trading costs for both broker-assisted and unassisted transactions. Of particular interest are the numerous comments gleaned from internet news groups and chat rooms on the experiences (good and bad) that investors have had with the discount and/or on-line brokers. The website address and telephone number for each broker are given. In only a few instances was information provided as to whether naked options are permitted and the extent to which stop limit orders can be accommodated.

17

SELECTED BIBLIOGRAPHY

As I pointed out earlier, Amazon.com lists over 300 books currently available on options or closely related topics. The list below discusses the ones I have read.

1. *Guide to the Markets,* Investors Business Daily, John Wiley & Sons, New York, NY, 277 pp., 1996, ISBN 0-471-15482-2, $16.95 (softcover). One of the best books ever written about long-term investments. Its chapter on options is a model of clarity. A copy should be on every investor's desk.

2. *How the Options Market Work,* Joseph A. Walker, The New York Institute of Finance (A Division of Simon & Schuster), New York, NY, 229 pp., 1991, ISBN 0-13-400888-X, $17.95 (softcover). This delightful book is one of the most readable introductions to options in print today. Although written before the introduction of LEAPS, it deserves a place on every option player's bookshelf.

3. *LEAPS (Long-Term Equity Anticipation Securities),* Harrison Roth, Irwin Professional Publishing, Burr Ridge, IL, 322 pp., 1994, ISBN 1-55623-819-3, $45.00 (hardcover). This was the first book ever devoted specifically to LEAPS. It is an intermediate-level text that explains a great many strategies—including spreads, straddles, and strangles—involving long-term options. At the time this book was written there were LEAPS available on 127 issues.

4. *Listed Stock Options (Revised Edition)*, Carl F. Luft and Richard K. Shiener, Irwin Professional Publishing, Burr Ridge, IL, 236 pp., 1994, ISBN 1-55738-520-3, $24.95 (softcover). A very clear and well-written introduction to options, one which includes a chapter on LEAPS and their distinguishing features. There are numerous case histories throughout the text, with extremely sharp analyses of the interplay between the underlying stocks and corresponding option prices. I like this one very much.

5. *McMillan on Options*, Lawrence G. McMillan, John Wiley & Sons, New York, NY, 570 pp., 1996, ISBN 0-471-11960-1, $65 (hardcover). This is a companion text to the author's earlier book, *Options as a Strategic Investment*, and it focuses on options trading techniques by means of seemingly countless examples drawn from actual situations. The examples are both enlightening and entertaining, and much can be learned from them, even by nontraders. The formulas presented in the appendix contain transcription errors in some instances and should not be relied on.

6. *The Option Advisor*, Bernie Schaeffer, John Wiley & Sons, New York, NY, 316 pp., 1997, ISBN 0-471-18539-6, $59.95 (hardcover). An intermediate-level book for options traders. What makes this book a useful addition to my library is the detailed treatment of LEAPS and the lovely section on navigating the Internet, with its many website addresses for obtaining relevant financial and investment information.

7. *Option Volatility & Pricing*, Sheldon Natenberg, Irwin Professional Publishing, Burr Ridge, IL, 469 pp., 1994, ISBN 1-55738-486-X, $50.00 (hardcover). This is an advanced text on options strategies, with detailed discussion and analysis of how option volatility affects option pricing. There is little discussion of LEAPS.

8. *Options (3rd Edition)*, Robert W. Kolb, Blackwell Publishers, Malden, MA, 347 pp., 1997, ISBN 1-57718-064-X, $64.95 (hardcover). One of the latest books containing both practical and theoretical treatments of option pricing and evaluation. This is one of very few books that treat the subject of exotic options of almost every description. Although the book names over 80 people as having reviewed various sections of the text, there are, unfortunately, several inconsistencies in the mathematical formulas (and occasionally outright transcription errors). Accompanying the book is a diskette that contains the pricing and sensitivity formulas for both European- and American-style options. The programming code appears to be error free, however, as the program arrived at the proper solution in the numerous cases that I tested it for.

9. *Options as a Strategic Investment (3rd Edition)*, Lawrence G. McMillan, New York Institute of Finance (A Simon & Schuster Company), New York, NY, 882 pp., 1993, ISBN 0-13-636002-5, $44.95 (hardcover). This is a very complete text on basic option strategies written by an acknowledged master. The book contains an excellent 43-page chapter on LEAPS. Pricing formulas and numerical examples are all based on the original Black-Scholes model, without taking into consideration early exercise or dividends.

10. *Options for the Stock Investor*, James B. Bittman, Irwin Professional Publishing, Chicago, IL, 273 pp., 1996, ISBN 1-55738-872-5, $29.95 (hardcover). This is an intermediate-level text for investors seeking to enhance their investment yield or protect the asset values of their stock portfolios through the use of options. Included with the book is a diskette containing a computer program based on the Black-Scholes formula to calculate option premiums given the price of the underlying issue, the strike price, the dividend yield, the risk-free interest rate, the number of days to expiration, and the volatility. The program can also calculate implied volatility from option premiums. The techniques presented deal with conventional options, with little reference to their long-term counterparts.

11. *The Options Manual (Third Edition)*, Gary L. Gastineau, McGraw-Hill, Inc., New York, NY, 440 pp., 1995, ISBN 0-07-022981-3, $49.95 (hardcover). This intermediate to advanced text is perhaps the best reference book on options that is available. Besides the usual treatment of option strategies, it contains unparalleled discussions of the history of options, their regulatory framework, taxation, and institutional usage. The only drawback is that the main body of the book was last updated in 1987, and so does not contain any discussion of LEAPS or other changes that have taken place in the option markets subsequent to that date.

12. *Options Markets,* John C. Cox and Mark Rubinstein, Prentice Hall, Englewood Cliffs, NJ, 498 pp., 1985, ISBN 0-13-638205-3, $76 (hardcover). Although LEAPS had not yet been invented at the time of its writing, this book remains the classic source for the theoretical evaluation of option strategies and alternative approaches to option pricing. Readers not familiar with advanced mathematical techniques will appreciate the sections describing clearing operations and the roles of market makers, participating brokers, and exchanges in options market activities.

13. *Understanding The Options Markets,* Commodity Research Bureau, New York, NY, 52 pp., 1989. This pamphlet is long outdated and precedes the introduction of LEAPS, but it was ordered in such large numbers by brokerage firms that it is still being given away free to customers. The writing is often unclear and the pamphlet's primary virtue is as a curiosity piece for those compiling a history of options trading.

APPENDICES AND INDEX

EUROPEAN PUT PREMIUMS

The tables that follow show the option premiums for European-style LEAP puts based on the formulas contained in Chapter 14. They are based on a stock price of $100 and exercise (strike) prices ranging from $120 down to $60 in steps of $5. Each table is presented in matrix format, with volatilities ranging from a low of 0.15 through a high of 0.65. Time to expiration ranges from one month to a maximum of 30 months. A dividend rate of zero and risk-free interest rate of 6% are assumed in all instances.

To obtain premiums for stock prices other than $100, simply scale or interpolate the tables. For example, suppose you want to know the put premium for a stock price of $50, strike price of $45, for a volatility of 0.40 and expiration date 24 months away. From Table A.7, we see that the premium for a $100 stock with strike $90 for volatility 0.40 and 24 month expiration is $11.452. The premium for the $50 stock with strike $45 is therefore half this amount, or $5.726 (i.e., $572.60 per contract).

Suppose the stock price is $60, strike price is $50, for the same volatility and expiration. From Table A.8, we see that the premium for a $100 stock with strike $85 is $9.527, and from Table A.9, we see that the premium for a $100 stock with strike $80 is $7.782. Multiplying each of these figures by 0.60 shows that the premium for a $60 stock with strike $51 is $5.716, and the premium for a $60 stock with strike $48 is $4.669. The premium for the $60 stock with strike $50 is therefore $4.669 + 0.667 x ($5.716 - $4.669), or $5.367 (i.e., $536.70 per contract).

Table A.1: European-Style Put Premiums as a Function of Time and Volatility
Stock Price = $100
Strike Price = $120

Mo	Volatility										
	0.15	0.20	0.25	0.30	0.35	0.40	0.45	0.50	0.55	0.60	0.65
1	19.402	19.403	19.419	19.472	19.577	19.742	19.962	20.235	20.551	20.905	21.292
2	18.811	18.862	19.015	19.287	19.668	20.137	20.677	21.272	21.910	22.583	23.284
3	18.250	18.425	18.782	19.297	19.932	20.657	21.447	22.286	23.163	24.068	24.996
4	17.734	18.077	18.645	19.382	20.236	21.173	22.168	23.205	24.274	25.366	26.476
5	17.266	17.790	18.560	19.495	20.539	21.657	22.827	24.033	25.265	26.516	27.780
6	16.840	17.548	18.504	19.616	20.828	22.106	23.428	24.782	26.156	27.545	28.945
7	16.450	17.336	18.464	19.736	21.099	22.520	23.979	25.463	26.965	28.478	29.998
8	16.091	17.147	18.433	19.852	21.351	22.901	24.483	26.087	27.704	29.329	30.958
9	15.757	16.974	18.406	19.960	21.584	23.253	24.948	26.661	28.384	30.111	31.839
10	15.445	16.814	18.382	20.060	21.800	23.578	25.378	27.192	29.012	30.834	32.652
11	15.152	16.664	18.359	20.152	21.999	23.879	25.777	27.684	29.595	31.503	33.406
12	14.874	16.522	18.335	20.236	22.184	24.159	26.148	28.143	30.137	32.126	34.107
13	14.611	16.386	18.310	20.312	22.354	24.418	26.493	28.570	30.642	32.707	34.762
14	14.360	16.255	18.284	20.380	22.512	24.660	26.815	28.968	31.115	33.251	35.374
15	14.120	16.128	18.256	20.442	22.657	24.885	27.116	29.342	31.558	33.762	35.949
16	13.889	16.005	18.226	20.497	22.792	25.095	27.398	29.692	31.974	34.241	36.489
17	13.668	15.884	18.194	20.546	22.916	25.291	27.661	30.021	32.365	34.692	36.998
18	13.454	15.767	18.160	20.589	23.031	25.474	27.908	30.329	32.734	35.117	37.477
19	13.247	15.651	18.124	20.626	23.137	25.644	28.140	30.620	33.081	35.518	37.930
20	13.047	15.538	18.087	20.658	23.234	25.802	28.357	30.894	33.408	35.897	38.358
21	12.853	15.426	18.048	20.685	23.323	25.950	28.562	31.152	33.718	36.256	38.762
22	12.665	15.316	18.006	20.708	23.405	26.088	28.754	31.395	34.010	36.594	39.145
23	12.482	15.207	17.964	20.726	23.479	26.217	28.934	31.625	34.286	36.915	39.508
24	12.304	15.100	17.919	20.739	23.547	26.337	29.103	31.841	34.548	37.219	39.851
25	12.131	14.994	17.873	20.749	23.609	26.449	29.262	32.046	34.795	37.506	40.177
26	11.962	14.889	17.826	20.754	23.665	26.553	29.412	32.239	35.029	37.779	40.486
27	11.797	14.785	17.777	20.756	23.715	26.649	29.552	32.421	35.250	38.037	40.778
28	11.636	14.683	17.726	20.754	23.761	26.739	29.684	32.592	35.460	38.282	41.056
29	11.479	14.581	17.674	20.750	23.801	26.822	29.808	32.754	35.658	38.514	41.319
30	11.325	14.479	17.621	20.742	23.836	26.898	29.924	32.907	35.845	38.734	41.569

Table A.2: European-Style Put Premiums
as a Function of Time and Volatility
Stock Price = $100
Strike Price = $115

Mo	\multicolumn{11}{c}{Volatility}
	0.15	0.20	0.25	0.30	0.35	0.40	0.45	0.50	0.55	0.60	0.65
1	14.428	14.447	14.519	14.665	14.884	15.167	15.503	15.882	16.296	16.737	17.201
2	13.896	14.063	14.382	14.826	15.363	15.967	16.621	17.312	18.030	18.770	19.527
3	13.447	13.829	14.400	15.100	15.887	16.733	17.620	18.538	19.477	20.432	21.400
4	13.073	13.673	14.468	15.384	16.375	17.417	18.493	19.594	20.711	21.841	22.979
5	12.753	13.561	14.553	15.653	16.819	18.028	19.264	20.520	21.789	23.067	24.350
6	12.474	13.472	14.639	15.902	17.221	18.576	19.953	21.345	22.747	24.155	25.565
7	12.225	13.397	14.722	16.130	17.586	19.071	20.574	22.089	23.610	25.133	26.657
8	11.998	13.330	14.798	16.337	17.917	19.521	21.139	22.765	24.394	26.022	27.648
9	11.789	13.268	14.867	16.527	18.220	19.933	21.656	23.383	25.111	26.836	28.555
10	11.594	13.209	14.929	16.699	18.498	20.311	22.131	23.953	25.772	27.585	29.391
11	11.410	13.152	14.983	16.857	18.753	20.660	22.571	24.479	26.383	28.278	30.164
12	11.236	13.095	15.030	17.001	18.988	20.983	22.978	24.968	26.950	28.923	30.883
13	11.070	13.039	15.071	17.132	19.206	21.283	23.356	25.423	27.479	29.524	31.554
14	10.911	12.982	15.106	17.252	19.407	21.561	23.709	25.847	27.974	30.086	32.182
15	10.758	12.925	15.135	17.361	19.592	21.819	24.038	26.245	28.437	30.613	32.771
16	10.610	12.867	15.158	17.461	19.764	22.060	24.346	26.617	28.873	31.109	33.324
17	10.467	12.809	15.177	17.552	19.923	22.285	24.634	26.968	29.282	31.575	33.846
18	10.328	12.750	15.192	17.635	20.071	22.496	24.905	27.297	29.668	32.015	34.338
19	10.193	12.691	15.201	17.709	20.208	22.692	25.160	27.607	30.031	32.431	34.802
20	10.062	12.631	15.207	17.777	20.335	22.877	25.399	27.900	30.375	32.823	35.241
21	9.933	12.571	15.209	17.838	20.452	23.049	25.624	28.176	30.700	33.194	35.657
22	9.808	12.510	15.207	17.892	20.561	23.211	25.837	28.436	31.007	33.546	36.051
23	9.686	12.448	15.201	17.941	20.662	23.362	26.036	28.683	31.298	33.879	36.424
24	9.567	12.386	15.193	17.984	20.756	23.504	26.225	28.916	31.573	34.195	36.778
25	9.450	12.322	15.181	18.023	20.842	23.637	26.402	29.136	31.834	34.495	37.114
26	9.335	12.258	15.167	18.056	20.922	23.761	26.570	29.344	32.082	34.779	37.433
27	9.221	12.194	15.150	18.085	20.996	23.878	26.727	29.542	32.316	35.049	37.736
28	9.110	12.129	15.130	18.110	21.063	23.987	26.876	29.728	32.539	35.305	38.023
29	9.001	12.064	15.109	18.131	21.125	24.089	27.016	29.905	32.750	35.548	38.296
30	8.893	11.998	15.085	18.148	21.182	24.184	27.148	30.072	32.950	35.779	38.556

Table A.3: European-Style Put Premiums
as a Function of Time and Volatility
Stock Price = $100
Strike Price = $110

Mo	\	\	\	\	Volatility	\	\	\	\	\	\
	0.15	0.20	0.25	0.30	0.35	0.40	0.45	0.50	0.55	0.60	0.65
1	9.482	9.604	9.832	10.147	10.525	10.949	11.407	11.891	12.393	12.910	13.439
2	9.143	9.557	10.106	10.741	11.429	12.154	12.904	13.671	14.451	15.241	16.037
3	8.930	9.606	10.408	11.279	12.194	13.136	14.097	15.070	16.052	17.040	18.032
4	8.776	9.677	10.683	11.747	12.844	13.962	15.094	16.235	17.381	18.531	19.682
5	8.654	9.747	10.928	12.154	13.408	14.676	15.955	17.239	18.526	19.814	21.101
6	8.549	9.811	11.144	12.514	13.904	15.305	16.712	18.123	19.534	20.943	22.350
7	8.455	9.867	11.336	12.833	14.346	15.866	17.390	18.914	20.436	21.954	23.468
8	8.368	9.914	11.506	13.120	14.744	16.372	18.002	19.628	21.251	22.869	24.480
9	8.284	9.954	11.658	13.378	15.105	16.833	18.559	20.280	21.996	23.704	25.404
10	8.204	9.986	11.793	13.612	15.434	17.253	19.069	20.878	22.680	24.472	26.255
11	8.126	10.011	11.915	13.825	15.734	17.640	19.539	21.430	23.312	25.183	27.042
12	8.049	10.030	12.024	14.019	16.011	17.997	19.975	21.943	23.899	25.843	27.773
13	7.974	10.044	12.121	14.196	16.266	18.327	20.379	22.419	24.446	26.459	28.455
14	7.900	10.053	12.208	14.358	16.501	18.634	20.756	22.864	24.957	27.035	29.094
15	7.826	10.057	12.285	14.507	16.719	18.920	21.108	23.281	25.437	27.575	29.693
16	7.754	10.057	12.354	14.643	16.922	19.187	21.437	23.671	25.887	28.082	30.256
17	7.682	10.052	12.416	14.769	17.110	19.436	21.747	24.039	26.310	28.560	30.787
18	7.609	10.044	12.470	14.884	17.285	19.670	22.037	24.384	26.710	29.012	31.288
19	7.537	10.033	12.517	14.990	17.448	19.889	22.310	24.710	27.087	29.438	31.761
20	7.466	10.018	12.559	15.088	17.600	20.094	22.568	25.018	27.443	29.841	32.209
21	7.394	10.000	12.596	15.177	17.742	20.287	22.810	25.309	27.781	30.223	32.633
22	7.323	9.980	12.627	15.259	17.874	20.469	23.039	25.584	28.100	30.585	33.035
23	7.252	9.958	12.654	15.335	17.998	20.639	23.256	25.845	28.403	30.928	33.417
24	7.181	9.933	12.676	15.404	18.113	20.800	23.460	26.091	28.690	31.254	33.779
25	7.111	9.906	12.694	15.467	18.221	20.951	23.653	26.325	28.963	31.563	34.124
26	7.041	9.878	12.709	15.525	18.321	21.093	23.836	26.546	29.221	31.857	34.451
27	6.972	9.848	12.720	15.577	18.415	21.227	24.008	26.756	29.467	32.137	34.762
28	6.903	9.816	12.727	15.625	18.502	21.352	24.172	26.956	29.700	32.402	35.058
29	6.835	9.783	12.732	15.668	18.583	21.471	24.326	27.145	29.922	32.655	35.339
30	6.768	9.748	12.734	15.707	18.659	21.582	24.472	27.324	30.133	32.895	35.607

Table A.4: European-Style Put Premiums
as a Function of Time and Volatility
Stock Price = $100
Strike Price = $105

Mo	Volatility										
	0.15	0.20	0.25	0.30	0.35	0.40	0.45	0.50	0.55	0.60	0.65
1	4.837	5.239	5.707	6.211	6.738	7.279	7.829	8.387	8.950	9.516	10.085
2	4.952	5.666	6.423	7.204	7.997	8.798	9.605	10.415	11.227	12.041	12.856
3	5.064	6.003	6.970	7.952	8.941	9.935	10.931	11.929	12.927	13.924	14.920
4	5.156	6.275	7.412	8.558	9.708	10.860	12.012	13.163	14.313	15.461	16.607
5	5.228	6.500	7.782	9.069	10.357	11.645	12.931	14.215	15.496	16.774	18.048
6	5.284	6.689	8.099	9.510	10.920	12.328	13.733	15.134	16.532	17.925	19.313
7	5.327	6.850	8.374	9.897	11.417	12.933	14.446	15.953	17.456	18.952	20.442
8	5.359	6.989	8.616	10.240	11.861	13.477	15.087	16.692	18.290	19.881	21.464
9	5.382	7.108	8.830	10.548	12.262	13.969	15.671	17.365	19.051	20.728	22.396
10	5.397	7.211	9.021	10.826	12.626	14.419	16.205	17.982	19.750	21.507	23.254
11	5.404	7.300	9.192	11.079	12.959	14.832	16.697	18.551	20.395	22.228	24.048
12	5.405	7.378	9.347	11.310	13.266	15.214	17.152	19.079	20.995	22.897	24.785
13	5.402	7.445	9.486	11.521	13.548	15.567	17.575	19.571	21.553	23.521	25.474
14	5.394	7.503	9.612	11.715	13.810	15.895	17.969	20.030	22.076	24.105	26.118
15	5.382	7.554	9.726	11.894	14.053	16.202	18.338	20.460	22.565	24.653	26.722
16	5.368	7.597	9.830	12.059	14.279	16.488	18.683	20.863	23.026	25.169	27.291
17	5.350	7.634	9.925	12.211	14.490	16.756	19.008	21.243	23.459	25.655	27.827
18	5.330	7.666	10.011	12.353	14.686	17.007	19.313	21.601	23.868	26.113	28.334
19	5.308	7.692	10.089	12.484	14.870	17.244	19.601	21.939	24.255	26.547	28.813
20	5.284	7.714	10.159	12.605	15.042	17.466	19.872	22.258	24.621	26.958	29.266
21	5.258	7.731	10.224	12.718	15.203	17.675	20.128	22.560	24.967	27.347	29.696
22	5.231	7.745	10.282	12.823	15.355	17.872	20.371	22.846	25.296	27.716	30.105
23	5.202	7.755	10.335	12.920	15.496	18.058	20.600	23.118	25.608	28.067	30.492
24	5.172	7.761	10.382	13.010	15.630	18.234	20.817	23.375	25.904	28.400	30.861
25	5.141	7.765	10.425	13.094	15.755	18.400	21.023	23.619	26.185	28.717	31.211
26	5.109	7.766	10.464	13.171	15.872	18.556	21.218	23.851	26.453	29.019	31.545
27	5.076	7.764	10.498	13.243	15.982	18.704	21.403	24.072	26.708	29.306	31.862
28	5.042	7.760	10.528	13.310	16.086	18.844	21.578	24.282	26.950	29.579	32.164
29	5.008	7.754	10.555	13.372	16.183	18.976	21.744	24.481	27.181	29.839	32.452
30	4.973	7.746	10.578	13.429	16.274	19.101	21.902	24.670	27.400	30.087	32.727

Table A.5: European-Style At-the-Money Put Premiums as a Function of Time and Volatility
Stock Price = $100
Strike Price = $100

Mo	\multicolumn{11}{c}{Volatility}
	0.15	0.20	0.25	0.30	0.35	0.40	0.45	0.50	0.55	0.60	0.65
1	1.485	2.057	2.629	3.202	3.776	4.349	4.922	5.495	6.067	6.639	7.211
2	1.965	2.767	3.572	4.378	5.185	5.991	6.797	7.603	8.408	9.212	10.015
3	2.283	3.258	4.237	5.220	6.202	7.185	8.167	9.149	10.128	11.107	12.083
4	2.520	3.636	4.760	5.888	7.018	8.147	9.275	10.401	11.526	12.649	13.769
5	2.705	3.943	5.192	6.447	7.703	8.959	10.214	11.466	12.716	13.963	15.207
6	2.854	4.199	5.560	6.927	8.296	9.665	11.032	12.397	13.758	15.115	16.468
7	2.976	4.419	5.879	7.348	8.819	10.290	11.760	13.225	14.687	16.143	17.594
8	3.079	4.608	6.160	7.722	9.287	10.852	12.414	13.973	15.526	17.073	18.613
9	3.164	4.774	6.410	8.058	9.709	11.361	13.009	14.653	16.291	17.921	19.544
10	3.237	4.920	6.634	8.362	10.094	11.826	13.555	15.278	16.994	18.702	20.400
11	3.298	5.049	6.836	8.639	10.446	12.254	14.057	15.855	17.644	19.423	21.192
12	3.349	5.165	7.020	8.892	10.771	12.649	14.523	16.390	18.248	20.095	21.929
13	3.393	5.267	7.187	9.125	11.071	13.016	14.956	16.889	18.811	20.721	22.617
14	3.429	5.360	7.339	9.340	11.349	13.358	15.361	17.355	19.338	21.307	23.262
15	3.460	5.442	7.479	9.539	11.608	13.677	15.739	17.792	19.832	21.858	23.867
16	3.485	5.516	7.607	9.724	11.850	13.975	16.094	18.203	20.298	22.377	24.437
17	3.505	5.583	7.725	9.895	12.076	14.256	16.429	18.590	20.737	22.866	24.975
18	3.521	5.642	7.834	10.055	12.287	14.519	16.743	18.955	21.151	23.328	25.483
19	3.533	5.696	7.934	10.204	12.486	14.767	17.041	19.300	21.543	23.765	25.964
20	3.542	5.744	8.026	10.343	12.672	15.001	17.321	19.627	21.915	24.180	26.420
21	3.548	5.787	8.111	10.472	12.847	15.222	17.587	19.937	22.267	24.573	26.853
22	3.552	5.825	8.189	10.594	13.012	15.431	17.839	20.231	22.601	24.947	27.264
23	3.553	5.859	8.262	10.707	13.168	15.628	18.077	20.509	22.919	25.302	27.655
24	3.551	5.889	8.329	10.813	13.314	15.815	18.304	20.774	23.222	25.640	28.027
25	3.548	5.915	8.390	10.913	13.452	15.992	18.519	21.026	23.509	25.962	28.382
26	3.543	5.938	8.447	11.006	13.583	16.159	18.723	21.266	23.783	26.269	28.719
27	3.536	5.957	8.499	11.093	13.706	16.318	18.917	21.495	24.044	26.561	29.041
28	3.527	5.974	8.547	11.174	13.822	16.469	19.102	21.712	24.293	26.840	29.348
29	3.517	5.988	8.591	11.251	13.932	16.612	19.277	21.919	24.531	27.106	29.640
30	3.506	6.000	8.631	11.322	14.035	16.747	19.444	22.117	24.757	27.360	29.920

Table A.6: European-Style Put Premiums
as a Function of Time and Volatility
Stock Price = $100
Strike Price = $95

Mo	Volatility										
	0.15	0.20	0.25	0.30	0.35	0.40	0.45	0.50	0.55	0.60	0.65
1	0.192	0.490	0.874	1.308	1.774	2.262	2.764	3.278	3.798	4.325	4.856
2	0.494	1.037	1.667	2.345	3.053	3.779	4.518	5.265	6.019	6.777	7.538
3	0.750	1.470	2.278	3.134	4.018	4.920	5.833	6.754	7.681	8.611	9.543
4	0.964	1.825	2.777	3.777	4.806	5.852	6.909	7.973	9.042	10.113	11.186
5	1.144	2.125	3.199	4.324	5.476	6.647	7.827	9.015	10.206	11.400	12.593
6	1.298	2.383	3.565	4.799	6.061	7.342	8.632	9.929	11.229	12.530	13.830
7	1.430	2.608	3.887	5.219	6.581	7.960	9.350	10.746	12.144	13.542	14.937
8	1.546	2.806	4.173	5.595	7.048	8.518	9.999	11.484	12.972	14.457	15.940
9	1.647	2.983	4.430	5.935	7.471	9.026	10.590	12.159	13.728	15.295	16.857
10	1.736	3.142	4.663	6.245	7.859	9.491	11.133	12.779	14.424	16.066	17.702
11	1.815	3.285	4.876	6.529	8.215	9.920	11.635	13.353	15.069	16.780	18.485
12	1.885	3.414	5.070	6.790	8.544	10.318	12.101	13.886	15.669	17.445	19.214
13	1.947	3.531	5.248	7.031	8.850	10.688	12.535	14.384	16.229	18.067	19.895
14	2.002	3.638	5.412	7.255	9.135	11.034	12.941	14.850	16.754	18.650	20.534
15	2.051	3.736	5.563	7.463	9.400	11.357	13.323	15.288	17.247	19.197	21.135
16	2.094	3.825	5.703	7.657	9.649	11.661	13.681	15.700	17.712	19.714	21.701
17	2.133	3.906	5.833	7.838	9.882	11.947	14.019	16.089	18.151	20.201	22.236
18	2.168	3.981	5.954	8.007	10.101	12.216	14.337	16.456	18.566	20.663	22.742
19	2.198	4.050	6.067	8.166	10.308	12.470	14.639	16.804	18.960	21.100	23.222
20	2.225	4.113	6.171	8.315	10.502	12.710	14.924	17.134	19.333	21.515	23.677
21	2.249	4.170	6.269	8.455	10.686	12.937	15.195	17.447	19.687	21.909	24.110
22	2.270	4.223	6.360	8.586	10.859	13.153	15.452	17.745	20.024	22.284	24.521
23	2.288	4.272	6.444	8.710	11.023	13.357	15.696	18.028	20.345	22.641	24.912
24	2.303	4.316	6.524	8.827	11.178	13.551	15.928	18.297	20.650	22.981	25.285
25	2.317	4.357	6.597	8.936	11.325	13.735	16.149	18.553	20.941	23.305	25.641
26	2.328	4.394	6.666	9.040	11.464	13.910	16.359	18.798	21.219	23.615	25.980
27	2.337	4.428	6.731	9.137	11.596	14.076	16.559	19.031	21.484	23.910	26.304
28	2.345	4.459	6.791	9.229	11.721	14.234	16.750	19.254	21.737	24.192	26.613
29	2.351	4.487	6.847	9.316	11.839	14.385	16.932	19.466	21.979	24.461	26.908
30	2.355	4.513	6.899	9.398	11.952	14.528	17.106	19.669	22.209	24.719	27.190

Table A.7: European-Style Put Premiums
as a Function of Time and Volatility
Stock Price = $100
Strike Price = $90

Mo	Volatility										
	0.15	0.20	0.25	0.30	0.35	0.40	0.45	0.50	0.55	0.60	0.65
1	0.007	0.058	0.187	0.394	0.666	0.989	1.352	1.745	2.161	2.596	3.046
2	0.066	0.274	0.622	1.074	1.599	2.175	2.788	3.429	4.089	4.766	5.453
3	0.162	0.524	1.051	1.688	2.399	3.159	3.954	4.773	5.611	6.461	7.322
4	0.268	0.765	1.440	2.228	3.088	3.997	4.938	5.903	6.884	7.877	8.878
5	0.374	0.988	1.790	2.706	3.693	4.728	5.794	6.883	7.987	9.101	10.223
6	0.474	1.193	2.105	3.132	4.232	5.378	6.554	7.752	8.964	10.185	11.412
7	0.568	1.380	2.390	3.518	4.717	5.962	7.238	8.534	9.842	11.160	12.482
8	0.656	1.550	2.650	3.868	5.158	6.494	7.860	9.245	10.642	12.046	13.454
9	0.736	1.707	2.887	4.189	5.562	6.982	8.430	9.897	11.375	12.860	14.346
10	0.811	1.851	3.106	4.484	5.935	7.431	8.956	10.499	12.052	13.611	15.170
11	0.879	1.983	3.308	4.757	6.279	7.848	9.445	11.058	12.681	14.309	15.935
12	0.942	2.105	3.494	5.010	6.600	8.236	9.899	11.579	13.268	14.959	16.648
13	1.000	2.218	3.667	5.245	6.899	8.598	10.325	12.067	13.817	15.569	17.316
14	1.053	2.323	3.828	5.465	7.179	8.938	10.724	12.525	14.333	16.141	17.944
15	1.102	2.420	3.979	5.671	7.441	9.257	11.100	12.957	14.819	16.680	18.535
16	1.146	2.510	4.119	5.864	7.688	9.558	11.454	13.364	15.278	17.189	19.092
17	1.188	2.593	4.250	6.046	7.920	9.841	11.788	13.748	15.712	17.670	19.620
18	1.226	2.671	4.373	6.216	8.140	10.110	12.105	14.113	16.123	18.126	20.119
19	1.261	2.744	4.489	6.377	8.347	10.363	12.405	14.458	16.512	18.559	20.594
20	1.293	2.811	4.597	6.529	8.543	10.604	12.690	14.787	16.883	18.971	21.044
21	1.322	2.874	4.699	6.672	8.729	10.832	12.961	15.099	17.235	19.362	21.473
22	1.349	2.933	4.794	6.807	8.905	11.049	13.218	15.396	17.571	19.735	21.881
23	1.373	2.987	4.884	6.935	9.072	11.256	13.464	15.680	17.891	20.090	22.270
24	1.396	3.038	4.969	7.056	9.230	11.452	13.697	15.950	18.196	20.429	22.641
25	1.416	3.086	5.049	7.171	9.381	11.639	13.920	16.207	18.488	20.753	22.995
26	1.435	3.130	5.124	7.280	9.525	11.817	14.133	16.454	18.766	21.062	23.334
27	1.452	3.171	5.195	7.383	9.661	11.987	14.336	16.689	19.032	21.357	23.657
28	1.467	3.210	5.262	7.481	9.791	12.150	14.530	16.914	19.287	21.640	23.966
29	1.481	3.245	5.325	7.573	9.915	12.304	14.716	17.129	19.530	21.911	24.262
30	1.493	3.278	5.384	7.661	10.032	12.452	14.893	17.335	19.764	22.170	24.545

Table A.8: European-Style Put Premiums
as a Function of Time and Volatility
Stock Price = $100
Strike Price = $85

Mo	Volatility										
	0.15	0.20	0.25	0.30	0.35	0.40	0.45	0.50	0.55	0.60	0.65
1	0.000	0.003	0.023	0.080	0.188	0.347	0.555	0.806	1.092	1.410	1.752
2	0.004	0.046	0.175	0.404	0.723	1.118	1.571	2.072	2.609	3.175	3.764
3	0.020	0.139	0.400	0.795	1.295	1.875	2.515	3.200	3.919	4.665	5.432
4	0.050	0.256	0.645	1.185	1.837	2.568	3.359	4.192	5.059	5.949	6.859
5	0.088	0.383	0.889	1.556	2.337	3.198	4.116	5.076	6.067	7.081	8.111
6	0.132	0.512	1.123	1.903	2.797	3.772	4.802	5.873	6.973	8.094	9.230
7	0.178	0.638	1.346	2.226	3.222	4.298	5.429	6.599	7.796	9.013	10.244
8	0.226	0.760	1.556	2.527	3.616	4.783	6.005	7.264	8.550	9.854	11.170
9	0.273	0.877	1.753	2.809	3.982	5.233	6.538	7.879	9.246	10.629	12.024
10	0.319	0.989	1.939	3.072	4.323	5.652	7.033	8.451	9.892	11.349	12.815
11	0.364	1.094	2.113	3.318	4.641	6.043	7.496	8.984	10.494	12.019	13.553
12	0.407	1.194	2.278	3.549	4.940	6.409	7.929	9.483	11.058	12.647	14.242
13	0.449	1.289	2.432	3.767	5.221	6.754	8.336	9.952	11.588	13.236	14.890
14	0.488	1.378	2.578	3.972	5.486	7.078	8.720	10.394	12.087	13.791	15.499
15	0.525	1.462	2.716	4.165	5.736	7.384	9.082	10.811	12.558	14.315	16.074
16	0.561	1.542	2.846	4.348	5.972	7.674	9.425	11.206	13.004	14.811	16.618
17	0.594	1.617	2.969	4.520	6.196	7.948	9.749	11.580	13.427	15.281	17.133
18	0.626	1.688	3.085	4.684	6.408	8.209	10.058	11.935	13.828	15.727	17.622
19	0.656	1.755	3.195	4.839	6.609	8.456	10.351	12.273	14.210	16.151	18.087
20	0.684	1.818	3.299	4.986	6.800	8.691	10.630	12.595	14.573	16.554	18.529
21	0.710	1.878	3.397	5.126	6.982	8.916	10.896	12.902	14.920	16.939	18.950
22	0.735	1.935	3.491	5.259	7.155	9.129	11.149	13.194	15.250	17.306	19.352
23	0.758	1.988	3.579	5.385	7.320	9.333	11.391	13.474	15.566	17.656	19.735
24	0.780	2.039	3.664	5.506	7.478	9.527	11.622	13.741	15.868	17.991	20.101
25	0.801	2.086	3.743	5.620	7.628	9.713	11.843	13.996	16.156	18.311	20.452
26	0.820	2.131	3.819	5.729	7.771	9.891	12.055	14.241	16.433	18.617	20.786
27	0.838	2.174	3.891	5.833	7.908	10.060	12.257	14.475	16.697	18.911	21.107
28	0.855	2.214	3.960	5.932	8.038	10.223	12.451	14.699	16.950	19.192	21.414
29	0.870	2.252	4.024	6.027	8.163	10.379	12.637	14.914	17.193	19.461	21.708
30	0.885	2.287	4.086	6.117	8.283	10.527	12.815	15.120	17.426	19.719	21.990

Table A.9: European-Style Put Premiums
as a Function of Time and Volatility
Stock Price = $100
Strike Price = $80

Mo	Volatility										
	0.15	0.20	0.25	0.30	0.35	0.40	0.45	0.50	0.55	0.60	0.65
1	0.000	0.000	0.001	0.010	0.037	0.093	0.184	0.312	0.477	0.676	0.907
2	0.000	0.005	0.035	0.119	0.273	0.500	0.792	1.143	1.541	1.981	2.454
3	0.001	0.025	0.120	0.318	0.619	1.012	1.482	2.013	2.595	3.216	3.870
4	0.006	0.065	0.242	0.556	0.994	1.533	2.152	2.834	3.564	4.333	5.132
5	0.014	0.118	0.382	0.808	1.369	2.036	2.784	3.593	4.450	5.343	6.265
6	0.026	0.182	0.530	1.059	1.731	2.512	3.373	4.294	5.262	6.264	7.293
7	0.042	0.251	0.681	1.305	2.078	2.960	3.922	4.944	6.010	7.109	8.232
8	0.060	0.323	0.831	1.543	2.408	3.382	4.436	5.548	6.703	7.889	9.099
9	0.081	0.396	0.977	1.771	2.720	3.779	4.917	6.112	7.348	8.614	9.902
10	0.102	0.469	1.120	1.989	3.016	4.153	5.369	6.640	7.951	9.291	10.650
11	0.125	0.542	1.257	2.198	3.297	4.507	5.794	7.136	8.517	9.924	11.350
12	0.148	0.612	1.389	2.396	3.563	4.841	6.195	7.603	9.049	10.519	12.007
13	0.171	0.681	1.516	2.585	3.816	5.158	6.575	8.045	9.551	11.081	12.626
14	0.194	0.748	1.637	2.766	4.057	5.458	6.934	8.462	10.025	11.611	13.210
15	0.217	0.813	1.754	2.938	4.285	5.743	7.275	8.858	10.475	12.113	13.763
16	0.239	0.875	1.865	3.102	4.503	6.014	7.600	9.234	10.902	12.589	14.287
17	0.261	0.935	1.972	3.258	4.710	6.272	7.908	9.592	11.308	13.042	14.785
18	0.283	0.993	2.074	3.408	4.908	6.519	8.202	9.933	11.694	13.472	15.258
19	0.303	1.049	2.171	3.550	5.097	6.754	8.482	10.258	12.062	13.883	15.709
20	0.323	1.102	2.265	3.687	5.277	6.978	8.750	10.568	12.414	14.274	16.139
21	0.343	1.152	2.354	3.817	5.450	7.192	9.006	10.865	12.750	14.648	16.549
22	0.361	1.201	2.439	3.942	5.615	7.398	9.251	11.148	13.071	15.005	16.940
23	0.379	1.248	2.521	4.061	5.773	7.594	9.485	11.420	13.378	15.347	17.315
24	0.396	1.292	2.599	4.175	5.924	7.782	9.710	11.680	13.673	15.675	17.673
25	0.413	1.335	2.674	4.285	6.069	7.963	9.925	11.929	13.955	15.988	18.016
26	0.428	1.376	2.745	4.389	6.207	8.135	10.132	12.168	14.226	16.289	18.345
27	0.443	1.415	2.814	4.490	6.341	8.301	10.330	12.398	14.485	16.577	18.660
28	0.457	1.452	2.879	4.586	6.468	8.461	10.520	12.618	14.734	16.853	18.962
29	0.471	1.487	2.942	4.678	6.591	8.613	10.703	12.830	14.974	17.119	19.252
30	0.484	1.521	3.002	4.766	6.708	8.760	10.878	13.033	15.204	17.373	19.530

Table A.10: European-Style Put Premiums
as a Function of Time and Volatility
Stock Price = $100
Strike Price = $75

Mo	Volatility										
	0.15	0.20	0.25	0.30	0.35	0.40	0.45	0.50	0.55	0.60	0.65
1	0.000	0.000	0.000	0.001	0.005	0.018	0.047	0.098	0.174	0.279	0.412
2	0.000	0.000	0.004	0.026	0.083	0.189	0.349	0.564	0.830	1.142	1.494
3	0.000	0.003	0.027	0.104	0.255	0.486	0.795	1.173	1.611	2.098	2.628
4	0.000	0.012	0.073	0.224	0.480	0.837	1.284	1.805	2.388	3.022	3.697
5	0.001	0.028	0.137	0.370	0.730	1.205	1.774	2.421	3.130	3.889	4.687
6	0.003	0.051	0.216	0.531	0.990	1.572	2.252	3.010	3.829	4.698	5.604
7	0.007	0.081	0.303	0.699	1.250	1.930	2.710	3.568	4.487	5.453	6.455
8	0.012	0.115	0.396	0.869	1.507	2.277	3.148	4.097	5.105	6.159	7.247
9	0.018	0.153	0.491	1.038	1.757	2.611	3.566	4.597	5.687	6.821	7.988
10	0.025	0.193	0.589	1.205	2.000	2.930	3.963	5.071	6.236	7.444	8.682
11	0.034	0.235	0.686	1.368	2.234	3.237	4.341	5.520	6.755	8.031	9.336
12	0.043	0.278	0.782	1.527	2.459	3.530	4.701	5.947	7.247	8.585	9.952
13	0.054	0.322	0.876	1.681	2.676	3.810	5.045	6.352	7.713	9.111	10.535
14	0.064	0.366	0.969	1.830	2.884	4.078	5.372	6.738	8.156	9.609	11.087
15	0.075	0.409	1.060	1.975	3.085	4.335	5.685	7.106	8.577	10.083	11.612
16	0.087	0.452	1.148	2.114	3.277	4.581	5.984	7.457	8.979	10.534	12.110
17	0.098	0.495	1.234	2.248	3.462	4.817	6.270	7.792	9.362	10.963	12.585
18	0.110	0.536	1.317	2.378	3.640	5.043	6.544	8.113	9.728	11.374	13.037
19	0.122	0.577	1.397	2.503	3.811	5.260	6.806	8.420	10.078	11.765	13.470
20	0.134	0.617	1.475	2.623	3.975	5.468	7.058	8.714	10.413	12.140	13.882
21	0.145	0.656	1.551	2.739	4.133	5.668	7.299	8.996	10.734	12.499	14.277
22	0.157	0.694	1.624	2.851	4.285	5.860	7.531	9.266	11.042	12.843	14.655
23	0.168	0.730	1.694	2.958	4.431	6.045	7.754	9.525	11.337	13.172	15.017
24	0.179	0.766	1.762	3.062	4.571	6.222	7.968	9.775	11.621	13.488	15.365
25	0.190	0.800	1.827	3.162	4.707	6.393	8.173	10.014	11.893	13.792	15.698
26	0.201	0.834	1.891	3.258	4.837	6.557	8.371	10.245	12.154	14.083	16.017
27	0.211	0.866	1.952	3.351	4.963	6.716	8.561	10.466	12.406	14.363	16.324
28	0.221	0.897	2.010	3.440	5.083	6.868	8.745	10.679	12.648	14.632	16.618
29	0.231	0.927	2.067	3.526	5.200	7.015	8.921	10.885	12.881	14.891	16.901
30	0.240	0.956	2.122	3.609	5.312	7.156	9.091	11.082	13.105	15.140	17.173

Table A.11: European-Style Put Premiums as a Function of Time and Volatility
Stock Price = $100
Strike Price = $70

Mo	\multicolumn{11}{c}{Volatility}
	0.15	0.20	0.25	0.30	0.35	0.40	0.45	0.50	0.55	0.60	0.65
1	0.000	0.000	0.000	0.000	0.000	0.002	0.009	0.023	0.051	0.096	0.160
2	0.000	0.000	0.000	0.004	0.019	0.058	0.130	0.243	0.399	0.598	0.838
3	0.000	0.000	0.004	0.026	0.087	0.203	0.381	0.623	0.925	1.280	1.683
4	0.000	0.001	0.017	0.075	0.202	0.410	0.702	1.070	1.505	2.000	2.544
5	0.000	0.005	0.040	0.146	0.348	0.653	1.053	1.537	2.093	2.710	3.376
6	0.000	0.011	0.073	0.234	0.514	0.912	1.414	2.005	2.669	3.393	4.167
7	0.001	0.020	0.115	0.334	0.692	1.178	1.775	2.463	3.224	4.045	4.914
8	0.002	0.033	0.164	0.443	0.876	1.446	2.130	2.906	3.757	4.665	5.621
9	0.003	0.049	0.218	0.556	1.061	1.710	2.475	3.334	4.265	5.254	6.288
10	0.005	0.067	0.276	0.673	1.246	1.969	2.810	3.744	4.751	5.814	6.920
11	0.007	0.087	0.337	0.790	1.429	2.221	3.133	4.138	5.215	6.346	7.518
12	0.010	0.109	0.399	0.908	1.609	2.467	3.445	4.516	5.657	6.852	8.086
13	0.013	0.132	0.463	1.024	1.785	2.705	3.746	4.879	6.080	7.334	8.626
14	0.017	0.157	0.527	1.140	1.957	2.935	4.035	5.226	6.485	7.794	9.139
15	0.021	0.182	0.591	1.253	2.124	3.158	4.314	5.559	6.872	8.233	9.629
16	0.026	0.208	0.655	1.364	2.287	3.373	4.582	5.879	7.242	8.653	10.096
17	0.031	0.235	0.718	1.473	2.445	3.581	4.840	6.187	7.598	9.054	10.543
18	0.036	0.261	0.781	1.579	2.598	3.782	5.088	6.482	7.938	9.439	10.970
19	0.041	0.288	0.842	1.682	2.746	3.976	5.327	6.766	8.265	9.808	11.379
20	0.047	0.315	0.903	1.783	2.890	4.164	5.558	7.038	8.579	10.161	11.770
21	0.053	0.341	0.962	1.880	3.029	4.344	5.780	7.301	8.881	10.501	12.146
22	0.059	0.367	1.019	1.976	3.163	4.519	5.995	7.554	9.171	10.827	12.506
23	0.065	0.393	1.076	2.068	3.294	4.688	6.201	7.797	9.450	11.140	12.852
24	0.071	0.419	1.131	2.158	3.420	4.851	6.400	8.032	9.719	11.441	13.184
25	0.077	0.444	1.185	2.245	3.542	5.008	6.593	8.258	9.978	11.731	13.503
26	0.083	0.468	1.237	2.329	3.660	5.161	6.778	8.476	10.227	12.010	13.810
27	0.089	0.492	1.288	2.411	3.775	5.308	6.958	8.687	10.467	12.279	14.106
28	0.095	0.516	1.338	2.490	3.885	5.450	7.131	8.890	10.699	12.538	14.390
29	0.101	0.539	1.386	2.567	3.993	5.587	7.298	9.086	10.922	12.787	14.664
30	0.106	0.562	1.433	2.642	4.096	5.720	7.459	9.275	11.138	13.027	14.927

Table A.12: European-Style Put Premiums
as a Function of Time and Volatility
Stock Price = $100
Strike Price = $65

Mo	Volatility										
	0.15	0.20	0.25	0.30	0.35	0.40	0.45	0.50	0.55	0.60	0.65
1	0.000	0.000	0.000	0.000	0.000	0.000	0.001	0.004	0.012	0.026	0.051
2	0.000	0.000	0.000	0.000	0.003	0.014	0.040	0.089	0.167	0.279	0.424
3	0.000	0.000	0.000	0.005	0.024	0.071	0.159	0.295	0.483	0.720	1.005
4	0.000	0.000	0.003	0.020	0.071	0.176	0.345	0.581	0.882	1.242	1.657
5	0.000	0.001	0.009	0.048	0.144	0.317	0.573	0.908	1.318	1.792	2.322
6	0.000	0.002	0.020	0.088	0.238	0.483	0.825	1.256	1.766	2.343	2.978
7	0.000	0.004	0.036	0.140	0.346	0.664	1.090	1.610	2.213	2.884	3.613
8	0.000	0.007	0.057	0.200	0.465	0.855	1.360	1.964	2.652	3.409	4.223
9	0.000	0.012	0.083	0.268	0.591	1.050	1.630	2.313	3.080	3.916	4.808
10	0.001	0.019	0.113	0.340	0.721	1.247	1.899	2.655	3.496	4.405	5.368
11	0.001	0.026	0.146	0.417	0.854	1.444	2.163	2.988	3.897	4.874	5.903
12	0.002	0.036	0.181	0.496	0.988	1.639	2.422	3.311	4.284	5.324	6.415
13	0.002	0.046	0.219	0.577	1.122	1.831	2.674	3.624	4.658	5.757	6.905
14	0.003	0.058	0.259	0.659	1.255	2.020	2.920	3.928	5.018	6.172	7.374
15	0.005	0.070	0.299	0.741	1.387	2.205	3.160	4.221	5.365	6.571	7.824
16	0.006	0.084	0.341	0.824	1.517	2.385	3.392	4.505	5.699	6.954	8.254
17	0.008	0.098	0.383	0.906	1.645	2.562	3.617	4.779	6.021	7.322	8.667
18	0.009	0.112	0.426	0.987	1.770	2.734	3.836	5.044	6.331	7.677	9.064
19	0.011	0.127	0.469	1.067	1.893	2.901	4.048	5.300	6.630	8.017	9.445
20	0.014	0.143	0.512	1.146	2.013	3.063	4.254	5.548	6.919	8.346	9.811
21	0.016	0.159	0.554	1.224	2.130	3.222	4.453	5.787	7.197	8.662	10.163
22	0.018	0.175	0.597	1.301	2.245	3.375	4.646	6.019	7.466	8.966	10.501
23	0.021	0.191	0.639	1.376	2.356	3.525	4.833	6.242	7.725	9.259	10.827
24	0.024	0.207	0.680	1.449	2.465	3.670	5.014	6.459	7.976	9.542	11.141
25	0.026	0.224	0.721	1.521	2.571	3.811	5.189	6.668	8.218	9.815	11.444
26	0.029	0.240	0.761	1.592	2.675	3.947	5.359	6.871	8.451	10.079	11.735
27	0.032	0.256	0.801	1.661	2.775	4.080	5.524	7.067	8.677	10.333	12.016
28	0.035	0.272	0.840	1.728	2.873	4.209	5.684	7.256	8.895	10.578	12.287
29	0.038	0.288	0.878	1.793	2.968	4.335	5.839	7.440	9.106	10.815	12.548
30	0.041	0.304	0.915	1.857	3.061	4.456	5.989	7.618	9.311	11.044	12.800

Table A.13: European-Style Put Premiums
as a Function of Time and Volatility
Stock Price = $100
Strike Price = $60

Mo	Volatility										
	0.15	0.20	0.25	0.30	0.35	0.40	0.45	0.50	0.55	0.60	0.65
1	0.000	0.000	0.000	0.000	0.000	0.000	0.000	0.000	0.002	0.005	0.013
2	0.000	0.000	0.000	0.000	0.000	0.002	0.009	0.026	0.059	0.112	0.190
3	0.000	0.000	0.000	0.001	0.005	0.020	0.056	0.122	0.224	0.367	0.550
4	0.000	0.000	0.000	0.004	0.021	0.064	0.149	0.283	0.472	0.714	1.009
5	0.000	0.000	0.001	0.012	0.051	0.135	0.280	0.492	0.770	1.111	1.511
6	0.000	0.000	0.004	0.027	0.095	0.229	0.439	0.730	1.096	1.531	2.028
7	0.000	0.000	0.009	0.049	0.153	0.339	0.618	0.986	1.436	1.959	2.545
8	0.000	0.001	0.016	0.078	0.221	0.463	0.809	1.251	1.781	2.385	3.053
9	0.000	0.002	0.026	0.113	0.297	0.596	1.007	1.521	2.125	2.805	3.550
10	0.000	0.004	0.039	0.153	0.381	0.735	1.210	1.792	2.466	3.217	4.031
11	0.000	0.006	0.054	0.197	0.469	0.878	1.414	2.060	2.800	3.617	4.497
12	0.000	0.009	0.071	0.245	0.561	1.023	1.618	2.326	3.128	4.006	4.947
13	0.000	0.013	0.091	0.295	0.656	1.170	1.820	2.586	3.447	4.384	5.381
14	0.000	0.017	0.112	0.348	0.752	1.316	2.021	2.842	3.758	4.749	5.800
15	0.001	0.023	0.135	0.403	0.849	1.462	2.218	3.091	4.060	5.102	6.203
16	0.001	0.028	0.159	0.459	0.946	1.606	2.411	3.335	4.353	5.444	6.592
17	0.001	0.035	0.184	0.516	1.044	1.748	2.601	3.572	4.637	5.774	6.967
18	0.002	0.041	0.210	0.574	1.141	1.889	2.787	3.803	4.913	6.094	7.328
19	0.002	0.049	0.237	0.632	1.237	2.027	2.968	4.028	5.180	6.402	7.677
20	0.003	0.057	0.264	0.689	1.332	2.162	3.145	4.247	5.439	6.701	8.013
21	0.004	0.065	0.292	0.747	1.426	2.295	3.318	4.459	5.691	6.990	8.338
22	0.005	0.073	0.321	0.805	1.518	2.426	3.486	4.665	5.934	7.269	8.651
23	0.005	0.082	0.349	0.862	1.610	2.553	3.650	4.866	6.170	7.539	8.953
24	0.006	0.091	0.378	0.919	1.699	2.677	3.810	5.061	6.399	7.800	9.245
25	0.007	0.100	0.406	0.975	1.787	2.799	3.966	5.250	6.620	8.052	9.528
26	0.008	0.110	0.435	1.030	1.873	2.918	4.118	5.434	6.835	8.297	9.800
27	0.010	0.120	0.463	1.085	1.958	3.034	4.265	5.612	7.043	8.534	10.064
28	0.011	0.129	0.491	1.139	2.041	3.147	4.409	5.786	7.245	8.763	10.318
29	0.012	0.139	0.520	1.192	2.122	3.258	4.549	5.954	7.441	8.985	10.564
30	0.013	0.149	0.547	1.244	2.201	3.365	4.685	6.118	7.631	9.199	10.802

B

APPENDIX B

AMERICAN PUT PREMIUMS

The tables that follow show the option premiums for American-style LEAP puts based on the formulas contained in Chapter 15. They are based on a stock price of $100 and exercise (strike) prices ranging from $120 down to $60 in steps of $5. Dividend rates of zero, 1%, 2%, and 3% are considered. Each table is presented in matrix format, with volatilities ranging from a low of 0.150 through a high of 0.650. Time to expiration ranges from one month to a maximum of 30 months. The risk-free interest rate in all instances is 6%.

To obtain premiums for stock prices other than $100, simply scale the tables. For example, suppose you want to know the put premium for a stock price of $50, strike price of $45, for a volatility of 0.40, expiration date 24 months away, and annual dividend rate of 2%. From Table B.33, we see that the premium for a $100 stock with strike $90 for volatility 0.40, 24-month expiration, and 2% dividend is $13.430. The premium for the $50 stock with strike $45 is therefore half this amount, or $6.715 (i.e., $671.50 per contract).

Suppose the stock price was $60, strike price was $50, for the same volatility and expiration. From Table B.34, we see that the premium for a $100 stock with strike $85 is $11.213, and from Table B.35, we see that the premium for a $100 stock with strike $80 is $9.201. Multiplying each of these figures by 0.60 shows that the premium for a $60 stock with strike $51 is $6.728, and the premium for a $60 stock with strike $48 is $5.521. The premium for the $60 stock with strike $50 is therefore $5.521 + 0.667 x ($6.728 - $5.521), or $6.326 (i.e., $632.60 per contract).

Table B.1: American-Style Put Premiums
as a Function of Time and Volatility
Stock Price = $100
Strike Price = $120
Dividend Rate = 0%

Mo	Volatility										
	0.15	0.20	0.25	0.30	0.35	0.40	0.45	0.50	0.55	0.60	0.65
1	20.000	20.000	20.000	20.000	20.000	20.036	20.183	20.409	20.695	21.029	21.400
2	20.000	20.000	20.000	20.001	20.161	20.512	20.981	21.529	22.135	22.785	23.468
3	20.000	20.000	20.000	20.106	20.528	21.132	21.847	22.636	23.477	24.357	25.265
4	20.000	20.000	20.001	20.306	20.943	21.754	22.669	23.653	24.683	25.748	26.836
5	20.000	20.000	20.038	20.540	21.362	22.349	23.434	24.582	25.773	26.994	28.237
6	20.000	20.000	20.111	20.786	21.769	22.910	24.144	25.436	26.768	28.127	29.504
7	20.000	20.000	20.205	21.033	22.159	23.438	24.804	26.226	27.684	29.166	30.663
8	20.000	20.000	20.310	21.276	22.532	23.935	25.423	26.962	28.534	30.128	31.734
9	20.000	20.000	20.420	21.512	22.887	24.405	26.003	27.650	29.328	31.024	32.731
10	20.000	20.000	20.533	21.741	23.226	24.849	26.550	28.297	30.072	31.864	33.662
11	20.000	20.000	20.647	21.962	23.549	25.271	27.068	28.909	30.774	32.653	34.538
12	20.000	20.003	20.760	22.176	23.858	25.673	27.560	29.488	31.438	33.400	35.365
13	20.000	20.013	20.872	22.381	24.154	26.056	28.027	30.038	32.068	34.107	36.148
14	20.000	20.027	20.981	22.580	24.438	26.422	28.474	30.561	32.667	34.780	36.892
15	20.000	20.044	21.089	22.771	24.710	26.772	28.900	31.061	33.239	35.421	37.601
16	20.000	20.064	21.194	22.956	24.971	27.108	29.308	31.539	33.785	36.034	38.278
17	20.000	20.086	21.296	23.134	25.223	27.431	29.699	31.998	34.309	36.621	38.926
18	20.000	20.110	21.396	23.306	25.465	27.741	30.075	32.438	34.811	37.183	39.547
19	20.000	20.135	21.493	23.473	25.699	28.040	30.437	32.861	35.294	37.724	40.144
20	20.000	20.160	21.588	23.634	25.924	28.327	30.785	33.269	35.759	38.245	40.718
21	20.000	20.186	21.680	23.790	26.142	28.605	31.122	33.662	36.207	38.746	41.270
22	20.000	20.212	21.770	23.941	26.352	28.873	31.446	34.041	36.640	39.230	41.803
23	20.000	20.239	21.858	24.087	26.555	29.132	31.760	34.408	37.058	39.697	42.318
24	20.000	20.266	21.943	24.229	26.752	29.383	32.064	34.763	37.462	40.149	42.815
25	20.000	20.292	22.026	24.366	26.943	29.627	32.358	35.107	37.854	40.587	43.296
26	20.000	20.319	22.107	24.499	27.128	29.862	32.643	35.440	38.233	41.010	43.762
27	20.000	20.346	22.185	24.629	27.308	30.091	32.920	35.763	38.601	41.421	44.213
28	20.000	20.372	22.261	24.754	27.482	30.313	33.189	36.077	38.958	41.819	44.651
29	20.000	20.398	22.336	24.876	27.652	30.529	33.450	36.381	39.305	42.206	45.076
30	20.000	20.423	22.408	24.995	27.816	30.739	33.704	36.678	39.641	42.582	45.488

Table B.2: American-Style Put Premiums
as a Function of Time and Volatility
Stock Price = $100
Strike Price = $115
Dividend Rate = 0%

Mo	Volatility										
	0.15	0.20	0.25	0.30	0.35	0.40	0.45	0.50	0.55	0.60	0.65
1	15.000	15.000	15.000	15.002	15.111	15.336	15.637	15.993	16.391	16.822	17.277
2	15.000	15.000	15.007	15.241	15.673	16.217	16.832	17.497	18.197	18.924	19.670
3	15.000	15.000	15.125	15.614	16.291	17.071	17.916	18.804	19.722	20.662	21.617
4	15.000	15.000	15.306	16.004	16.878	17.848	18.878	19.945	21.039	22.151	23.277
5	15.000	15.010	15.506	16.380	17.422	18.554	19.741	20.961	22.205	23.465	24.734
6	15.000	15.048	15.711	16.738	17.927	19.200	20.524	21.880	23.255	24.644	26.041
7	15.000	15.102	15.912	17.076	18.395	19.796	21.243	22.719	24.214	25.719	27.230
8	15.000	15.165	16.107	17.395	18.833	20.348	21.908	23.495	25.097	26.707	28.321
9	15.000	15.232	16.295	17.696	19.242	20.864	22.528	24.216	25.917	27.624	29.333
10	15.000	15.303	16.475	17.980	19.628	21.348	23.108	24.890	26.683	28.480	30.277
11	15.000	15.373	16.648	18.250	19.992	21.804	23.654	25.523	27.402	29.283	31.162
12	15.000	15.444	16.813	18.507	20.337	22.236	24.169	26.121	28.080	30.040	31.996
13	15.000	15.514	16.972	18.751	20.665	22.645	24.658	26.687	28.722	30.756	32.785
14	15.000	15.583	17.124	18.984	20.977	23.034	25.122	27.225	29.332	31.436	33.534
15	15.000	15.650	17.271	19.207	21.275	23.404	25.564	27.737	29.912	32.084	34.246
16	15.000	15.716	17.411	19.420	21.559	23.758	25.986	28.226	30.467	32.702	34.926
17	15.000	15.780	17.546	19.625	21.831	24.097	26.391	28.694	30.998	33.293	35.576
18	15.000	15.842	17.676	19.821	22.093	24.422	26.778	29.143	31.506	33.860	36.199
19	15.000	15.903	17.802	20.010	22.343	24.734	27.151	29.575	31.995	34.404	36.797
20	15.000	15.962	17.922	20.191	22.585	25.035	27.509	29.990	32.465	34.927	37.371
21	15.000	16.019	18.038	20.365	22.817	25.324	27.854	30.389	32.918	35.431	37.925
22	15.000	16.074	18.150	20.534	23.041	25.603	28.187	30.775	33.354	35.917	38.458
23	15.000	16.128	18.258	20.696	23.258	25.873	28.509	31.147	33.776	36.386	38.972
24	15.000	16.180	18.363	20.853	23.467	26.134	28.820	31.507	34.183	36.839	39.469
25	15.000	16.230	18.463	21.005	23.669	26.386	29.121	31.856	34.577	37.278	39.950
26	15.001	16.279	18.561	21.152	23.865	26.630	29.412	32.193	34.959	37.702	40.415
27	15.002	16.326	18.655	21.294	24.055	26.867	29.695	32.520	35.329	38.114	40.866
28	15.003	16.372	18.747	21.432	24.239	27.096	29.969	32.838	35.688	38.512	41.303
29	15.005	16.416	18.835	21.565	24.417	27.319	30.235	33.146	36.037	38.900	41.727
30	15.007	16.458	18.921	21.695	24.591	27.536	30.494	33.445	36.376	39.276	42.138

Table B.3: American-Style Put Premiums
as a Function of Time and Volatility
Stock Price = $100
Strike Price = $110
Dividend Rate = 0%

Mo	Volatility										
	0.15	0.20	0.25	0.30	0.35	0.40	0.45	0.50	0.55	0.60	0.65
1	10.000	10.000	10.062	10.301	10.641	11.043	11.487	11.960	12.456	12.968	13.492
2	10.000	10.048	10.422	10.976	11.620	12.317	13.049	13.803	14.573	15.356	16.147
3	10.000	10.201	10.818	11.600	12.464	13.374	14.312	15.270	16.241	17.220	18.206
4	10.000	10.379	11.189	12.155	13.196	14.278	15.385	16.508	17.642	18.782	19.927
5	10.003	10.558	11.531	12.653	13.844	15.073	16.324	17.589	18.863	20.142	21.422
6	10.021	10.730	11.845	13.103	14.427	15.785	17.164	18.555	19.952	21.352	22.753
7	10.049	10.894	12.135	13.515	14.957	16.433	17.927	19.430	20.939	22.448	23.957
8	10.083	11.049	12.404	13.894	15.445	17.027	18.626	20.233	21.843	23.452	25.059
9	10.120	11.195	12.655	14.247	15.898	17.578	19.273	20.975	22.679	24.380	26.078
10	10.158	11.333	12.889	14.576	16.320	18.091	19.876	21.666	23.457	25.245	27.027
11	10.196	11.464	13.110	14.884	16.715	18.572	20.441	22.314	24.187	26.055	27.916
12	10.235	11.588	13.317	15.175	17.086	19.024	20.972	22.924	24.873	26.817	28.752
13	10.272	11.705	13.514	15.449	17.437	19.451	21.475	23.500	25.523	27.538	29.542
14	10.309	11.817	13.700	15.708	17.770	19.856	21.951	24.047	26.138	28.221	30.291
15	10.345	11.923	13.876	15.954	18.086	20.241	22.404	24.567	26.724	28.871	31.004
16	10.380	12.024	14.043	16.189	18.387	20.608	22.837	25.063	27.283	29.491	31.683
17	10.413	12.120	14.203	16.413	18.675	20.959	23.250	25.538	27.817	30.083	32.332
18	10.445	12.212	14.356	16.627	18.950	21.295	23.645	25.992	28.329	30.651	32.954
19	10.476	12.299	14.501	16.831	19.214	21.617	24.025	26.428	28.820	31.195	33.550
20	10.505	12.382	14.641	17.028	19.467	21.926	24.390	26.847	29.292	31.718	34.123
21	10.533	12.462	14.775	17.217	19.711	22.224	24.741	27.251	29.746	32.222	34.674
22	10.559	12.539	14.904	17.398	19.945	22.511	25.080	27.640	30.184	32.708	35.205
23	10.584	12.612	15.027	17.573	20.171	22.788	25.406	28.015	30.607	33.176	35.718
24	10.608	12.683	15.146	17.742	20.389	23.055	25.722	28.378	31.015	33.629	36.213
25	10.631	12.750	15.261	17.904	20.600	23.314	26.027	28.729	31.410	34.066	36.691
26	10.654	12.815	15.372	18.062	20.804	23.564	26.322	29.068	31.793	34.490	37.154
27	10.675	12.878	15.479	18.214	21.001	23.806	26.609	29.397	32.163	34.900	37.603
28	10.696	12.938	15.582	18.361	21.193	24.041	26.886	29.717	32.523	35.298	38.037
29	10.717	12.996	15.682	18.503	21.378	24.269	27.156	30.027	32.872	35.684	38.459
30	10.736	13.052	15.778	18.642	21.558	24.490	27.417	30.327	33.211	36.059	38.868

Table B.4: American-Style Put Premiums
as a Function of Time and Volatility
Stock Price = $100
Strike Price = $105
Dividend Rate = 0%

Mo	Volatility										
	0.15	0.20	0.25	0.30	0.35	0.40	0.45	0.50	0.55	0.60	0.65
1	5.047	5.360	5.793	6.279	6.795	7.330	7.876	8.430	8.990	9.554	10.122
2	5.255	5.865	6.578	7.334	8.112	8.903	9.703	10.507	11.316	12.126	12.938
3	5.461	6.282	7.196	8.148	9.118	10.099	11.086	12.077	13.070	14.064	15.058
4	5.646	6.635	7.711	8.822	9.950	11.087	12.229	13.373	14.518	15.662	16.806
5	5.811	6.941	8.156	9.404	10.668	11.939	13.214	14.490	15.767	17.041	18.314
6	5.958	7.212	8.549	9.918	11.302	12.693	14.086	15.480	16.873	18.264	19.651
7	6.091	7.455	8.902	10.380	11.872	13.371	14.872	16.373	17.871	19.366	20.857
8	6.212	7.675	9.222	10.800	12.392	13.990	15.590	17.188	18.784	20.374	21.960
9	6.322	7.876	9.515	11.185	12.870	14.560	16.251	17.940	19.625	21.305	22.977
10	6.423	8.061	9.785	11.542	13.313	15.089	16.866	18.640	20.408	22.170	23.924
11	6.515	8.232	10.037	11.875	13.727	15.584	17.440	19.294	21.141	22.980	24.809
12	6.600	8.391	10.271	12.186	14.114	16.048	17.980	19.908	21.829	23.741	25.642
13	6.679	8.539	10.491	12.478	14.480	16.486	18.490	20.489	22.480	24.460	26.428
14	6.753	8.678	10.699	12.755	14.825	16.900	18.972	21.039	23.096	25.141	27.173
15	6.822	8.809	10.894	13.016	15.153	17.293	19.431	21.562	23.682	25.789	27.881
16	6.886	8.933	11.080	13.265	15.464	17.668	19.868	22.060	24.240	26.407	28.556
17	6.947	9.049	11.256	13.501	15.762	18.025	20.285	22.536	24.774	26.996	29.200
18	7.004	9.160	11.423	13.727	16.045	18.367	20.684	22.992	25.285	27.561	29.817
19	7.058	9.266	11.583	13.942	16.317	18.695	21.067	23.429	25.775	28.103	30.409
20	7.109	9.366	11.736	14.149	16.578	19.009	21.435	23.849	26.246	28.624	30.978
21	7.157	9.462	11.882	14.347	16.828	19.312	21.789	24.253	26.699	29.125	31.525
22	7.203	9.553	12.022	14.538	17.069	19.603	22.129	24.642	27.136	29.607	32.052
23	7.246	9.640	12.157	14.721	17.301	19.884	22.458	25.018	27.558	30.073	32.560
24	7.288	9.724	12.286	14.897	17.525	20.155	22.776	25.381	27.965	30.523	33.051
25	7.327	9.804	12.410	15.067	17.741	20.416	23.082	25.732	28.358	30.957	33.525
26	7.364	9.881	12.530	15.231	17.950	20.670	23.379	26.071	28.739	31.378	33.984
27	7.400	9.955	12.645	15.390	18.152	20.915	23.667	26.400	29.109	31.786	34.428
28	7.434	10.026	12.757	15.543	18.348	21.153	23.946	26.720	29.466	32.181	34.859
29	7.466	10.094	12.864	15.691	18.537	21.383	24.217	27.029	29.814	32.565	35.277
30	7.497	10.160	12.968	15.835	18.721	21.607	24.479	27.330	30.151	32.937	35.682

Table B.5: American-Style Put Premiums
as a Function of Time and Volatility
Stock Price = $100
Strike Price = $100
Dividend Rate = 0%

Mo	Volatility										
	0.15	0.20	0.25	0.30	0.35	0.40	0.45	0.50	0.55	0.60	0.65
1	1.521	2.090	2.660	3.232	3.804	4.376	4.948	5.520	6.092	6.664	7.236
2	2.048	2.844	3.645	4.448	5.252	6.057	6.862	7.666	8.470	9.274	10.076
3	2.418	3.384	4.358	5.336	6.316	7.296	8.277	9.257	10.236	11.214	12.191
4	2.707	3.815	4.932	6.056	7.181	8.308	9.435	10.561	11.685	12.808	13.929
5	2.947	4.176	5.419	6.668	7.921	9.175	10.428	11.681	12.931	14.180	15.425
6	3.151	4.489	5.843	7.205	8.571	9.938	11.305	12.671	14.034	15.393	16.749
7	3.330	4.765	6.220	7.684	9.154	10.624	12.094	13.562	15.027	16.488	17.943
8	3.488	5.013	6.561	8.119	9.683	11.249	12.814	14.376	15.934	17.487	19.034
9	3.630	5.238	6.872	8.518	10.170	11.824	13.476	15.125	16.770	18.409	20.040
10	3.759	5.444	7.158	8.885	10.620	12.356	14.091	15.822	17.547	19.266	20.976
11	3.876	5.634	7.423	9.228	11.040	12.854	14.666	16.473	18.274	20.067	21.851
12	3.983	5.810	7.670	9.547	11.433	13.320	15.205	17.085	18.957	20.821	22.673
13	4.083	5.973	7.901	9.848	11.803	13.760	15.714	17.662	19.602	21.532	23.450
14	4.175	6.127	8.119	10.131	12.153	14.176	16.196	18.209	20.213	22.206	24.185
15	4.260	6.270	8.324	10.399	12.484	14.570	16.653	18.729	20.794	22.847	24.885
16	4.340	6.406	8.518	10.653	12.799	14.946	17.089	19.224	21.348	23.458	25.551
17	4.414	6.534	8.702	10.895	13.099	15.305	17.505	19.697	21.877	24.041	26.187
18	4.484	6.655	8.877	11.126	13.386	15.647	17.903	20.150	22.383	24.599	26.797
19	4.550	6.770	9.044	11.346	13.660	15.976	18.285	20.584	22.868	25.135	27.381
20	4.612	6.879	9.204	11.557	13.924	16.291	18.652	21.001	23.335	25.650	27.942
21	4.670	6.983	9.356	11.760	14.176	16.594	19.004	21.403	23.784	26.145	28.482
22	4.725	7.082	9.502	11.954	14.419	16.885	19.344	21.789	24.217	26.622	29.002
23	4.777	7.176	9.642	12.141	14.653	17.166	19.671	22.162	24.634	27.082	29.504
24	4.827	7.267	9.777	12.321	14.879	17.438	19.988	22.523	25.037	27.527	29.988
25	4.874	7.353	9.906	12.494	15.097	17.700	20.294	22.871	25.427	27.957	30.456
26	4.919	7.436	10.030	12.661	15.307	17.953	20.589	23.208	25.804	28.373	30.909
27	4.961	7.516	10.150	12.823	15.511	18.199	20.876	23.535	26.170	28.776	31.348
28	5.002	7.593	10.266	12.979	15.708	18.437	21.154	23.852	26.524	29.166	31.773
29	5.040	7.666	10.378	13.130	15.899	18.667	21.423	24.159	26.868	29.545	32.185
30	5.077	7.737	10.486	13.276	16.084	18.891	21.685	24.458	27.202	29.913	32.585

Table B.6: American-Style Put Premiums
as a Function of Time and Volatility
Stock Price = $100
Strike Price = $95
Dividend Rate = 0%

Mo	Volatility										
	0.15	0.20	0.25	0.30	0.35	0.40	0.45	0.50	0.55	0.60	0.65
1	0.197	0.499	0.884	1.320	1.787	2.276	2.779	3.292	3.813	4.340	4.872
2	0.516	1.066	1.700	2.382	3.091	3.819	4.559	5.308	6.062	6.821	7.583
3	0.793	1.525	2.341	3.201	4.089	4.993	5.909	6.832	7.761	8.692	9.626
4	1.032	1.911	2.874	3.881	4.914	5.964	7.025	8.092	9.164	10.238	11.313
5	1.240	2.244	3.333	4.466	5.626	6.802	7.988	9.180	10.375	11.573	12.770
6	1.423	2.538	3.738	4.984	6.256	7.543	8.841	10.144	11.450	12.756	14.062
7	1.587	2.801	4.102	5.449	6.823	8.212	9.610	11.014	12.419	13.825	15.228
8	1.735	3.039	4.432	5.873	7.339	8.822	10.313	11.809	13.306	14.802	16.294
9	1.870	3.257	4.735	6.262	7.815	9.384	10.961	12.542	14.124	15.703	17.278
10	1.993	3.457	5.015	6.622	8.256	9.906	11.563	13.225	14.885	16.542	18.193
11	2.106	3.643	5.275	6.958	8.668	10.394	12.127	13.863	15.597	17.327	19.050
12	2.211	3.815	5.518	7.272	9.054	10.852	12.656	14.463	16.267	18.065	19.856
13	2.308	3.977	5.747	7.568	9.418	11.284	13.156	15.030	16.900	18.763	20.616
14	2.398	4.128	5.961	7.848	9.763	11.693	13.630	15.567	17.499	19.424	21.338
15	2.483	4.271	6.164	8.112	10.089	12.081	14.080	16.078	18.069	20.052	22.023
16	2.562	4.405	6.357	8.364	10.400	12.452	14.509	16.564	18.613	20.651	22.676
17	2.636	4.532	6.540	8.603	10.696	12.805	14.918	17.029	19.132	21.224	23.301
18	2.706	4.653	6.714	8.831	10.980	13.143	15.310	17.474	19.630	21.772	23.898
19	2.772	4.768	6.880	9.050	11.251	13.467	15.686	17.902	20.107	22.298	24.472
20	2.835	4.877	7.038	9.259	11.511	13.778	16.047	18.312	20.566	22.803	25.022
21	2.893	4.981	7.190	9.460	11.761	14.077	16.395	18.707	21.007	23.290	25.552
22	2.949	5.081	7.336	9.653	12.001	14.365	16.730	19.088	21.432	23.759	26.063
23	3.002	5.176	7.475	9.838	12.233	14.642	17.053	19.455	21.843	24.211	26.555
24	3.053	5.267	7.610	10.017	12.457	14.910	17.365	19.810	22.239	24.648	27.031
25	3.101	5.354	7.739	10.189	12.673	15.169	17.666	20.153	22.623	25.070	27.491
26	3.146	5.438	7.863	10.356	12.881	15.420	17.958	20.485	22.994	25.479	27.935
27	3.190	5.518	7.983	10.516	13.083	15.663	18.241	20.807	23.354	25.875	28.366
28	3.231	5.595	8.099	10.672	13.278	15.898	18.515	21.119	23.703	26.259	28.784
29	3.271	5.670	8.211	10.822	13.468	16.126	18.781	21.422	24.041	26.632	29.189
30	3.309	5.741	8.319	10.968	13.652	16.347	19.040	21.716	24.370	26.994	29.582

Table B.7: American-Style Put Premiums
as a Function of Time and Volatility
Stock Price = $100
Strike Price = $90
Dividend Rate = 0%

Mo	Volatility										
	0.15	0.20	0.25	0.30	0.35	0.40	0.45	0.50	0.55	0.60	0.65
1	0.008	0.060	0.190	0.398	0.672	0.996	1.359	1.753	2.170	2.606	3.056
2	0.072	0.284	0.637	1.092	1.620	2.199	2.815	3.457	4.119	4.797	5.486
3	0.175	0.547	1.082	1.726	2.442	3.207	4.005	4.828	5.669	6.522	7.386
4	0.292	0.804	1.493	2.290	3.159	4.074	5.021	5.990	6.976	7.973	8.978
5	0.410	1.047	1.866	2.796	3.794	4.838	5.912	7.008	8.118	9.238	10.365
6	0.525	1.273	2.208	3.253	4.367	5.524	6.711	7.917	9.138	10.367	11.602
7	0.635	1.484	2.523	3.672	4.889	6.149	7.437	8.744	10.063	11.390	12.722
8	0.740	1.680	2.814	4.058	5.369	6.723	8.104	9.502	10.913	12.330	13.750
9	0.839	1.864	3.084	4.416	5.815	7.255	8.721	10.205	11.699	13.199	14.701
10	0.932	2.035	3.337	4.751	6.230	7.751	9.298	10.860	12.432	14.009	15.586
11	1.020	2.197	3.575	5.064	6.620	8.216	9.838	11.475	13.120	14.769	16.416
12	1.103	2.349	3.798	5.360	6.987	8.655	10.347	12.054	13.768	15.484	17.198
13	1.182	2.492	4.009	5.639	7.334	9.070	10.829	12.602	14.381	16.161	17.936
14	1.256	2.628	4.209	5.903	7.663	9.463	11.286	13.121	14.962	16.802	18.637
15	1.327	2.757	4.399	6.155	7.977	9.837	11.721	13.616	15.516	17.413	19.304
16	1.394	2.880	4.579	6.394	8.275	10.195	12.136	14.089	16.044	17.996	19.940
17	1.457	2.996	4.752	6.623	8.560	10.536	12.533	14.540	16.549	18.553	20.547
18	1.518	3.107	4.916	6.842	8.833	10.863	12.913	14.973	17.033	19.087	21.130
19	1.575	3.214	5.074	7.051	9.095	11.177	13.279	15.389	17.498	19.599	21.688
20	1.629	3.315	5.224	7.253	9.347	11.479	13.630	15.788	17.945	20.092	22.225
21	1.681	3.412	5.369	7.446	9.589	11.769	13.968	16.173	18.375	20.566	22.742
22	1.731	3.505	5.508	7.632	9.822	12.049	14.294	16.544	18.790	21.024	23.240
23	1.778	3.595	5.642	7.811	10.047	12.319	14.609	16.903	19.190	21.465	23.721
24	1.824	3.680	5.771	7.984	10.264	12.580	14.913	17.249	19.578	21.891	24.185
25	1.867	3.763	5.895	8.151	10.474	12.833	15.207	17.584	19.952	22.304	24.634
26	1.908	3.842	6.015	8.313	10.677	13.077	15.492	17.908	20.315	22.704	25.069
27	1.948	3.919	6.131	8.469	10.874	13.314	15.768	18.223	20.666	23.091	25.490
28	1.986	3.992	6.243	8.620	11.064	13.543	16.036	18.528	21.007	23.466	25.898
29	2.022	4.063	6.351	8.766	11.249	13.766	16.296	18.824	21.338	23.830	26.294
30	2.057	4.132	6.456	8.908	11.428	13.982	16.549	19.112	21.660	24.184	26.679

Table B.8: American-Style Put Premiums
as a Function of Time and Volatility
Stock Price = $100
Strike Price = $85
Dividend Rate = 0%

Mo	Volatility										
	0.15	0.20	0.25	0.30	0.35	0.40	0.45	0.50	0.55	0.60	0.65
1	0.000	0.003	0.024	0.082	0.190	0.350	0.559	0.810	1.098	1.415	1.759
2	0.005	0.050	0.181	0.412	0.735	1.132	1.587	2.090	2.629	3.196	3.787
3	0.024	0.148	0.415	0.816	1.321	1.906	2.549	3.238	3.961	4.710	5.479
4	0.057	0.273	0.673	1.222	1.881	2.620	3.416	4.256	5.127	6.023	6.937
5	0.101	0.411	0.931	1.611	2.403	3.274	4.201	5.169	6.167	7.187	8.224
6	0.151	0.552	1.183	1.980	2.889	3.876	4.918	5.999	7.108	8.238	9.383
7	0.205	0.693	1.425	2.327	3.342	4.434	5.579	6.761	7.970	9.199	10.440
8	0.261	0.830	1.657	2.655	3.766	4.953	6.191	7.466	8.767	10.085	11.414
9	0.318	0.964	1.877	2.964	4.164	5.438	6.764	8.124	9.508	10.908	12.319
10	0.374	1.093	2.087	3.257	4.539	5.895	7.301	8.740	10.202	11.679	13.164
11	0.430	1.218	2.288	3.534	4.894	6.326	7.807	9.320	10.855	12.403	13.959
12	0.484	1.338	2.479	3.798	5.230	6.734	8.286	9.868	11.472	13.087	14.708
13	0.537	1.453	2.661	4.050	5.550	7.122	8.740	10.389	12.056	13.735	15.418
14	0.589	1.563	2.836	4.289	5.855	7.491	9.173	10.884	12.613	14.351	16.093
15	0.639	1.670	3.003	4.519	6.146	7.843	9.586	11.356	13.143	14.938	16.735
16	0.687	1.772	3.164	4.738	6.424	8.180	9.980	11.808	13.650	15.499	17.348
17	0.734	1.870	3.318	4.949	6.692	8.504	10.359	12.240	14.135	16.036	17.935
18	0.779	1.964	3.465	5.151	6.948	8.814	10.722	12.655	14.601	16.551	18.498
19	0.822	2.055	3.608	5.346	7.195	9.113	11.071	13.054	15.049	17.046	19.038
20	0.864	2.143	3.745	5.533	7.433	9.400	11.408	13.439	15.480	17.523	19.558
21	0.904	2.227	3.877	5.714	7.662	9.677	11.732	13.809	15.896	17.981	20.059
22	0.943	2.309	4.004	5.888	7.883	9.945	12.045	14.167	16.297	18.424	20.541
23	0.981	2.387	4.127	6.056	8.097	10.203	12.348	14.513	16.684	18.852	21.007
24	1.017	2.463	4.246	6.219	8.303	10.453	12.641	14.847	17.059	19.265	21.458
25	1.052	2.536	4.361	6.376	8.503	10.695	12.924	15.171	17.421	19.665	21.894
26	1.085	2.607	4.472	6.529	8.697	10.930	13.199	15.485	17.773	20.052	22.316
27	1.118	2.675	4.579	6.677	8.885	11.158	13.466	15.789	18.114	20.428	22.725
28	1.149	2.741	4.683	6.820	9.067	11.379	13.724	16.084	18.445	20.793	23.121
29	1.179	2.805	4.785	6.959	9.245	11.593	13.976	16.372	18.766	21.147	23.506
30	1.209	2.867	4.883	7.094	9.417	11.802	14.220	16.651	19.078	21.491	23.880

Table B.9: American-Style Put Premiums
as a Function of Time and Volatility
Stock Price = $100
Strike Price = $80
Dividend Rate = 0%

Mo	Volatility										
	0.15	0.20	0.25	0.30	0.35	0.40	0.45	0.50	0.55	0.60	0.65
1	0.000	0.000	0.002	0.011	0.038	0.094	0.186	0.315	0.480	0.680	0.910
2	0.000	0.006	0.037	0.123	0.279	0.508	0.802	1.154	1.554	1.995	2.470
3	0.002	0.029	0.127	0.328	0.634	1.031	1.504	2.039	2.624	3.248	3.905
4	0.008	0.072	0.256	0.577	1.021	1.567	2.192	2.879	3.614	4.388	5.191
5	0.018	0.131	0.405	0.841	1.412	2.088	2.844	3.661	4.525	5.425	6.353
6	0.033	0.201	0.564	1.107	1.792	2.585	3.457	4.389	5.366	6.377	7.414
7	0.052	0.278	0.727	1.370	2.160	3.057	4.033	5.068	6.146	7.256	8.391
8	0.075	0.359	0.891	1.627	2.512	3.505	4.576	5.704	6.874	8.075	9.298
9	0.099	0.442	1.053	1.875	2.849	3.931	5.089	6.303	7.557	8.841	10.145
10	0.126	0.527	1.212	2.115	3.171	4.335	5.575	6.869	8.201	9.561	10.939
11	0.154	0.611	1.368	2.347	3.480	4.721	6.036	7.404	8.809	10.240	11.689
12	0.183	0.694	1.519	2.570	3.776	5.089	6.475	7.913	9.387	10.884	12.398
13	0.212	0.777	1.666	2.785	4.060	5.441	6.894	8.398	9.936	11.497	13.072
14	0.242	0.858	1.808	2.992	4.332	5.778	7.295	8.861	10.460	12.080	13.713
15	0.272	0.937	1.946	3.191	4.594	6.101	7.679	9.304	10.961	12.637	14.325
16	0.301	1.014	2.080	3.384	4.846	6.412	8.047	9.729	11.441	13.171	14.911
17	0.331	1.090	2.210	3.570	5.089	6.711	8.401	10.137	11.901	13.683	15.472
18	0.360	1.163	2.335	3.750	5.323	6.999	8.742	10.529	12.344	14.174	16.011
19	0.388	1.235	2.457	3.924	5.549	7.276	9.070	10.907	12.770	14.647	16.529
20	0.416	1.305	2.575	4.093	5.768	7.545	9.387	11.272	13.181	15.103	17.028
21	0.444	1.373	2.690	4.255	5.979	7.804	9.694	11.624	13.577	15.542	17.509
22	0.470	1.439	2.801	4.413	6.184	8.055	9.990	11.964	13.961	15.967	17.973
23	0.497	1.503	2.909	4.566	6.382	8.298	10.276	12.293	14.331	16.378	18.422
24	0.522	1.566	3.013	4.715	6.574	8.533	10.554	12.612	14.690	16.775	18.856
25	0.547	1.627	3.115	4.859	6.761	8.762	10.824	12.922	15.038	17.160	19.276
26	0.572	1.686	3.214	4.999	6.942	8.983	11.085	13.222	15.375	17.533	19.682
27	0.596	1.743	3.310	5.135	7.118	9.199	11.339	13.513	15.703	17.895	20.077
28	0.619	1.799	3.403	5.267	7.289	9.408	11.586	13.796	16.021	18.246	20.460
29	0.641	1.854	3.494	5.396	7.455	9.612	11.826	14.072	16.330	18.587	20.832
30	0.663	1.907	3.583	5.521	7.617	9.810	12.060	14.339	16.631	18.919	21.193

Table B.10: American-Style Put Premiums
as a Function of Time and Volatility
Stock Price = $100
Strike Price = $75
Dividend Rate = 0%

Mo	\multicolumn{11}{c}{Volatility}										
	0.15	0.20	0.25	0.30	0.35	0.40	0.45	0.50	0.55	0.60	0.65
1	0.000	0.000	0.000	0.001	0.005	0.018	0.048	0.099	0.176	0.281	0.414
2	0.000	0.001	0.005	0.028	0.086	0.193	0.355	0.571	0.838	1.152	1.506
3	0.000	0.004	0.030	0.109	0.263	0.498	0.810	1.190	1.630	2.121	2.653
4	0.001	0.015	0.079	0.235	0.496	0.859	1.310	1.836	2.424	3.062	3.741
5	0.003	0.033	0.149	0.389	0.757	1.239	1.816	2.470	3.185	3.950	4.755
6	0.006	0.060	0.234	0.560	1.029	1.621	2.311	3.079	3.908	4.785	5.699
7	0.011	0.094	0.329	0.739	1.305	1.998	2.791	3.661	4.591	5.568	6.581
8	0.017	0.133	0.431	0.922	1.578	2.365	3.252	4.216	5.238	6.306	7.407
9	0.025	0.176	0.537	1.105	1.846	2.720	3.695	4.745	5.852	7.002	8.185
10	0.035	0.223	0.645	1.288	2.108	3.064	4.119	5.249	6.435	7.662	8.919
11	0.046	0.272	0.754	1.468	2.364	3.395	4.526	5.731	6.990	8.288	9.616
12	0.059	0.323	0.863	1.645	2.612	3.715	4.917	6.192	7.519	8.885	10.277
13	0.072	0.375	0.972	1.818	2.853	4.024	5.293	6.634	8.025	9.454	10.907
14	0.086	0.428	1.079	1.988	3.086	4.322	5.655	7.058	8.510	9.998	11.509
15	0.101	0.480	1.185	2.153	3.313	4.610	6.003	7.465	8.976	10.520	12.086
16	0.116	0.533	1.289	2.314	3.533	4.888	6.339	7.858	9.423	11.020	12.638
17	0.131	0.586	1.392	2.471	3.746	5.157	6.664	8.236	9.853	11.501	13.168
18	0.147	0.638	1.492	2.624	3.953	5.418	6.977	8.600	10.268	11.965	13.679
19	0.163	0.690	1.590	2.773	4.154	5.670	7.280	8.953	10.668	12.411	14.170
20	0.179	0.741	1.686	2.919	4.349	5.915	7.573	9.293	11.055	12.842	14.644
21	0.196	0.791	1.781	3.060	4.538	6.152	7.857	9.623	11.429	13.259	15.102
22	0.212	0.841	1.873	3.198	4.723	6.382	8.132	9.942	11.791	13.662	15.544
23	0.228	0.889	1.963	3.332	4.902	6.606	8.399	10.252	12.141	14.052	15.972
24	0.244	0.937	2.050	3.463	5.076	6.823	8.659	10.552	12.481	14.430	16.386
25	0.260	0.984	2.136	3.590	5.246	7.035	8.911	10.844	12.811	14.796	16.787
26	0.275	1.030	2.220	3.715	5.411	7.240	9.156	11.127	13.131	15.152	17.177
27	0.291	1.075	2.302	3.836	5.572	7.440	9.394	11.403	13.442	15.497	17.554
28	0.306	1.120	2.382	3.954	5.729	7.635	9.627	11.671	13.745	15.833	17.921
29	0.321	1.163	2.461	4.069	5.882	7.825	9.853	11.932	14.039	16.160	18.278
30	0.336	1.205	2.537	4.182	6.031	8.010	10.073	12.186	14.326	16.477	18.624

Table B.11: American-Style Put Premiums
as a Function of Time and Volatility
Stock Price = $100
Strike Price = $70
Dividend Rate = 0%

Mo	Volatility										
	0.15	0.20	0.25	0.30	0.35	0.40	0.45	0.50	0.55	0.60	0.65
1	0.000	0.000	0.000	0.000	0.000	0.003	0.009	0.024	0.052	0.097	0.161
2	0.000	0.000	0.001	0.005	0.021	0.060	0.133	0.247	0.404	0.604	0.845
3	0.000	0.001	0.006	0.029	0.092	0.210	0.390	0.634	0.938	1.296	1.701
4	0.000	0.002	0.020	0.081	0.211	0.424	0.719	1.091	1.531	2.029	2.577
5	0.000	0.007	0.046	0.156	0.364	0.675	1.081	1.571	2.133	2.755	3.427
6	0.001	0.015	0.083	0.251	0.539	0.945	1.456	2.055	2.727	3.459	4.240
7	0.002	0.026	0.129	0.358	0.727	1.225	1.832	2.531	3.303	4.134	5.013
8	0.004	0.042	0.183	0.476	0.922	1.507	2.205	2.995	3.858	4.780	5.748
9	0.006	0.060	0.244	0.599	1.121	1.787	2.570	3.445	4.393	5.397	6.446
10	0.008	0.082	0.309	0.726	1.321	2.065	2.926	3.880	4.906	5.987	7.111
11	0.012	0.106	0.378	0.856	1.520	2.337	3.273	4.301	5.400	6.552	7.746
12	0.016	0.133	0.449	0.986	1.717	2.603	3.610	4.707	5.874	7.094	8.352
13	0.021	0.161	0.522	1.117	1.911	2.864	3.936	5.099	6.331	7.613	8.933
14	0.026	0.191	0.596	1.246	2.102	3.118	4.253	5.478	6.771	8.112	9.489
15	0.032	0.222	0.671	1.375	2.290	3.365	4.561	5.845	7.195	8.592	10.024
16	0.039	0.254	0.746	1.503	2.474	3.606	4.859	6.199	7.604	9.054	10.538
17	0.046	0.287	0.820	1.628	2.653	3.841	5.149	6.543	7.999	9.500	11.033
18	0.053	0.320	0.895	1.752	2.829	4.070	5.430	6.875	8.381	9.931	11.510
19	0.060	0.353	0.969	1.874	3.001	4.293	5.703	7.197	8.751	10.347	11.970
20	0.068	0.387	1.042	1.993	3.169	4.510	5.968	7.510	9.110	10.750	12.415
21	0.077	0.421	1.115	2.111	3.334	4.721	6.226	7.813	9.457	11.139	12.846
22	0.085	0.455	1.187	2.226	3.494	4.928	6.477	8.108	9.794	11.517	13.262
23	0.094	0.489	1.257	2.339	3.651	5.129	6.721	8.394	10.121	11.883	13.666
24	0.102	0.522	1.327	2.449	3.805	5.324	6.959	8.672	10.438	12.238	14.057
25	0.111	0.556	1.396	2.558	3.955	5.516	7.191	8.943	10.747	12.583	14.437
26	0.120	0.589	1.463	2.664	4.101	5.702	7.416	9.207	11.048	12.919	14.806
27	0.129	0.622	1.530	2.769	4.244	5.884	7.636	9.464	11.340	13.245	15.164
28	0.138	0.654	1.595	2.871	4.384	6.062	7.851	9.714	11.624	13.562	15.513
29	0.147	0.686	1.659	2.971	4.521	6.236	8.060	9.958	11.902	13.871	15.852
30	0.155	0.718	1.723	3.069	4.655	6.405	8.265	10.196	12.172	14.172	16.182

Table B.12: American-Style Put Premiums
as a Function of Time and Volatility
Stock Price = $100
Strike Price = $65
Dividend Rate = 0%

Mo	Volatility										
	0.15	0.20	0.25	0.30	0.35	0.40	0.45	0.50	0.55	0.60	0.65
1	0.000	0.000	0.000	0.000	0.000	0.000	0.001	0.004	0.012	0.027	0.052
2	0.000	0.000	0.000	0.001	0.004	0.015	0.041	0.091	0.170	0.282	0.429
3	0.000	0.000	0.001	0.006	0.026	0.075	0.164	0.302	0.491	0.730	1.018
4	0.000	0.000	0.004	0.023	0.077	0.184	0.356	0.595	0.899	1.263	1.681
5	0.000	0.001	0.012	0.053	0.154	0.331	0.591	0.932	1.346	1.825	2.361
6	0.000	0.003	0.025	0.098	0.253	0.504	0.853	1.291	1.807	2.392	3.033
7	0.000	0.006	0.043	0.154	0.368	0.695	1.129	1.659	2.271	2.951	3.689
8	0.001	0.011	0.068	0.220	0.495	0.896	1.413	2.029	2.728	3.497	4.322
9	0.001	0.018	0.097	0.294	0.630	1.103	1.698	2.395	3.177	4.027	4.933
10	0.002	0.026	0.131	0.374	0.771	1.314	1.983	2.757	3.615	4.541	5.521
11	0.003	0.036	0.169	0.458	0.915	1.526	2.265	3.111	4.040	5.037	6.086
12	0.004	0.048	0.210	0.546	1.062	1.737	2.544	3.457	4.454	5.517	6.631
13	0.005	0.061	0.254	0.637	1.209	1.946	2.817	3.795	4.855	5.980	7.155
14	0.007	0.076	0.300	0.730	1.357	2.153	3.085	4.124	5.244	6.428	7.660
15	0.009	0.091	0.348	0.823	1.504	2.358	3.348	4.444	5.622	6.862	8.148
16	0.011	0.108	0.397	0.917	1.650	2.559	3.605	4.756	5.988	7.281	8.618
17	0.014	0.126	0.447	1.011	1.795	2.756	3.856	5.060	6.344	7.687	9.073
18	0.017	0.145	0.498	1.106	1.938	2.950	4.101	5.356	6.690	8.080	9.513
19	0.020	0.164	0.550	1.200	2.079	3.140	4.341	5.644	7.025	8.462	9.938
20	0.023	0.184	0.602	1.293	2.218	3.327	4.575	5.925	7.351	8.832	10.351
21	0.027	0.205	0.654	1.385	2.355	3.510	4.803	6.199	7.668	9.191	10.750
22	0.030	0.225	0.706	1.477	2.490	3.689	5.026	6.465	7.977	9.540	11.138
23	0.034	0.247	0.758	1.567	2.622	3.865	5.245	6.725	8.277	9.879	11.514
24	0.038	0.268	0.809	1.657	2.753	4.036	5.458	6.978	8.569	10.209	11.880
25	0.042	0.290	0.861	1.745	2.881	4.205	5.666	7.226	8.854	10.530	12.235
26	0.047	0.312	0.912	1.832	3.007	4.370	5.870	7.467	9.132	10.842	12.580
27	0.051	0.333	0.963	1.918	3.130	4.531	6.069	7.702	9.402	11.146	12.916
28	0.056	0.355	1.014	2.003	3.251	4.689	6.263	7.932	9.666	11.443	13.244
29	0.060	0.377	1.063	2.087	3.370	4.845	6.454	8.157	9.924	11.731	13.562
30	0.065	0.399	1.113	2.169	3.487	4.996	6.640	8.377	10.175	12.013	13.873

Table B.13: American-Style Put Premiums
as a Function of Time and Volatility
Stock Price = $100
Strike Price = $60
Dividend Rate = 0%

Mo	Volatility										
	0.15	0.20	0.25	0.30	0.35	0.40	0.45	0.50	0.55	0.60	0.65
1	0.000	0.000	0.000	0.000	0.000	0.000	0.000	0.001	0.002	0.006	0.013
2	0.000	0.000	0.000	0.000	0.001	0.003	0.010	0.028	0.061	0.115	0.193
3	0.000	0.000	0.000	0.001	0.006	0.022	0.059	0.126	0.229	0.373	0.559
4	0.000	0.000	0.001	0.005	0.023	0.069	0.155	0.292	0.483	0.728	1.026
5	0.000	0.000	0.003	0.015	0.056	0.143	0.292	0.507	0.789	1.135	1.539
6	0.000	0.001	0.006	0.032	0.104	0.242	0.458	0.754	1.125	1.566	2.069
7	0.000	0.002	0.012	0.057	0.166	0.359	0.644	1.020	1.477	2.008	2.602
8	0.000	0.003	0.022	0.089	0.239	0.490	0.845	1.297	1.836	2.451	3.129
9	0.000	0.005	0.034	0.128	0.322	0.632	1.055	1.581	2.197	2.889	3.646
10	0.000	0.007	0.049	0.173	0.413	0.781	1.270	1.866	2.555	3.321	4.150
11	0.001	0.011	0.067	0.222	0.509	0.935	1.488	2.152	2.909	3.744	4.641
12	0.001	0.015	0.088	0.276	0.610	1.092	1.707	2.435	3.257	4.157	5.118
13	0.001	0.020	0.111	0.333	0.714	1.251	1.925	2.715	3.599	4.560	5.581
14	0.002	0.026	0.136	0.393	0.821	1.411	2.143	2.991	3.934	4.952	6.030
15	0.002	0.033	0.163	0.456	0.929	1.572	2.358	3.262	4.261	5.334	6.465
16	0.003	0.041	0.192	0.520	1.039	1.732	2.571	3.529	4.581	5.706	6.888
17	0.004	0.049	0.222	0.586	1.149	1.891	2.781	3.790	4.893	6.068	7.298
18	0.005	0.059	0.254	0.652	1.259	2.048	2.988	4.047	5.198	6.420	7.696
19	0.006	0.068	0.287	0.720	1.369	2.204	3.191	4.298	5.495	6.763	8.083
20	0.007	0.079	0.320	0.788	1.479	2.359	3.392	4.543	5.786	7.097	8.458
21	0.008	0.090	0.354	0.857	1.587	2.511	3.588	4.784	6.069	7.422	8.824
22	0.010	0.101	0.389	0.925	1.696	2.661	3.781	5.019	6.346	7.739	9.179
23	0.011	0.113	0.425	0.994	1.803	2.810	3.971	5.250	6.617	8.048	9.525
24	0.013	0.125	0.460	1.062	1.909	2.956	4.157	5.476	6.881	8.349	9.861
25	0.014	0.138	0.496	1.130	2.014	3.099	4.340	5.696	7.139	8.643	10.189
26	0.016	0.151	0.532	1.198	2.118	3.241	4.519	5.913	7.391	8.929	10.508
27	0.018	0.164	0.569	1.266	2.220	3.380	4.695	6.124	7.637	9.209	10.820
28	0.020	0.177	0.605	1.333	2.322	3.517	4.867	6.332	7.878	9.482	11.123
29	0.022	0.191	0.641	1.399	2.422	3.651	5.036	6.535	8.114	9.748	11.419
30	0.024	0.204	0.677	1.465	2.520	3.784	5.202	6.733	8.344	10.009	11.708

Table B.14: American-Style Put Premiums
as a Function of Time and Volatility
Stock Price = $100
Strike Price = $120
Dividend Rate = 1%

Mo	Volatility										
	0.15	0.20	0.25	0.30	0.35	0.40	0.45	0.50	0.55	0.60	0.65
1	20.000	20.000	20.000	20.000	20.000	20.057	20.217	20.451	20.742	21.077	21.450
2	20.000	20.000	20.000	20.011	20.214	20.585	21.063	21.617	22.225	22.876	23.559
3	20.000	20.000	20.000	20.167	20.625	21.246	21.969	22.761	23.604	24.484	25.391
4	20.000	20.000	20.020	20.407	21.077	21.903	22.826	23.812	24.843	25.907	26.995
5	20.000	20.000	20.097	20.676	21.529	22.531	23.622	24.773	25.964	27.184	28.425
6	20.000	20.000	20.205	20.954	21.967	23.122	24.361	25.656	26.987	28.344	29.719
7	20.000	20.000	20.330	21.231	22.387	23.678	25.050	26.474	27.931	29.410	30.905
8	20.000	20.000	20.464	21.501	22.787	24.203	25.695	27.235	28.806	30.397	32.000
9	20.000	20.001	20.601	21.764	23.168	24.698	26.301	27.948	29.624	31.317	33.020
10	20.000	20.013	20.740	22.018	23.532	25.167	26.873	28.620	30.392	32.180	33.975
11	20.000	20.034	20.877	22.263	23.879	25.613	27.414	29.254	31.117	32.992	34.872
12	20.000	20.061	21.013	22.499	24.211	26.037	27.928	29.855	31.803	33.760	35.720
13	20.000	20.092	21.146	22.726	24.528	26.442	28.417	30.427	32.454	34.488	36.523
14	20.000	20.127	21.277	22.946	24.833	26.829	28.884	30.971	33.074	35.181	37.286
15	20.000	20.165	21.404	23.158	25.126	27.200	29.331	31.492	33.665	35.841	38.014
16	20.000	20.204	21.529	23.362	25.407	27.556	29.760	31.990	34.231	36.473	38.709
17	20.000	20.244	21.650	23.560	25.678	27.899	30.171	32.467	34.773	37.078	39.375
18	20.000	20.285	21.768	23.751	25.940	28.228	30.566	32.926	35.294	37.658	40.013
19	20.000	20.326	21.883	23.935	26.192	28.545	30.946	33.367	35.794	38.216	40.626
20	20.000	20.368	21.994	24.114	26.436	28.851	31.312	33.793	36.276	38.753	41.216
21	20.000	20.409	22.103	24.287	26.671	29.147	31.666	34.203	36.741	39.271	41.784
22	20.000	20.450	22.209	24.455	26.899	29.432	32.008	34.599	37.190	39.771	42.332
23	20.000	20.491	22.312	24.618	27.119	29.709	32.339	34.983	37.624	40.253	42.861
24	20.000	20.532	22.413	24.776	27.333	29.977	32.659	35.353	38.044	40.720	43.373
25	20.000	20.572	22.511	24.930	27.540	30.236	32.969	35.713	38.451	41.172	43.868
26	20.000	20.612	22.606	25.079	27.741	30.488	33.270	36.061	38.845	41.609	44.347
27	20.000	20.651	22.699	25.224	27.936	30.732	33.562	36.399	39.227	42.034	44.811
28	20.000	20.690	22.790	25.364	28.126	30.970	33.846	36.728	39.598	42.446	45.262
29	20.000	20.728	22.878	25.501	28.311	31.201	34.122	37.047	39.959	42.846	45.699
30	20.000	20.765	22.964	25.634	28.490	31.425	34.390	37.357	40.309	43.234	46.123

Table B.15: American-Style Put Premiums
as a Function of Time and Volatility
Stock Price = $100
Strike Price = $115
Dividend Rate = 1%

Mo	Volatility										
	0.15	0.20	0.25	0.30	0.35	0.40	0.45	0.50	0.55	0.60	0.65
1	15.000	15.000	15.000	15.010	15.141	15.376	15.682	16.041	16.440	16.871	17.326
2	15.000	15.000	15.027	15.301	15.749	16.300	16.919	17.585	18.285	19.011	19.757
3	15.000	15.000	15.188	15.714	16.405	17.191	18.038	18.927	19.844	20.783	21.738
4	15.000	15.006	15.406	16.137	17.025	18.001	19.032	20.100	21.193	22.304	23.427
5	15.000	15.050	15.638	16.545	17.600	18.737	19.925	21.145	22.388	23.645	24.913
6	15.000	15.119	15.872	16.931	18.133	19.411	20.737	22.091	23.465	24.852	26.246
7	15.000	15.201	16.100	17.296	18.628	20.033	21.482	22.957	24.449	25.952	27.460
8	15.000	15.290	16.321	17.640	19.091	20.612	22.172	23.758	25.357	26.965	28.576
9	15.000	15.382	16.532	17.965	19.525	21.152	22.816	24.502	26.201	27.905	29.610
10	15.000	15.474	16.736	18.273	19.934	21.659	23.420	25.200	26.990	28.783	30.576
11	15.000	15.566	16.930	18.566	20.321	22.138	23.988	25.856	27.731	29.608	31.482
12	15.000	15.657	17.117	18.844	20.688	22.591	24.525	26.475	28.431	30.386	32.337
13	15.000	15.746	17.296	19.109	21.037	23.021	25.035	27.062	29.093	31.122	33.145
14	15.000	15.833	17.467	19.362	21.369	23.431	25.520	27.620	29.723	31.822	33.913
15	15.000	15.918	17.632	19.604	21.687	23.822	25.982	28.152	30.323	32.488	34.644
16	15.001	16.001	17.791	19.837	21.991	24.196	26.424	28.661	30.896	33.125	35.341
17	15.004	16.081	17.944	20.060	22.282	24.554	26.847	29.148	31.445	33.734	36.008
18	15.009	16.159	18.091	20.274	22.562	24.898	27.253	29.615	31.972	34.318	36.648
19	15.015	16.235	18.233	20.481	22.831	25.228	27.644	30.064	32.477	34.878	37.262
20	15.023	16.308	18.370	20.679	23.090	25.546	28.020	30.496	32.964	35.418	37.852
21	15.031	16.380	18.502	20.871	23.340	25.853	28.382	30.912	33.433	35.938	38.420
22	15.040	16.449	18.630	21.056	23.581	26.149	28.732	31.314	33.886	36.439	38.968
23	15.050	16.517	18.754	21.235	23.814	26.435	29.070	31.703	34.323	36.923	39.497
24	15.060	16.582	18.873	21.407	24.039	26.712	29.397	32.078	34.745	37.390	40.008
25	15.070	16.646	18.989	21.575	24.258	26.980	29.714	32.442	35.154	37.843	40.502
26	15.081	16.708	19.101	21.737	24.469	27.240	30.021	32.794	35.551	38.281	40.980
27	15.092	16.768	19.210	21.894	24.674	27.492	30.318	33.136	35.935	38.706	41.444
28	15.103	16.826	19.315	22.047	24.873	27.737	30.607	33.468	36.308	39.118	41.893
29	15.114	16.882	19.417	22.195	25.067	27.974	30.888	33.790	36.670	39.519	42.329
30	15.124	16.937	19.516	22.339	25.254	28.205	31.161	34.103	37.022	39.907	42.753

Table B.16: American-Style Put Premiums
as a Function of Time and Volatility
Stock Price = $100
Strike Price = $110
Dividend Rate = 1%

Mo	\multicolumn{11}{c}{Volatility}										
	0.15	0.20	0.25	0.30	0.35	0.40	0.45	0.50	0.55	0.60	0.65
1	10.000	10.000	10.087	10.340	10.685	11.089	11.534	12.007	12.502	13.014	13.538
2	10.000	10.084	10.490	11.055	11.703	12.401	13.133	13.886	14.656	15.438	16.228
3	10.000	10.274	10.920	11.712	12.580	13.491	14.429	15.386	16.355	17.334	18.318
4	10.003	10.482	11.322	12.298	13.342	14.425	15.532	16.654	17.786	18.925	20.068
5	10.031	10.689	11.691	12.823	14.018	15.248	16.499	17.763	19.035	20.312	21.590
6	10.075	10.887	12.031	13.300	14.627	15.987	17.365	18.754	20.150	21.548	22.947
7	10.127	11.074	12.346	13.737	15.183	16.660	18.153	19.655	21.162	22.669	24.175
8	10.182	11.251	12.638	14.140	15.695	17.278	18.877	20.482	22.089	23.696	25.300
9	10.238	11.419	12.911	14.515	16.171	17.853	19.547	21.247	22.948	24.647	26.342
10	10.294	11.577	13.166	14.866	16.615	18.388	20.173	21.961	23.749	25.533	27.312
11	10.350	11.726	13.407	15.196	17.032	18.891	20.759	22.631	24.500	26.364	28.221
12	10.404	11.868	13.634	15.507	17.425	19.364	21.312	23.261	25.207	27.147	29.077
13	10.457	12.003	13.850	15.801	17.797	19.812	21.835	23.858	25.876	27.887	29.886
14	10.508	12.132	14.054	16.080	18.149	20.237	22.331	24.425	26.512	28.589	30.653
15	10.557	12.255	14.249	16.345	18.485	20.642	22.804	24.964	27.116	29.257	31.384
16	10.605	12.372	14.435	16.599	18.805	21.028	23.255	25.479	27.693	29.895	32.080
17	10.652	12.484	14.612	16.841	19.111	21.397	23.687	25.971	28.245	30.504	32.746
18	10.697	12.591	14.781	17.072	19.404	21.751	24.100	26.443	28.774	31.089	33.384
19	10.740	12.694	14.944	17.294	19.685	22.091	24.497	26.896	29.282	31.649	33.996
20	10.782	12.792	15.099	17.508	19.956	22.418	24.879	27.332	29.770	32.189	34.584
21	10.821	12.886	15.249	17.713	20.216	22.732	25.247	27.752	30.240	32.708	35.150
22	10.860	12.977	15.393	17.911	20.467	23.036	25.602	28.157	30.694	33.208	35.696
23	10.896	13.064	15.532	18.102	20.710	23.329	25.945	28.548	31.132	33.691	36.222
24	10.931	13.148	15.666	18.286	20.944	23.612	26.276	28.926	31.555	34.158	36.731
25	10.965	13.229	15.795	18.464	21.170	23.886	26.597	29.292	31.965	34.610	37.222
26	10.998	13.307	15.920	18.636	21.389	24.151	26.907	29.646	32.361	35.047	37.698
27	11.029	13.382	16.041	18.803	21.602	24.409	27.208	29.990	32.746	35.471	38.159
28	11.059	13.455	16.158	18.964	21.807	24.658	27.500	30.323	33.119	35.881	38.606
29	11.088	13.525	16.271	19.121	22.007	24.900	27.784	30.647	33.481	36.280	39.040
30	11.116	13.593	16.381	19.273	22.201	25.136	28.059	30.961	33.833	36.667	39.460

Table B.17: American-Style Put Premiums
as a Function of Time and Volatility
Stock Price = $100
Strike Price = $105
Dividend Rate = 1%

Mo	0.15	0.20	0.25	0.30	0.35	0.40	0.45	0.50	0.55	0.60	0.65
1	5.070	5.398	5.835	6.322	6.839	7.372	7.918	8.472	9.031	9.595	10.162
2	5.312	5.937	6.653	7.410	8.188	8.979	9.778	10.582	11.390	12.200	13.011
3	5.546	6.382	7.301	8.254	9.224	10.205	11.192	12.182	13.174	14.167	15.160
4	5.755	6.761	7.843	8.956	10.084	11.221	12.362	13.506	14.650	15.793	16.936
5	5.942	7.091	8.312	9.563	10.828	12.100	13.374	14.650	15.925	17.199	18.470
6	6.110	7.384	8.729	10.102	11.487	12.878	14.272	15.665	17.057	18.446	19.831
7	6.261	7.648	9.104	10.587	12.082	13.581	15.082	16.582	18.079	19.572	21.061
8	6.400	7.889	9.447	11.030	12.624	14.223	15.823	17.420	19.014	20.603	22.186
9	6.528	8.110	9.761	11.438	13.125	14.816	16.507	18.195	19.878	21.555	23.225
10	6.646	8.314	10.052	11.816	13.590	15.367	17.143	18.915	20.682	22.441	24.192
11	6.755	8.504	10.323	12.169	14.024	15.882	17.739	19.590	21.435	23.271	25.097
12	6.856	8.681	10.577	12.500	14.432	16.367	18.299	20.225	22.144	24.052	25.949
13	6.950	8.847	10.816	12.812	14.818	16.825	18.828	20.826	22.813	24.790	26.753
14	7.038	9.003	11.042	13.107	15.182	17.258	19.330	21.395	23.448	25.490	27.516
15	7.121	9.150	11.255	13.387	15.529	17.671	19.808	21.936	24.053	26.155	28.241
16	7.199	9.290	11.458	13.654	15.859	18.064	20.263	22.452	24.629	26.790	28.933
17	7.272	9.422	11.651	13.908	16.174	18.439	20.698	22.946	25.180	27.397	29.594
18	7.342	9.548	11.835	14.150	16.475	18.799	21.115	23.419	25.707	27.978	30.227
19	7.408	9.668	12.011	14.383	16.764	19.143	21.515	23.873	26.214	28.535	30.834
20	7.471	9.783	12.180	14.606	17.041	19.475	21.899	24.309	26.701	29.071	31.417
21	7.531	9.892	12.341	14.820	17.308	19.794	22.269	24.729	27.170	29.587	31.979
22	7.588	9.997	12.496	15.026	17.565	20.101	22.626	25.134	27.622	30.085	32.520
23	7.642	10.098	12.646	15.225	17.813	20.397	22.970	25.525	28.058	30.565	33.042
24	7.694	10.195	12.789	15.417	18.052	20.684	23.303	25.903	28.480	31.028	33.546
25	7.744	10.288	12.928	15.602	18.284	20.961	23.625	26.269	28.887	31.477	34.033
26	7.791	10.377	13.062	15.780	18.507	21.229	23.936	26.623	29.282	31.911	34.505
27	7.837	10.463	13.191	15.953	18.724	21.489	24.238	26.966	29.665	32.332	34.961
28	7.880	10.546	13.316	16.121	18.934	21.741	24.531	27.298	30.036	32.739	35.404
29	7.922	10.626	13.436	16.283	19.138	21.985	24.816	27.622	30.396	33.135	35.834
30	7.962	10.704	13.553	16.440	19.335	22.223	25.092	27.935	30.746	33.520	36.251

Table B.18: American-Style Put Premiums
as a Function of Time and Volatility
Stock Price = $100
Strike Price = $100
Dividend Rate = 1%

Mo	Volatility										
	0.15	0.20	0.25	0.30	0.35	0.40	0.45	0.50	0.55	0.60	0.65
1	1.551	2.121	2.692	3.264	3.837	4.409	4.982	5.554	6.126	6.698	7.270
2	2.103	2.903	3.705	4.510	5.315	6.120	6.925	7.730	8.534	9.338	10.140
3	2.496	3.467	4.445	5.425	6.406	7.387	8.368	9.349	10.328	11.306	12.283
4	2.806	3.921	5.043	6.170	7.297	8.425	9.553	10.679	11.803	12.926	14.046
5	3.066	4.304	5.553	6.806	8.061	9.317	10.571	11.824	13.075	14.322	15.567
6	3.289	4.638	5.999	7.366	8.735	10.104	11.472	12.838	14.201	15.560	16.915
7	3.486	4.935	6.398	7.868	9.341	10.813	12.284	13.752	15.217	16.677	18.131
8	3.662	5.202	6.759	8.324	9.892	11.460	13.026	14.588	16.146	17.698	19.244
9	3.820	5.446	7.090	8.743	10.400	12.056	13.709	15.359	17.003	18.641	20.270
10	3.965	5.670	7.396	9.131	10.871	12.610	14.345	16.076	17.801	19.518	21.226
11	4.098	5.877	7.680	9.493	11.310	13.127	14.940	16.747	18.547	20.339	22.120
12	4.220	6.070	7.945	9.832	11.723	13.613	15.499	17.379	19.250	21.111	22.961
13	4.334	6.250	8.194	10.151	12.112	14.072	16.027	17.975	19.914	21.841	23.755
14	4.440	6.420	8.429	10.452	12.480	14.507	16.528	18.540	20.543	22.533	24.508
15	4.539	6.579	8.651	10.738	12.830	14.920	17.003	19.078	21.141	23.191	25.224
16	4.632	6.730	8.862	11.010	13.163	15.313	17.457	19.591	21.712	23.818	25.907
17	4.720	6.873	9.063	11.269	13.480	15.689	17.890	20.081	22.258	24.418	26.559
18	4.803	7.009	9.254	11.516	13.784	16.049	18.305	20.550	22.780	24.992	27.184
19	4.881	7.138	9.436	11.753	14.075	16.394	18.704	21.001	23.282	25.543	27.783
20	4.955	7.261	9.611	11.980	14.354	16.725	19.086	21.434	23.764	26.073	28.359
21	5.025	7.379	9.778	12.198	14.623	17.044	19.455	21.851	24.228	26.583	28.913
22	5.091	7.491	9.939	12.407	14.882	17.351	19.810	22.253	24.676	27.075	29.447
23	5.155	7.599	10.093	12.609	15.131	17.648	20.153	22.641	25.107	27.549	29.962
24	5.215	7.703	10.242	12.804	15.372	17.934	20.484	23.016	25.525	28.007	30.459
25	5.273	7.802	10.385	12.992	15.604	18.211	20.804	23.378	25.928	28.450	30.940
26	5.328	7.898	10.523	13.173	15.829	18.479	21.115	23.730	26.319	28.879	31.405
27	5.381	7.990	10.657	13.349	16.047	18.739	21.415	24.070	26.698	29.295	31.856
28	5.432	8.078	10.785	13.519	16.258	18.991	21.707	24.400	27.066	29.698	32.293
29	5.480	8.164	10.910	13.683	16.463	19.235	21.990	24.721	27.422	30.089	32.717
30	5.526	8.246	11.031	13.843	16.662	19.472	22.265	25.032	27.769	30.469	33.128

Table B.19: American-Style Put Premiums
as a Function of Time and Volatility
Stock Price = $100
Strike Price = $95
Dividend Rate = 1%

Mo	Volatility										
	0.15	0.20	0.25	0.30	0.35	0.40	0.45	0.50	0.55	0.60	0.65
1	0.204	0.511	0.899	1.338	1.807	2.298	2.802	3.317	3.839	4.366	4.898
2	0.537	1.097	1.738	2.423	3.136	3.867	4.609	5.359	6.114	6.874	7.637
3	0.832	1.576	2.400	3.266	4.158	5.066	5.984	6.909	7.838	8.771	9.706
4	1.087	1.981	2.954	3.968	5.007	6.061	7.124	8.193	9.266	10.341	11.418
5	1.312	2.334	3.434	4.576	5.741	6.921	8.110	9.304	10.501	11.700	12.898
6	1.511	2.646	3.860	5.114	6.393	7.685	8.986	10.291	11.598	12.906	14.212
7	1.691	2.927	4.243	5.600	6.981	8.375	9.777	11.183	12.590	13.996	15.399
8	1.854	3.183	4.592	6.044	7.518	9.006	10.501	11.999	13.497	14.993	16.486
9	2.004	3.418	4.914	6.452	8.014	9.588	11.169	12.753	14.336	15.915	17.490
10	2.141	3.635	5.212	6.832	8.474	10.130	11.792	13.455	15.117	16.773	18.424
11	2.269	3.837	5.490	7.186	8.905	10.637	12.375	14.113	15.848	17.577	19.299
12	2.387	4.025	5.750	7.519	9.310	11.114	12.923	14.732	16.536	18.334	20.123
13	2.498	4.202	5.995	7.832	9.693	11.565	13.441	15.317	17.187	19.049	20.901
14	2.602	4.369	6.227	8.129	10.055	11.992	13.933	15.871	17.804	19.727	21.639
15	2.699	4.527	6.446	8.410	10.399	12.398	14.400	16.399	18.391	20.372	22.340
16	2.791	4.676	6.654	8.678	10.726	12.785	14.846	16.903	18.951	20.988	23.010
17	2.878	4.818	6.852	8.934	11.039	13.155	15.273	17.385	19.487	21.576	23.649
18	2.960	4.952	7.042	9.178	11.339	13.510	15.681	17.846	20.000	22.140	24.262
19	3.038	5.081	7.223	9.413	11.626	13.850	16.073	18.289	20.493	22.681	24.850
20	3.111	5.204	7.396	9.637	11.902	14.176	16.450	18.715	20.966	23.201	25.415
21	3.182	5.321	7.562	9.853	12.168	14.491	16.813	19.125	21.422	23.702	25.958
22	3.249	5.433	7.722	10.061	12.423	14.794	17.163	19.520	21.862	24.184	26.482
23	3.313	5.541	7.876	10.261	12.670	15.087	17.500	19.902	22.287	24.650	26.988
24	3.374	5.645	8.024	10.454	12.908	15.370	17.827	20.271	22.697	25.100	27.476
25	3.432	5.745	8.166	10.640	13.138	15.643	18.143	20.628	23.094	25.536	27.948
26	3.488	5.841	8.304	10.821	13.361	15.908	18.448	20.974	23.479	25.957	28.405
27	3.542	5.933	8.437	10.995	13.577	16.164	18.745	21.309	23.851	26.366	28.848
28	3.593	6.022	8.566	11.164	13.786	16.413	19.032	21.635	24.213	26.762	29.277
29	3.642	6.108	8.690	11.328	13.989	16.655	19.312	21.950	24.564	27.147	29.693
30	3.689	6.191	8.811	11.486	14.186	16.889	19.583	22.257	24.905	27.520	30.098

Table B.20: American-Style Put Premiums
as a Function of Time and Volatility
Stock Price = $100
Strike Price = $90
Dividend Rate = 1%

Mo	Volatility										
	0.15	0.20	0.25	0.30	0.35	0.40	0.45	0.50	0.55	0.60	0.65
1	0.008	0.062	0.195	0.405	0.681	1.008	1.373	1.769	2.187	2.624	3.076
2	0.076	0.295	0.654	1.116	1.648	2.231	2.850	3.495	4.159	4.839	5.530
3	0.186	0.570	1.116	1.768	2.491	3.260	4.063	4.889	5.732	6.588	7.453
4	0.312	0.842	1.543	2.351	3.227	4.148	5.100	6.073	7.061	8.061	9.068
5	0.440	1.099	1.934	2.875	3.883	4.933	6.013	7.112	8.225	9.348	10.477
6	0.567	1.340	2.293	3.352	4.475	5.640	6.832	8.043	9.266	10.498	11.735
7	0.688	1.565	2.625	3.789	5.017	6.284	7.578	8.890	10.213	11.542	12.876
8	0.804	1.776	2.933	4.193	5.516	6.878	8.265	9.668	11.082	12.501	13.923
9	0.915	1.975	3.220	4.569	5.980	7.429	8.902	10.391	11.888	13.390	14.893
10	1.020	2.161	3.489	4.921	6.414	7.944	9.497	11.065	12.640	14.219	15.797
11	1.119	2.337	3.743	5.252	6.821	8.428	10.056	11.698	13.346	14.996	16.644
12	1.214	2.503	3.982	5.564	7.206	8.884	10.583	12.295	14.012	15.729	17.443
13	1.304	2.661	4.208	5.860	7.570	9.316	11.082	12.860	14.642	16.423	18.198
14	1.390	2.810	4.424	6.140	7.916	9.727	11.557	13.397	15.240	17.081	18.915
15	1.471	2.953	4.629	6.408	8.246	10.118	12.009	13.909	15.810	17.708	19.598
16	1.549	3.089	4.824	6.663	8.560	10.491	12.440	14.397	16.355	18.307	20.249
17	1.623	3.219	5.011	6.907	8.862	10.849	12.853	14.865	16.875	18.879	20.872
18	1.694	3.343	5.190	7.141	9.150	11.192	13.250	15.313	17.375	19.428	21.468
19	1.762	3.462	5.361	7.366	9.428	11.521	13.630	15.744	17.854	19.955	22.041
20	1.827	3.576	5.526	7.581	9.694	11.838	13.997	16.159	18.316	20.462	22.592
21	1.889	3.685	5.685	7.789	9.951	12.143	14.350	16.558	18.760	20.950	23.122
22	1.949	3.791	5.837	7.990	10.199	12.438	14.690	16.944	19.189	21.421	23.633
23	2.006	3.892	5.984	8.183	10.438	12.723	15.019	17.316	19.603	21.875	24.127
24	2.061	3.990	6.126	8.370	10.669	12.998	15.338	17.676	20.004	22.315	24.603
25	2.114	4.084	6.263	8.550	10.893	13.264	15.646	18.025	20.392	22.740	25.064
26	2.164	4.174	6.396	8.725	11.110	13.522	15.944	18.362	20.767	23.152	25.511
27	2.213	4.262	6.524	8.894	11.320	13.772	16.234	18.690	21.131	23.551	25.943
28	2.260	4.347	6.649	9.058	11.524	14.015	16.515	19.008	21.485	23.938	26.363
29	2.305	4.429	6.769	9.217	11.721	14.251	16.788	19.316	21.828	24.314	26.770
30	2.349	4.508	6.886	9.372	11.914	14.480	17.053	19.616	22.161	24.679	27.165

Table B.21: American-Style Put Premiums
as a Function of Time and Volatility
Stock Price = $100
Strike Price = $85
Dividend Rate = 1%

Mo	Volatility										
	0.15	0.20	0.25	0.30	0.35	0.40	0.45	0.50	0.55	0.60	0.65
1	0.000	0.003	0.024	0.084	0.193	0.355	0.566	0.819	1.108	1.427	1.771
2	0.005	0.052	0.187	0.423	0.750	1.151	1.610	2.116	2.657	3.227	3.820
3	0.026	0.155	0.431	0.839	1.352	1.942	2.591	3.284	4.010	4.762	5.534
4	0.062	0.288	0.700	1.259	1.928	2.674	3.477	4.321	5.196	6.095	7.012
5	0.110	0.435	0.971	1.664	2.467	3.346	4.281	5.254	6.256	7.280	8.320
6	0.166	0.586	1.236	2.048	2.970	3.967	5.016	6.103	7.217	8.351	9.499
7	0.226	0.737	1.492	2.411	3.440	4.542	5.695	6.884	8.098	9.330	10.575
8	0.289	0.886	1.737	2.755	3.881	5.079	6.326	7.608	8.913	10.235	11.568
9	0.353	1.032	1.972	3.080	4.295	5.582	6.916	8.284	9.673	11.077	12.490
10	0.417	1.172	2.196	3.388	4.687	6.056	7.471	8.917	10.385	11.865	13.353
11	0.480	1.309	2.410	3.681	5.058	6.504	7.994	9.515	11.055	12.607	14.165
12	0.543	1.440	2.615	3.960	5.411	6.928	8.490	10.080	11.689	13.307	14.931
13	0.604	1.567	2.812	4.227	5.746	7.332	8.961	10.617	12.290	13.972	15.657
14	0.664	1.689	3.000	4.481	6.067	7.718	9.410	11.129	12.862	14.604	16.347
15	0.722	1.807	3.181	4.725	6.373	8.086	9.839	11.617	13.409	15.207	17.005
16	0.779	1.921	3.355	4.959	6.667	8.439	10.249	12.084	13.931	15.783	17.633
17	0.834	2.030	3.522	5.184	6.949	8.777	10.643	12.532	14.432	16.335	18.234
18	0.887	2.136	3.683	5.401	7.221	9.102	11.022	12.962	14.912	16.864	18.811
19	0.939	2.238	3.838	5.609	7.482	9.416	11.386	13.376	15.375	17.373	19.365
20	0.989	2.337	3.988	5.810	7.734	9.718	11.737	13.775	15.820	17.863	19.898
21	1.038	2.433	4.132	6.004	7.977	10.009	12.075	14.159	16.249	18.335	20.411
22	1.085	2.525	4.272	6.192	8.212	10.291	12.402	14.531	16.664	18.791	20.906
23	1.130	2.614	4.408	6.374	8.439	10.563	12.719	14.890	17.064	19.231	21.385
24	1.175	2.701	4.538	6.549	8.659	10.827	13.025	15.238	17.452	19.657	21.847
25	1.217	2.784	4.665	6.720	8.873	11.082	13.322	15.575	17.827	20.070	22.295
26	1.259	2.866	4.788	6.885	9.080	11.330	13.610	15.901	18.191	20.469	22.728
27	1.299	2.944	4.908	7.045	9.280	11.571	13.889	16.219	18.544	20.857	23.149
28	1.338	3.021	5.024	7.201	9.475	11.804	14.161	16.526	18.887	21.233	23.556
29	1.376	3.095	5.136	7.352	9.665	12.032	14.425	16.826	19.220	21.598	23.952
30	1.413	3.167	5.245	7.499	9.849	12.253	14.681	17.117	19.544	21.953	24.336

Table B.22: American-Style Put Premiums
as a Function of Time and Volatility
Stock Price = $100
Strike Price = $80
Dividend Rate = 1%

Mo	Volatility										
	0.15	0.20	0.25	0.30	0.35	0.40	0.45	0.50	0.55	0.60	0.65
1	0.000	0.000	0.002	0.011	0.039	0.096	0.188	0.318	0.485	0.686	0.918
2	0.000	0.006	0.038	0.126	0.286	0.517	0.815	1.170	1.574	2.017	2.494
3	0.002	0.030	0.133	0.339	0.650	1.053	1.531	2.071	2.660	3.288	3.948
4	0.008	0.076	0.267	0.597	1.050	1.603	2.235	2.928	3.668	4.446	5.253
5	0.020	0.140	0.424	0.872	1.454	2.139	2.903	3.727	4.596	5.501	6.433
6	0.037	0.215	0.593	1.150	1.848	2.652	3.533	4.472	5.455	6.471	7.512
7	0.058	0.298	0.766	1.426	2.230	3.139	4.126	5.168	6.253	7.368	8.507
8	0.083	0.387	0.940	1.695	2.597	3.603	4.685	5.822	6.998	8.204	9.431
9	0.112	0.478	1.113	1.957	2.949	4.044	5.214	6.437	7.698	8.987	10.295
10	0.142	0.570	1.284	2.210	3.286	4.465	5.716	7.019	8.358	9.724	11.106
11	0.175	0.663	1.450	2.455	3.609	4.866	6.193	7.571	8.983	10.420	11.872
12	0.208	0.755	1.613	2.691	3.919	5.249	6.648	8.096	9.576	11.080	12.597
13	0.243	0.846	1.771	2.920	4.217	5.616	7.083	8.596	10.141	11.707	13.286
14	0.278	0.936	1.925	3.140	4.504	5.968	7.498	9.074	10.681	12.306	13.943
15	0.313	1.025	2.075	3.353	4.780	6.306	7.897	9.533	11.197	12.878	14.569
16	0.348	1.111	2.221	3.559	5.046	6.631	8.280	9.972	11.691	13.426	15.169
17	0.383	1.196	2.362	3.758	5.303	6.944	8.649	10.395	12.166	13.952	15.745
18	0.418	1.279	2.499	3.951	5.551	7.246	9.004	10.801	12.623	14.458	16.297
19	0.452	1.360	2.632	4.137	5.790	7.538	9.346	11.193	13.063	14.944	16.828
20	0.486	1.439	2.762	4.318	6.022	7.820	9.677	11.572	13.487	15.413	17.340
21	0.520	1.517	2.888	4.494	6.247	8.092	9.997	11.937	13.897	15.866	17.833
22	0.553	1.592	3.010	4.664	6.464	8.357	10.307	12.291	14.294	16.303	18.310
23	0.585	1.666	3.129	4.829	6.675	8.613	10.606	12.633	14.677	16.726	18.770
24	0.617	1.737	3.245	4.990	6.880	8.861	10.897	12.965	15.049	17.136	19.215
25	0.648	1.807	3.357	5.146	7.079	9.102	11.179	13.287	15.409	17.532	19.647
26	0.678	1.875	3.467	5.297	7.273	9.337	11.453	13.599	15.758	17.917	20.065
27	0.708	1.942	3.574	5.445	7.461	9.564	11.720	13.903	16.098	18.290	20.470
28	0.737	2.007	3.678	5.589	7.644	9.786	11.979	14.198	16.427	18.653	20.864
29	0.766	2.070	3.779	5.729	7.822	10.002	12.231	14.485	16.748	19.005	21.246
30	0.794	2.132	3.878	5.865	7.996	10.212	12.476	14.764	17.060	19.347	21.618

Table B.23: American-Style Put Premiums
as a Function of Time and Volatility
Stock Price = $100
Strike Price = $75
Dividend Rate = 1%

Mo	Volatility										
	0.15	0.20	0.25	0.30	0.35	0.40	0.45	0.50	0.55	0.60	0.65
1	0.000	0.000	0.000	0.001	0.005	0.019	0.048	0.100	0.178	0.284	0.418
2	0.000	0.000	0.005	0.029	0.088	0.197	0.361	0.580	0.850	1.166	1.522
3	0.000	0.004	0.031	0.113	0.270	0.510	0.826	1.211	1.655	2.149	2.685
4	0.001	0.015	0.083	0.244	0.512	0.881	1.338	1.870	2.463	3.106	3.789
5	0.003	0.035	0.157	0.405	0.782	1.273	1.857	2.518	3.240	4.010	4.820
6	0.006	0.065	0.247	0.584	1.065	1.668	2.367	3.143	3.978	4.861	5.780
7	0.012	0.101	0.348	0.772	1.352	2.057	2.861	3.740	4.678	5.660	6.678
8	0.019	0.144	0.457	0.965	1.637	2.437	3.336	4.310	5.340	6.414	7.521
9	0.029	0.192	0.571	1.159	1.917	2.806	3.793	4.854	5.969	7.126	8.314
10	0.040	0.244	0.687	1.352	2.192	3.164	4.232	5.373	6.567	7.801	9.064
11	0.053	0.298	0.805	1.543	2.460	3.509	4.654	5.870	7.137	8.443	9.776
12	0.068	0.355	0.923	1.731	2.721	3.842	5.059	6.346	7.682	9.054	10.452
13	0.083	0.413	1.040	1.916	2.974	4.165	5.449	6.802	8.203	9.638	11.097
14	0.100	0.472	1.157	2.096	3.220	4.476	5.825	7.240	8.702	10.197	11.713
15	0.118	0.531	1.272	2.273	3.460	4.777	6.187	7.662	9.182	10.732	12.303
16	0.136	0.591	1.386	2.445	3.692	5.069	6.537	8.068	9.643	11.247	12.869
17	0.155	0.650	1.498	2.614	3.918	5.351	6.875	8.460	10.087	11.741	13.413
18	0.174	0.709	1.608	2.778	4.137	5.625	7.201	8.838	10.515	12.218	13.936
19	0.194	0.768	1.716	2.939	4.350	5.890	7.517	9.203	10.928	12.678	14.440
20	0.214	0.826	1.822	3.095	4.557	6.147	7.823	9.557	11.328	13.121	14.927
21	0.234	0.884	1.926	3.247	4.759	6.397	8.120	9.899	11.714	13.550	15.396
22	0.254	0.941	2.027	3.396	4.955	6.640	8.408	10.231	12.089	13.965	15.850
23	0.274	0.997	2.127	3.542	5.146	6.876	8.688	10.553	12.451	14.367	16.290
24	0.294	1.052	2.224	3.683	5.332	7.105	8.959	10.866	12.803	14.757	16.715
25	0.314	1.107	2.320	3.822	5.513	7.328	9.224	11.169	13.145	15.135	17.128
26	0.334	1.160	2.413	3.957	5.690	7.546	9.481	11.465	13.477	15.502	17.528
27	0.354	1.213	2.505	4.089	5.862	7.758	9.731	11.752	13.799	15.858	17.916
28	0.374	1.264	2.594	4.218	6.030	7.964	9.974	12.031	14.113	16.205	18.293
29	0.393	1.315	2.682	4.343	6.194	8.165	10.212	12.303	14.419	16.542	18.660
30	0.412	1.365	2.768	4.467	6.354	8.362	10.443	12.569	14.716	16.870	19.016

Table B.24: American-Style Put Premiums
as a Function of Time and Volatility
Stock Price = $100
Strike Price = $70
Dividend Rate = 1%

Mo	Volatility										
	0.15	0.20	0.25	0.30	0.35	0.40	0.45	0.50	0.55	0.60	0.65
1	0.000	0.000	0.000	0.000	0.000	0.003	0.009	0.024	0.053	0.098	0.163
2	0.000	0.000	0.001	0.005	0.021	0.061	0.136	0.252	0.410	0.612	0.855
3	0.000	0.001	0.006	0.030	0.094	0.215	0.399	0.646	0.953	1.315	1.723
4	0.000	0.003	0.021	0.084	0.218	0.436	0.736	1.113	1.558	2.060	2.613
5	0.000	0.007	0.048	0.163	0.377	0.695	1.108	1.605	2.173	2.801	3.478
6	0.001	0.016	0.087	0.263	0.560	0.975	1.494	2.101	2.780	3.519	4.305
7	0.002	0.028	0.137	0.376	0.756	1.264	1.882	2.590	3.370	4.208	5.093
8	0.004	0.045	0.196	0.500	0.960	1.557	2.267	3.067	3.939	4.868	5.842
9	0.006	0.066	0.261	0.631	1.169	1.849	2.645	3.531	4.488	5.500	6.555
10	0.010	0.090	0.331	0.766	1.378	2.138	3.013	3.979	5.015	6.104	7.235
11	0.014	0.117	0.406	0.904	1.588	2.422	3.373	4.413	5.522	6.683	7.883
12	0.019	0.147	0.483	1.043	1.795	2.700	3.722	4.833	6.010	7.238	8.504
13	0.024	0.179	0.562	1.182	2.000	2.972	4.061	5.238	6.480	7.771	9.098
14	0.031	0.213	0.643	1.321	2.202	3.238	4.391	5.630	6.933	8.284	9.667
15	0.038	0.248	0.725	1.459	2.400	3.498	4.711	6.010	7.371	8.777	10.215
16	0.046	0.284	0.807	1.596	2.595	3.751	5.022	6.377	7.793	9.252	10.742
17	0.055	0.321	0.889	1.731	2.785	3.997	5.324	6.733	8.201	9.711	11.249
18	0.064	0.359	0.971	1.864	2.972	4.238	5.617	7.078	8.596	10.154	11.739
19	0.073	0.398	1.053	1.995	3.155	4.472	5.902	7.412	8.978	10.582	12.211
20	0.083	0.437	1.134	2.125	3.334	4.701	6.180	7.737	9.348	10.997	12.668
21	0.093	0.476	1.215	2.252	3.509	4.924	6.449	8.052	9.708	11.398	13.110
22	0.104	0.515	1.294	2.376	3.681	5.141	6.712	8.359	10.056	11.787	13.538
23	0.115	0.554	1.373	2.499	3.848	5.354	6.968	8.656	10.395	12.165	13.953
24	0.126	0.594	1.451	2.619	4.012	5.561	7.217	8.946	10.724	12.531	14.355
25	0.137	0.633	1.528	2.738	4.172	5.763	7.460	9.229	11.044	12.887	14.745
26	0.149	0.671	1.603	2.854	4.329	5.960	7.697	9.504	11.355	13.234	15.125
27	0.160	0.710	1.678	2.967	4.483	6.153	7.928	9.771	11.658	13.570	15.493
28	0.172	0.748	1.751	3.079	4.633	6.342	8.153	10.033	11.954	13.898	15.851
29	0.183	0.786	1.823	3.188	4.781	6.526	8.374	10.287	12.241	14.217	16.200
30	0.195	0.824	1.895	3.296	4.925	6.706	8.589	10.536	12.522	14.528	16.539

Table B.25: American-Style Put Premiums
as a Function of Time and Volatility
Stock Price = $100
Strike Price = $65
Dividend Rate = 1%

Mo	\multicolumn{11}{c}{Volatility}
	0.15	0.20	0.25	0.30	0.35	0.40	0.45	0.50	0.55	0.60	0.65
1	0.000	0.000	0.000	0.000	0.000	0.000	0.001	0.004	0.012	0.027	0.052
2	0.000	0.000	0.000	0.001	0.004	0.015	0.042	0.093	0.173	0.286	0.434
3	0.000	0.000	0.001	0.006	0.027	0.077	0.168	0.309	0.500	0.742	1.032
4	0.000	0.000	0.004	0.024	0.079	0.190	0.365	0.608	0.916	1.284	1.706
5	0.000	0.001	0.012	0.056	0.160	0.342	0.607	0.954	1.373	1.857	2.398
6	0.000	0.003	0.026	0.102	0.263	0.522	0.877	1.322	1.846	2.436	3.083
7	0.000	0.007	0.046	0.162	0.384	0.719	1.163	1.701	2.320	3.008	3.752
8	0.001	0.012	0.072	0.232	0.517	0.929	1.456	2.082	2.790	3.566	4.398
9	0.001	0.019	0.104	0.310	0.659	1.145	1.752	2.460	3.251	4.109	5.022
10	0.002	0.029	0.141	0.396	0.807	1.365	2.047	2.832	3.701	4.635	5.623
11	0.003	0.040	0.183	0.486	0.959	1.586	2.340	3.198	4.139	5.144	6.201
12	0.005	0.053	0.228	0.581	1.114	1.807	2.629	3.556	4.564	5.637	6.758
13	0.006	0.068	0.276	0.678	1.270	2.026	2.914	3.905	4.978	6.113	7.295
14	0.008	0.085	0.326	0.777	1.427	2.243	3.193	4.246	5.379	6.573	7.813
15	0.011	0.103	0.379	0.878	1.583	2.458	3.467	4.578	5.769	7.019	8.313
16	0.014	0.122	0.433	0.979	1.738	2.669	3.735	4.902	6.147	7.450	8.795
17	0.017	0.143	0.488	1.081	1.892	2.877	3.997	5.218	6.515	7.868	9.262
18	0.020	0.164	0.545	1.183	2.044	3.081	4.253	5.525	6.872	8.273	9.713
19	0.024	0.187	0.602	1.284	2.194	3.282	4.503	5.825	7.219	8.666	10.150
20	0.028	0.210	0.659	1.385	2.343	3.479	4.748	6.116	7.556	9.047	10.573
21	0.033	0.234	0.718	1.486	2.489	3.672	4.988	6.401	7.884	9.417	10.984
22	0.038	0.258	0.776	1.586	2.633	3.861	5.222	6.679	8.204	9.777	11.382
23	0.043	0.283	0.834	1.684	2.775	4.047	5.451	6.949	8.515	10.127	11.769
24	0.048	0.308	0.892	1.782	2.915	4.229	5.674	7.213	8.818	10.467	12.145
25	0.053	0.334	0.950	1.878	3.052	4.407	5.893	7.471	9.113	10.798	12.510
26	0.059	0.360	1.008	1.974	3.187	4.582	6.107	7.723	9.401	11.121	12.865
27	0.065	0.385	1.065	2.068	3.320	4.754	6.316	7.969	9.682	11.435	13.211
28	0.071	0.411	1.122	2.161	3.451	4.922	6.521	8.209	9.956	11.741	13.548
29	0.077	0.438	1.178	2.252	3.579	5.087	6.721	8.444	10.224	12.040	13.876
30	0.083	0.464	1.234	2.343	3.705	5.248	6.918	8.673	10.485	12.331	14.195

Table B.26: American-Style Put Premiums
as a Function of Time and Volatility
Stock Price = $100
Strike Price = $60
Dividend Rate = 1%

Mo	Volatility										
	0.15	0.20	0.25	0.30	0.35	0.40	0.45	0.50	0.55	0.60	0.65
1	0.000	0.000	0.000	0.000	0.000	0.000	0.000	0.001	0.002	0.006	0.013
2	0.000	0.000	0.000	0.000	0.001	0.003	0.010	0.028	0.062	0.116	0.195
3	0.000	0.000	0.000	0.001	0.006	0.023	0.060	0.129	0.234	0.380	0.567
4	0.000	0.000	0.001	0.005	0.024	0.071	0.160	0.299	0.493	0.742	1.042
5	0.000	0.000	0.003	0.016	0.058	0.148	0.300	0.520	0.806	1.157	1.565
6	0.000	0.001	0.007	0.034	0.108	0.251	0.472	0.773	1.151	1.598	2.106
7	0.000	0.002	0.013	0.060	0.173	0.373	0.665	1.048	1.512	2.050	2.650
8	0.000	0.003	0.023	0.094	0.251	0.510	0.873	1.334	1.881	2.503	3.188
9	0.000	0.005	0.036	0.136	0.338	0.657	1.090	1.626	2.252	2.953	3.717
10	0.001	0.008	0.053	0.183	0.434	0.813	1.314	1.922	2.620	3.395	4.233
11	0.001	0.012	0.072	0.236	0.536	0.974	1.540	2.217	2.985	3.829	4.735
12	0.001	0.017	0.095	0.294	0.643	1.139	1.768	2.510	3.344	4.253	5.223
13	0.002	0.023	0.121	0.356	0.753	1.307	1.996	2.800	3.697	4.667	5.697
14	0.002	0.030	0.148	0.421	0.867	1.475	2.223	3.086	4.042	5.071	6.157
15	0.003	0.038	0.179	0.488	0.982	1.644	2.448	3.368	4.380	5.464	6.604
16	0.004	0.046	0.211	0.558	1.098	1.812	2.671	3.645	4.710	5.847	7.038
17	0.005	0.056	0.244	0.629	1.216	1.980	2.890	3.916	5.033	6.219	7.459
18	0.006	0.067	0.280	0.702	1.333	2.146	3.107	4.183	5.349	6.582	7.868
19	0.007	0.078	0.316	0.775	1.451	2.311	3.320	4.444	5.657	6.936	8.265
20	0.009	0.091	0.353	0.849	1.568	2.474	3.530	4.700	5.958	7.280	8.651
21	0.010	0.103	0.392	0.924	1.685	2.636	3.736	4.951	6.251	7.616	9.027
22	0.012	0.117	0.431	0.999	1.801	2.795	3.939	5.196	6.538	7.943	9.392
23	0.014	0.131	0.471	1.074	1.916	2.952	4.138	5.437	6.819	8.262	9.747
24	0.016	0.146	0.511	1.149	2.030	3.107	4.333	5.672	7.093	8.573	10.094
25	0.019	0.160	0.552	1.224	2.143	3.260	4.525	5.903	7.361	8.876	10.431
26	0.021	0.176	0.593	1.298	2.255	3.410	4.714	6.128	7.622	9.172	10.760
27	0.024	0.192	0.634	1.373	2.366	3.558	4.899	6.350	7.878	9.461	11.080
28	0.026	0.208	0.675	1.446	2.475	3.704	5.081	6.566	8.129	9.744	11.392
29	0.029	0.224	0.716	1.519	2.583	3.847	5.259	6.779	8.373	10.019	11.697
30	0.032	0.241	0.758	1.592	2.689	3.988	5.434	6.987	8.613	10.289	11.995

Table B.27: American-Style Put Premiums
as a Function of Time and Volatility
Stock Price = $100
Strike Price = $120
Dividend Rate = 2%

Mo	Volatility										
	0.15	0.20	0.25	0.30	0.35	0.40	0.45	0.50	0.55	0.60	0.65
1	20.000	20.000	20.000	20.000	20.002	20.083	20.255	20.496	20.790	21.127	21.501
2	20.000	20.000	20.000	20.036	20.276	20.664	21.150	21.707	22.318	22.969	23.652
3	20.000	20.000	20.002	20.242	20.731	21.366	22.095	22.891	23.734	24.613	25.520
4	20.000	20.000	20.066	20.523	21.222	22.060	22.988	23.976	25.007	26.070	27.156
5	20.000	20.000	20.184	20.829	21.709	22.721	23.817	24.969	26.159	27.377	28.616
6	20.000	20.000	20.328	21.140	22.178	23.343	24.587	25.882	27.212	28.566	29.938
7	20.000	20.001	20.486	21.447	22.628	23.929	25.305	26.728	28.183	29.659	31.150
8	20.000	20.017	20.650	21.747	23.056	24.482	25.977	27.516	29.085	30.672	32.271
9	20.000	20.048	20.816	22.037	23.465	25.004	26.609	28.255	29.928	31.617	33.315
10	20.000	20.089	20.981	22.317	23.854	25.499	27.206	28.951	30.720	32.503	34.292
11	20.000	20.137	21.144	22.587	24.226	25.969	27.771	29.609	31.468	33.338	35.212
12	20.000	20.189	21.304	22.848	24.582	26.417	28.308	30.233	32.176	34.128	36.081
13	20.000	20.245	21.461	23.099	24.923	26.845	28.820	30.827	32.849	34.877	36.904
14	20.000	20.303	21.614	23.341	25.250	27.254	29.309	31.393	33.490	35.590	37.688
15	20.000	20.362	21.763	23.574	25.565	27.646	29.777	31.934	34.101	36.270	38.434
16	20.000	20.422	21.909	23.800	25.867	28.023	30.226	32.452	34.687	36.921	39.148
17	20.000	20.482	22.050	24.018	26.159	28.386	30.657	32.949	35.248	37.544	39.831
18	20.000	20.542	22.188	24.229	26.440	28.735	31.072	33.427	35.787	38.143	40.487
19	20.000	20.602	22.322	24.433	26.712	29.072	31.472	33.887	36.306	38.718	41.116
20	20.000	20.662	22.452	24.630	26.974	29.397	31.857	34.331	36.806	39.272	41.722
21	20.000	20.720	22.579	24.822	27.228	29.711	32.229	34.759	37.288	39.806	42.306
22	20.000	20.779	22.702	25.008	27.474	30.015	32.588	35.173	37.753	40.322	42.870
23	20.000	20.836	22.823	25.189	27.713	30.309	32.936	35.573	38.204	40.820	43.414
24	20.000	20.892	22.940	25.364	27.944	30.594	33.274	35.960	38.639	41.302	43.939
25	20.000	20.948	23.054	25.534	28.169	30.871	33.600	36.335	39.061	41.768	44.448
26	20.000	21.002	23.165	25.700	28.386	31.139	33.918	36.700	39.470	42.220	44.941
27	20.000	21.056	23.274	25.861	28.598	31.400	34.226	37.053	39.867	42.658	45.419
28	20.000	21.109	23.380	26.018	28.804	31.653	34.525	37.396	40.253	43.084	45.882
29	20.000	21.161	23.483	26.171	29.005	31.900	34.816	37.730	40.627	43.497	46.332
30	20.000	21.212	23.584	26.320	29.200	32.140	35.099	38.055	40.991	43.899	46.768

Table B.28: American-Style Put Premiums
as a Function of Time and Volatility
Stock Price = $100
Strike Price = $115
Dividend Rate = 2%

Mo	Volatility										
	0.15	0.20	0.25	0.30	0.35	0.40	0.45	0.50	0.55	0.60	0.65
1	15.000	15.000	15.000	15.025	15.175	15.419	15.729	16.090	16.490	16.921	17.376
2	15.000	15.000	15.059	15.368	15.830	16.388	17.009	17.675	18.376	19.101	19.846
3	15.000	15.000	15.266	15.822	16.525	17.316	18.164	19.053	19.969	20.907	21.860
4	15.000	15.040	15.521	16.280	17.179	18.159	19.191	20.258	21.350	22.459	23.581
5	15.000	15.121	15.787	16.721	17.786	18.927	20.115	21.334	22.575	23.830	25.095
6	15.000	15.223	16.051	17.137	18.348	19.630	20.955	22.308	23.680	25.064	26.455
7	15.000	15.335	16.308	17.530	18.872	20.280	21.728	23.201	24.691	26.190	27.694
8	15.000	15.451	16.556	17.901	19.361	20.884	22.445	24.027	25.624	27.228	28.834
9	15.000	15.569	16.793	18.252	19.821	21.450	23.113	24.797	26.492	28.192	29.892
10	15.000	15.686	17.021	18.585	20.255	21.982	23.741	25.518	27.304	29.093	30.880
11	15.002	15.801	17.239	18.900	20.665	22.484	24.332	26.197	28.068	29.940	31.808
12	15.009	15.914	17.448	19.201	21.055	22.960	24.892	26.838	28.789	30.739	32.683
13	15.020	16.024	17.649	19.488	21.426	23.412	25.424	27.447	29.473	31.496	33.511
14	15.035	16.131	17.841	19.763	21.779	23.843	25.930	28.026	30.123	32.215	34.298
15	15.052	16.236	18.027	20.026	22.118	24.255	26.413	28.578	30.743	32.901	35.048
16	15.071	16.337	18.205	20.278	22.442	24.649	26.875	29.106	31.335	33.556	35.763
17	15.091	16.436	18.377	20.521	22.754	25.027	27.318	29.613	31.903	34.183	36.448
18	15.112	16.531	18.543	20.755	23.053	25.391	27.743	30.098	32.447	34.784	37.104
19	15.134	16.624	18.703	20.980	23.342	25.740	28.152	30.565	32.971	35.362	37.734
20	15.157	16.714	18.857	21.197	23.619	26.077	28.546	31.015	33.475	35.918	38.340
21	15.179	16.802	19.007	21.407	23.887	26.401	28.927	31.449	33.960	36.453	38.924
22	15.202	16.887	19.152	21.610	24.146	26.715	29.294	31.868	34.429	36.970	39.487
23	15.225	16.970	19.292	21.806	24.397	27.019	29.649	32.273	34.882	37.469	40.030
24	15.248	17.050	19.428	21.996	24.639	27.313	29.992	32.664	35.320	37.952	40.555
25	15.271	17.128	19.560	22.180	24.874	27.597	30.325	33.044	35.744	38.419	41.063
26	15.293	17.205	19.688	22.358	25.102	27.873	30.648	33.412	36.155	38.871	41.555
27	15.316	17.279	19.812	22.531	25.323	28.141	30.961	33.769	36.554	39.310	42.031
28	15.338	17.351	19.933	22.700	25.538	28.401	31.265	34.115	36.941	39.736	42.493
29	15.360	17.421	20.050	22.863	25.747	28.654	31.561	34.452	37.317	40.149	42.941
30	15.382	17.489	20.164	23.022	25.950	28.900	31.848	34.779	37.682	40.550	43.377

Table B.29: American-Style Put Premiums
as a Function of Time and Volatility
Stock Price = $100
Strike Price = $110
Dividend Rate = 2%

Mo	\multicolumn{11}{c}{Volatility}
	0.15	0.20	0.25	0.30	0.35	0.40	0.45	0.50	0.55	0.60	0.65
1	10.000	10.000	10.117	10.382	10.731	11.137	11.582	12.055	12.550	13.061	13.585
2	10.000	10.131	10.564	11.137	11.789	12.488	13.219	13.972	14.740	15.521	16.310
3	10.001	10.359	11.029	11.830	12.700	13.611	14.549	15.504	16.472	17.449	18.432
4	10.034	10.600	11.463	12.447	13.493	14.576	15.682	16.802	17.933	19.070	20.211
5	10.093	10.836	11.862	13.002	14.199	15.428	16.678	17.940	19.210	20.484	21.761
6	10.165	11.061	12.230	13.506	14.835	16.195	17.571	18.959	20.352	21.748	23.143
7	10.241	11.274	12.570	13.969	15.418	16.894	18.385	19.885	21.389	22.893	24.396
8	10.320	11.475	12.887	14.397	15.955	17.538	19.134	20.737	22.341	23.945	25.545
9	10.398	11.665	13.183	14.797	16.455	18.136	19.829	21.526	23.224	24.919	26.609
10	10.474	11.845	13.462	15.171	16.922	18.695	20.478	22.263	24.047	25.827	27.601
11	10.549	12.016	13.724	15.523	17.362	19.220	21.087	22.955	24.820	26.679	28.531
12	10.622	12.178	13.973	15.855	17.777	19.716	21.661	23.607	25.548	27.482	29.407
13	10.692	12.333	14.209	16.171	18.170	20.185	22.206	24.225	26.238	28.242	30.235
14	10.760	12.480	14.433	16.471	18.544	20.631	22.723	24.811	26.893	28.964	31.021
15	10.826	12.621	14.647	16.756	18.900	21.056	23.215	25.370	27.517	29.651	31.770
16	10.889	12.756	14.852	17.029	19.240	21.462	23.686	25.904	28.112	30.306	32.484
17	10.950	12.885	15.048	17.290	19.565	21.851	24.136	26.415	28.682	30.934	33.166
18	11.009	13.009	15.236	17.541	19.877	22.223	24.569	26.905	29.229	31.535	33.821
19	11.067	13.128	15.416	17.781	20.177	22.582	24.984	27.376	29.754	32.112	34.449
20	11.122	13.243	15.589	18.013	20.466	22.926	25.383	27.829	30.259	32.667	35.052
21	11.175	13.353	15.756	18.236	20.744	23.259	25.769	28.266	30.745	33.202	35.633
22	11.227	13.460	15.917	18.451	21.012	23.579	26.140	28.687	31.215	33.718	36.193
23	11.277	13.562	16.072	18.658	21.271	23.889	26.500	29.095	31.668	34.216	36.734
24	11.325	13.661	16.222	18.859	21.522	24.189	26.847	29.488	32.107	34.697	37.256
25	11.371	13.757	16.367	19.053	21.765	24.479	27.184	29.870	32.531	35.163	37.762
26	11.416	13.849	16.508	19.241	22.000	24.760	27.510	30.239	32.942	35.614	38.251
27	11.460	13.938	16.644	19.424	22.228	25.033	27.826	30.597	33.341	36.051	38.724
28	11.501	14.025	16.775	19.601	22.449	25.298	28.133	30.945	33.727	36.475	39.183
29	11.542	14.109	16.903	19.772	22.664	25.555	28.431	31.283	34.103	36.887	39.629
30	11.581	14.190	17.027	19.939	22.873	25.805	28.721	31.611	34.468	37.287	40.062

Table B.30: American-Style Put Premiums
as a Function of Time and Volatility
Stock Price = $100
Strike Price = $105
Dividend Rate = 2%

Mo	Volatility										
	0.15	0.20	0.25	0.30	0.35	0.40	0.45	0.50	0.55	0.60	0.65
1	5.098	5.439	5.879	6.367	6.883	7.416	7.961	8.514	9.073	9.637	10.203
2	5.375	6.012	6.732	7.489	8.267	9.057	9.855	10.659	11.465	12.275	13.085
3	5.640	6.488	7.410	8.363	9.334	10.314	11.299	12.289	13.280	14.272	15.264
4	5.875	6.894	7.980	9.094	10.222	11.358	12.499	13.641	14.784	15.927	17.068
5	6.086	7.250	8.476	9.728	10.993	12.264	13.538	14.813	16.086	17.358	18.628
6	6.276	7.567	8.918	10.292	11.678	13.069	14.462	15.853	17.244	18.631	20.014
7	6.449	7.854	9.317	10.803	12.298	13.797	15.297	16.795	18.290	19.781	21.268
8	6.608	8.117	9.682	11.269	12.865	14.464	16.062	17.657	19.249	20.835	22.415
9	6.754	8.359	10.019	11.700	13.389	15.079	16.769	18.455	20.135	21.810	23.476
10	6.890	8.584	10.332	12.101	13.876	15.653	17.428	19.198	20.961	22.717	24.464
11	7.017	8.794	10.625	12.475	14.333	16.190	18.045	19.894	21.735	23.568	25.389
12	7.136	8.991	10.899	12.828	14.762	16.696	18.627	20.550	22.465	24.369	26.260
13	7.248	9.176	11.158	13.160	15.168	17.175	19.176	21.170	23.154	25.126	27.084
14	7.353	9.350	11.403	13.475	15.553	17.628	19.698	21.759	23.808	25.844	27.865
15	7.452	9.516	11.636	13.775	15.919	18.060	20.195	22.319	24.431	26.528	28.608
16	7.545	9.673	11.857	14.060	16.268	18.472	20.669	22.854	25.025	27.180	29.317
17	7.634	9.822	12.068	14.333	16.602	18.866	21.122	23.366	25.594	27.804	29.994
18	7.718	9.965	12.270	14.594	16.921	19.244	21.557	23.856	26.139	28.402	30.643
19	7.798	10.101	12.463	14.844	17.228	19.607	21.975	24.328	26.662	28.976	31.266
20	7.875	10.232	12.649	15.085	17.523	19.956	22.376	24.781	27.165	29.527	31.864
21	7.948	10.357	12.827	15.316	17.807	20.292	22.763	25.217	27.650	30.059	32.440
22	8.018	10.477	12.999	15.539	18.081	20.616	23.136	25.638	28.118	30.571	32.995
23	8.085	10.593	13.164	15.754	18.346	20.929	23.497	26.045	28.569	31.065	33.531
24	8.149	10.704	13.323	15.962	18.601	21.231	23.845	26.438	29.005	31.543	34.049
25	8.211	10.812	13.477	16.163	18.848	21.524	24.183	26.819	29.428	32.006	34.549
26	8.270	10.915	13.626	16.357	19.088	21.808	24.510	27.187	29.837	32.453	35.034
27	8.327	11.015	13.770	16.545	19.320	22.083	24.827	27.545	30.233	32.887	35.503
28	8.382	11.112	13.910	16.728	19.545	22.350	25.134	27.892	30.618	33.308	35.958
29	8.436	11.205	14.045	16.905	19.764	22.609	25.433	28.229	30.991	33.716	36.399
30	8.487	11.295	14.176	17.077	19.976	22.861	25.723	28.556	31.354	34.113	36.827

Table B.31: American-Style Put Premiums
as a Function of Time and Volatility
Stock Price = $100
Strike Price = $100
Dividend Rate = 2%

Mo	\multicolumn{11}{c	}{Volatility}
	0.15	0.20	0.25	0.30	0.35	0.40	0.45	0.50	0.55	0.60	0.65
1	1.583	2.154	2.726	3.298	3.871	4.443	5.016	5.588	6.161	6.732	7.304
2	2.161	2.963	3.768	4.573	5.379	6.185	6.990	7.795	8.599	9.403	10.205
3	2.578	3.554	4.534	5.516	6.498	7.480	8.462	9.442	10.421	11.399	12.375
4	2.911	4.032	5.159	6.287	7.416	8.545	9.673	10.799	11.923	13.046	14.165
5	3.192	4.439	5.693	6.949	8.206	9.462	10.717	11.970	13.220	14.467	15.711
6	3.436	4.795	6.162	7.533	8.904	10.274	11.643	13.008	14.371	15.729	17.083
7	3.653	5.113	6.584	8.058	9.533	11.007	12.478	13.946	15.410	16.869	18.322
8	3.847	5.401	6.967	8.537	10.108	11.677	13.243	14.805	16.361	17.912	19.456
9	4.024	5.665	7.319	8.978	10.637	12.295	13.949	15.598	17.241	18.876	20.504
10	4.186	5.909	7.645	9.387	11.130	12.870	14.606	16.336	18.059	19.774	21.480
11	4.336	6.135	7.949	9.770	11.590	13.408	15.221	17.028	18.826	20.615	22.393
12	4.475	6.346	8.234	10.129	12.023	13.915	15.801	17.679	19.548	21.407	23.253
13	4.605	6.544	8.502	10.467	12.432	14.394	16.349	18.295	20.231	22.155	24.066
14	4.727	6.731	8.756	10.788	12.820	14.848	16.868	18.879	20.879	22.865	24.836
15	4.842	6.908	8.996	11.092	13.188	15.280	17.363	19.436	21.496	23.541	25.570
16	4.950	7.076	9.225	11.382	13.540	15.692	17.835	19.966	22.084	24.185	26.269
17	5.052	7.235	9.442	11.659	13.875	16.085	18.286	20.474	22.647	24.802	26.937
18	5.149	7.387	9.650	11.924	14.197	16.463	18.719	20.961	23.186	25.392	27.577
19	5.241	7.531	9.850	12.178	14.505	16.825	19.134	21.428	23.704	25.959	28.192
20	5.328	7.670	10.041	12.422	14.801	17.174	19.533	21.877	24.202	26.504	28.782
21	5.412	7.803	10.224	12.656	15.087	17.509	19.918	22.310	24.681	27.029	29.351
22	5.491	7.930	10.401	12.882	15.362	17.833	20.289	22.728	25.144	27.535	29.898
23	5.568	8.053	10.571	13.100	15.627	18.145	20.648	23.131	25.591	28.024	30.427
24	5.641	8.170	10.734	13.310	15.884	18.447	20.994	23.521	26.023	28.496	30.937
25	5.711	8.284	10.893	13.514	16.132	18.740	21.330	23.898	26.440	28.952	31.431
26	5.778	8.393	11.045	13.710	16.372	19.023	21.655	24.264	26.845	29.395	31.909
27	5.843	8.499	11.193	13.901	16.605	19.297	21.970	24.618	27.237	29.823	32.372
28	5.905	8.601	11.337	14.086	16.831	19.564	22.276	24.962	27.618	30.239	32.821
29	5.965	8.699	11.475	14.265	17.051	19.822	22.573	25.296	27.988	30.642	33.256
30	6.022	8.795	11.610	14.439	17.264	20.074	22.862	25.621	28.347	31.034	33.679

Table B.32: American-Style Put Premiums
as a Function of Time and Volatility
Stock Price = $100
Strike Price = $95
Dividend Rate = 2%

Mo	\multicolumn{11}{c}{Volatility}
	0.15	0.20	0.25	0.30	0.35	0.40	0.45	0.50	0.55	0.60	0.65
1	0.211	0.523	0.915	1.356	1.828	2.320	2.826	3.341	3.864	4.392	4.925
2	0.560	1.129	1.776	2.466	3.182	3.915	4.659	5.411	6.167	6.928	7.691
3	0.872	1.629	2.461	3.333	4.229	5.140	6.060	6.987	7.918	8.851	9.786
4	1.146	2.055	3.037	4.058	5.102	6.159	7.225	8.296	9.370	10.447	11.523
5	1.388	2.427	3.539	4.689	5.860	7.043	8.235	9.431	10.630	11.829	13.027
6	1.605	2.759	3.986	5.249	6.534	7.830	9.134	10.441	11.750	13.058	14.364
7	1.801	3.060	4.390	5.757	7.144	8.542	9.947	11.355	12.763	14.170	15.573
8	1.981	3.334	4.759	6.221	7.702	9.195	10.693	12.193	13.692	15.189	16.680
9	2.147	3.588	5.100	6.650	8.219	9.798	11.383	12.968	14.552	16.131	17.704
10	2.300	3.823	5.418	7.049	8.700	10.361	12.026	13.691	15.352	17.009	18.658
11	2.443	4.042	5.714	7.423	9.151	10.888	12.629	14.368	16.103	17.832	19.552
12	2.577	4.248	5.993	7.775	9.575	11.385	13.197	15.006	16.810	18.607	20.394
13	2.703	4.442	6.256	8.107	9.976	11.854	13.734	15.610	17.480	19.340	21.190
14	2.821	4.625	6.505	8.422	10.357	12.300	14.244	16.183	18.115	20.036	21.945
15	2.933	4.799	6.741	8.721	10.719	12.724	14.729	16.729	18.719	20.698	22.663
16	3.039	4.964	6.967	9.007	11.065	13.129	15.193	17.250	19.296	21.330	23.348
17	3.139	5.121	7.182	9.280	11.395	13.517	15.636	17.748	19.849	21.935	24.004
18	3.235	5.271	7.387	9.541	11.712	13.889	16.062	18.226	20.378	22.514	24.631
19	3.326	5.415	7.584	9.792	12.016	14.245	16.470	18.685	20.887	23.070	25.234
20	3.413	5.552	7.773	10.033	12.308	14.589	16.863	19.127	21.376	23.605	25.813
21	3.496	5.684	7.955	10.264	12.590	14.919	17.242	19.553	21.847	24.121	26.371
22	3.576	5.811	8.130	10.488	12.862	15.238	17.607	19.963	22.301	24.618	26.908
23	3.652	5.933	8.299	10.703	13.124	15.546	17.960	20.360	22.740	25.097	27.427
24	3.725	6.050	8.462	10.912	13.377	15.844	18.302	20.744	23.165	25.561	27.928
25	3.795	6.163	8.619	11.113	13.623	16.133	18.632	21.115	23.576	26.010	28.413
26	3.863	6.273	8.771	11.308	13.860	16.412	18.953	21.475	23.974	26.444	28.882
27	3.928	6.378	8.918	11.497	14.091	16.683	19.263	21.824	24.359	26.865	29.337
28	3.991	6.480	9.060	11.680	14.314	16.946	19.565	22.162	24.734	27.274	29.778
29	4.051	6.579	9.199	11.858	14.531	17.202	19.858	22.491	25.097	27.670	30.206
30	4.109	6.675	9.333	12.031	14.742	17.450	20.142	22.811	25.451	28.055	30.621

Table B.33: American-Style Put Premiums
as a Function of Time and Volatility
Stock Price = $100
Strike Price = $90
Dividend Rate = 2%

Mo	\multicolumn{11}{c}{Volatility}										
	0.15	0.20	0.25	0.30	0.35	0.40	0.45	0.50	0.55	0.60	0.65
1	0.008	0.064	0.199	0.413	0.691	1.020	1.387	1.784	2.204	2.642	3.095
2	0.080	0.306	0.672	1.140	1.677	2.264	2.886	3.533	4.200	4.881	5.573
3	0.198	0.594	1.151	1.812	2.540	3.315	4.121	4.950	5.796	6.654	7.520
4	0.334	0.880	1.596	2.414	3.298	4.225	5.181	6.158	7.149	8.150	9.159
5	0.473	1.153	2.005	2.958	3.974	5.031	6.116	7.219	8.335	9.460	10.590
6	0.611	1.410	2.382	3.454	4.587	5.759	6.957	8.171	9.398	10.631	11.870
7	0.745	1.651	2.731	3.910	5.148	6.424	7.724	9.039	10.365	11.697	13.031
8	0.874	1.878	3.057	4.333	5.667	7.037	8.431	9.838	11.255	12.676	14.099
9	0.997	2.092	3.362	4.728	6.151	7.608	9.088	10.580	12.080	13.584	15.088
10	1.115	2.294	3.648	5.098	6.603	8.142	9.702	11.274	12.852	14.432	16.010
11	1.227	2.485	3.919	5.447	7.030	8.645	10.280	11.926	13.577	15.228	16.876
12	1.334	2.667	4.175	5.777	7.432	9.120	10.826	12.541	14.261	15.979	17.692
13	1.437	2.840	4.418	6.090	7.814	9.570	11.343	13.125	14.909	16.690	18.465
14	1.535	3.004	4.649	6.388	8.178	9.998	11.835	13.679	15.524	17.365	19.198
15	1.629	3.162	4.870	6.672	8.525	10.407	12.304	14.208	16.111	18.008	19.896
16	1.719	3.312	5.082	6.944	8.856	10.797	12.753	14.713	16.672	18.623	20.563
17	1.805	3.456	5.284	7.204	9.174	11.172	13.183	15.197	17.209	19.211	21.201
18	1.888	3.594	5.478	7.454	9.479	11.531	13.595	15.662	17.724	19.775	21.812
19	1.967	3.727	5.665	7.694	9.773	11.877	13.992	16.108	18.218	20.317	22.400
20	2.044	3.855	5.845	7.926	10.055	12.209	14.374	16.538	18.695	20.838	22.964
21	2.118	3.978	6.018	8.149	10.327	12.530	14.742	16.953	19.154	21.340	23.508
22	2.188	4.097	6.185	8.364	10.590	12.840	15.098	17.353	19.597	21.825	24.032
23	2.257	4.211	6.346	8.572	10.845	13.140	15.442	17.740	20.025	22.293	24.539
24	2.323	4.322	6.502	8.773	11.091	13.430	15.775	18.114	20.439	22.746	25.028
25	2.386	4.429	6.653	8.968	11.329	13.711	16.097	18.476	20.840	23.184	25.501
26	2.448	4.532	6.799	9.157	11.560	13.983	16.410	18.828	21.229	23.608	25.960
27	2.507	4.632	6.941	9.340	11.784	14.247	16.713	19.168	21.606	24.020	26.404
28	2.564	4.729	7.079	9.518	12.002	14.504	17.007	19.499	21.972	24.419	26.835
29	2.620	4.823	7.212	9.691	12.213	14.753	17.293	19.821	22.327	24.807	27.253
30	2.674	4.915	7.342	9.859	12.419	14.996	17.572	20.133	22.673	25.183	27.659

Table B.34: American-Style Put Premiums as a Function of Time and Volatility
Stock Price = $100
Strike Price = $85
Dividend Rate = 2%

Mo	Volatility										
	0.15	0.20	0.25	0.30	0.35	0.40	0.45	0.50	0.55	0.60	0.65
1	0.000	0.003	0.025	0.085	0.197	0.360	0.573	0.827	1.118	1.438	1.784
2	0.006	0.054	0.193	0.434	0.765	1.170	1.634	2.142	2.687	3.259	3.854
3	0.028	0.163	0.447	0.863	1.383	1.979	2.633	3.330	4.060	4.814	5.589
4	0.067	0.304	0.728	1.298	1.976	2.729	3.538	4.388	5.267	6.169	7.088
5	0.120	0.460	1.012	1.719	2.533	3.421	4.362	5.341	6.347	7.375	8.417
6	0.181	0.622	1.292	2.119	3.053	4.060	5.117	6.210	7.328	8.465	9.616
7	0.248	0.785	1.562	2.499	3.541	4.654	5.815	7.010	8.229	9.464	10.712
8	0.319	0.946	1.822	2.859	3.999	5.209	6.465	7.753	9.063	10.388	11.723
9	0.391	1.103	2.071	3.200	4.432	5.730	7.073	8.447	9.841	11.249	12.665
10	0.463	1.257	2.310	3.525	4.840	6.222	7.646	9.099	10.571	12.055	13.546
11	0.535	1.405	2.539	3.834	5.229	6.687	8.187	9.714	11.259	12.814	14.374
12	0.607	1.550	2.759	4.129	5.598	7.129	8.700	10.297	11.910	13.532	15.157
13	0.677	1.689	2.970	4.412	5.950	7.550	9.188	10.851	12.529	14.213	15.900
14	0.746	1.824	3.173	4.682	6.287	7.952	9.654	11.379	13.118	14.862	16.606
15	0.814	1.954	3.369	4.941	6.610	8.336	10.099	11.884	13.680	15.480	17.278
16	0.880	2.081	3.557	5.191	6.919	8.705	10.526	12.367	14.218	16.072	17.922
17	0.945	2.203	3.738	5.431	7.217	9.060	10.936	12.831	14.735	16.639	18.537
18	1.008	2.321	3.913	5.662	7.504	9.401	11.330	13.276	15.230	17.183	19.128
19	1.069	2.435	4.082	5.885	7.780	9.729	11.709	13.705	15.707	17.706	19.696
20	1.128	2.546	4.245	6.101	8.047	10.046	12.075	14.119	16.167	18.210	20.243
21	1.186	2.654	4.404	6.309	8.305	10.352	12.429	14.518	16.610	18.696	20.769
22	1.243	2.758	4.557	6.511	8.555	10.649	12.770	14.904	17.039	19.165	21.278
23	1.298	2.859	4.705	6.707	8.796	10.935	13.101	15.277	17.453	19.619	21.769
24	1.351	2.958	4.849	6.896	9.030	11.213	13.421	15.639	17.854	20.057	22.243
25	1.403	3.053	4.989	7.080	9.258	11.483	13.732	15.989	18.242	20.482	22.703
26	1.454	3.146	5.125	7.259	9.478	11.744	14.033	16.329	18.619	20.894	23.148
27	1.503	3.236	5.257	7.432	9.692	11.998	14.326	16.659	18.984	21.293	23.579
28	1.551	3.324	5.385	7.601	9.901	12.245	14.611	16.980	19.339	21.681	23.998
29	1.598	3.409	5.510	7.765	10.104	12.486	14.887	17.291	19.684	22.057	24.405
30	1.643	3.492	5.632	7.925	10.301	12.720	15.157	17.594	20.020	22.424	24.800

Table B.35: American-Style Put Premiums
as a Function of Time and Volatility
Stock Price = $100
Strike Price = $80
Dividend Rate = 2%

Mo	Volatility										
	0.15	0.20	0.25	0.30	0.35	0.40	0.45	0.50	0.55	0.60	0.65
1	0.000	0.000	0.002	0.011	0.039	0.097	0.191	0.322	0.490	0.692	0.925
2	0.000	0.006	0.040	0.130	0.292	0.528	0.829	1.187	1.593	2.039	2.519
3	0.002	0.032	0.138	0.350	0.667	1.076	1.559	2.104	2.696	3.328	3.991
4	0.009	0.081	0.279	0.618	1.080	1.640	2.279	2.977	3.722	4.504	5.315
5	0.022	0.149	0.445	0.904	1.497	2.192	2.964	3.794	4.669	5.579	6.514
6	0.040	0.230	0.623	1.195	1.906	2.720	3.610	4.557	5.546	6.567	7.612
7	0.065	0.320	0.807	1.484	2.303	3.225	4.220	5.271	6.362	7.482	8.625
8	0.093	0.416	0.992	1.767	2.685	3.705	4.797	5.942	7.125	8.336	9.567
9	0.125	0.516	1.177	2.042	3.052	4.162	5.343	6.574	7.842	9.136	10.448
10	0.161	0.617	1.359	2.310	3.404	4.598	5.861	7.173	8.519	9.890	11.276
11	0.198	0.719	1.538	2.568	3.743	5.015	6.355	7.742	9.161	10.602	12.059
12	0.237	0.820	1.713	2.819	4.068	5.414	6.826	8.283	9.770	11.279	12.800
13	0.277	0.921	1.883	3.061	4.381	5.797	7.276	8.799	10.351	11.922	13.504
14	0.318	1.021	2.050	3.296	4.683	6.164	7.708	9.293	10.906	12.536	14.176
15	0.359	1.120	2.212	3.522	4.974	6.517	8.122	9.767	11.438	13.124	14.818
16	0.401	1.216	2.370	3.742	5.254	6.858	8.520	10.222	11.947	13.687	15.432
17	0.442	1.311	2.524	3.955	5.525	7.186	8.904	10.659	12.437	14.227	16.021
18	0.484	1.405	2.673	4.161	5.788	7.502	9.274	11.081	12.908	14.747	16.587
19	0.525	1.496	2.819	4.361	6.041	7.808	9.631	11.487	13.363	15.247	17.132
20	0.566	1.585	2.960	4.555	6.287	8.105	9.976	11.879	13.801	15.730	17.657
21	0.606	1.673	3.098	4.744	6.525	8.391	10.310	12.259	14.225	16.196	18.163
22	0.646	1.758	3.233	4.927	6.757	8.669	10.633	12.626	14.634	16.646	18.652
23	0.685	1.842	3.364	5.106	6.981	8.939	10.947	12.982	15.031	17.081	19.124
24	0.724	1.924	3.491	5.279	7.199	9.201	11.251	13.327	15.415	17.503	19.581
25	0.763	2.004	3.616	5.448	7.412	9.455	11.546	13.662	15.788	17.912	20.024
26	0.800	2.082	3.737	5.612	7.618	9.703	11.833	13.987	16.150	18.308	20.454
27	0.837	2.159	3.855	5.772	7.819	9.943	12.112	14.303	16.501	18.693	20.870
28	0.873	2.234	3.971	5.928	8.015	10.178	12.384	14.611	16.843	19.067	21.274
29	0.909	2.307	4.084	6.080	8.205	10.406	12.648	14.910	17.175	19.430	21.667
30	0.944	2.378	4.194	6.229	8.391	10.628	12.906	15.201	17.498	19.783	22.049

Table B.36: American-Style Put Premiums
as a Function of Time and Volatility
Stock Price = $100
Strike Price = $75
Dividend Rate = 2%

Mo	Volatility										
	0.15	0.20	0.25	0.30	0.35	0.40	0.45	0.50	0.55	0.60	0.65
1	0.000	0.000	0.000	0.001	0.005	0.019	0.049	0.101	0.180	0.287	0.422
2	0.000	0.000	0.006	0.029	0.090	0.201	0.368	0.589	0.861	1.180	1.538
3	0.000	0.004	0.033	0.117	0.278	0.522	0.843	1.232	1.680	2.178	2.717
4	0.001	0.016	0.087	0.254	0.528	0.904	1.368	1.905	2.503	3.150	3.838
5	0.003	0.038	0.165	0.422	0.808	1.308	1.900	2.568	3.296	4.072	4.885
6	0.007	0.069	0.261	0.609	1.102	1.715	2.424	3.208	4.050	4.938	5.863
7	0.013	0.109	0.369	0.807	1.401	2.118	2.933	3.821	4.766	5.755	6.777
8	0.022	0.156	0.485	1.010	1.698	2.512	3.423	4.406	5.444	6.524	7.636
9	0.032	0.209	0.607	1.215	1.991	2.895	3.895	4.966	6.089	7.253	8.446
10	0.046	0.266	0.732	1.419	2.279	3.267	4.349	5.500	6.703	7.944	9.212
11	0.061	0.326	0.859	1.622	2.560	3.626	4.785	6.012	7.289	8.601	9.939
12	0.078	0.389	0.986	1.822	2.834	3.974	5.206	6.503	7.848	9.227	10.630
13	0.096	0.454	1.114	2.018	3.101	4.310	5.610	6.974	8.384	9.826	11.290
14	0.116	0.520	1.240	2.211	3.360	4.636	6.000	7.427	8.898	10.399	11.921
15	0.137	0.586	1.366	2.399	3.612	4.951	6.377	7.864	9.392	10.949	12.525
16	0.159	0.653	1.490	2.584	3.858	5.256	6.741	8.284	9.868	11.478	13.105
17	0.182	0.720	1.612	2.764	4.097	5.552	7.092	8.690	10.326	11.986	13.662
18	0.205	0.787	1.732	2.940	4.329	5.839	7.433	9.082	10.767	12.476	14.198
19	0.229	0.854	1.850	3.113	4.555	6.118	7.762	9.461	11.194	12.949	14.715
20	0.253	0.920	1.967	3.281	4.775	6.388	8.082	9.828	11.607	13.406	15.214
21	0.278	0.986	2.081	3.445	4.989	6.651	8.392	10.183	12.007	13.848	15.696
22	0.303	1.051	2.193	3.606	5.198	6.907	8.693	10.528	12.394	14.275	16.162
23	0.328	1.115	2.303	3.763	5.401	7.156	8.985	10.863	12.769	14.689	16.613
24	0.353	1.179	2.411	3.916	5.599	7.398	9.270	11.188	13.133	15.091	17.050
25	0.378	1.241	2.517	4.066	5.793	7.633	9.546	11.504	13.487	15.481	17.474
26	0.403	1.303	2.620	4.213	5.982	7.863	9.816	11.811	13.830	15.859	17.884
27	0.427	1.364	2.722	4.356	6.166	8.087	10.078	12.110	14.165	16.227	18.283
28	0.452	1.424	2.822	4.496	6.346	8.305	10.333	12.402	14.490	16.584	18.671
29	0.477	1.483	2.920	4.633	6.521	8.519	10.583	12.685	14.807	16.932	19.048
30	0.501	1.541	3.016	4.768	6.693	8.727	10.826	12.962	15.115	17.270	19.414

Table B.37: American-Style Put Premiums
as a Function of Time and Volatility
Stock Price = $100
Strike Price = $70
Dividend Rate = 2%

Mo	Volatility										
	0.15	0.20	0.25	0.30	0.35	0.40	0.45	0.50	0.55	0.60	0.65
1	0.000	0.000	0.000	0.000	0.000	0.003	0.009	0.025	0.053	0.099	0.165
2	0.000	0.000	0.001	0.005	0.022	0.063	0.139	0.256	0.417	0.620	0.865
3	0.000	0.001	0.006	0.031	0.097	0.221	0.408	0.659	0.969	1.334	1.746
4	0.000	0.003	0.022	0.087	0.226	0.448	0.754	1.136	1.585	2.093	2.649
5	0.000	0.008	0.051	0.171	0.391	0.716	1.136	1.640	2.214	2.847	3.529
6	0.001	0.017	0.093	0.275	0.581	1.005	1.533	2.148	2.835	3.579	4.371
7	0.002	0.031	0.146	0.395	0.786	1.306	1.934	2.651	3.439	4.284	5.174
8	0.004	0.049	0.209	0.526	1.000	1.610	2.331	3.141	4.022	4.958	5.938
9	0.007	0.072	0.279	0.664	1.218	1.913	2.721	3.618	4.585	5.604	6.666
10	0.011	0.099	0.355	0.808	1.438	2.214	3.103	4.081	5.126	6.223	7.360
11	0.016	0.129	0.435	0.954	1.658	2.510	3.476	4.528	5.647	6.816	8.023
12	0.022	0.162	0.519	1.102	1.877	2.800	3.838	4.962	6.150	7.386	8.657
13	0.028	0.198	0.606	1.251	2.093	3.085	4.191	5.381	6.633	7.933	9.265
14	0.036	0.236	0.694	1.400	2.306	3.363	4.533	5.786	7.100	8.459	9.849
15	0.045	0.276	0.783	1.548	2.515	3.635	4.866	6.179	7.551	8.965	10.410
16	0.055	0.317	0.873	1.694	2.721	3.900	5.190	6.559	7.986	9.454	10.950
17	0.065	0.360	0.964	1.840	2.924	4.159	5.505	6.928	8.407	9.926	11.470
18	0.076	0.403	1.054	1.983	3.122	4.412	5.811	7.286	8.815	10.381	11.972
19	0.088	0.447	1.144	2.125	3.316	4.659	6.108	7.633	9.210	10.822	12.457
20	0.100	0.492	1.233	2.264	3.507	4.900	6.398	7.970	9.593	11.249	12.925
21	0.113	0.537	1.322	2.401	3.693	5.134	6.680	8.298	9.964	11.662	13.379
22	0.126	0.582	1.411	2.536	3.876	5.364	6.955	8.617	10.325	12.063	13.819
23	0.140	0.627	1.498	2.669	4.054	5.588	7.223	8.927	10.676	12.453	14.245
24	0.154	0.673	1.584	2.800	4.230	5.807	7.484	9.228	11.016	12.831	14.658
25	0.168	0.718	1.670	2.928	4.401	6.020	7.739	9.522	11.348	13.198	15.059
26	0.183	0.763	1.754	3.054	4.569	6.229	7.987	9.809	11.670	13.555	15.449
27	0.197	0.808	1.837	3.178	4.734	6.434	8.230	10.088	11.985	13.902	15.828
28	0.212	0.853	1.920	3.300	4.895	6.633	8.466	10.360	12.291	14.241	16.196
29	0.227	0.897	2.001	3.420	5.053	6.829	8.698	10.626	12.589	14.570	16.554
30	0.242	0.942	2.081	3.537	5.208	7.020	8.924	10.885	12.880	14.891	16.903

Table B.38: American-Style Put Premiums
as a Function of Time and Volatility
Stock Price = $100
Strike Price = $65
Dividend Rate = 2%

Mo	Volatility										
	0.15	0.20	0.25	0.30	0.35	0.40	0.45	0.50	0.55	0.60	0.65
1	0.000	0.000	0.000	0.000	0.000	0.000	0.001	0.004	0.012	0.027	0.053
2	0.000	0.000	0.000	0.001	0.004	0.015	0.043	0.095	0.176	0.291	0.440
3	0.000	0.000	0.001	0.006	0.028	0.079	0.172	0.315	0.509	0.754	1.046
4	0.000	0.000	0.004	0.025	0.082	0.195	0.375	0.622	0.934	1.306	1.732
5	0.000	0.001	0.013	0.058	0.166	0.353	0.624	0.976	1.401	1.891	2.436
6	0.000	0.003	0.027	0.107	0.274	0.539	0.902	1.355	1.885	2.481	3.134
7	0.000	0.007	0.049	0.170	0.400	0.745	1.197	1.744	2.371	3.066	3.816
8	0.001	0.013	0.077	0.245	0.540	0.963	1.500	2.136	2.853	3.637	4.476
9	0.002	0.021	0.112	0.328	0.689	1.188	1.807	2.526	3.326	4.193	5.113
10	0.002	0.031	0.152	0.419	0.845	1.417	2.113	2.910	3.789	4.732	5.727
11	0.004	0.044	0.197	0.516	1.006	1.648	2.417	3.288	4.239	5.254	6.319
12	0.005	0.059	0.246	0.617	1.169	1.879	2.718	3.658	4.678	5.759	6.889
13	0.007	0.076	0.299	0.721	1.334	2.109	3.014	4.019	5.104	6.248	7.438
14	0.010	0.095	0.354	0.827	1.500	2.337	3.304	4.372	5.517	6.721	7.969
15	0.013	0.115	0.412	0.936	1.665	2.562	3.590	4.717	5.919	7.179	8.481
16	0.016	0.137	0.471	1.045	1.830	2.784	3.869	5.052	6.310	7.623	8.975
17	0.020	0.161	0.533	1.155	1.993	3.003	4.142	5.380	6.690	8.053	9.454
18	0.025	0.186	0.595	1.265	2.155	3.218	4.410	5.699	7.058	8.469	9.917
19	0.029	0.212	0.658	1.375	2.316	3.429	4.672	6.010	7.417	8.874	10.365
20	0.035	0.239	0.722	1.484	2.474	3.637	4.928	6.314	7.766	9.267	10.800
21	0.040	0.266	0.787	1.593	2.630	3.841	5.179	6.609	8.106	9.649	11.222
22	0.046	0.295	0.852	1.701	2.784	4.041	5.424	6.898	8.437	10.019	11.631
23	0.053	0.324	0.917	1.809	2.936	4.237	5.664	7.180	8.759	10.380	12.028
24	0.060	0.353	0.982	1.915	3.085	4.430	5.898	7.455	9.073	10.731	12.415
25	0.067	0.383	1.046	2.020	3.233	4.619	6.128	7.724	9.379	11.073	12.790
26	0.074	0.413	1.111	2.124	3.378	4.804	6.353	7.986	9.678	11.406	13.156
27	0.082	0.444	1.176	2.227	3.520	4.986	6.573	8.243	9.969	11.730	13.511
28	0.090	0.475	1.240	2.329	3.660	5.164	6.788	8.494	10.253	12.047	13.858
29	0.098	0.506	1.303	2.429	3.798	5.339	6.999	8.739	10.531	12.355	14.195
30	0.106	0.537	1.366	2.528	3.934	5.511	7.205	8.978	10.802	12.656	14.524

Table B.39: American-Style Put Premiums
as a Function of Time and Volatility
Stock Price = $100
Strike Price = $60
Dividend Rate = 2%

Mo	\multicolumn{11}{c}{Volatility}
	0.15	0.20	0.25	0.30	0.35	0.40	0.45	0.50	0.55	0.60	0.65
1	0.000	0.000	0.000	0.000	0.000	0.000	0.000	0.001	0.002	0.006	0.014
2	0.000	0.000	0.000	0.000	0.001	0.003	0.011	0.029	0.063	0.118	0.198
3	0.000	0.000	0.000	0.001	0.006	0.023	0.062	0.132	0.238	0.386	0.576
4	0.000	0.000	0.001	0.006	0.025	0.073	0.164	0.306	0.503	0.755	1.059
5	0.000	0.000	0.003	0.016	0.060	0.153	0.309	0.533	0.824	1.179	1.592
6	0.000	0.001	0.007	0.036	0.113	0.260	0.486	0.794	1.177	1.630	2.143
7	0.000	0.002	0.014	0.063	0.181	0.387	0.686	1.076	1.548	2.092	2.698
8	0.000	0.003	0.024	0.100	0.263	0.530	0.902	1.371	1.927	2.556	3.248
9	0.000	0.005	0.039	0.144	0.355	0.684	1.127	1.673	2.308	3.017	3.789
10	0.001	0.009	0.057	0.195	0.456	0.847	1.360	1.979	2.688	3.471	4.316
11	0.001	0.013	0.078	0.252	0.564	1.016	1.595	2.284	3.063	3.917	4.830
12	0.001	0.018	0.103	0.314	0.677	1.189	1.833	2.587	3.433	4.352	5.330
13	0.002	0.025	0.131	0.380	0.794	1.364	2.070	2.888	3.797	4.778	5.816
14	0.003	0.033	0.162	0.450	0.915	1.541	2.307	3.185	4.153	5.193	6.288
15	0.003	0.042	0.195	0.523	1.037	1.719	2.541	3.477	4.502	5.597	6.746
16	0.005	0.052	0.231	0.598	1.161	1.896	2.774	3.764	4.843	5.991	7.191
17	0.006	0.064	0.268	0.676	1.286	2.073	3.003	4.047	5.177	6.375	7.623
18	0.007	0.076	0.307	0.754	1.412	2.249	3.230	4.324	5.504	6.749	8.043
19	0.009	0.089	0.348	0.834	1.537	2.423	3.453	4.595	5.822	7.113	8.451
20	0.011	0.104	0.390	0.915	1.663	2.595	3.673	4.862	6.134	7.468	8.848
21	0.013	0.119	0.433	0.996	1.788	2.766	3.889	5.123	6.438	7.814	9.233
22	0.015	0.135	0.477	1.078	1.912	2.935	4.102	5.379	6.736	8.152	9.609
23	0.018	0.151	0.521	1.160	2.036	3.101	4.311	5.629	7.027	8.481	9.975
24	0.021	0.168	0.567	1.242	2.158	3.265	4.517	5.875	7.311	8.802	10.331
25	0.024	0.186	0.613	1.324	2.280	3.427	4.718	6.115	7.589	9.115	10.678
26	0.027	0.204	0.659	1.406	2.400	3.587	4.917	6.351	7.860	9.421	11.016
27	0.030	0.223	0.705	1.487	2.519	3.744	5.112	6.582	8.126	9.720	11.345
28	0.034	0.242	0.752	1.568	2.637	3.899	5.303	6.809	8.386	10.011	11.667
29	0.037	0.262	0.799	1.649	2.754	4.052	5.491	7.031	8.640	10.296	11.981
30	0.041	0.282	0.846	1.729	2.869	4.202	5.675	7.248	8.889	10.575	12.287

Table B.40: American-Style Put Premiums
as a Function of Time and Volatility
Stock Price = $100
Strike Price = $120
Dividend Rate = 3%

Mo	Volatility										
	0.15	0.20	0.25	0.30	0.35	0.40	0.45	0.50	0.55	0.60	0.65
1	20.000	20.000	20.000	20.000	20.012	20.114	20.297	20.543	20.840	21.179	21.553
2	20.000	20.000	20.000	20.074	20.346	20.748	21.241	21.801	22.413	23.064	23.746
3	20.000	20.000	20.026	20.331	20.847	21.493	22.227	23.024	23.868	24.746	25.651
4	20.000	20.000	20.140	20.655	21.377	22.225	23.156	24.145	25.175	26.236	27.320
5	20.000	20.000	20.300	20.999	21.900	22.921	24.019	25.170	26.359	27.575	28.810
6	20.000	20.009	20.482	21.345	22.403	23.575	24.820	26.114	27.442	28.793	30.161
7	20.000	20.045	20.674	21.684	22.884	24.192	25.568	26.989	28.441	29.914	31.400
8	20.000	20.097	20.870	22.014	23.342	24.773	26.268	27.805	29.370	30.952	32.546
9	20.000	20.161	21.066	22.334	23.778	25.322	26.927	28.571	30.239	31.922	33.615
10	20.000	20.233	21.259	22.641	24.195	25.844	27.550	29.292	31.056	32.832	34.616
11	20.000	20.310	21.450	22.938	24.593	26.340	28.140	29.974	31.827	33.691	35.558
12	20.000	20.389	21.636	23.224	24.974	26.812	28.702	30.621	32.558	34.503	36.448
13	20.000	20.471	21.818	23.500	25.339	27.264	29.237	31.238	33.253	35.273	37.293
14	20.000	20.554	21.995	23.765	25.690	27.696	29.748	31.826	33.915	36.007	38.096
15	20.000	20.637	22.167	24.022	26.027	28.111	30.238	32.388	34.548	36.708	38.862
16	20.000	20.720	22.335	24.270	26.352	28.510	30.708	32.927	35.153	37.378	39.594
17	20.000	20.802	22.498	24.510	26.665	28.893	31.160	33.445	35.734	38.020	40.295
18	20.000	20.883	22.657	24.742	26.967	29.263	31.595	33.943	36.292	38.636	40.968
19	20.000	20.964	22.812	24.967	27.259	29.620	32.014	34.422	36.830	39.229	41.615
20	20.001	21.043	22.962	25.184	27.541	29.965	32.419	34.884	37.347	39.801	42.237
21	20.003	21.122	23.109	25.396	27.815	30.298	32.810	35.330	37.847	40.351	42.837
22	20.008	21.199	23.252	25.601	28.080	30.621	33.188	35.761	38.329	40.883	43.416
23	20.014	21.274	23.391	25.800	28.337	30.934	33.554	36.179	38.796	41.397	43.975
24	20.022	21.348	23.526	25.994	28.587	31.237	33.908	36.583	39.248	41.894	44.515
25	20.030	21.421	23.658	26.182	28.829	31.531	34.252	36.975	39.685	42.375	45.038
26	20.040	21.493	23.787	26.366	29.065	31.817	34.586	37.355	40.110	42.842	45.544
27	20.050	21.563	23.913	26.544	29.294	32.094	34.911	37.724	40.522	43.295	46.035
28	20.061	21.632	24.035	26.718	29.517	32.364	35.226	38.083	40.922	43.734	46.511
29	20.073	21.700	24.155	26.888	29.734	32.627	35.533	38.432	41.311	44.160	46.974
30	20.085	21.766	24.272	27.053	29.946	32.883	35.831	38.771	41.689	44.575	47.423

Table B.41: American-Style Put Premiums
as a Function of Time and Volatility
Stock Price = $100
Strike Price = $115
Dividend Rate = 3%

Mo	Volatility										
	0.15	0.20	0.25	0.30	0.35	0.40	0.45	0.50	0.55	0.60	0.65
1	15.000	15.000	15.000	15.047	15.213	15.465	15.779	16.141	16.542	16.972	17.427
2	15.000	15.000	15.105	15.443	15.917	16.479	17.102	17.768	18.468	19.192	19.936
3	15.000	15.018	15.358	15.939	16.651	17.445	18.294	19.182	20.097	21.033	21.985
4	15.000	15.104	15.652	16.434	17.341	18.323	19.355	20.421	21.511	22.617	23.736
5	15.000	15.224	15.954	16.908	17.981	19.123	20.310	21.528	22.766	24.018	25.280
6	15.000	15.361	16.251	17.357	18.574	19.857	21.181	22.531	23.900	25.280	26.667
7	15.000	15.505	16.538	17.779	19.127	20.535	21.982	23.452	24.937	26.432	27.932
8	15.003	15.651	16.814	18.178	19.644	21.167	22.725	24.304	25.896	27.495	29.097
9	15.018	15.796	17.079	18.556	20.131	21.759	23.420	25.099	26.789	28.484	30.179
10	15.040	15.939	17.332	18.915	20.590	22.316	24.072	25.844	27.625	29.408	31.190
11	15.069	16.080	17.575	19.256	21.025	22.843	24.687	26.547	28.412	30.277	32.139
12	15.101	16.217	17.809	19.581	21.439	23.342	25.271	27.211	29.156	31.098	33.035
13	15.136	16.350	18.033	19.891	21.833	23.817	25.825	27.842	29.861	31.876	33.884
14	15.173	16.480	18.248	20.188	22.209	24.271	26.353	28.442	30.532	32.616	34.690
15	15.212	16.606	18.455	20.473	22.570	24.704	26.857	29.016	31.172	33.321	35.458
16	15.251	16.728	18.655	20.747	22.915	25.120	27.340	29.564	31.784	33.995	36.192
17	15.291	16.847	18.847	21.011	23.247	25.519	27.803	30.090	32.370	34.640	36.894
18	15.331	16.962	19.033	21.265	23.567	25.902	28.248	30.595	32.933	35.259	37.568
19	15.371	17.074	19.213	21.510	23.876	26.271	28.676	31.080	33.475	35.854	38.214
20	15.411	17.183	19.387	21.746	24.173	26.627	29.089	31.548	33.996	36.427	38.836
21	15.450	17.288	19.555	21.975	24.460	26.971	29.488	32.000	34.499	36.979	39.436
22	15.490	17.391	19.719	22.197	24.738	27.303	29.873	32.436	34.984	37.512	40.013
23	15.528	17.491	19.877	22.412	25.007	27.624	30.245	32.858	35.453	38.026	40.571
24	15.567	17.588	20.030	22.619	25.267	27.936	30.606	33.266	35.907	38.524	41.111
25	15.604	17.683	20.180	22.821	25.520	28.238	30.955	33.661	36.347	39.005	41.632
26	15.641	17.775	20.325	23.017	25.765	28.530	31.295	34.045	36.773	39.472	42.137
27	15.678	17.865	20.466	23.208	26.003	28.815	31.624	34.417	37.186	39.925	42.627
28	15.714	17.952	20.603	23.393	26.234	29.091	31.944	34.779	37.587	40.364	43.102
29	15.749	18.038	20.737	23.573	26.460	29.360	32.255	35.130	37.977	40.790	43.562
30	15.784	18.121	20.867	23.748	26.679	29.622	32.557	35.472	38.356	41.204	44.010

Table B.42: American-Style Put Premiums
as a Function of Time and Volatility
Stock Price = $100
Strike Price = $110
Dividend Rate = 3%

Mo	Volatility										
	0.15	0.20	0.25	0.30	0.35	0.40	0.45	0.50	0.55	0.60	0.65
1	10.000	10.006	10.153	10.427	10.780	11.186	11.631	12.105	12.599	13.109	13.632
2	10.000	10.190	10.644	11.225	11.878	12.577	13.307	14.059	14.826	15.606	16.394
3	10.023	10.457	11.147	11.953	12.824	13.735	14.671	15.625	16.592	17.567	18.548
4	10.095	10.733	11.614	12.603	13.650	14.732	15.836	16.955	18.083	19.218	20.357
5	10.188	11.000	12.044	13.189	14.386	15.614	16.862	18.121	19.389	20.660	21.934
6	10.290	11.255	12.441	13.722	15.052	16.409	17.784	19.168	20.558	21.950	23.343
7	10.395	11.495	12.809	14.213	15.661	17.135	18.624	20.121	21.621	23.122	24.621
8	10.499	11.722	13.152	14.667	16.225	17.805	19.398	20.998	22.598	24.198	25.794
9	10.601	11.937	13.474	15.092	16.750	18.429	20.118	21.812	23.505	25.195	26.881
10	10.701	12.141	13.777	15.491	17.242	19.012	20.791	22.572	24.351	26.126	27.895
11	10.797	12.335	14.063	15.866	17.705	19.561	21.424	23.287	25.146	27.000	28.846
12	10.891	12.519	14.334	16.222	18.143	20.080	22.021	23.961	25.897	27.824	29.742
13	10.981	12.695	14.592	16.559	18.559	20.571	22.587	24.600	26.607	28.605	30.590
14	11.069	12.863	14.838	16.881	18.954	21.039	23.125	25.208	27.282	29.346	31.395
15	11.153	13.024	15.073	17.188	19.332	21.485	23.638	25.787	27.925	30.051	32.162
16	11.234	13.178	15.297	17.482	19.692	21.911	24.129	26.340	28.540	30.726	32.894
17	11.313	13.326	15.513	17.764	20.038	22.320	24.599	26.870	29.129	31.371	33.594
18	11.389	13.469	15.721	18.034	20.370	22.712	25.051	27.379	29.693	31.989	34.265
19	11.462	13.606	15.920	18.294	20.690	23.090	25.485	27.868	30.236	32.584	34.909
20	11.534	13.739	16.113	18.545	20.997	23.453	25.903	28.339	30.758	33.155	35.528
21	11.602	13.867	16.298	18.786	21.294	23.804	26.306	28.793	31.261	33.706	36.124
22	11.669	13.990	16.477	19.020	21.580	24.142	26.695	29.231	31.747	34.237	36.699
23	11.734	14.110	16.650	19.245	21.858	24.470	27.071	29.655	32.216	34.750	37.254
24	11.796	14.225	16.817	19.463	22.126	24.787	27.435	30.065	32.670	35.246	37.790
25	11.857	14.337	16.979	19.675	22.386	25.094	27.788	30.462	33.109	35.726	38.309
26	11.916	14.446	17.137	19.880	22.638	25.391	28.130	30.846	33.535	36.191	38.811
27	11.973	14.551	17.289	20.079	22.882	25.680	28.462	31.220	33.948	36.642	39.298
28	12.029	14.653	17.437	20.272	23.120	25.961	28.784	31.582	34.349	37.079	39.769
29	12.083	14.752	17.581	20.460	23.351	26.234	29.097	31.934	34.738	37.504	40.227
30	12.135	14.848	17.721	20.643	23.575	26.499	29.402	32.277	35.116	37.916	40.672

Table B.43: American-Style Put Premiums
as a Function of Time and Volatility
Stock Price = $100
Strike Price = $105
Dividend Rate = 3%

Mo	\multicolumn{11}{c}{Volatility}
	0.15	0.20	0.25	0.30	0.35	0.40	0.45	0.50	0.55	0.60	0.65
1	5.131	5.483	5.924	6.413	6.928	7.461	8.005	8.558	9.116	9.679	10.245
2	5.447	6.093	6.813	7.570	8.348	9.137	9.934	10.736	11.542	12.351	13.160
3	5.743	6.601	7.524	8.477	9.446	10.425	11.410	12.398	13.388	14.379	15.370
4	6.007	7.036	8.124	9.237	10.365	11.500	12.639	13.780	14.921	16.062	17.201
5	6.244	7.419	8.648	9.900	11.164	12.433	13.706	14.979	16.251	17.521	18.789
6	6.459	7.762	9.116	10.491	11.876	13.266	14.656	16.046	17.434	18.819	20.200
7	6.656	8.074	9.541	11.027	12.522	14.019	15.517	17.013	18.506	19.994	21.478
8	6.837	8.361	9.931	11.519	13.114	14.711	16.307	17.900	19.489	21.072	22.648
9	7.005	8.626	10.291	11.974	13.662	15.351	17.038	18.721	20.398	22.069	23.731
10	7.161	8.873	10.628	12.398	14.173	15.948	17.720	19.487	21.246	22.998	24.740
11	7.308	9.104	10.943	12.795	14.652	16.508	18.360	20.205	22.042	23.870	25.686
12	7.446	9.322	11.239	13.170	15.104	17.036	18.963	20.882	22.792	24.691	26.577
13	7.576	9.528	11.519	13.524	15.531	17.536	19.534	21.523	23.502	25.468	27.420
14	7.700	9.723	11.785	13.860	15.937	18.010	20.076	22.132	24.176	26.205	28.219
15	7.817	9.908	12.038	14.180	16.324	18.463	20.593	22.712	24.817	26.907	28.980
16	7.928	10.084	12.279	14.486	16.693	18.895	21.087	23.266	25.430	27.578	29.706
17	8.034	10.252	12.510	14.778	17.046	19.308	21.559	23.796	26.017	28.219	30.400
18	8.135	10.413	12.731	15.059	17.385	19.705	22.012	24.305	26.579	28.834	31.065
19	8.232	10.568	12.943	15.328	17.711	20.086	22.448	24.794	27.120	29.424	31.704
20	8.325	10.716	13.146	15.587	18.025	20.453	22.867	25.264	27.640	29.992	32.318
21	8.414	10.858	13.342	15.836	18.327	20.807	23.272	25.717	28.141	30.539	32.909
22	8.499	10.995	13.532	16.077	18.618	21.148	23.662	26.155	28.624	31.066	33.478
23	8.581	11.128	13.714	16.309	18.900	21.478	24.039	26.578	29.091	31.575	34.028
24	8.660	11.255	13.890	16.534	19.173	21.798	24.404	26.987	29.542	32.068	34.559
25	8.736	11.378	14.061	16.752	19.437	22.107	24.757	27.383	29.979	32.544	35.073
26	8.809	11.497	14.226	16.963	19.692	22.407	25.100	27.766	30.403	33.005	35.570
27	8.880	11.613	14.386	17.167	19.941	22.698	25.432	28.139	30.813	33.452	36.052
28	8.949	11.725	14.542	17.366	20.182	22.980	25.755	28.500	31.212	33.886	36.519
29	9.015	11.833	14.692	17.559	20.416	23.254	26.068	28.851	31.599	34.307	36.973
30	9.079	11.938	14.839	17.746	20.643	23.521	26.373	29.192	31.975	34.716	37.413

Table B.44: American-Style Put Premiums
as a Function of Time and Volatility
Stock Price = $100
Strike Price = $100
Dividend Rate = 3%

Mo	Volatility										
	0.15	0.20	0.25	0.30	0.35	0.40	0.45	0.50	0.55	0.60	0.65
1	1.615	2.187	2.760	3.333	3.905	4.478	5.051	5.623	6.195	6.767	7.339
2	2.222	3.026	3.832	4.638	5.445	6.251	7.056	7.861	8.665	9.468	10.271
3	2.664	3.644	4.627	5.610	6.593	7.575	8.557	9.537	10.516	11.494	12.470
4	3.022	4.149	5.278	6.409	7.539	8.668	9.795	10.922	12.046	13.167	14.286
5	3.327	4.580	5.838	7.096	8.354	9.611	10.866	12.119	13.368	14.615	15.858
6	3.593	4.960	6.332	7.706	9.078	10.449	11.817	13.182	14.544	15.901	17.254
7	3.831	5.302	6.778	8.255	9.732	11.206	12.677	14.144	15.607	17.064	18.516
8	4.046	5.612	7.184	8.758	10.330	11.899	13.465	15.026	16.581	18.130	19.672
9	4.243	5.897	7.559	9.221	10.883	12.541	14.194	15.842	17.483	19.116	20.741
10	4.425	6.162	7.907	9.653	11.397	13.138	14.873	16.602	18.323	20.035	21.737
11	4.594	6.409	8.232	10.057	11.880	13.698	15.510	17.315	19.111	20.896	22.671
12	4.751	6.640	8.538	10.437	12.334	14.226	16.111	17.987	19.853	21.708	23.550
13	4.899	6.858	8.826	10.797	12.764	14.725	16.679	18.623	20.555	22.475	24.381
14	5.039	7.064	9.100	11.137	13.172	15.199	17.218	19.227	21.222	23.204	25.170
15	5.170	7.259	9.360	11.462	13.560	15.651	17.732	19.802	21.857	23.897	25.920
16	5.295	7.445	9.607	11.771	13.930	16.082	18.223	20.351	22.464	24.559	26.636
17	5.413	7.622	9.844	12.067	14.285	16.495	18.693	20.877	23.044	25.193	27.321
18	5.526	7.791	10.070	12.350	14.625	16.891	19.143	21.381	23.600	25.800	27.977
19	5.634	7.953	10.287	12.622	14.952	17.271	19.576	21.865	24.135	26.383	28.607
20	5.737	8.109	10.496	12.884	15.266	17.637	19.993	22.331	24.649	26.943	29.212
21	5.836	8.258	10.697	13.136	15.569	17.990	20.395	22.781	25.144	27.483	29.795
22	5.930	8.402	10.890	13.379	15.861	18.330	20.782	23.214	25.622	28.004	30.357
23	6.021	8.540	11.077	13.614	16.144	18.659	21.157	23.633	26.084	28.507	30.899
24	6.108	8.674	11.257	13.841	16.417	18.978	21.520	24.038	26.531	28.993	31.423
25	6.193	8.803	11.431	14.061	16.681	19.286	21.871	24.431	26.963	29.464	31.930
26	6.274	8.927	11.600	14.274	16.937	19.585	22.211	24.811	27.382	29.919	32.420
27	6.352	9.048	11.764	14.480	17.186	19.875	22.541	25.180	27.788	30.361	32.896
28	6.427	9.164	11.922	14.680	17.427	20.156	22.861	25.538	28.182	30.789	33.356
29	6.500	9.278	12.076	14.875	17.662	20.430	23.173	25.886	28.565	31.205	33.803
30	6.571	9.387	12.226	15.064	17.890	20.696	23.476	26.224	28.937	31.609	34.238

Table B.45: American-Style Put Premiums
as a Function of Time and Volatility
Stock Price = $100
Strike Price = $95
Dividend Rate = 3%

Mo	Volatility										
	0.15	0.20	0.25	0.30	0.35	0.40	0.45	0.50	0.55	0.60	0.65
1	0.219	0.535	0.931	1.375	1.849	2.343	2.850	3.366	3.890	4.419	4.952
2	0.585	1.162	1.815	2.510	3.229	3.965	4.710	5.463	6.221	6.983	7.746
3	0.915	1.684	2.524	3.402	4.302	5.215	6.138	7.066	7.998	8.932	9.868
4	1.207	2.132	3.124	4.151	5.199	6.260	7.328	8.401	9.476	10.553	11.630
5	1.468	2.525	3.648	4.805	5.981	7.169	8.363	9.561	10.760	11.960	13.158
6	1.704	2.878	4.117	5.389	6.679	7.979	9.285	10.594	11.904	13.212	14.518
7	1.919	3.199	4.543	5.919	7.312	8.714	10.122	11.532	12.940	14.347	15.749
8	2.117	3.494	4.934	6.405	7.893	9.389	10.890	12.392	13.891	15.387	16.878
9	2.301	3.767	5.296	6.855	8.431	10.015	11.602	13.188	14.772	16.350	17.923
10	2.472	4.021	5.633	7.276	8.933	10.599	12.266	13.932	15.593	17.248	18.896
11	2.632	4.260	5.950	7.670	9.405	11.147	12.889	14.629	16.364	18.091	19.809
12	2.782	4.484	6.248	8.042	9.850	11.663	13.477	15.287	17.090	18.885	20.670
13	2.925	4.696	6.530	8.394	10.271	12.153	14.034	15.910	17.778	19.637	21.483
14	3.059	4.897	6.798	8.728	10.671	12.618	14.563	16.502	18.432	20.350	22.256
15	3.187	5.089	7.053	9.046	11.052	13.061	15.067	17.066	19.054	21.030	22.991
16	3.308	5.271	7.296	9.350	11.416	13.485	15.549	17.605	19.649	21.679	23.692
17	3.424	5.445	7.529	9.641	11.765	13.890	16.010	18.121	20.218	22.300	24.364
18	3.535	5.612	7.752	9.920	12.100	14.280	16.453	18.616	20.764	22.895	25.007
19	3.641	5.772	7.966	10.188	12.421	14.654	16.879	19.091	21.289	23.467	25.624
20	3.742	5.925	8.172	10.447	12.731	15.014	17.288	19.550	21.794	24.017	26.218
21	3.840	6.073	8.371	10.695	13.030	15.361	17.683	19.991	22.280	24.547	26.790
22	3.934	6.216	8.562	10.935	13.318	15.697	18.065	20.417	22.750	25.059	27.341
23	4.024	6.353	8.747	11.168	13.596	16.021	18.434	20.829	23.203	25.553	27.873
24	4.111	6.485	8.925	11.392	13.866	16.335	18.790	21.228	23.642	26.030	28.388
25	4.195	6.614	9.098	11.609	14.127	16.639	19.136	21.614	24.067	26.492	28.885
26	4.275	6.738	9.266	11.820	14.380	16.933	19.471	21.988	24.479	26.940	29.367
27	4.354	6.858	9.428	12.024	14.626	17.219	19.796	22.351	24.878	27.373	29.833
28	4.429	6.974	9.585	12.223	14.865	17.497	20.112	22.703	25.266	27.794	30.286
29	4.502	7.087	9.738	12.415	15.097	17.767	20.419	23.046	25.642	28.203	30.725
30	4.573	7.196	9.887	12.603	15.322	18.030	20.718	23.379	26.008	28.600	31.152

Table B.46: American-Style Put Premiums
as a Function of Time and Volatility
Stock Price = $100
Strike Price = $90
Dividend Rate = 3%

Mo	Volatility										
	0.15	0.20	0.25	0.30	0.35	0.40	0.45	0.50	0.55	0.60	0.65
1	0.009	0.066	0.204	0.420	0.701	1.032	1.401	1.800	2.222	2.661	3.114
2	0.084	0.318	0.691	1.164	1.707	2.298	2.923	3.573	4.241	4.924	5.618
3	0.211	0.620	1.187	1.856	2.591	3.371	4.181	5.013	5.861	6.721	7.589
4	0.357	0.921	1.650	2.479	3.370	4.303	5.264	6.244	7.237	8.241	9.251
5	0.509	1.210	2.078	3.043	4.068	5.132	6.221	7.328	8.446	9.573	10.705
6	0.660	1.484	2.474	3.559	4.702	5.881	7.084	8.302	9.531	10.767	12.007
7	0.807	1.742	2.843	4.036	5.284	6.567	7.872	9.192	10.520	11.854	13.190
8	0.949	1.986	3.187	4.479	5.824	7.202	8.600	10.012	11.431	12.854	14.277
9	1.086	2.217	3.510	4.893	6.327	7.793	9.278	10.774	12.277	13.782	15.286
10	1.218	2.436	3.815	5.282	6.800	8.347	9.912	11.488	13.068	14.649	16.227
11	1.344	2.644	4.104	5.650	7.245	8.869	10.510	12.159	13.812	15.464	17.112
12	1.465	2.842	4.378	5.999	7.667	9.363	11.074	12.794	14.515	16.233	17.946
13	1.582	3.031	4.639	6.330	8.068	9.832	11.611	13.395	15.181	16.962	18.735
14	1.694	3.211	4.887	6.646	8.450	10.279	12.121	13.968	15.814	17.654	19.485
15	1.801	3.384	5.125	6.948	8.815	10.705	12.608	14.515	16.418	18.314	20.200
16	1.905	3.551	5.354	7.237	9.164	11.114	13.074	15.037	16.995	18.945	20.883
17	2.005	3.710	5.573	7.515	9.499	11.505	13.521	15.538	17.549	19.549	21.536
18	2.101	3.864	5.783	7.781	9.821	11.882	13.951	16.019	18.080	20.128	22.162
19	2.193	4.012	5.986	8.038	10.131	12.244	14.364	16.481	18.590	20.685	22.764
20	2.283	4.155	6.182	8.286	10.430	12.593	14.762	16.927	19.082	21.222	23.343
21	2.369	4.292	6.371	8.525	10.719	12.930	15.146	17.357	19.556	21.738	23.900
22	2.453	4.426	6.553	8.757	10.998	13.256	15.518	17.772	20.014	22.237	24.438
23	2.534	4.555	6.730	8.980	11.268	13.571	15.877	18.174	20.456	22.719	24.957
24	2.612	4.679	6.901	9.197	11.530	13.877	16.224	18.562	20.884	23.185	25.459
25	2.688	4.800	7.067	9.407	11.783	14.173	16.561	18.939	21.299	23.636	25.945
26	2.762	4.918	7.228	9.611	12.029	14.460	16.888	19.304	21.701	24.073	26.416
27	2.834	5.032	7.384	9.809	12.268	14.739	17.206	19.659	22.091	24.497	26.872
28	2.903	5.142	7.536	10.002	12.501	15.010	17.514	20.003	22.470	24.908	27.314
29	2.970	5.250	7.683	10.189	12.727	15.274	17.814	20.338	22.838	25.308	27.743
30	3.036	5.354	7.827	10.371	12.946	15.530	18.106	20.663	23.195	25.696	28.160

Table B.47: American-Style Put Premiums
as a Function of Time and Volatility
Stock Price = $100
Strike Price = $85
Dividend Rate = 3%

Mo	Volatility										
	0.15	0.20	0.25	0.30	0.35	0.40	0.45	0.50	0.55	0.60	0.65
1	0.000	0.003	0.026	0.087	0.200	0.366	0.580	0.836	1.128	1.450	1.797
2	0.006	0.057	0.199	0.445	0.781	1.191	1.658	2.169	2.716	3.291	3.888
3	0.029	0.171	0.463	0.888	1.415	2.017	2.676	3.377	4.110	4.868	5.645
4	0.073	0.321	0.757	1.339	2.025	2.786	3.601	4.455	5.339	6.244	7.166
5	0.130	0.487	1.056	1.776	2.600	3.497	4.445	5.429	6.440	7.470	8.515
6	0.198	0.661	1.350	2.193	3.139	4.155	5.220	6.318	7.441	8.582	9.735
7	0.273	0.836	1.635	2.590	3.645	4.768	5.937	7.138	8.362	9.601	10.851
8	0.352	1.010	1.911	2.967	4.122	5.342	6.607	7.901	9.216	10.544	11.882
9	0.432	1.180	2.176	3.326	4.572	5.882	7.234	8.614	10.013	11.424	12.842
10	0.514	1.347	2.431	3.667	4.999	6.392	7.825	9.285	10.761	12.248	13.741
11	0.596	1.509	2.676	3.994	5.405	6.876	8.385	9.919	11.468	13.026	14.587
12	0.678	1.667	2.911	4.306	5.792	7.336	8.916	10.520	12.137	13.761	15.387
13	0.758	1.820	3.138	4.605	6.162	7.774	9.422	11.091	12.772	14.459	16.146
14	0.838	1.969	3.356	4.892	6.516	8.194	9.905	11.636	13.378	15.124	16.868
15	0.916	2.113	3.567	5.168	6.855	8.595	10.367	12.158	13.957	15.759	17.557
16	0.993	2.253	3.770	5.433	7.182	8.981	10.811	12.658	14.512	16.366	18.215
17	1.068	2.388	3.967	5.689	7.496	9.352	11.237	13.137	15.044	16.949	18.846
18	1.142	2.520	4.157	5.936	7.798	9.709	11.647	13.599	15.555	17.508	19.451
19	1.214	2.648	4.341	6.175	8.091	10.053	12.042	14.043	16.047	18.046	20.033
20	1.284	2.772	4.519	6.406	8.373	10.386	12.424	14.472	16.522	18.564	20.593
21	1.353	2.893	4.692	6.630	8.647	10.708	12.792	14.886	16.979	19.064	21.134
22	1.420	3.011	4.859	6.847	8.911	11.019	13.149	15.287	17.422	19.546	21.655
23	1.486	3.125	5.022	7.057	9.168	11.321	13.494	15.674	17.850	20.013	22.158
24	1.550	3.236	5.180	7.261	9.417	11.613	13.829	16.050	18.264	20.465	22.645
25	1.612	3.344	5.334	7.459	9.659	11.897	14.154	16.414	18.666	20.902	23.117
26	1.673	3.450	5.483	7.652	9.894	12.173	14.470	16.767	19.055	21.326	23.574
27	1.733	3.552	5.629	7.840	10.122	12.442	14.776	17.111	19.434	21.738	24.017
28	1.791	3.652	5.771	8.022	10.345	12.703	15.074	17.444	19.801	22.137	24.447
29	1.848	3.750	5.909	8.200	10.561	12.956	15.364	17.768	20.158	22.525	24.864
30	1.904	3.845	6.044	8.374	10.772	13.204	15.647	18.084	20.506	22.903	25.270

Table B.48: American-Style Put Premiums
as a Function of Time and Volatility
Stock Price = $100
Strike Price = $80
Dividend Rate = 3%

Mo	\multicolumn{11}{c}{Volatility}										
	0.15	0.20	0.25	0.30	0.35	0.40	0.45	0.50	0.55	0.60	0.65
1	0.000	0.000	0.002	0.011	0.040	0.099	0.194	0.326	0.495	0.699	0.933
2	0.000	0.006	0.041	0.134	0.299	0.538	0.842	1.204	1.613	2.062	2.543
3	0.003	0.033	0.144	0.362	0.685	1.099	1.588	2.137	2.734	3.369	4.034
4	0.010	0.086	0.292	0.640	1.110	1.679	2.324	3.028	3.778	4.564	5.378
5	0.024	0.159	0.466	0.938	1.542	2.246	3.026	3.863	4.743	5.657	6.596
6	0.044	0.246	0.655	1.242	1.966	2.791	3.690	4.644	5.639	6.664	7.713
7	0.072	0.344	0.850	1.545	2.379	3.312	4.318	5.376	6.473	7.598	8.744
8	0.104	0.448	1.047	1.842	2.776	3.809	4.912	6.065	7.254	8.470	9.705
9	0.141	0.557	1.244	2.132	3.159	4.283	5.475	6.715	7.989	9.288	10.603
10	0.181	0.667	1.439	2.414	3.528	4.736	6.011	7.331	8.684	10.059	11.449
11	0.224	0.779	1.631	2.687	3.882	5.170	6.521	7.917	9.342	10.789	12.248
12	0.269	0.891	1.819	2.953	4.223	5.585	7.009	8.475	9.969	11.481	13.006
13	0.315	1.003	2.002	3.210	4.552	5.984	7.476	9.008	10.566	12.141	13.726
14	0.363	1.113	2.182	3.459	4.869	6.367	7.923	9.518	11.137	12.771	14.413
15	0.411	1.223	2.358	3.700	5.175	6.736	8.354	10.007	11.684	13.374	15.070
16	0.460	1.330	2.529	3.934	5.471	7.092	8.768	10.478	12.209	13.952	15.699
17	0.509	1.437	2.696	4.162	5.757	7.436	9.167	10.931	12.714	14.507	16.303
18	0.558	1.541	2.858	4.382	6.035	7.768	9.552	11.367	13.200	15.042	16.883
19	0.607	1.644	3.017	4.597	6.303	8.089	9.924	11.788	13.669	15.556	17.441
20	0.656	1.744	3.172	4.805	6.564	8.400	10.284	12.195	14.122	16.052	17.979
21	0.704	1.843	3.323	5.008	6.816	8.701	10.632	12.589	14.559	16.532	18.498
22	0.752	1.940	3.471	5.205	7.062	8.993	10.970	12.971	14.983	16.995	18.999
23	0.800	2.035	3.614	5.397	7.301	9.277	11.297	13.340	15.393	17.443	19.484
24	0.847	2.128	3.755	5.584	7.533	9.553	11.615	13.699	15.790	17.878	19.953
25	0.893	2.219	3.892	5.766	7.759	9.821	11.924	14.047	16.176	18.298	20.408
26	0.939	2.309	4.026	5.944	7.979	10.082	12.225	14.385	16.550	18.707	20.849
27	0.984	2.396	4.157	6.117	8.193	10.336	12.517	14.714	16.914	19.103	21.276
28	1.029	2.482	4.285	6.286	8.402	10.584	12.801	15.034	17.267	19.489	21.691
29	1.073	2.566	4.410	6.451	8.606	10.825	13.079	15.346	17.611	19.863	22.095
30	1.116	2.649	4.532	6.612	8.805	11.061	13.349	15.649	17.946	20.228	22.487

Table B.49: American-Style Put Premiums
as a Function of Time and Volatility
Stock Price = $100
Strike Price = $75
Dividend Rate = 3%

Mo	Volatility										
	0.15	0.20	0.25	0.30	0.35	0.40	0.45	0.50	0.55	0.60	0.65
1	0.000	0.000	0.000	0.001	0.005	0.019	0.050	0.103	0.182	0.290	0.426
2	0.000	0.000	0.006	0.030	0.093	0.206	0.375	0.598	0.873	1.194	1.555
3	0.000	0.005	0.034	0.121	0.286	0.535	0.860	1.254	1.706	2.207	2.749
4	0.001	0.017	0.092	0.264	0.544	0.927	1.398	1.941	2.544	3.196	3.887
5	0.003	0.040	0.174	0.440	0.835	1.343	1.944	2.619	3.353	4.134	4.952
6	0.007	0.075	0.276	0.636	1.141	1.765	2.483	3.275	4.124	5.018	5.947
7	0.014	0.118	0.391	0.844	1.451	2.182	3.006	3.903	4.856	5.850	6.878
8	0.024	0.170	0.515	1.058	1.762	2.590	3.512	4.505	5.551	6.637	7.754
9	0.037	0.227	0.645	1.274	2.068	2.988	4.000	5.080	6.212	7.382	8.580
10	0.052	0.290	0.780	1.490	2.370	3.374	4.469	5.631	6.842	8.089	9.362
11	0.069	0.357	0.916	1.705	2.664	3.748	4.921	6.159	7.443	8.762	10.105
12	0.089	0.427	1.054	1.917	2.952	4.110	5.356	6.665	8.018	9.404	10.812
13	0.111	0.498	1.192	2.126	3.233	4.461	5.776	7.151	8.570	10.018	11.486
14	0.134	0.572	1.329	2.331	3.506	4.801	6.181	7.620	9.099	10.606	12.132
15	0.159	0.646	1.465	2.532	3.772	5.131	6.572	8.071	9.608	11.171	12.750
16	0.185	0.722	1.600	2.729	4.031	5.451	6.951	8.506	10.098	11.714	13.344
17	0.213	0.797	1.733	2.923	4.284	5.761	7.317	8.926	10.570	12.236	13.915
18	0.241	0.873	1.865	3.112	4.529	6.062	7.671	9.332	11.026	12.740	14.465
19	0.270	0.948	1.994	3.297	4.769	6.354	8.015	9.725	11.467	13.226	14.995
20	0.299	1.023	2.122	3.478	5.002	6.639	8.348	10.106	11.893	13.696	15.507
21	0.329	1.098	2.247	3.655	5.230	6.915	8.672	10.475	12.306	14.151	16.001
22	0.359	1.172	2.371	3.828	5.452	7.184	8.987	10.833	12.706	14.591	16.479
23	0.389	1.245	2.492	3.997	5.668	7.446	9.292	11.181	13.094	15.018	16.942
24	0.420	1.318	2.611	4.163	5.880	7.701	9.590	11.519	13.471	15.432	17.391
25	0.451	1.390	2.728	4.325	6.086	7.950	9.879	11.848	13.837	15.833	17.825
26	0.482	1.461	2.843	4.484	6.287	8.193	10.162	12.168	14.193	16.223	18.247
27	0.513	1.531	2.956	4.639	6.484	8.429	10.436	12.479	14.539	16.602	18.657
28	0.543	1.600	3.067	4.792	6.676	8.660	10.704	12.782	14.876	16.970	19.055
29	0.574	1.669	3.176	4.941	6.864	8.886	10.966	13.078	15.204	17.329	19.442
30	0.605	1.736	3.283	5.087	7.048	9.106	11.221	13.366	15.524	17.678	19.819

Table B.50: American-Style Put Premiums
as a Function of Time and Volatility
Stock Price = $100
Strike Price = $70
Dividend Rate = 3%

Mo	Volatility										
	0.15	0.20	0.25	0.30	0.35	0.40	0.45	0.50	0.55	0.60	0.65
1	0.000	0.000	0.000	0.000	0.000	0.003	0.009	0.025	0.054	0.100	0.166
2	0.000	0.000	0.001	0.005	0.022	0.064	0.142	0.260	0.423	0.629	0.875
3	0.000	0.001	0.006	0.032	0.101	0.226	0.417	0.671	0.985	1.353	1.769
4	0.000	0.003	0.023	0.091	0.233	0.461	0.772	1.159	1.614	2.126	2.686
5	0.000	0.008	0.053	0.178	0.405	0.737	1.165	1.676	2.256	2.894	3.581
6	0.001	0.018	0.098	0.288	0.603	1.037	1.574	2.197	2.890	3.641	4.438
7	0.002	0.033	0.155	0.415	0.817	1.348	1.987	2.713	3.509	4.360	5.257
8	0.005	0.053	0.223	0.553	1.041	1.664	2.397	3.217	4.107	5.050	6.036
9	0.008	0.079	0.298	0.700	1.270	1.980	2.801	3.709	4.684	5.711	6.779
10	0.012	0.108	0.380	0.852	1.501	2.293	3.196	4.185	5.240	6.345	7.488
11	0.018	0.142	0.468	1.008	1.732	2.601	3.582	4.647	5.776	6.953	8.166
12	0.025	0.179	0.559	1.166	1.962	2.905	3.958	5.094	6.292	7.536	8.814
13	0.033	0.220	0.653	1.324	2.190	3.202	4.324	5.527	6.790	8.097	9.436
14	0.042	0.262	0.749	1.483	2.415	3.493	4.680	5.947	7.271	8.637	10.034
15	0.053	0.307	0.846	1.642	2.636	3.778	5.027	6.353	7.735	9.158	10.608
16	0.064	0.354	0.945	1.799	2.854	4.056	5.364	6.747	8.185	9.660	11.161
17	0.077	0.402	1.044	1.955	3.068	4.328	5.692	7.129	8.619	10.145	11.694
18	0.090	0.451	1.143	2.109	3.279	4.593	6.011	7.500	9.040	10.614	12.209
19	0.105	0.501	1.242	2.261	3.485	4.853	6.321	7.861	9.448	11.067	12.706
20	0.120	0.552	1.340	2.412	3.687	5.106	6.624	8.211	9.844	11.507	13.187
21	0.136	0.604	1.439	2.560	3.886	5.354	6.919	8.551	10.228	11.932	13.653
22	0.152	0.656	1.536	2.706	4.080	5.595	7.206	8.882	10.601	12.345	14.104
23	0.169	0.708	1.633	2.850	4.271	5.832	7.487	9.205	10.963	12.746	14.542
24	0.187	0.761	1.729	2.992	4.458	6.063	7.760	9.519	11.316	13.136	14.966
25	0.204	0.813	1.824	3.131	4.641	6.288	8.027	9.824	11.659	13.515	15.378
26	0.223	0.865	1.918	3.268	4.821	6.509	8.287	10.123	11.993	13.883	15.779
27	0.241	0.918	2.010	3.403	4.997	6.725	8.541	10.414	12.319	14.241	16.168
28	0.260	0.970	2.102	3.535	5.170	6.937	8.790	10.697	12.636	14.590	16.546
29	0.279	1.022	2.193	3.666	5.339	7.144	9.033	10.974	12.946	14.930	16.915
30	0.298	1.073	2.282	3.794	5.505	7.346	9.270	11.245	13.248	15.262	17.273

Table B.51: American-Style Put Premiums
as a Function of Time and Volatility
Stock Price = $100
Strike Price = $65
Dividend Rate = 3%

Mo	Volatility										
	0.15	0.20	0.25	0.30	0.35	0.40	0.45	0.50	0.55	0.60	0.65
1	0.000	0.000	0.000	0.000	0.000	0.000	0.001	0.004	0.012	0.028	0.054
2	0.000	0.000	0.000	0.001	0.004	0.016	0.044	0.096	0.179	0.295	0.446
3	0.000	0.000	0.001	0.007	0.029	0.081	0.177	0.322	0.518	0.766	1.061
4	0.000	0.000	0.004	0.026	0.085	0.201	0.384	0.636	0.952	1.328	1.758
5	0.000	0.001	0.013	0.061	0.172	0.365	0.641	0.999	1.430	1.925	2.475
6	0.000	0.004	0.029	0.113	0.285	0.558	0.928	1.388	1.925	2.528	3.186
7	0.000	0.008	0.052	0.179	0.417	0.771	1.233	1.788	2.424	3.125	3.881
8	0.001	0.014	0.083	0.258	0.564	0.998	1.546	2.192	2.918	3.710	4.555
9	0.002	0.023	0.120	0.347	0.721	1.233	1.864	2.594	3.404	4.279	5.205
10	0.003	0.034	0.164	0.444	0.885	1.472	2.181	2.991	3.879	4.831	5.833
11	0.004	0.048	0.213	0.547	1.054	1.713	2.497	3.381	4.343	5.366	6.438
12	0.006	0.065	0.266	0.655	1.227	1.955	2.809	3.763	4.794	5.885	7.021
13	0.008	0.084	0.323	0.767	1.401	2.196	3.117	4.137	5.233	6.386	7.584
14	0.011	0.106	0.384	0.881	1.577	2.435	3.420	4.502	5.659	6.872	8.127
15	0.015	0.129	0.448	0.997	1.752	2.671	3.717	4.859	6.074	7.343	8.652
16	0.019	0.154	0.513	1.115	1.927	2.904	4.008	5.207	6.477	7.799	9.159
17	0.024	0.181	0.581	1.233	2.100	3.134	4.293	5.547	6.869	8.241	9.650
18	0.029	0.210	0.650	1.352	2.273	3.360	4.573	5.878	7.250	8.670	10.125
19	0.035	0.240	0.720	1.471	2.443	3.583	4.847	6.201	7.621	9.087	10.585
20	0.042	0.271	0.791	1.590	2.612	3.802	5.115	6.516	7.982	9.492	11.031
21	0.049	0.303	0.862	1.708	2.778	4.017	5.377	6.824	8.333	9.885	11.464
22	0.057	0.336	0.934	1.825	2.943	4.228	5.634	7.125	8.676	10.267	11.885
23	0.065	0.369	1.007	1.942	3.105	4.436	5.885	7.418	9.009	10.639	12.293
24	0.073	0.404	1.079	2.057	3.265	4.639	6.131	7.705	9.335	11.001	12.690
25	0.082	0.439	1.152	2.172	3.423	4.839	6.372	7.985	9.652	11.354	13.076
26	0.092	0.474	1.224	2.285	3.578	5.035	6.607	8.258	9.961	11.697	13.451
27	0.101	0.510	1.296	2.398	3.731	5.228	6.838	8.526	10.263	12.032	13.817
28	0.112	0.546	1.368	2.509	3.882	5.417	7.064	8.787	10.558	12.359	14.173
29	0.122	0.582	1.440	2.619	4.030	5.603	7.286	9.043	10.846	12.677	14.520
30	0.133	0.619	1.511	2.727	4.176	5.785	7.503	9.293	11.128	12.988	14.859

Table B.52: American-Style Put Premiums
as a Function of Time and Volatility
Stock Price = $100
Strike Price = $60
Dividend Rate = 3%

Mo	Volatility										
	0.15	0.20	0.25	0.30	0.35	0.40	0.45	0.50	0.55	0.60	0.65
1	0.000	0.000	0.000	0.000	0.000	0.000	0.000	0.001	0.002	0.006	0.014
2	0.000	0.000	0.000	0.000	0.001	0.003	0.011	0.029	0.064	0.120	0.201
3	0.000	0.000	0.000	0.001	0.006	0.024	0.063	0.134	0.243	0.393	0.585
4	0.000	0.000	0.001	0.006	0.026	0.075	0.169	0.314	0.514	0.769	1.077
5	0.000	0.000	0.003	0.017	0.063	0.159	0.318	0.547	0.842	1.202	1.619
6	0.000	0.001	0.007	0.037	0.118	0.269	0.502	0.815	1.205	1.663	2.181
7	0.000	0.002	0.015	0.067	0.189	0.402	0.709	1.106	1.585	2.136	2.748
8	0.000	0.003	0.026	0.105	0.275	0.551	0.932	1.410	1.974	2.611	3.310
9	0.000	0.006	0.041	0.153	0.372	0.712	1.166	1.722	2.366	3.083	3.862
10	0.001	0.009	0.061	0.207	0.479	0.882	1.407	2.037	2.756	3.549	4.402
11	0.001	0.014	0.085	0.268	0.593	1.059	1.652	2.353	3.143	4.006	4.928
12	0.001	0.020	0.112	0.335	0.713	1.241	1.899	2.667	3.524	4.454	5.440
13	0.002	0.028	0.143	0.406	0.837	1.425	2.147	2.979	3.899	4.891	5.937
14	0.003	0.037	0.177	0.482	0.965	1.611	2.393	3.286	4.267	5.317	6.421
15	0.004	0.047	0.213	0.560	1.095	1.798	2.638	3.589	4.627	5.733	6.891
16	0.005	0.059	0.253	0.642	1.228	1.984	2.881	3.888	4.980	6.139	7.347
17	0.007	0.072	0.294	0.725	1.361	2.171	3.121	4.181	5.325	6.534	7.790
18	0.009	0.086	0.338	0.811	1.495	2.356	3.358	4.469	5.663	6.919	8.221
19	0.011	0.102	0.383	0.897	1.629	2.540	3.592	4.751	5.993	7.294	8.640
20	0.013	0.118	0.430	0.985	1.763	2.722	3.822	5.029	6.315	7.660	9.048
21	0.016	0.136	0.478	1.074	1.897	2.902	4.049	5.300	6.630	8.017	9.444
22	0.019	0.155	0.527	1.163	2.030	3.081	4.272	5.567	6.939	8.365	9.830
23	0.022	0.174	0.577	1.252	2.162	3.257	4.491	5.828	7.240	8.705	10.206
24	0.026	0.194	0.628	1.342	2.294	3.431	4.707	6.084	7.534	9.036	10.572
25	0.029	0.215	0.679	1.431	2.424	3.603	4.919	6.335	7.823	9.360	10.929
26	0.034	0.237	0.731	1.521	2.554	3.772	5.127	6.581	8.105	9.675	11.277
27	0.038	0.259	0.784	1.610	2.682	3.939	5.332	6.822	8.380	9.984	11.616
28	0.043	0.282	0.837	1.699	2.809	4.104	5.534	7.059	8.650	10.285	11.947
29	0.048	0.305	0.890	1.787	2.934	4.266	5.731	7.291	8.914	10.580	12.270
30	0.053	0.329	0.943	1.875	3.058	4.426	5.926	7.518	9.173	10.868	12.585

C

IN-THE-MONEY PROBABILITIES

The tables that follow show the probability of a put option winding up in the money by the expiration date, based upon Equations 13.2 and 13.13. They are based on a stock price of $100 and exercise (strike) prices ranging from $120 down to $80 in steps of $5. Annual earnings growth rates of 0%, 5%, 10%, 15%, and 20% are considered. Each table is presented in matrix format, with volatilities ranging from a low of 0.150 through a high of 0.650. Time to expiration ranges from one month to a maximum of 30 months. The dividend rate is zero and risk-free interest rate is 6% in all instances.

For example, suppose you wanted to know the probability of winding up in the money for an at-the-money LEAP put with stock and strike price of $100, volatility of 0.40, with an expiration date of 24 months away, no dividend and risk-free interest rate of 6%. From Table C.5, we see that for a zero growth in earnings (and accompanying stock price), the associated probability is 0.310. For a 5% growth rate in earnings, Table C.14 shows this probability to fall to 0.251. For a 10% growth rate in earnings, Table C.23 shows this probability to fall to 0.198. For a 15% growth rate in earnings, Table C.32 shows this probability to fall to 0.153. And for a 20% growth rate in earnings, Table C.41 shows this probability to fall to just 0.115. These probabilities hold independently of whether a European- or American-style pricing formula is used to determine premiums.

Table C.1: Probability of a Put Expiring in the Money as a Function of Time and Volatility
Stock Price = $100
Strike Price = $120
Annual Growth Rate = 0%

Mo	Volatility										
	0.15	0.20	0.25	0.30	0.35	0.40	0.45	0.50	0.55	0.60	0.65
1	1.000	0.999	0.992	0.977	0.956	0.930	0.903	0.876	0.850	0.826	0.803
2	0.997	0.981	0.949	0.911	0.872	0.835	0.801	0.771	0.744	0.719	0.697
3	0.986	0.948	0.899	0.851	0.807	0.769	0.736	0.707	0.681	0.658	0.638
4	0.966	0.911	0.854	0.802	0.759	0.722	0.690	0.662	0.638	0.616	0.597
5	0.943	0.876	0.814	0.763	0.720	0.684	0.654	0.628	0.605	0.584	0.566
6	0.917	0.843	0.780	0.730	0.689	0.654	0.625	0.600	0.578	0.558	0.540
7	0.890	0.813	0.750	0.701	0.662	0.629	0.601	0.577	0.556	0.537	0.519
8	0.865	0.785	0.724	0.677	0.639	0.607	0.581	0.557	0.537	0.518	0.501
9	0.839	0.760	0.701	0.655	0.618	0.588	0.563	0.540	0.520	0.502	0.485
10	0.815	0.737	0.679	0.635	0.600	0.571	0.546	0.525	0.505	0.487	0.471
11	0.792	0.715	0.660	0.618	0.584	0.556	0.532	0.511	0.491	0.474	0.458
12	0.770	0.696	0.642	0.602	0.569	0.542	0.519	0.498	0.479	0.462	0.446
13	0.750	0.677	0.626	0.587	0.556	0.529	0.507	0.486	0.468	0.450	0.435
14	0.730	0.660	0.611	0.573	0.543	0.518	0.495	0.475	0.457	0.440	0.424
15	0.711	0.644	0.596	0.561	0.531	0.507	0.485	0.465	0.447	0.430	0.415
16	0.693	0.628	0.583	0.549	0.520	0.496	0.475	0.456	0.438	0.421	0.406
17	0.676	0.614	0.571	0.537	0.510	0.487	0.466	0.447	0.429	0.413	0.397
18	0.659	0.600	0.559	0.527	0.500	0.477	0.457	0.438	0.421	0.404	0.389
19	0.644	0.588	0.548	0.517	0.491	0.469	0.449	0.430	0.413	0.397	0.381
20	0.629	0.575	0.537	0.508	0.483	0.461	0.441	0.423	0.406	0.389	0.374
21	0.614	0.564	0.527	0.499	0.474	0.453	0.433	0.415	0.398	0.382	0.367
22	0.600	0.552	0.518	0.490	0.466	0.445	0.426	0.408	0.392	0.376	0.360
23	0.587	0.542	0.509	0.482	0.459	0.438	0.419	0.402	0.385	0.369	0.354
24	0.574	0.531	0.500	0.474	0.452	0.431	0.413	0.395	0.379	0.363	0.348
25	0.562	0.522	0.491	0.466	0.445	0.425	0.407	0.389	0.373	0.357	0.342
26	0.550	0.512	0.483	0.459	0.438	0.419	0.400	0.383	0.367	0.351	0.336
27	0.539	0.503	0.476	0.452	0.432	0.412	0.395	0.378	0.361	0.346	0.330
28	0.528	0.494	0.468	0.446	0.425	0.407	0.389	0.372	0.356	0.340	0.325
29	0.517	0.486	0.461	0.439	0.419	0.401	0.383	0.367	0.351	0.335	0.320
30	0.507	0.478	0.454	0.433	0.414	0.395	0.378	0.362	0.345	0.330	0.315

Table C.2: Probability of a Put Expiring in the Money
as a Function of Time and Volatility
Stock Price = $100
Strike Price = $115
Annual Growth Rate = 0%

Mo	Volatility										
	0.15	0.20	0.25	0.30	0.35	0.40	0.45	0.50	0.55	0.60	0.65
1	0.999	0.989	0.966	0.935	0.900	0.866	0.835	0.806	0.779	0.755	0.734
2	0.982	0.939	0.889	0.841	0.799	0.762	0.731	0.703	0.679	0.658	0.639
3	0.948	0.884	0.825	0.775	0.734	0.700	0.671	0.646	0.624	0.605	0.588
4	0.910	0.836	0.776	0.727	0.688	0.657	0.630	0.607	0.586	0.568	0.552
5	0.872	0.795	0.736	0.690	0.654	0.624	0.599	0.577	0.558	0.541	0.525
6	0.837	0.760	0.703	0.660	0.625	0.597	0.574	0.553	0.535	0.519	0.504
7	0.804	0.729	0.675	0.634	0.602	0.575	0.553	0.533	0.516	0.500	0.485
8	0.774	0.702	0.650	0.612	0.582	0.557	0.535	0.516	0.499	0.484	0.469
9	0.747	0.677	0.629	0.593	0.564	0.540	0.519	0.501	0.484	0.469	0.455
10	0.721	0.656	0.610	0.576	0.548	0.525	0.505	0.487	0.471	0.456	0.442
11	0.698	0.636	0.593	0.560	0.534	0.512	0.493	0.475	0.459	0.444	0.431
12	0.676	0.617	0.577	0.546	0.521	0.500	0.481	0.464	0.448	0.434	0.420
13	0.656	0.601	0.562	0.533	0.509	0.489	0.470	0.454	0.438	0.424	0.410
14	0.637	0.585	0.549	0.521	0.498	0.478	0.460	0.444	0.429	0.414	0.401
15	0.619	0.571	0.537	0.510	0.488	0.469	0.451	0.435	0.420	0.406	0.392
16	0.602	0.557	0.525	0.500	0.478	0.460	0.442	0.427	0.412	0.397	0.384
17	0.586	0.544	0.514	0.490	0.469	0.451	0.434	0.419	0.404	0.390	0.376
18	0.571	0.532	0.504	0.481	0.461	0.443	0.426	0.411	0.396	0.382	0.369
19	0.557	0.521	0.494	0.472	0.453	0.435	0.419	0.404	0.389	0.375	0.362
20	0.543	0.510	0.485	0.464	0.445	0.428	0.412	0.397	0.382	0.368	0.355
21	0.530	0.500	0.476	0.456	0.438	0.421	0.405	0.390	0.376	0.362	0.348
22	0.518	0.490	0.468	0.448	0.431	0.415	0.399	0.384	0.370	0.356	0.342
23	0.506	0.480	0.460	0.441	0.424	0.408	0.393	0.378	0.364	0.350	0.336
24	0.495	0.471	0.452	0.434	0.418	0.402	0.387	0.372	0.358	0.344	0.331
25	0.484	0.463	0.445	0.428	0.412	0.396	0.381	0.367	0.353	0.339	0.325
26	0.474	0.455	0.437	0.421	0.406	0.391	0.376	0.361	0.347	0.333	0.320
27	0.464	0.447	0.431	0.415	0.400	0.385	0.371	0.356	0.342	0.328	0.315
28	0.454	0.439	0.424	0.409	0.394	0.380	0.365	0.351	0.337	0.323	0.310
29	0.445	0.432	0.418	0.403	0.389	0.375	0.360	0.346	0.332	0.318	0.305
30	0.436	0.424	0.412	0.398	0.384	0.370	0.356	0.342	0.328	0.314	0.300

Table C.3: Probability of a Put Expiring in the Money
as a Function of Time and Volatility
Stock Price = $100
Strike Price = $110
Annual Growth Rate = 0%

Mo	Volatility										
	0.15	0.20	0.25	0.30	0.35	0.40	0.45	0.50	0.55	0.60	0.65
1	0.980	0.938	0.888	0.841	0.800	0.766	0.736	0.710	0.688	0.668	0.651
2	0.913	0.842	0.784	0.737	0.700	0.670	0.645	0.624	0.606	0.589	0.575
3	0.849	0.774	0.719	0.677	0.645	0.619	0.597	0.578	0.561	0.547	0.534
4	0.796	0.724	0.673	0.636	0.607	0.583	0.564	0.546	0.531	0.518	0.505
5	0.751	0.684	0.639	0.605	0.579	0.557	0.539	0.523	0.508	0.495	0.483
6	0.713	0.652	0.611	0.580	0.556	0.536	0.518	0.503	0.489	0.477	0.465
7	0.681	0.625	0.587	0.559	0.537	0.518	0.501	0.487	0.473	0.461	0.450
8	0.652	0.601	0.567	0.541	0.520	0.502	0.487	0.473	0.460	0.447	0.436
9	0.626	0.581	0.549	0.525	0.506	0.489	0.474	0.460	0.447	0.435	0.424
10	0.604	0.562	0.534	0.511	0.493	0.477	0.462	0.449	0.436	0.424	0.413
11	0.583	0.546	0.519	0.499	0.481	0.466	0.451	0.438	0.426	0.414	0.403
12	0.564	0.531	0.506	0.487	0.470	0.456	0.442	0.429	0.417	0.405	0.393
13	0.546	0.517	0.495	0.476	0.461	0.446	0.433	0.420	0.408	0.396	0.385
14	0.530	0.504	0.484	0.467	0.451	0.437	0.424	0.412	0.400	0.388	0.376
15	0.515	0.492	0.473	0.457	0.443	0.429	0.416	0.404	0.392	0.380	0.369
16	0.501	0.480	0.464	0.449	0.435	0.422	0.409	0.397	0.385	0.373	0.361
17	0.487	0.470	0.455	0.441	0.427	0.414	0.402	0.390	0.378	0.366	0.354
18	0.475	0.460	0.446	0.433	0.420	0.407	0.395	0.383	0.371	0.359	0.348
19	0.463	0.450	0.438	0.425	0.413	0.401	0.389	0.377	0.365	0.353	0.341
20	0.452	0.441	0.430	0.418	0.407	0.395	0.383	0.371	0.359	0.347	0.335
21	0.441	0.433	0.423	0.412	0.400	0.389	0.377	0.365	0.353	0.341	0.330
22	0.431	0.425	0.416	0.405	0.394	0.383	0.371	0.359	0.348	0.336	0.324
23	0.421	0.417	0.409	0.399	0.389	0.377	0.366	0.354	0.342	0.330	0.319
24	0.412	0.410	0.403	0.393	0.383	0.372	0.361	0.349	0.337	0.325	0.313
25	0.403	0.402	0.396	0.388	0.378	0.367	0.356	0.344	0.332	0.320	0.308
26	0.395	0.395	0.390	0.382	0.373	0.362	0.351	0.339	0.327	0.315	0.303
27	0.386	0.389	0.385	0.377	0.368	0.357	0.346	0.334	0.323	0.311	0.299
28	0.378	0.382	0.379	0.372	0.363	0.352	0.341	0.330	0.318	0.306	0.294
29	0.371	0.376	0.374	0.367	0.358	0.348	0.337	0.325	0.314	0.302	0.290
30	0.363	0.370	0.368	0.362	0.354	0.344	0.333	0.321	0.309	0.297	0.285

Table C.4: Probability of a Put Expiring in the Money
as a Function of Time and Volatility
Stock Price = $100
Strike Price = $105
Annual Growth Rate = 0%

Mo	\multicolumn{11}{Volatility}										
	0.15	0.20	0.25	0.30	0.35	0.40	0.45	0.50	0.55	0.60	0.65
1	0.839	0.767	0.716	0.678	0.649	0.626	0.607	0.591	0.578	0.566	0.556
2	0.727	0.668	0.629	0.601	0.579	0.562	0.547	0.535	0.524	0.514	0.505
3	0.660	0.613	0.582	0.560	0.542	0.527	0.515	0.504	0.494	0.485	0.477
4	0.614	0.576	0.551	0.532	0.517	0.504	0.492	0.482	0.473	0.464	0.456
5	0.578	0.548	0.527	0.510	0.497	0.485	0.475	0.465	0.456	0.447	0.439
6	0.549	0.525	0.507	0.493	0.481	0.470	0.460	0.451	0.442	0.433	0.425
7	0.525	0.506	0.491	0.478	0.467	0.457	0.448	0.438	0.430	0.421	0.413
8	0.504	0.489	0.476	0.465	0.455	0.446	0.437	0.428	0.419	0.410	0.402
9	0.486	0.474	0.464	0.454	0.445	0.436	0.427	0.418	0.409	0.400	0.392
10	0.469	0.461	0.452	0.444	0.435	0.426	0.417	0.409	0.400	0.391	0.383
11	0.454	0.449	0.442	0.434	0.426	0.418	0.409	0.400	0.392	0.383	0.374
12	0.440	0.438	0.433	0.426	0.418	0.410	0.401	0.393	0.384	0.375	0.366
13	0.428	0.428	0.424	0.418	0.410	0.402	0.394	0.385	0.377	0.368	0.359
14	0.416	0.418	0.415	0.410	0.403	0.395	0.387	0.379	0.370	0.361	0.352
15	0.405	0.409	0.408	0.403	0.396	0.389	0.381	0.372	0.363	0.354	0.345
16	0.395	0.401	0.400	0.396	0.390	0.383	0.375	0.366	0.357	0.348	0.338
17	0.385	0.393	0.393	0.390	0.384	0.377	0.369	0.360	0.351	0.342	0.332
18	0.376	0.386	0.387	0.384	0.378	0.371	0.363	0.354	0.345	0.336	0.326
19	0.367	0.378	0.380	0.378	0.373	0.366	0.358	0.349	0.340	0.330	0.321
20	0.359	0.372	0.374	0.372	0.367	0.360	0.352	0.344	0.335	0.325	0.315
21	0.351	0.365	0.369	0.367	0.362	0.355	0.348	0.339	0.330	0.320	0.310
22	0.344	0.359	0.363	0.362	0.357	0.351	0.343	0.334	0.325	0.315	0.305
23	0.336	0.353	0.358	0.357	0.352	0.346	0.338	0.329	0.320	0.310	0.300
24	0.329	0.347	0.353	0.352	0.348	0.341	0.334	0.325	0.315	0.306	0.296
25	0.323	0.342	0.348	0.347	0.343	0.337	0.329	0.320	0.311	0.301	0.291
26	0.316	0.336	0.343	0.343	0.339	0.333	0.325	0.316	0.307	0.297	0.287
27	0.310	0.331	0.338	0.339	0.335	0.329	0.321	0.312	0.303	0.293	0.282
28	0.304	0.326	0.334	0.334	0.331	0.325	0.317	0.308	0.299	0.289	0.278
29	0.298	0.321	0.329	0.330	0.327	0.321	0.313	0.304	0.295	0.285	0.274
30	0.293	0.316	0.325	0.326	0.323	0.317	0.309	0.300	0.291	0.281	0.270

Table C.5: Probability of a Put Expiring in the Money
as a Function of Time and Volatility
Stock Price = $100
Strike Price = $100
Annual Growth Rate = 0%

Mo	\multicolumn{11}{c}{Volatility}
	0.15	0.20	0.25	0.30	0.35	0.40	0.45	0.50	0.55	0.60	0.65
1	0.445	0.454	0.458	0.460	0.460	0.460	0.459	0.457	0.456	0.454	0.452
2	0.423	0.435	0.441	0.443	0.444	0.443	0.442	0.440	0.438	0.435	0.432
3	0.406	0.421	0.428	0.431	0.431	0.431	0.429	0.427	0.424	0.421	0.417
4	0.392	0.409	0.417	0.420	0.421	0.420	0.418	0.415	0.412	0.409	0.405
5	0.380	0.398	0.407	0.411	0.412	0.411	0.409	0.406	0.402	0.398	0.394
6	0.368	0.389	0.398	0.402	0.403	0.402	0.400	0.397	0.393	0.389	0.384
7	0.358	0.380	0.390	0.395	0.396	0.395	0.392	0.389	0.385	0.380	0.375
8	0.349	0.372	0.383	0.388	0.389	0.388	0.385	0.381	0.377	0.372	0.367
9	0.340	0.365	0.376	0.381	0.382	0.381	0.378	0.374	0.370	0.365	0.359
10	0.332	0.358	0.369	0.375	0.376	0.375	0.372	0.368	0.363	0.358	0.352
11	0.325	0.351	0.363	0.369	0.370	0.369	0.366	0.362	0.357	0.351	0.345
12	0.317	0.345	0.358	0.363	0.365	0.363	0.360	0.356	0.350	0.345	0.338
13	0.311	0.339	0.352	0.358	0.359	0.358	0.355	0.350	0.345	0.339	0.332
14	0.304	0.333	0.347	0.353	0.354	0.353	0.349	0.345	0.339	0.333	0.326
15	0.298	0.327	0.342	0.348	0.349	0.348	0.344	0.340	0.334	0.327	0.320
16	0.292	0.322	0.337	0.343	0.345	0.343	0.340	0.335	0.329	0.322	0.315
17	0.286	0.317	0.332	0.339	0.340	0.339	0.335	0.330	0.324	0.317	0.310
18	0.280	0.312	0.327	0.334	0.336	0.334	0.330	0.325	0.319	0.312	0.305
19	0.275	0.307	0.323	0.330	0.331	0.330	0.326	0.321	0.314	0.307	0.300
20	0.270	0.303	0.319	0.326	0.327	0.326	0.322	0.316	0.310	0.303	0.295
21	0.265	0.298	0.315	0.322	0.323	0.322	0.318	0.312	0.306	0.298	0.290
22	0.260	0.294	0.311	0.318	0.320	0.318	0.314	0.308	0.302	0.294	0.286
23	0.255	0.290	0.307	0.314	0.316	0.314	0.310	0.304	0.297	0.290	0.282
24	0.251	0.286	0.303	0.310	0.312	0.310	0.306	0.300	0.294	0.286	0.278
25	0.246	0.282	0.299	0.307	0.309	0.307	0.303	0.297	0.290	0.282	0.273
26	0.242	0.278	0.296	0.303	0.305	0.303	0.299	0.293	0.286	0.278	0.270
27	0.238	0.274	0.292	0.300	0.302	0.300	0.295	0.289	0.282	0.274	0.266
28	0.234	0.271	0.289	0.296	0.298	0.296	0.292	0.286	0.279	0.271	0.262
29	0.230	0.267	0.285	0.293	0.295	0.293	0.289	0.283	0.275	0.267	0.258
30	0.226	0.264	0.282	0.290	0.292	0.290	0.286	0.279	0.272	0.264	0.255

Table C.6: Probability of a Put Expiring in the Money
as a Function of Time and Volatility
Stock Price = $100
Strike Price = $95
Annual Growth Rate = 0%

Mo	Volatility										
	0.15	0.20	0.25	0.30	0.35	0.40	0.45	0.50	0.55	0.60	0.65
1	0.093	0.158	0.207	0.244	0.272	0.293	0.309	0.322	0.332	0.340	0.347
2	0.151	0.214	0.257	0.287	0.308	0.324	0.335	0.344	0.350	0.355	0.358
3	0.178	0.238	0.277	0.303	0.321	0.333	0.342	0.348	0.353	0.355	0.357
4	0.193	0.250	0.286	0.309	0.325	0.336	0.343	0.348	0.351	0.352	0.353
5	0.201	0.256	0.290	0.312	0.326	0.336	0.342	0.345	0.347	0.348	0.348
6	0.206	0.259	0.292	0.312	0.326	0.334	0.339	0.342	0.343	0.343	0.342
7	0.209	0.261	0.292	0.312	0.324	0.332	0.336	0.338	0.339	0.338	0.337
8	0.210	0.261	0.291	0.310	0.322	0.329	0.333	0.334	0.334	0.333	0.331
9	0.210	0.260	0.290	0.308	0.319	0.326	0.329	0.330	0.330	0.328	0.325
10	0.209	0.259	0.288	0.306	0.317	0.323	0.326	0.326	0.325	0.323	0.320
11	0.208	0.258	0.286	0.304	0.314	0.320	0.322	0.322	0.321	0.318	0.315
12	0.207	0.256	0.284	0.301	0.311	0.316	0.318	0.318	0.317	0.314	0.310
13	0.205	0.254	0.282	0.299	0.308	0.313	0.315	0.314	0.312	0.309	0.305
14	0.203	0.252	0.280	0.296	0.305	0.310	0.311	0.310	0.308	0.305	0.300
15	0.201	0.249	0.277	0.293	0.302	0.306	0.308	0.307	0.304	0.300	0.296
16	0.199	0.247	0.275	0.290	0.299	0.303	0.304	0.303	0.300	0.296	0.291
17	0.197	0.245	0.272	0.288	0.296	0.300	0.301	0.299	0.296	0.292	0.287
18	0.195	0.242	0.269	0.285	0.293	0.297	0.297	0.296	0.292	0.288	0.282
19	0.192	0.240	0.267	0.282	0.290	0.294	0.294	0.292	0.289	0.284	0.278
20	0.190	0.237	0.264	0.280	0.287	0.291	0.291	0.289	0.285	0.280	0.274
21	0.188	0.235	0.262	0.277	0.285	0.288	0.288	0.285	0.281	0.276	0.270
22	0.185	0.232	0.259	0.274	0.282	0.285	0.285	0.282	0.278	0.273	0.267
23	0.183	0.230	0.257	0.272	0.279	0.282	0.282	0.279	0.275	0.269	0.263
24	0.180	0.228	0.254	0.269	0.276	0.279	0.278	0.276	0.271	0.266	0.259
25	0.178	0.225	0.252	0.266	0.274	0.276	0.276	0.273	0.268	0.262	0.256
26	0.176	0.223	0.249	0.264	0.271	0.273	0.273	0.270	0.265	0.259	0.252
27	0.173	0.220	0.247	0.261	0.269	0.271	0.270	0.267	0.262	0.256	0.249
28	0.171	0.218	0.245	0.259	0.266	0.268	0.267	0.264	0.259	0.252	0.245
29	0.169	0.216	0.242	0.257	0.263	0.265	0.264	0.261	0.256	0.249	0.242
30	0.167	0.213	0.240	0.254	0.261	0.263	0.262	0.258	0.253	0.246	0.239

Table C.7: Probability of a Put Expiring in the Money
as a Function of Time and Volatility
Stock Price = $100
Strike Price = $90
Annual Growth Rate = 0%

Mo	Volatility										
	0.15	0.20	0.25	0.30	0.35	0.40	0.45	0.50	0.55	0.60	0.65
1	0.005	0.026	0.059	0.094	0.127	0.155	0.180	0.201	0.219	0.235	0.248
2	0.028	0.073	0.119	0.158	0.190	0.215	0.236	0.252	0.266	0.276	0.285
3	0.050	0.105	0.153	0.190	0.219	0.241	0.259	0.272	0.283	0.291	0.297
4	0.068	0.126	0.173	0.209	0.235	0.255	0.270	0.281	0.290	0.296	0.301
5	0.082	0.141	0.187	0.221	0.245	0.263	0.276	0.286	0.293	0.298	0.301
6	0.092	0.152	0.197	0.228	0.251	0.268	0.279	0.288	0.294	0.298	0.300
7	0.100	0.160	0.203	0.234	0.255	0.270	0.281	0.288	0.293	0.296	0.298
8	0.106	0.166	0.208	0.237	0.257	0.271	0.281	0.288	0.292	0.294	0.295
9	0.111	0.170	0.211	0.239	0.259	0.272	0.281	0.286	0.290	0.291	0.292
10	0.114	0.173	0.213	0.241	0.259	0.272	0.280	0.285	0.288	0.289	0.288
11	0.117	0.175	0.215	0.241	0.259	0.271	0.278	0.283	0.285	0.286	0.285
12	0.120	0.177	0.216	0.242	0.259	0.270	0.277	0.281	0.282	0.282	0.281
13	0.121	0.178	0.216	0.241	0.258	0.269	0.275	0.278	0.280	0.279	0.278
14	0.122	0.179	0.216	0.241	0.257	0.267	0.273	0.276	0.277	0.276	0.274
15	0.123	0.179	0.216	0.240	0.256	0.265	0.271	0.274	0.274	0.273	0.270
16	0.124	0.179	0.216	0.239	0.254	0.264	0.269	0.271	0.271	0.270	0.267
17	0.124	0.179	0.215	0.238	0.253	0.262	0.267	0.268	0.268	0.266	0.263
18	0.124	0.179	0.214	0.237	0.251	0.260	0.264	0.266	0.265	0.263	0.260
19	0.124	0.178	0.214	0.236	0.250	0.258	0.262	0.263	0.263	0.260	0.257
20	0.124	0.178	0.213	0.235	0.248	0.256	0.260	0.261	0.260	0.257	0.253
21	0.123	0.177	0.211	0.233	0.246	0.254	0.258	0.258	0.257	0.254	0.250
22	0.123	0.176	0.210	0.232	0.245	0.252	0.255	0.256	0.254	0.251	0.247
23	0.122	0.175	0.209	0.230	0.243	0.250	0.253	0.253	0.251	0.248	0.244
24	0.121	0.174	0.208	0.229	0.241	0.248	0.251	0.251	0.249	0.245	0.240
25	0.121	0.173	0.206	0.227	0.239	0.246	0.248	0.248	0.246	0.242	0.237
26	0.120	0.172	0.205	0.225	0.237	0.244	0.246	0.246	0.243	0.239	0.234
27	0.119	0.171	0.204	0.224	0.236	0.242	0.244	0.243	0.241	0.237	0.231
28	0.118	0.170	0.202	0.222	0.234	0.240	0.242	0.241	0.238	0.234	0.229
29	0.117	0.168	0.201	0.221	0.232	0.238	0.240	0.239	0.236	0.231	0.226
30	0.116	0.167	0.199	0.219	0.230	0.236	0.237	0.236	0.233	0.229	0.223

Table C.8: Probability of a Put Expiring in the Money as a Function of Time and Volatility
Stock Price = $100
Strike Price = $85
Annual Growth Rate = 0%

Mo	Volatility										
	0.15	0.20	0.25	0.30	0.35	0.40	0.45	0.50	0.55	0.60	0.65
1	0.000	0.002	0.009	0.024	0.044	0.066	0.088	0.109	0.128	0.146	0.162
2	0.002	0.016	0.041	0.071	0.100	0.128	0.151	0.172	0.189	0.204	0.217
3	0.008	0.034	0.069	0.104	0.135	0.162	0.184	0.202	0.217	0.229	0.239
4	0.016	0.051	0.091	0.127	0.158	0.183	0.203	0.219	0.232	0.242	0.250
5	0.024	0.065	0.107	0.143	0.173	0.196	0.215	0.229	0.240	0.249	0.256
6	0.031	0.076	0.119	0.155	0.184	0.206	0.222	0.235	0.245	0.253	0.258
7	0.037	0.085	0.129	0.164	0.191	0.212	0.228	0.239	0.248	0.255	0.259
8	0.043	0.093	0.137	0.171	0.197	0.217	0.231	0.242	0.250	0.255	0.259
9	0.048	0.099	0.143	0.177	0.202	0.220	0.234	0.243	0.250	0.255	0.258
10	0.053	0.105	0.148	0.181	0.205	0.222	0.235	0.244	0.250	0.254	0.256
11	0.056	0.109	0.152	0.184	0.207	0.224	0.236	0.244	0.249	0.253	0.254
12	0.060	0.113	0.155	0.186	0.209	0.225	0.236	0.244	0.248	0.251	0.252
13	0.062	0.116	0.158	0.188	0.210	0.225	0.236	0.243	0.247	0.249	0.250
14	0.065	0.118	0.160	0.190	0.211	0.225	0.235	0.242	0.246	0.247	0.248
15	0.067	0.120	0.161	0.191	0.211	0.225	0.235	0.241	0.244	0.245	0.245
16	0.069	0.122	0.162	0.191	0.211	0.225	0.234	0.239	0.242	0.243	0.242
17	0.070	0.123	0.163	0.192	0.211	0.224	0.233	0.238	0.240	0.241	0.240
18	0.071	0.124	0.164	0.192	0.211	0.224	0.232	0.236	0.238	0.239	0.237
19	0.072	0.125	0.165	0.192	0.210	0.223	0.230	0.235	0.236	0.236	0.235
20	0.073	0.126	0.165	0.192	0.210	0.222	0.229	0.233	0.234	0.234	0.232
21	0.074	0.126	0.165	0.191	0.209	0.221	0.228	0.231	0.232	0.232	0.229
22	0.074	0.127	0.165	0.191	0.208	0.219	0.226	0.229	0.230	0.229	0.227
23	0.075	0.127	0.165	0.191	0.208	0.218	0.225	0.228	0.228	0.227	0.224
24	0.075	0.127	0.165	0.190	0.207	0.217	0.223	0.226	0.226	0.224	0.222
25	0.075	0.127	0.164	0.189	0.206	0.216	0.221	0.224	0.224	0.222	0.219
26	0.076	0.127	0.164	0.189	0.205	0.214	0.220	0.222	0.222	0.220	0.216
27	0.076	0.127	0.163	0.188	0.203	0.213	0.218	0.220	0.220	0.218	0.214
28	0.076	0.127	0.163	0.187	0.202	0.212	0.217	0.218	0.218	0.215	0.212
29	0.076	0.126	0.162	0.186	0.201	0.210	0.215	0.216	0.216	0.213	0.209
30	0.075	0.126	0.162	0.185	0.200	0.209	0.213	0.215	0.214	0.211	0.207

Table C.9: Probability of a Put Expiring in the Money
as a Function of Time and Volatility
Stock Price = $100
Strike Price = $80
Annual Growth Rate = 0%

Mo	Volatility										
	0.15	0.20	0.25	0.30	0.35	0.40	0.45	0.50	0.55	0.60	0.65
1	0.000	0.000	0.001	0.004	0.010	0.021	0.034	0.049	0.065	0.080	0.095
2	0.000	0.002	0.010	0.025	0.044	0.066	0.087	0.107	0.125	0.141	0.156
3	0.001	0.008	0.025	0.048	0.074	0.098	0.121	0.141	0.158	0.173	0.185
4	0.002	0.015	0.039	0.068	0.096	0.121	0.143	0.162	0.178	0.191	0.202
5	0.005	0.023	0.053	0.084	0.113	0.138	0.159	0.176	0.190	0.202	0.212
6	0.007	0.031	0.064	0.097	0.126	0.150	0.170	0.186	0.199	0.209	0.218
7	0.010	0.039	0.074	0.107	0.136	0.159	0.178	0.193	0.205	0.214	0.221
8	0.014	0.045	0.082	0.116	0.144	0.166	0.184	0.198	0.209	0.217	0.223
9	0.017	0.051	0.089	0.123	0.150	0.172	0.189	0.202	0.212	0.219	0.224
10	0.020	0.056	0.095	0.128	0.155	0.176	0.192	0.204	0.213	0.220	0.225
11	0.022	0.061	0.100	0.133	0.159	0.179	0.195	0.206	0.214	0.220	0.224
12	0.025	0.065	0.104	0.137	0.163	0.182	0.196	0.207	0.215	0.220	0.223
13	0.027	0.068	0.108	0.140	0.165	0.184	0.198	0.208	0.215	0.220	0.222
14	0.029	0.071	0.111	0.143	0.167	0.186	0.199	0.208	0.215	0.219	0.221
15	0.031	0.074	0.114	0.145	0.169	0.187	0.199	0.208	0.214	0.218	0.220
16	0.033	0.077	0.116	0.147	0.171	0.187	0.200	0.208	0.213	0.217	0.218
17	0.035	0.079	0.118	0.149	0.172	0.188	0.200	0.207	0.212	0.215	0.216
18	0.036	0.081	0.120	0.150	0.172	0.188	0.199	0.207	0.211	0.214	0.214
19	0.038	0.082	0.121	0.151	0.173	0.188	0.199	0.206	0.210	0.212	0.212
20	0.039	0.084	0.122	0.152	0.173	0.188	0.199	0.205	0.209	0.211	0.211
21	0.040	0.085	0.124	0.153	0.174	0.188	0.198	0.204	0.208	0.209	0.209
22	0.041	0.086	0.124	0.153	0.174	0.188	0.197	0.203	0.206	0.207	0.207
23	0.042	0.087	0.125	0.153	0.174	0.187	0.196	0.202	0.205	0.205	0.204
24	0.042	0.088	0.126	0.154	0.173	0.187	0.196	0.201	0.203	0.204	0.202
25	0.043	0.088	0.126	0.154	0.173	0.186	0.195	0.200	0.202	0.202	0.200
26	0.044	0.089	0.126	0.154	0.173	0.186	0.194	0.198	0.200	0.200	0.198
27	0.044	0.089	0.127	0.154	0.172	0.185	0.193	0.197	0.199	0.198	0.196
28	0.045	0.090	0.127	0.153	0.172	0.184	0.192	0.196	0.197	0.196	0.194
29	0.045	0.090	0.127	0.153	0.171	0.183	0.191	0.194	0.195	0.195	0.192
30	0.045	0.090	0.127	0.153	0.171	0.182	0.189	0.193	0.194	0.193	0.190

Table C.10: Probability of a Put Expiring in the Money
as a Function of Time and Volatility
Stock Price = $100
Strike Price = $120
Annual Growth Rate = 5%

Mo	\multicolumn{11}{c}{Volatility}										
	0.15	0.20	0.25	0.30	0.35	0.40	0.45	0.50	0.55	0.60	0.65
1	1.000	0.999	0.991	0.975	0.952	0.925	0.898	0.870	0.844	0.819	0.796
2	0.996	0.975	0.940	0.899	0.859	0.822	0.788	0.758	0.732	0.708	0.686
3	0.979	0.933	0.880	0.831	0.787	0.750	0.718	0.689	0.665	0.643	0.623
4	0.949	0.886	0.826	0.775	0.732	0.697	0.667	0.641	0.618	0.598	0.579
5	0.913	0.840	0.778	0.728	0.688	0.655	0.627	0.603	0.582	0.563	0.546
6	0.874	0.797	0.736	0.689	0.652	0.621	0.595	0.573	0.553	0.535	0.519
7	0.835	0.757	0.700	0.656	0.621	0.593	0.568	0.547	0.528	0.511	0.496
8	0.796	0.721	0.667	0.626	0.594	0.568	0.545	0.525	0.507	0.491	0.476
9	0.759	0.688	0.638	0.600	0.571	0.546	0.524	0.506	0.489	0.473	0.459
10	0.724	0.657	0.611	0.577	0.549	0.526	0.506	0.488	0.472	0.457	0.443
11	0.690	0.629	0.587	0.556	0.530	0.508	0.490	0.472	0.457	0.442	0.428
12	0.658	0.603	0.565	0.536	0.513	0.492	0.474	0.458	0.443	0.429	0.415
13	0.628	0.579	0.545	0.518	0.496	0.477	0.460	0.445	0.430	0.416	0.403
14	0.600	0.556	0.526	0.502	0.482	0.464	0.448	0.432	0.418	0.405	0.392
15	0.573	0.535	0.508	0.486	0.468	0.451	0.435	0.421	0.407	0.394	0.381
16	0.547	0.516	0.492	0.472	0.455	0.439	0.424	0.410	0.397	0.384	0.372
17	0.524	0.497	0.476	0.458	0.442	0.428	0.414	0.400	0.387	0.374	0.362
18	0.501	0.479	0.462	0.446	0.431	0.417	0.404	0.391	0.378	0.365	0.353
19	0.480	0.463	0.448	0.434	0.420	0.407	0.394	0.381	0.369	0.357	0.345
20	0.459	0.447	0.435	0.422	0.410	0.397	0.385	0.373	0.361	0.349	0.337
21	0.440	0.432	0.422	0.411	0.400	0.388	0.376	0.365	0.353	0.341	0.329
22	0.422	0.418	0.410	0.401	0.391	0.380	0.368	0.357	0.345	0.334	0.322
23	0.405	0.405	0.399	0.391	0.382	0.371	0.360	0.349	0.338	0.326	0.315
24	0.388	0.392	0.388	0.382	0.373	0.363	0.353	0.342	0.331	0.320	0.308
25	0.373	0.380	0.378	0.373	0.365	0.356	0.346	0.335	0.324	0.313	0.302
26	0.358	0.368	0.368	0.364	0.357	0.348	0.339	0.328	0.318	0.307	0.296
27	0.344	0.357	0.359	0.356	0.350	0.341	0.332	0.322	0.312	0.301	0.290
28	0.330	0.346	0.350	0.348	0.342	0.335	0.326	0.316	0.306	0.295	0.284
29	0.318	0.336	0.341	0.340	0.335	0.328	0.319	0.310	0.300	0.289	0.278
30	0.305	0.326	0.333	0.333	0.328	0.322	0.313	0.304	0.294	0.284	0.273

Table C.11: Probability of a Put Expiring in the Money
as a Function of Time and Volatility
Stock Price = $100
Strike Price = $115
Annual Growth Rate = 5%

Mo	\multicolumn{11}{c}{Volatility}
	0.15	0.20	0.25	0.30	0.35	0.40	0.45	0.50	0.55	0.60	0.65
1	0.999	0.987	0.962	0.929	0.893	0.858	0.826	0.797	0.771	0.748	0.726
2	0.975	0.926	0.873	0.824	0.782	0.746	0.715	0.689	0.666	0.646	0.627
3	0.928	0.858	0.798	0.750	0.710	0.678	0.650	0.627	0.607	0.589	0.573
4	0.874	0.798	0.740	0.694	0.659	0.630	0.605	0.584	0.566	0.550	0.535
5	0.822	0.746	0.692	0.651	0.619	0.593	0.571	0.552	0.535	0.519	0.506
6	0.772	0.701	0.652	0.615	0.587	0.563	0.543	0.525	0.509	0.495	0.482
7	0.727	0.662	0.618	0.585	0.559	0.538	0.519	0.503	0.488	0.474	0.462
8	0.685	0.627	0.588	0.559	0.536	0.516	0.499	0.483	0.469	0.456	0.444
9	0.646	0.596	0.562	0.536	0.515	0.497	0.481	0.466	0.453	0.441	0.429
10	0.611	0.568	0.539	0.515	0.496	0.480	0.465	0.451	0.438	0.426	0.415
11	0.579	0.543	0.517	0.497	0.480	0.464	0.450	0.437	0.425	0.413	0.402
12	0.549	0.519	0.498	0.480	0.464	0.450	0.437	0.424	0.413	0.401	0.390
13	0.521	0.498	0.480	0.464	0.450	0.437	0.425	0.413	0.401	0.390	0.379
14	0.496	0.478	0.463	0.450	0.437	0.425	0.413	0.402	0.391	0.380	0.369
15	0.472	0.459	0.448	0.436	0.425	0.413	0.402	0.391	0.381	0.370	0.359
16	0.450	0.442	0.433	0.423	0.413	0.403	0.392	0.382	0.371	0.361	0.350
17	0.429	0.426	0.420	0.412	0.403	0.393	0.383	0.373	0.362	0.352	0.342
18	0.409	0.411	0.407	0.400	0.392	0.383	0.374	0.364	0.354	0.344	0.334
19	0.391	0.396	0.395	0.390	0.383	0.374	0.365	0.356	0.346	0.336	0.326
20	0.374	0.383	0.383	0.380	0.374	0.366	0.357	0.348	0.339	0.329	0.319
21	0.358	0.370	0.373	0.370	0.365	0.358	0.350	0.341	0.331	0.322	0.312
22	0.342	0.358	0.362	0.361	0.357	0.350	0.342	0.334	0.324	0.315	0.305
23	0.328	0.346	0.353	0.352	0.349	0.343	0.335	0.327	0.318	0.308	0.298
24	0.314	0.335	0.343	0.344	0.341	0.336	0.328	0.320	0.311	0.302	0.292
25	0.301	0.325	0.334	0.336	0.334	0.329	0.322	0.314	0.305	0.296	0.286
26	0.289	0.315	0.326	0.329	0.327	0.322	0.316	0.308	0.299	0.290	0.280
27	0.277	0.305	0.317	0.321	0.320	0.316	0.310	0.302	0.294	0.284	0.275
28	0.266	0.296	0.310	0.314	0.314	0.310	0.304	0.296	0.288	0.279	0.270
29	0.256	0.287	0.302	0.307	0.307	0.304	0.298	0.291	0.283	0.274	0.264
30	0.245	0.279	0.295	0.301	0.301	0.298	0.293	0.286	0.277	0.269	0.259

Table C.12: Probability of a Put Expiring in the Money
as a Function of Time and Volatility
Stock Price = $100
Strike Price = $110
Annual Growth Rate = 5%

Mo	Volatility										
	0.15	0.20	0.25	0.30	0.35	0.40	0.45	0.50	0.55	0.60	0.65
1	0.975	0.928	0.876	0.829	0.789	0.754	0.725	0.700	0.678	0.659	0.643
2	0.890	0.816	0.759	0.715	0.680	0.652	0.628	0.608	0.591	0.576	0.563
3	0.807	0.735	0.684	0.647	0.618	0.594	0.575	0.558	0.543	0.530	0.518
4	0.737	0.674	0.631	0.599	0.575	0.555	0.538	0.523	0.510	0.498	0.487
5	0.678	0.625	0.589	0.563	0.542	0.525	0.510	0.497	0.485	0.474	0.463
6	0.628	0.585	0.556	0.533	0.516	0.500	0.487	0.475	0.464	0.453	0.443
7	0.585	0.551	0.527	0.509	0.493	0.480	0.468	0.456	0.446	0.436	0.426
8	0.547	0.521	0.502	0.487	0.474	0.462	0.451	0.440	0.430	0.421	0.411
9	0.513	0.495	0.480	0.468	0.456	0.446	0.436	0.426	0.416	0.407	0.398
10	0.483	0.472	0.461	0.451	0.441	0.431	0.422	0.413	0.404	0.395	0.386
11	0.456	0.450	0.443	0.435	0.427	0.418	0.410	0.401	0.392	0.383	0.374
12	0.431	0.431	0.427	0.421	0.414	0.406	0.398	0.390	0.381	0.373	0.364
13	0.409	0.413	0.412	0.408	0.402	0.395	0.388	0.380	0.371	0.363	0.354
14	0.388	0.397	0.398	0.396	0.391	0.385	0.378	0.370	0.362	0.354	0.345
15	0.369	0.382	0.386	0.385	0.381	0.375	0.369	0.361	0.353	0.345	0.337
16	0.351	0.368	0.374	0.374	0.371	0.366	0.360	0.353	0.345	0.337	0.329
17	0.334	0.354	0.362	0.364	0.362	0.357	0.352	0.345	0.337	0.329	0.321
18	0.319	0.342	0.352	0.354	0.353	0.349	0.344	0.337	0.330	0.322	0.314
19	0.304	0.330	0.342	0.345	0.345	0.342	0.336	0.330	0.323	0.315	0.307
20	0.291	0.319	0.332	0.337	0.337	0.334	0.329	0.323	0.316	0.308	0.300
21	0.278	0.309	0.323	0.329	0.329	0.327	0.322	0.316	0.309	0.302	0.294
22	0.266	0.299	0.314	0.321	0.322	0.320	0.316	0.310	0.303	0.296	0.287
23	0.255	0.289	0.306	0.314	0.315	0.314	0.310	0.304	0.297	0.290	0.282
24	0.244	0.280	0.298	0.306	0.309	0.307	0.304	0.298	0.291	0.284	0.276
25	0.234	0.272	0.291	0.300	0.302	0.301	0.298	0.292	0.286	0.278	0.270
26	0.224	0.263	0.283	0.293	0.296	0.296	0.292	0.287	0.280	0.273	0.265
27	0.215	0.256	0.276	0.287	0.290	0.290	0.287	0.282	0.275	0.268	0.260
28	0.206	0.248	0.270	0.281	0.285	0.284	0.281	0.277	0.270	0.263	0.255
29	0.198	0.241	0.263	0.275	0.279	0.279	0.276	0.272	0.265	0.258	0.250
30	0.190	0.234	0.257	0.269	0.274	0.274	0.272	0.267	0.261	0.253	0.246

Table C.13: Probability of a Put Expiring in the Money
as a Function of Time and Volatility
Stock Price = $100
Strike Price = $105
Annual Growth Rate = 5%

Mo	Volatility										
	0.15	0.20	0.25	0.30	0.35	0.40	0.45	0.50	0.55	0.60	0.65
1	0.814	0.745	0.696	0.661	0.634	0.612	0.595	0.580	0.568	0.557	0.547
2	0.680	0.630	0.598	0.574	0.556	0.542	0.529	0.519	0.509	0.501	0.493
3	0.597	0.565	0.543	0.527	0.514	0.503	0.493	0.484	0.476	0.468	0.461
4	0.539	0.519	0.505	0.493	0.484	0.475	0.467	0.459	0.452	0.445	0.438
5	0.493	0.483	0.475	0.467	0.460	0.453	0.446	0.440	0.433	0.426	0.420
6	0.456	0.454	0.451	0.446	0.441	0.435	0.429	0.423	0.417	0.410	0.404
7	0.424	0.430	0.430	0.428	0.424	0.420	0.414	0.409	0.403	0.396	0.390
8	0.397	0.408	0.412	0.412	0.410	0.406	0.401	0.396	0.390	0.384	0.378
9	0.373	0.389	0.396	0.398	0.396	0.393	0.389	0.384	0.379	0.373	0.366
10	0.351	0.372	0.381	0.385	0.384	0.382	0.378	0.374	0.368	0.362	0.356
11	0.332	0.357	0.368	0.373	0.373	0.372	0.368	0.364	0.359	0.353	0.347
12	0.315	0.342	0.356	0.362	0.363	0.362	0.359	0.355	0.350	0.344	0.338
13	0.298	0.329	0.344	0.351	0.354	0.353	0.350	0.346	0.341	0.335	0.329
14	0.284	0.317	0.334	0.342	0.345	0.345	0.342	0.338	0.333	0.328	0.321
15	0.270	0.306	0.324	0.333	0.336	0.337	0.334	0.331	0.326	0.320	0.314
16	0.257	0.295	0.314	0.324	0.328	0.329	0.327	0.323	0.319	0.313	0.307
17	0.245	0.285	0.306	0.316	0.321	0.322	0.320	0.317	0.312	0.306	0.300
18	0.234	0.275	0.297	0.309	0.314	0.315	0.313	0.310	0.305	0.300	0.293
19	0.224	0.266	0.289	0.301	0.307	0.308	0.307	0.304	0.299	0.293	0.287
20	0.214	0.258	0.282	0.294	0.300	0.302	0.301	0.298	0.293	0.287	0.281
21	0.205	0.250	0.274	0.288	0.294	0.296	0.295	0.292	0.287	0.282	0.275
22	0.196	0.242	0.267	0.281	0.288	0.290	0.289	0.286	0.282	0.276	0.270
23	0.188	0.235	0.261	0.275	0.282	0.285	0.284	0.281	0.276	0.271	0.264
24	0.181	0.228	0.254	0.269	0.276	0.279	0.279	0.276	0.271	0.266	0.259
25	0.173	0.221	0.248	0.263	0.271	0.274	0.273	0.271	0.266	0.261	0.254
26	0.166	0.214	0.242	0.258	0.266	0.269	0.269	0.266	0.261	0.256	0.249
27	0.160	0.208	0.237	0.253	0.261	0.264	0.264	0.261	0.257	0.251	0.245
28	0.153	0.202	0.231	0.247	0.256	0.259	0.259	0.257	0.252	0.247	0.240
29	0.147	0.197	0.226	0.242	0.251	0.255	0.255	0.252	0.248	0.242	0.236
30	0.142	0.191	0.221	0.238	0.247	0.250	0.250	0.248	0.244	0.238	0.231

Table C.14: Probability of a Put Expiring in the Money
as a Function of Time and Volatility
Stock Price = $100
Strike Price = $100
Annual Growth Rate = 5%

Mo	\multicolumn{11}{c}{Volatility}										
	0.15	0.20	0.25	0.30	0.35	0.40	0.45	0.50	0.55	0.60	0.65
1	0.408	0.426	0.435	0.441	0.444	0.445	0.446	0.446	0.445	0.445	0.443
2	0.371	0.395	0.409	0.416	0.421	0.423	0.424	0.424	0.423	0.422	0.420
3	0.343	0.373	0.389	0.398	0.403	0.406	0.407	0.407	0.406	0.405	0.402
4	0.320	0.354	0.372	0.383	0.389	0.392	0.393	0.393	0.392	0.390	0.388
5	0.301	0.337	0.358	0.369	0.376	0.380	0.381	0.381	0.380	0.378	0.375
6	0.284	0.323	0.345	0.357	0.365	0.368	0.370	0.370	0.368	0.366	0.363
7	0.269	0.310	0.333	0.347	0.354	0.358	0.360	0.360	0.358	0.356	0.353
8	0.255	0.298	0.322	0.337	0.345	0.349	0.351	0.351	0.349	0.347	0.343
9	0.242	0.287	0.312	0.327	0.336	0.340	0.342	0.342	0.340	0.338	0.334
10	0.230	0.276	0.303	0.319	0.328	0.332	0.334	0.334	0.332	0.330	0.326
11	0.219	0.267	0.294	0.310	0.320	0.325	0.327	0.326	0.325	0.322	0.318
12	0.209	0.258	0.286	0.303	0.312	0.317	0.319	0.319	0.317	0.314	0.311
13	0.200	0.249	0.278	0.295	0.305	0.311	0.313	0.312	0.311	0.307	0.303
14	0.191	0.241	0.271	0.288	0.299	0.304	0.306	0.306	0.304	0.301	0.297
15	0.183	0.234	0.264	0.282	0.292	0.298	0.300	0.300	0.298	0.294	0.290
16	0.175	0.226	0.257	0.275	0.286	0.292	0.294	0.294	0.292	0.288	0.284
17	0.168	0.220	0.251	0.269	0.280	0.286	0.288	0.288	0.286	0.283	0.278
18	0.161	0.213	0.244	0.263	0.275	0.280	0.283	0.282	0.280	0.277	0.272
19	0.155	0.207	0.239	0.258	0.269	0.275	0.277	0.277	0.275	0.272	0.267
20	0.148	0.201	0.233	0.252	0.264	0.270	0.272	0.272	0.270	0.266	0.262
21	0.142	0.195	0.227	0.247	0.259	0.265	0.267	0.267	0.265	0.261	0.257
22	0.137	0.189	0.222	0.242	0.254	0.260	0.263	0.262	0.260	0.256	0.252
23	0.132	0.184	0.217	0.237	0.249	0.255	0.258	0.258	0.255	0.252	0.247
24	0.126	0.179	0.212	0.232	0.244	0.251	0.253	0.253	0.251	0.247	0.242
25	0.122	0.174	0.207	0.228	0.240	0.246	0.249	0.249	0.246	0.243	0.238
26	0.117	0.169	0.203	0.223	0.236	0.242	0.245	0.245	0.242	0.238	0.233
27	0.113	0.165	0.198	0.219	0.232	0.238	0.241	0.240	0.238	0.234	0.229
28	0.108	0.160	0.194	0.215	0.227	0.234	0.237	0.236	0.234	0.230	0.225
29	0.104	0.156	0.190	0.211	0.223	0.230	0.233	0.233	0.230	0.226	0.221
30	0.101	0.152	0.186	0.207	0.220	0.226	0.229	0.229	0.226	0.222	0.217

Table C.15: Probability of a Put Expiring in the Money
as a Function of Time and Volatility
Stock Price = $100
Strike Price = $95
Annual Growth Rate = 5%

Mo	\multicolumn{11}{c}{Volatility}										
	0.15	0.20	0.25	0.30	0.35	0.40	0.45	0.50	0.55	0.60	0.65
1	0.078	0.141	0.191	0.229	0.258	0.281	0.298	0.312	0.323	0.332	0.339
2	0.121	0.186	0.232	0.264	0.288	0.306	0.319	0.329	0.336	0.342	0.346
3	0.138	0.201	0.244	0.274	0.295	0.311	0.322	0.330	0.336	0.340	0.343
4	0.145	0.206	0.248	0.276	0.296	0.310	0.320	0.327	0.332	0.335	0.337
5	0.146	0.207	0.247	0.275	0.294	0.307	0.316	0.322	0.326	0.328	0.330
6	0.146	0.205	0.245	0.272	0.290	0.303	0.311	0.317	0.320	0.322	0.322
7	0.143	0.203	0.242	0.268	0.286	0.298	0.306	0.311	0.314	0.315	0.315
8	0.140	0.199	0.238	0.264	0.281	0.293	0.301	0.305	0.308	0.309	0.308
9	0.137	0.195	0.234	0.260	0.277	0.288	0.295	0.300	0.302	0.302	0.302
10	0.133	0.191	0.229	0.255	0.272	0.283	0.290	0.294	0.296	0.296	0.295
11	0.129	0.187	0.225	0.250	0.267	0.278	0.285	0.289	0.290	0.290	0.289
12	0.125	0.182	0.221	0.246	0.262	0.273	0.280	0.283	0.285	0.285	0.283
13	0.121	0.178	0.216	0.241	0.258	0.268	0.275	0.278	0.280	0.279	0.278
14	0.117	0.174	0.212	0.237	0.253	0.264	0.270	0.273	0.274	0.274	0.272
15	0.113	0.170	0.207	0.233	0.249	0.259	0.265	0.269	0.269	0.269	0.267
16	0.109	0.165	0.203	0.228	0.245	0.255	0.261	0.264	0.265	0.264	0.261
17	0.106	0.161	0.199	0.224	0.240	0.250	0.256	0.259	0.260	0.259	0.256
18	0.102	0.157	0.195	0.220	0.236	0.246	0.252	0.255	0.255	0.254	0.252
19	0.099	0.153	0.191	0.216	0.232	0.242	0.248	0.251	0.251	0.249	0.247
20	0.095	0.150	0.187	0.212	0.228	0.238	0.244	0.246	0.247	0.245	0.242
21	0.092	0.146	0.183	0.208	0.224	0.234	0.240	0.242	0.242	0.241	0.238
22	0.089	0.142	0.180	0.204	0.220	0.230	0.236	0.238	0.238	0.237	0.233
23	0.086	0.139	0.176	0.201	0.217	0.227	0.232	0.234	0.234	0.232	0.229
24	0.083	0.136	0.173	0.197	0.213	0.223	0.228	0.230	0.230	0.228	0.225
25	0.080	0.132	0.169	0.194	0.210	0.219	0.225	0.227	0.227	0.225	0.221
26	0.077	0.129	0.166	0.190	0.206	0.216	0.221	0.223	0.223	0.221	0.217
27	0.075	0.126	0.162	0.187	0.203	0.212	0.218	0.220	0.219	0.217	0.214
28	0.072	0.123	0.159	0.184	0.200	0.209	0.214	0.216	0.216	0.214	0.210
29	0.070	0.120	0.156	0.181	0.196	0.206	0.211	0.213	0.212	0.210	0.206
30	0.068	0.117	0.153	0.177	0.193	0.203	0.208	0.210	0.209	0.207	0.203

Table C.16: Probability of a Put Expiring in the Money
as a Function of Time and Volatility
Stock Price = $100
Strike Price = $90
Annual Growth Rate = 5%

Mo	Volatility										
	0.15	0.20	0.25	0.30	0.35	0.40	0.45	0.50	0.55	0.60	0.65
1	0.004	0.022	0.052	0.086	0.118	0.147	0.172	0.193	0.212	0.227	0.241
2	0.020	0.060	0.103	0.142	0.174	0.201	0.222	0.239	0.254	0.265	0.275
3	0.035	0.084	0.130	0.168	0.199	0.222	0.241	0.256	0.267	0.277	0.284
4	0.046	0.099	0.145	0.182	0.211	0.233	0.249	0.262	0.272	0.280	0.286
5	0.054	0.108	0.154	0.190	0.217	0.237	0.253	0.264	0.273	0.280	0.284
6	0.059	0.114	0.160	0.194	0.220	0.239	0.254	0.264	0.272	0.278	0.281
7	0.062	0.118	0.163	0.196	0.221	0.240	0.253	0.263	0.270	0.275	0.278
8	0.064	0.120	0.164	0.197	0.221	0.239	0.251	0.261	0.267	0.271	0.274
9	0.065	0.121	0.165	0.197	0.220	0.237	0.249	0.258	0.264	0.267	0.269
10	0.066	0.121	0.164	0.196	0.219	0.235	0.247	0.255	0.260	0.263	0.265
11	0.066	0.120	0.163	0.194	0.217	0.233	0.244	0.251	0.256	0.259	0.260
12	0.065	0.120	0.162	0.193	0.215	0.230	0.241	0.248	0.253	0.255	0.256
13	0.065	0.118	0.160	0.191	0.212	0.227	0.238	0.245	0.249	0.251	0.251
14	0.064	0.117	0.159	0.189	0.210	0.225	0.235	0.241	0.245	0.247	0.247
15	0.063	0.115	0.157	0.186	0.207	0.222	0.231	0.238	0.241	0.243	0.243
16	0.062	0.114	0.154	0.184	0.204	0.219	0.228	0.234	0.238	0.239	0.239
17	0.060	0.112	0.152	0.181	0.202	0.216	0.225	0.231	0.234	0.235	0.234
18	0.059	0.110	0.150	0.179	0.199	0.213	0.222	0.227	0.230	0.231	0.230
19	0.058	0.108	0.148	0.176	0.196	0.210	0.219	0.224	0.227	0.227	0.226
20	0.056	0.106	0.146	0.174	0.194	0.207	0.216	0.221	0.223	0.224	0.223
21	0.055	0.104	0.143	0.171	0.191	0.204	0.212	0.217	0.220	0.220	0.219
22	0.053	0.102	0.141	0.169	0.188	0.201	0.209	0.214	0.216	0.216	0.215
23	0.052	0.100	0.139	0.166	0.185	0.198	0.206	0.211	0.213	0.213	0.211
24	0.051	0.098	0.136	0.164	0.183	0.195	0.203	0.208	0.210	0.210	0.208
25	0.049	0.096	0.134	0.161	0.180	0.193	0.201	0.205	0.207	0.206	0.204
26	0.048	0.094	0.132	0.159	0.178	0.190	0.198	0.202	0.203	0.203	0.201
27	0.046	0.092	0.130	0.156	0.175	0.187	0.195	0.199	0.200	0.200	0.198
28	0.045	0.090	0.127	0.154	0.172	0.185	0.192	0.196	0.197	0.197	0.195
29	0.044	0.089	0.125	0.152	0.170	0.182	0.189	0.193	0.194	0.194	0.191
30	0.043	0.087	0.123	0.149	0.168	0.179	0.187	0.190	0.192	0.191	0.188

Table C.17: Probability of a Put Expiring in the Money
as a Function of Time and Volatility
Stock Price = $100
Strike Price = $85
Annual Growth Rate = 5%

Mo	Volatility										
	0.15	0.20	0.25	0.30	0.35	0.40	0.45	0.50	0.55	0.60	0.65
1	0.000	0.001	0.008	0.021	0.040	0.061	0.083	0.104	0.123	0.141	0.157
2	0.001	0.012	0.034	0.062	0.091	0.117	0.141	0.162	0.179	0.195	0.208
3	0.005	0.026	0.057	0.090	0.120	0.147	0.169	0.188	0.204	0.217	0.227
4	0.010	0.037	0.073	0.108	0.139	0.164	0.185	0.202	0.216	0.227	0.236
5	0.014	0.047	0.085	0.120	0.150	0.175	0.194	0.210	0.222	0.232	0.240
6	0.018	0.054	0.094	0.129	0.158	0.181	0.200	0.214	0.226	0.234	0.241
7	0.021	0.059	0.100	0.135	0.163	0.185	0.203	0.216	0.227	0.235	0.240
8	0.023	0.064	0.104	0.139	0.166	0.188	0.205	0.217	0.227	0.234	0.239
9	0.026	0.067	0.107	0.142	0.169	0.189	0.205	0.217	0.226	0.232	0.237
10	0.027	0.069	0.110	0.143	0.170	0.190	0.205	0.216	0.224	0.230	0.234
11	0.028	0.071	0.111	0.144	0.170	0.190	0.204	0.215	0.223	0.228	0.231
12	0.029	0.072	0.112	0.145	0.170	0.189	0.203	0.213	0.221	0.225	0.228
13	0.030	0.073	0.113	0.145	0.170	0.188	0.202	0.211	0.218	0.223	0.225
14	0.030	0.073	0.113	0.145	0.169	0.187	0.200	0.209	0.216	0.220	0.222
15	0.031	0.073	0.113	0.144	0.168	0.186	0.198	0.207	0.213	0.217	0.219
16	0.031	0.073	0.112	0.143	0.167	0.184	0.196	0.205	0.211	0.214	0.216
17	0.031	0.073	0.111	0.142	0.165	0.182	0.194	0.203	0.208	0.211	0.212
18	0.030	0.072	0.111	0.141	0.164	0.180	0.192	0.200	0.205	0.208	0.209
19	0.030	0.072	0.110	0.140	0.162	0.179	0.190	0.198	0.203	0.205	0.206
20	0.030	0.071	0.109	0.139	0.161	0.177	0.188	0.195	0.200	0.202	0.203
21	0.029	0.070	0.108	0.137	0.159	0.175	0.186	0.193	0.197	0.199	0.200
22	0.029	0.069	0.107	0.136	0.157	0.173	0.183	0.190	0.195	0.196	0.197
23	0.029	0.069	0.105	0.134	0.156	0.171	0.181	0.188	0.192	0.194	0.194
24	0.028	0.068	0.104	0.133	0.154	0.169	0.179	0.186	0.189	0.191	0.191
25	0.028	0.067	0.103	0.131	0.152	0.167	0.177	0.183	0.187	0.188	0.188
26	0.027	0.066	0.101	0.130	0.150	0.165	0.175	0.181	0.184	0.185	0.185
27	0.027	0.065	0.100	0.128	0.148	0.163	0.172	0.178	0.182	0.183	0.182
28	0.026	0.064	0.099	0.126	0.147	0.161	0.170	0.176	0.179	0.180	0.179
29	0.025	0.063	0.097	0.125	0.145	0.159	0.168	0.174	0.177	0.177	0.176
30	0.025	0.062	0.096	0.123	0.143	0.157	0.166	0.171	0.174	0.175	0.174

Table C.18: Probability of a Put Expiring in the Money
as a Function of Time and Volatility
Stock Price = $100
Strike Price = $80
Annual Growth Rate = 5%

Mo	Volatility										
	0.15	0.20	0.25	0.30	0.35	0.40	0.45	0.50	0.55	0.60	0.65
1	0.000	0.000	0.001	0.003	0.009	0.019	0.032	0.046	0.061	0.077	0.091
2	0.000	0.001	0.008	0.021	0.039	0.059	0.080	0.099	0.117	0.134	0.149
3	0.000	0.005	0.019	0.040	0.064	0.088	0.110	0.130	0.147	0.162	0.175
4	0.001	0.011	0.031	0.056	0.083	0.107	0.129	0.148	0.164	0.178	0.189
5	0.002	0.016	0.040	0.069	0.096	0.121	0.142	0.160	0.175	0.187	0.197
6	0.004	0.021	0.048	0.078	0.106	0.130	0.151	0.168	0.182	0.193	0.202
7	0.005	0.025	0.055	0.086	0.113	0.137	0.157	0.173	0.186	0.196	0.204
8	0.007	0.029	0.060	0.091	0.119	0.142	0.161	0.176	0.188	0.198	0.205
9	0.008	0.032	0.064	0.096	0.123	0.146	0.164	0.178	0.189	0.198	0.205
10	0.009	0.035	0.068	0.099	0.126	0.148	0.166	0.179	0.190	0.198	0.204
11	0.010	0.037	0.070	0.102	0.128	0.150	0.167	0.180	0.190	0.197	0.203
12	0.011	0.039	0.072	0.104	0.130	0.151	0.167	0.180	0.189	0.196	0.201
13	0.012	0.040	0.074	0.105	0.131	0.151	0.167	0.179	0.188	0.195	0.199
14	0.012	0.041	0.075	0.106	0.132	0.152	0.167	0.179	0.187	0.193	0.197
15	0.013	0.042	0.076	0.107	0.132	0.151	0.166	0.178	0.186	0.191	0.195
16	0.013	0.043	0.077	0.107	0.132	0.151	0.166	0.176	0.184	0.189	0.193
17	0.013	0.044	0.077	0.107	0.132	0.151	0.165	0.175	0.182	0.187	0.190
18	0.014	0.044	0.078	0.107	0.131	0.150	0.164	0.174	0.181	0.185	0.188
19	0.014	0.044	0.078	0.107	0.131	0.149	0.162	0.172	0.179	0.183	0.185
20	0.014	0.044	0.078	0.107	0.130	0.148	0.161	0.170	0.177	0.181	0.183
21	0.014	0.044	0.077	0.106	0.129	0.147	0.160	0.169	0.175	0.179	0.181
22	0.014	0.044	0.077	0.106	0.129	0.146	0.158	0.167	0.173	0.176	0.178
23	0.014	0.044	0.077	0.105	0.128	0.144	0.157	0.165	0.171	0.174	0.176
24	0.014	0.044	0.076	0.104	0.127	0.143	0.155	0.163	0.169	0.172	0.173
25	0.014	0.044	0.076	0.104	0.125	0.142	0.154	0.162	0.167	0.170	0.171
26	0.014	0.043	0.075	0.103	0.124	0.140	0.152	0.160	0.165	0.167	0.168
27	0.014	0.043	0.075	0.102	0.123	0.139	0.150	0.158	0.163	0.165	0.166
28	0.014	0.042	0.074	0.101	0.122	0.138	0.149	0.156	0.161	0.163	0.164
29	0.013	0.042	0.073	0.100	0.121	0.136	0.147	0.154	0.159	0.161	0.161
30	0.013	0.042	0.072	0.099	0.120	0.135	0.146	0.153	0.157	0.159	0.159

Table C.19: Probability of a Put Expiring in the Money
as a Function of Time and Volatility
Stock Price = $100
Strike Price = $120
Annual Growth Rate = 10%

Mo	Volatility										
	0.15	0.20	0.25	0.30	0.35	0.40	0.45	0.50	0.55	0.60	0.65
1	1.000	0.998	0.989	0.972	0.948	0.920	0.892	0.864	0.838	0.813	0.790
2	0.994	0.969	0.930	0.887	0.846	0.808	0.775	0.746	0.719	0.696	0.675
3	0.969	0.915	0.859	0.809	0.766	0.730	0.698	0.672	0.648	0.627	0.609
4	0.926	0.855	0.794	0.745	0.704	0.671	0.643	0.619	0.598	0.579	0.562
5	0.874	0.797	0.738	0.692	0.655	0.625	0.600	0.578	0.559	0.542	0.526
6	0.819	0.743	0.688	0.647	0.614	0.587	0.565	0.545	0.527	0.512	0.497
7	0.764	0.694	0.645	0.608	0.579	0.555	0.535	0.517	0.501	0.486	0.472
8	0.711	0.649	0.606	0.574	0.549	0.527	0.509	0.492	0.478	0.464	0.451
9	0.661	0.608	0.571	0.544	0.522	0.503	0.486	0.471	0.457	0.444	0.432
10	0.614	0.570	0.540	0.517	0.497	0.481	0.466	0.452	0.439	0.427	0.415
11	0.570	0.536	0.512	0.492	0.476	0.461	0.447	0.435	0.422	0.411	0.400
12	0.529	0.505	0.486	0.470	0.456	0.443	0.430	0.419	0.407	0.396	0.386
13	0.492	0.476	0.462	0.449	0.437	0.426	0.415	0.404	0.393	0.383	0.373
14	0.457	0.449	0.440	0.430	0.421	0.411	0.401	0.390	0.380	0.370	0.360
15	0.425	0.424	0.420	0.413	0.405	0.396	0.387	0.378	0.368	0.359	0.349
16	0.395	0.401	0.401	0.396	0.390	0.383	0.375	0.366	0.357	0.348	0.338
17	0.368	0.380	0.383	0.381	0.376	0.370	0.363	0.355	0.346	0.338	0.328
18	0.342	0.360	0.366	0.367	0.364	0.358	0.352	0.344	0.336	0.328	0.319
19	0.319	0.342	0.351	0.353	0.351	0.347	0.341	0.335	0.327	0.319	0.310
20	0.297	0.324	0.336	0.340	0.340	0.337	0.332	0.325	0.318	0.310	0.302
21	0.277	0.308	0.323	0.328	0.329	0.327	0.322	0.316	0.309	0.302	0.293
22	0.258	0.293	0.310	0.317	0.319	0.317	0.313	0.308	0.301	0.294	0.286
23	0.241	0.278	0.297	0.306	0.309	0.308	0.305	0.300	0.293	0.286	0.278
24	0.225	0.265	0.286	0.296	0.300	0.299	0.296	0.292	0.286	0.279	0.271
25	0.210	0.252	0.275	0.286	0.291	0.291	0.289	0.284	0.279	0.272	0.264
26	0.196	0.240	0.264	0.277	0.282	0.283	0.281	0.277	0.272	0.265	0.258
27	0.183	0.229	0.254	0.268	0.274	0.276	0.274	0.270	0.265	0.259	0.252
28	0.172	0.218	0.245	0.259	0.266	0.268	0.267	0.264	0.259	0.253	0.245
29	0.160	0.208	0.236	0.251	0.259	0.261	0.260	0.257	0.253	0.247	0.240
30	0.150	0.199	0.227	0.243	0.251	0.255	0.254	0.251	0.247	0.241	0.234

Table C.20: Probability of a Put Expiring in the Money
as a Function of Time and Volatility
Stock Price = $100
Strike Price = $115
Annual Growth Rate = 10%

Mo	Volatility										
	0.15	0.20	0.25	0.30	0.35	0.40	0.45	0.50	0.55	0.60	0.65
1	0.998	0.985	0.957	0.922	0.885	0.850	0.818	0.789	0.763	0.740	0.719
2	0.965	0.911	0.855	0.806	0.764	0.729	0.700	0.674	0.652	0.633	0.615
3	0.902	0.828	0.769	0.722	0.685	0.655	0.630	0.608	0.589	0.572	0.557
4	0.830	0.755	0.701	0.660	0.628	0.602	0.580	0.562	0.545	0.530	0.517
5	0.760	0.692	0.645	0.611	0.583	0.561	0.542	0.526	0.511	0.498	0.486
6	0.695	0.638	0.599	0.570	0.547	0.528	0.511	0.497	0.484	0.472	0.460
7	0.636	0.590	0.559	0.535	0.516	0.500	0.485	0.472	0.460	0.449	0.439
8	0.583	0.548	0.524	0.505	0.489	0.475	0.463	0.451	0.440	0.430	0.420
9	0.535	0.511	0.493	0.479	0.466	0.454	0.443	0.432	0.422	0.412	0.403
10	0.491	0.478	0.466	0.455	0.444	0.434	0.425	0.415	0.406	0.397	0.387
11	0.452	0.448	0.441	0.433	0.425	0.417	0.408	0.400	0.391	0.382	0.374
12	0.417	0.420	0.418	0.414	0.408	0.401	0.394	0.386	0.378	0.369	0.361
13	0.385	0.395	0.398	0.396	0.392	0.386	0.380	0.373	0.365	0.357	0.349
14	0.356	0.373	0.379	0.380	0.377	0.373	0.367	0.361	0.353	0.346	0.338
15	0.329	0.352	0.361	0.364	0.363	0.360	0.355	0.349	0.343	0.335	0.328
16	0.305	0.332	0.345	0.350	0.350	0.348	0.344	0.339	0.332	0.325	0.318
17	0.282	0.314	0.330	0.337	0.338	0.337	0.334	0.329	0.323	0.316	0.309
18	0.262	0.297	0.315	0.324	0.327	0.327	0.324	0.319	0.314	0.307	0.300
19	0.243	0.282	0.302	0.312	0.316	0.317	0.314	0.310	0.305	0.299	0.292
20	0.226	0.267	0.290	0.301	0.306	0.307	0.305	0.302	0.297	0.291	0.284
21	0.210	0.254	0.278	0.291	0.297	0.298	0.297	0.294	0.289	0.283	0.277
22	0.196	0.241	0.267	0.281	0.287	0.290	0.289	0.286	0.281	0.276	0.269
23	0.182	0.229	0.256	0.271	0.279	0.282	0.281	0.279	0.274	0.269	0.263
24	0.170	0.218	0.246	0.262	0.270	0.274	0.274	0.271	0.267	0.262	0.256
25	0.158	0.208	0.237	0.254	0.262	0.266	0.267	0.265	0.261	0.256	0.250
26	0.147	0.198	0.228	0.245	0.255	0.259	0.260	0.258	0.255	0.250	0.244
27	0.138	0.188	0.219	0.237	0.248	0.252	0.253	0.252	0.248	0.244	0.238
28	0.128	0.179	0.211	0.230	0.241	0.246	0.247	0.246	0.243	0.238	0.232
29	0.120	0.171	0.203	0.223	0.234	0.239	0.241	0.240	0.237	0.232	0.227
30	0.112	0.163	0.196	0.216	0.228	0.233	0.235	0.234	0.231	0.227	0.222

Table C.21: Probability of a Put Expiring in the Money
as a Function of Time and Volatility
Stock Price = $100
Strike Price = $110
Annual Growth Rate = 10%

Mo	Volatility										
	0.15	0.20	0.25	0.30	0.35	0.40	0.45	0.50	0.55	0.60	0.65
1	0.969	0.918	0.864	0.817	0.777	0.743	0.714	0.690	0.669	0.650	0.634
2	0.862	0.788	0.733	0.691	0.659	0.633	0.611	0.593	0.577	0.563	0.550
3	0.758	0.693	0.648	0.616	0.590	0.570	0.553	0.538	0.525	0.514	0.503
4	0.671	0.620	0.587	0.562	0.542	0.526	0.513	0.500	0.489	0.479	0.470
5	0.598	0.563	0.539	0.520	0.506	0.493	0.481	0.471	0.461	0.452	0.444
6	0.536	0.515	0.499	0.486	0.475	0.465	0.456	0.447	0.438	0.430	0.422
7	0.484	0.475	0.466	0.458	0.450	0.442	0.434	0.426	0.419	0.411	0.404
8	0.439	0.440	0.437	0.433	0.428	0.421	0.415	0.408	0.401	0.394	0.387
9	0.399	0.409	0.412	0.411	0.408	0.403	0.398	0.392	0.386	0.379	0.372
10	0.365	0.382	0.389	0.391	0.390	0.387	0.383	0.378	0.372	0.366	0.359
11	0.334	0.358	0.369	0.374	0.374	0.372	0.369	0.364	0.359	0.353	0.347
12	0.306	0.336	0.351	0.357	0.359	0.359	0.356	0.352	0.347	0.342	0.336
13	0.282	0.316	0.334	0.342	0.346	0.346	0.344	0.341	0.336	0.331	0.325
14	0.260	0.298	0.318	0.329	0.333	0.335	0.333	0.330	0.326	0.321	0.315
15	0.239	0.281	0.304	0.316	0.322	0.324	0.323	0.320	0.316	0.312	0.306
16	0.221	0.265	0.290	0.304	0.311	0.313	0.313	0.311	0.307	0.303	0.297
17	0.205	0.251	0.278	0.292	0.300	0.304	0.304	0.302	0.299	0.294	0.289
18	0.190	0.238	0.266	0.282	0.291	0.295	0.295	0.294	0.291	0.286	0.281
19	0.176	0.226	0.255	0.272	0.281	0.286	0.287	0.286	0.283	0.279	0.274
20	0.163	0.214	0.244	0.262	0.273	0.278	0.279	0.278	0.275	0.271	0.266
21	0.152	0.203	0.235	0.253	0.264	0.270	0.272	0.271	0.268	0.265	0.260
22	0.141	0.193	0.225	0.245	0.256	0.262	0.264	0.264	0.262	0.258	0.253
23	0.131	0.184	0.217	0.237	0.249	0.255	0.258	0.257	0.255	0.252	0.247
24	0.122	0.175	0.208	0.229	0.242	0.248	0.251	0.251	0.249	0.245	0.241
25	0.114	0.166	0.200	0.222	0.235	0.242	0.245	0.245	0.243	0.240	0.235
26	0.106	0.158	0.193	0.215	0.228	0.235	0.239	0.239	0.237	0.234	0.229
27	0.099	0.151	0.186	0.208	0.222	0.229	0.233	0.233	0.232	0.228	0.224
28	0.092	0.144	0.179	0.202	0.216	0.223	0.227	0.228	0.226	0.223	0.219
29	0.086	0.137	0.173	0.195	0.210	0.218	0.222	0.223	0.221	0.218	0.214
30	0.080	0.131	0.166	0.190	0.204	0.212	0.217	0.217	0.216	0.213	0.209

Table C.22: Probability of a Put Expiring in the Money
as a Function of Time and Volatility
Stock Price = $100
Strike Price = $105
Annual Growth Rate = 10%

Mo	Volatility										
	0.15	0.20	0.25	0.30	0.35	0.40	0.45	0.50	0.55	0.60	0.65
1	0.787	0.721	0.676	0.643	0.618	0.598	0.582	0.569	0.557	0.547	0.538
2	0.630	0.591	0.566	0.548	0.533	0.521	0.511	0.503	0.495	0.487	0.480
3	0.532	0.515	0.503	0.493	0.485	0.478	0.471	0.464	0.458	0.452	0.446
4	0.462	0.461	0.459	0.455	0.451	0.446	0.441	0.436	0.431	0.426	0.421
5	0.408	0.420	0.424	0.425	0.424	0.421	0.418	0.414	0.410	0.405	0.400
6	0.364	0.385	0.396	0.400	0.401	0.401	0.399	0.395	0.392	0.388	0.383
7	0.328	0.356	0.371	0.379	0.382	0.383	0.382	0.379	0.376	0.372	0.368
8	0.297	0.331	0.350	0.360	0.365	0.367	0.366	0.365	0.362	0.358	0.354
9	0.270	0.309	0.331	0.343	0.350	0.352	0.353	0.352	0.349	0.346	0.342
10	0.246	0.290	0.314	0.328	0.336	0.339	0.340	0.340	0.337	0.334	0.330
11	0.226	0.272	0.299	0.314	0.323	0.327	0.329	0.329	0.327	0.324	0.320
12	0.207	0.256	0.284	0.301	0.311	0.316	0.318	0.318	0.317	0.314	0.310
13	0.191	0.241	0.271	0.289	0.300	0.306	0.309	0.309	0.307	0.304	0.301
14	0.176	0.228	0.259	0.278	0.290	0.296	0.299	0.300	0.298	0.296	0.292
15	0.162	0.215	0.248	0.268	0.280	0.287	0.290	0.291	0.290	0.287	0.284
16	0.150	0.204	0.238	0.258	0.271	0.279	0.282	0.283	0.282	0.280	0.276
17	0.139	0.193	0.228	0.249	0.263	0.270	0.274	0.275	0.275	0.272	0.269
18	0.129	0.183	0.218	0.241	0.255	0.263	0.267	0.268	0.267	0.265	0.262
19	0.119	0.174	0.210	0.233	0.247	0.255	0.260	0.261	0.261	0.258	0.255
20	0.111	0.165	0.201	0.225	0.239	0.248	0.253	0.255	0.254	0.252	0.249
21	0.103	0.157	0.194	0.217	0.232	0.241	0.246	0.248	0.248	0.246	0.242
22	0.096	0.150	0.186	0.210	0.226	0.235	0.240	0.242	0.242	0.240	0.236
23	0.089	0.142	0.179	0.204	0.219	0.229	0.234	0.236	0.236	0.234	0.231
24	0.083	0.136	0.173	0.197	0.213	0.223	0.228	0.231	0.230	0.228	0.225
25	0.077	0.129	0.166	0.191	0.207	0.217	0.223	0.225	0.225	0.223	0.220
26	0.072	0.123	0.160	0.185	0.202	0.212	0.217	0.220	0.220	0.218	0.215
27	0.067	0.118	0.154	0.180	0.196	0.206	0.212	0.215	0.215	0.213	0.210
28	0.063	0.112	0.149	0.174	0.191	0.201	0.207	0.210	0.210	0.208	0.205
29	0.059	0.107	0.144	0.169	0.186	0.196	0.202	0.205	0.205	0.204	0.201
30	0.055	0.102	0.139	0.164	0.181	0.192	0.198	0.201	0.201	0.199	0.196

Table C.23: Probability of a Put Expiring in the Money
as a Function of Time and Volatility
Stock Price = $100
Strike Price = $100
Annual Growth Rate = 10%

Mo	Volatility										
	0.15	0.20	0.25	0.30	0.35	0.40	0.45	0.50	0.55	0.60	0.65
1	0.371	0.398	0.413	0.422	0.428	0.431	0.433	0.435	0.435	0.435	0.435
2	0.321	0.357	0.377	0.390	0.398	0.403	0.406	0.408	0.409	0.409	0.408
3	0.284	0.326	0.351	0.366	0.376	0.382	0.386	0.388	0.389	0.388	0.388
4	0.255	0.302	0.329	0.347	0.358	0.365	0.369	0.371	0.372	0.372	0.371
5	0.231	0.281	0.311	0.330	0.342	0.349	0.354	0.356	0.357	0.357	0.356
6	0.210	0.262	0.294	0.314	0.327	0.336	0.341	0.343	0.345	0.344	0.343
7	0.192	0.246	0.280	0.301	0.315	0.323	0.329	0.332	0.333	0.333	0.331
8	0.176	0.231	0.266	0.288	0.303	0.312	0.318	0.321	0.322	0.322	0.320
9	0.161	0.218	0.254	0.277	0.292	0.302	0.308	0.311	0.312	0.312	0.310
10	0.149	0.206	0.242	0.266	0.282	0.292	0.298	0.301	0.303	0.302	0.301
11	0.137	0.194	0.232	0.256	0.273	0.283	0.289	0.293	0.294	0.294	0.292
12	0.127	0.184	0.222	0.247	0.264	0.274	0.281	0.284	0.286	0.285	0.284
13	0.117	0.174	0.213	0.238	0.255	0.266	0.273	0.277	0.278	0.278	0.276
14	0.109	0.165	0.204	0.230	0.247	0.258	0.265	0.269	0.271	0.270	0.269
15	0.101	0.157	0.196	0.222	0.240	0.251	0.258	0.262	0.263	0.263	0.262
16	0.094	0.149	0.189	0.215	0.233	0.244	0.251	0.255	0.257	0.256	0.255
17	0.087	0.142	0.181	0.208	0.226	0.238	0.245	0.249	0.250	0.250	0.248
18	0.081	0.135	0.174	0.201	0.219	0.231	0.239	0.243	0.244	0.244	0.242
19	0.075	0.129	0.168	0.195	0.213	0.225	0.233	0.237	0.238	0.238	0.236
20	0.070	0.123	0.162	0.189	0.207	0.219	0.227	0.231	0.233	0.232	0.230
21	0.065	0.117	0.156	0.183	0.202	0.214	0.221	0.225	0.227	0.227	0.225
22	0.061	0.111	0.150	0.177	0.196	0.208	0.216	0.220	0.222	0.221	0.220
23	0.057	0.106	0.145	0.172	0.191	0.203	0.211	0.215	0.217	0.216	0.215
24	0.053	0.102	0.140	0.167	0.186	0.198	0.206	0.210	0.212	0.211	0.210
25	0.050	0.097	0.135	0.162	0.181	0.193	0.201	0.205	0.207	0.207	0.205
26	0.046	0.093	0.130	0.157	0.176	0.189	0.196	0.201	0.202	0.202	0.200
27	0.043	0.088	0.126	0.153	0.172	0.184	0.192	0.196	0.198	0.198	0.196
28	0.041	0.085	0.121	0.148	0.167	0.180	0.188	0.192	0.194	0.193	0.191
29	0.038	0.081	0.117	0.144	0.163	0.175	0.183	0.188	0.189	0.189	0.187
30	0.036	0.077	0.113	0.140	0.159	0.171	0.179	0.184	0.185	0.185	0.183

Table C.24: Probability of a Put Expiring in the Money as a Function of Time and Volatility
Stock Price = $100
Strike Price = $95
Annual Growth Rate = 10%

Mo	\multicolumn{11}{c}{Volatility}										
	0.15	0.20	0.25	0.30	0.35	0.40	0.45	0.50	0.55	0.60	0.65
1	0.065	0.125	0.176	0.215	0.245	0.268	0.287	0.302	0.313	0.323	0.331
2	0.096	0.160	0.208	0.243	0.269	0.288	0.303	0.314	0.323	0.330	0.335
3	0.105	0.168	0.214	0.247	0.271	0.289	0.302	0.312	0.319	0.325	0.329
4	0.105	0.168	0.213	0.245	0.268	0.285	0.297	0.306	0.313	0.317	0.320
5	0.103	0.164	0.208	0.240	0.263	0.279	0.291	0.299	0.305	0.309	0.312
6	0.098	0.159	0.203	0.234	0.256	0.272	0.284	0.292	0.297	0.301	0.303
7	0.093	0.153	0.197	0.228	0.250	0.266	0.277	0.284	0.290	0.293	0.295
8	0.088	0.147	0.191	0.221	0.243	0.259	0.270	0.277	0.282	0.285	0.287
9	0.083	0.141	0.184	0.215	0.237	0.252	0.263	0.270	0.275	0.278	0.279
10	0.078	0.135	0.178	0.209	0.230	0.246	0.256	0.263	0.268	0.271	0.272
11	0.073	0.129	0.172	0.202	0.224	0.239	0.250	0.257	0.261	0.264	0.265
12	0.069	0.124	0.166	0.196	0.218	0.233	0.244	0.251	0.255	0.257	0.258
13	0.065	0.118	0.160	0.191	0.212	0.227	0.238	0.245	0.249	0.251	0.251
14	0.061	0.113	0.155	0.185	0.207	0.222	0.232	0.239	0.243	0.245	0.245
15	0.057	0.108	0.149	0.180	0.201	0.216	0.226	0.233	0.237	0.239	0.239
16	0.053	0.104	0.144	0.174	0.196	0.211	0.221	0.228	0.231	0.233	0.233
17	0.050	0.099	0.139	0.169	0.191	0.206	0.216	0.222	0.226	0.228	0.228
18	0.047	0.095	0.135	0.164	0.186	0.201	0.211	0.217	0.221	0.222	0.222
19	0.044	0.091	0.130	0.160	0.181	0.196	0.206	0.212	0.216	0.217	0.217
20	0.041	0.087	0.126	0.155	0.176	0.191	0.201	0.207	0.211	0.213	0.212
21	0.038	0.083	0.122	0.151	0.172	0.187	0.197	0.203	0.206	0.208	0.207
22	0.036	0.080	0.118	0.147	0.167	0.182	0.192	0.198	0.202	0.203	0.203
23	0.034	0.076	0.114	0.142	0.163	0.178	0.188	0.194	0.197	0.199	0.198
24	0.032	0.073	0.110	0.138	0.159	0.174	0.184	0.190	0.193	0.194	0.194
25	0.030	0.070	0.106	0.135	0.155	0.170	0.180	0.186	0.189	0.190	0.190
26	0.028	0.067	0.103	0.131	0.151	0.166	0.176	0.182	0.185	0.186	0.186
27	0.026	0.064	0.100	0.127	0.148	0.162	0.172	0.178	0.181	0.182	0.182
28	0.025	0.061	0.096	0.124	0.144	0.159	0.168	0.174	0.177	0.178	0.178
29	0.023	0.059	0.093	0.121	0.141	0.155	0.165	0.171	0.174	0.175	0.174
30	0.022	0.056	0.090	0.117	0.137	0.152	0.161	0.167	0.170	0.171	0.170

Table C.25: Probability of a Put Expiring in the Money
as a Function of Time and Volatility
Stock Price = $100
Strike Price = $90
Annual Growth Rate = 10%

Mo	Volatility										
	0.15	0.20	0.25	0.30	0.35	0.40	0.45	0.50	0.55	0.60	0.65
1	0.003	0.019	0.046	0.079	0.110	0.139	0.164	0.186	0.204	0.220	0.234
2	0.014	0.049	0.089	0.127	0.160	0.187	0.209	0.227	0.242	0.254	0.264
3	0.024	0.066	0.110	0.148	0.179	0.204	0.224	0.240	0.253	0.263	0.271
4	0.030	0.076	0.121	0.158	0.188	0.211	0.229	0.244	0.255	0.264	0.271
5	0.034	0.081	0.126	0.162	0.191	0.213	0.230	0.244	0.254	0.262	0.268
6	0.036	0.084	0.128	0.164	0.191	0.213	0.229	0.242	0.251	0.258	0.263
7	0.037	0.084	0.128	0.163	0.190	0.211	0.227	0.238	0.247	0.254	0.258
8	0.037	0.084	0.127	0.162	0.188	0.208	0.223	0.235	0.243	0.249	0.253
9	0.036	0.083	0.125	0.159	0.185	0.205	0.220	0.231	0.238	0.244	0.248
10	0.035	0.081	0.123	0.157	0.182	0.202	0.216	0.226	0.234	0.239	0.242
11	0.034	0.079	0.120	0.154	0.179	0.198	0.212	0.222	0.229	0.234	0.237
12	0.033	0.077	0.118	0.150	0.175	0.194	0.208	0.217	0.224	0.229	0.232
13	0.031	0.075	0.115	0.147	0.172	0.190	0.203	0.213	0.220	0.224	0.227
14	0.030	0.072	0.112	0.144	0.168	0.186	0.199	0.209	0.215	0.219	0.222
15	0.028	0.070	0.109	0.140	0.165	0.182	0.195	0.204	0.211	0.215	0.217
16	0.027	0.067	0.106	0.137	0.161	0.179	0.191	0.200	0.206	0.210	0.212
17	0.026	0.065	0.103	0.134	0.157	0.175	0.187	0.196	0.202	0.206	0.207
18	0.024	0.063	0.100	0.131	0.154	0.171	0.183	0.192	0.198	0.201	0.203
19	0.023	0.060	0.097	0.127	0.150	0.167	0.180	0.188	0.194	0.197	0.198
20	0.022	0.058	0.094	0.124	0.147	0.164	0.176	0.184	0.190	0.193	0.194
21	0.021	0.056	0.092	0.121	0.144	0.160	0.172	0.181	0.186	0.189	0.190
22	0.019	0.054	0.089	0.118	0.140	0.157	0.169	0.177	0.182	0.185	0.186
23	0.018	0.052	0.086	0.115	0.137	0.154	0.165	0.173	0.178	0.181	0.182
24	0.017	0.050	0.084	0.112	0.134	0.150	0.162	0.170	0.175	0.177	0.178
25	0.016	0.048	0.081	0.109	0.131	0.147	0.159	0.166	0.171	0.174	0.174
26	0.015	0.046	0.079	0.107	0.128	0.144	0.155	0.163	0.168	0.170	0.171
27	0.015	0.044	0.077	0.104	0.125	0.141	0.152	0.160	0.164	0.167	0.167
28	0.014	0.043	0.074	0.101	0.122	0.138	0.149	0.157	0.161	0.163	0.164
29	0.013	0.041	0.072	0.099	0.120	0.135	0.146	0.153	0.158	0.160	0.161
30	0.012	0.040	0.070	0.096	0.117	0.132	0.143	0.150	0.155	0.157	0.157

Table C.26: Probability of a Put Expiring in the Money
as a Function of Time and Volatility
Stock Price = $100
Strike Price = $85
Annual Growth Rate = 10%

Mo	Volatility										
	0.15	0.20	0.25	0.30	0.35	0.40	0.45	0.50	0.55	0.60	0.65
1	0.000	0.001	0.007	0.019	0.037	0.057	0.078	0.098	0.118	0.135	0.151
2	0.001	0.009	0.028	0.054	0.081	0.107	0.131	0.152	0.170	0.185	0.199
3	0.003	0.019	0.046	0.077	0.107	0.133	0.156	0.175	0.191	0.205	0.216
4	0.006	0.027	0.058	0.091	0.121	0.147	0.168	0.186	0.201	0.213	0.223
5	0.008	0.033	0.067	0.100	0.130	0.155	0.175	0.192	0.205	0.216	0.225
6	0.010	0.037	0.072	0.106	0.135	0.159	0.178	0.194	0.207	0.217	0.224
7	0.011	0.040	0.076	0.109	0.138	0.161	0.180	0.195	0.206	0.216	0.223
8	0.012	0.042	0.078	0.111	0.139	0.162	0.180	0.194	0.205	0.213	0.220
9	0.013	0.043	0.079	0.112	0.139	0.161	0.179	0.192	0.203	0.211	0.217
10	0.013	0.043	0.079	0.112	0.139	0.160	0.177	0.190	0.200	0.208	0.213
11	0.013	0.044	0.079	0.111	0.138	0.159	0.175	0.188	0.198	0.205	0.210
12	0.013	0.043	0.079	0.110	0.136	0.157	0.173	0.185	0.195	0.201	0.206
13	0.013	0.043	0.078	0.109	0.135	0.155	0.171	0.183	0.191	0.198	0.202
14	0.013	0.042	0.077	0.108	0.133	0.153	0.168	0.180	0.188	0.194	0.198
15	0.012	0.042	0.075	0.106	0.131	0.151	0.165	0.177	0.185	0.191	0.194
16	0.012	0.041	0.074	0.104	0.129	0.148	0.163	0.174	0.182	0.187	0.191
17	0.012	0.040	0.073	0.102	0.127	0.146	0.160	0.171	0.178	0.184	0.187
18	0.011	0.039	0.071	0.100	0.124	0.143	0.157	0.168	0.175	0.180	0.183
19	0.011	0.038	0.070	0.098	0.122	0.141	0.154	0.165	0.172	0.177	0.179
20	0.010	0.037	0.068	0.096	0.120	0.138	0.152	0.162	0.169	0.173	0.176
21	0.010	0.036	0.066	0.095	0.118	0.135	0.149	0.159	0.166	0.170	0.172
22	0.009	0.034	0.065	0.093	0.115	0.133	0.146	0.156	0.162	0.167	0.169
23	0.009	0.033	0.063	0.091	0.113	0.130	0.144	0.153	0.159	0.163	0.166
24	0.009	0.032	0.062	0.089	0.111	0.128	0.141	0.150	0.156	0.160	0.162
25	0.008	0.031	0.060	0.087	0.109	0.126	0.138	0.147	0.153	0.157	0.159
26	0.008	0.030	0.058	0.085	0.106	0.123	0.136	0.145	0.151	0.154	0.156
27	0.007	0.029	0.057	0.083	0.104	0.121	0.133	0.142	0.148	0.151	0.153
28	0.007	0.028	0.055	0.081	0.102	0.118	0.131	0.139	0.145	0.148	0.150
29	0.007	0.027	0.054	0.079	0.100	0.116	0.128	0.137	0.142	0.146	0.147
30	0.006	0.026	0.053	0.077	0.098	0.114	0.126	0.134	0.140	0.143	0.144

Table C.27: Probability of a Put Expiring in the Money
as a Function of Time and Volatility
Stock Price = $100
Strike Price = $80
Annual Growth Rate = 10%

Mo	Volatility										
	0.15	0.20	0.25	0.30	0.35	0.40	0.45	0.50	0.55	0.60	0.65
1	0.000	0.000	0.000	0.003	0.008	0.018	0.030	0.044	0.058	0.073	0.088
2	0.000	0.001	0.006	0.018	0.034	0.054	0.073	0.092	0.110	0.127	0.141
3	0.000	0.004	0.015	0.034	0.056	0.078	0.100	0.119	0.137	0.152	0.165
4	0.001	0.007	0.023	0.046	0.071	0.095	0.116	0.135	0.152	0.166	0.178
5	0.001	0.010	0.030	0.056	0.081	0.105	0.127	0.145	0.160	0.173	0.184
6	0.002	0.013	0.036	0.062	0.089	0.113	0.133	0.151	0.165	0.177	0.187
7	0.002	0.016	0.040	0.067	0.094	0.117	0.137	0.154	0.168	0.179	0.188
8	0.003	0.018	0.043	0.071	0.097	0.120	0.140	0.156	0.169	0.179	0.188
9	0.003	0.019	0.045	0.073	0.100	0.122	0.141	0.156	0.169	0.179	0.186
10	0.004	0.020	0.047	0.075	0.101	0.123	0.142	0.156	0.168	0.178	0.185
11	0.004	0.021	0.048	0.076	0.102	0.124	0.141	0.156	0.167	0.176	0.183
12	0.004	0.022	0.049	0.077	0.102	0.123	0.141	0.155	0.166	0.174	0.180
13	0.004	0.022	0.049	0.077	0.102	0.123	0.140	0.153	0.164	0.172	0.178
14	0.005	0.022	0.049	0.077	0.101	0.122	0.139	0.152	0.162	0.169	0.175
15	0.005	0.023	0.049	0.076	0.101	0.121	0.137	0.150	0.160	0.167	0.172
16	0.005	0.022	0.049	0.076	0.100	0.120	0.136	0.148	0.157	0.164	0.169
17	0.005	0.022	0.048	0.075	0.099	0.118	0.134	0.146	0.155	0.162	0.166
18	0.004	0.022	0.048	0.074	0.098	0.117	0.132	0.144	0.153	0.159	0.164
19	0.004	0.022	0.047	0.073	0.096	0.115	0.130	0.142	0.150	0.157	0.161
20	0.004	0.021	0.047	0.072	0.095	0.114	0.128	0.140	0.148	0.154	0.158
21	0.004	0.021	0.046	0.071	0.094	0.112	0.127	0.138	0.146	0.151	0.155
22	0.004	0.021	0.045	0.070	0.092	0.110	0.125	0.135	0.143	0.149	0.152
23	0.004	0.020	0.044	0.069	0.091	0.109	0.123	0.133	0.141	0.146	0.149
24	0.004	0.020	0.043	0.068	0.089	0.107	0.121	0.131	0.138	0.144	0.147
25	0.004	0.019	0.042	0.067	0.088	0.105	0.119	0.129	0.136	0.141	0.144
26	0.004	0.019	0.042	0.065	0.086	0.103	0.117	0.127	0.134	0.139	0.141
27	0.003	0.018	0.041	0.064	0.085	0.102	0.115	0.125	0.131	0.136	0.139
28	0.003	0.018	0.040	0.063	0.083	0.100	0.113	0.122	0.129	0.134	0.136
29	0.003	0.017	0.039	0.062	0.082	0.098	0.111	0.120	0.127	0.131	0.134
30	0.003	0.017	0.038	0.060	0.080	0.097	0.109	0.118	0.125	0.129	0.131

Table C.28: Probability of a Put Expiring in the Money
as a Function of Time and Volatility
Stock Price = $100
Strike Price = $120
Annual Growth Rate = 15%

Mo	\multicolumn{11}{c}{Volatility}
	0.15	0.20	0.25	0.30	0.35	0.40	0.45	0.50	0.55	0.60	0.65
1	1.000	0.998	0.988	0.969	0.943	0.915	0.886	0.858	0.831	0.806	0.784
2	0.991	0.961	0.918	0.873	0.831	0.794	0.761	0.732	0.707	0.684	0.664
3	0.955	0.894	0.835	0.785	0.744	0.709	0.679	0.653	0.631	0.611	0.594
4	0.895	0.820	0.760	0.713	0.675	0.645	0.619	0.597	0.577	0.560	0.544
5	0.824	0.749	0.694	0.653	0.620	0.594	0.572	0.553	0.536	0.520	0.506
6	0.750	0.683	0.636	0.602	0.575	0.552	0.533	0.517	0.502	0.488	0.475
7	0.679	0.624	0.586	0.558	0.536	0.517	0.501	0.486	0.473	0.461	0.449
8	0.612	0.570	0.542	0.520	0.502	0.487	0.473	0.460	0.448	0.437	0.426
9	0.550	0.523	0.503	0.486	0.472	0.460	0.448	0.437	0.426	0.416	0.406
10	0.494	0.480	0.467	0.456	0.446	0.435	0.426	0.416	0.407	0.397	0.388
11	0.443	0.441	0.436	0.429	0.422	0.414	0.406	0.397	0.389	0.380	0.372
12	0.398	0.406	0.407	0.404	0.400	0.394	0.387	0.380	0.372	0.365	0.357
13	0.357	0.374	0.381	0.382	0.380	0.376	0.370	0.364	0.358	0.350	0.343
14	0.320	0.345	0.357	0.361	0.361	0.359	0.355	0.350	0.344	0.337	0.330
15	0.287	0.319	0.335	0.342	0.344	0.344	0.341	0.336	0.331	0.325	0.318
16	0.258	0.295	0.315	0.325	0.329	0.329	0.327	0.324	0.319	0.313	0.307
17	0.231	0.273	0.296	0.308	0.314	0.316	0.315	0.312	0.307	0.302	0.296
18	0.208	0.253	0.279	0.293	0.300	0.303	0.303	0.301	0.297	0.292	0.286
19	0.187	0.235	0.263	0.279	0.287	0.291	0.292	0.290	0.287	0.282	0.277
20	0.168	0.218	0.248	0.265	0.275	0.280	0.281	0.280	0.277	0.273	0.268
21	0.151	0.203	0.234	0.253	0.264	0.269	0.271	0.271	0.268	0.264	0.259
22	0.136	0.188	0.221	0.241	0.253	0.259	0.262	0.262	0.260	0.256	0.251
23	0.122	0.175	0.209	0.230	0.243	0.250	0.253	0.253	0.251	0.248	0.244
24	0.110	0.163	0.198	0.220	0.233	0.241	0.245	0.245	0.244	0.241	0.236
25	0.099	0.152	0.187	0.210	0.224	0.233	0.236	0.237	0.236	0.233	0.229
26	0.089	0.142	0.177	0.201	0.216	0.224	0.229	0.230	0.229	0.227	0.223
27	0.080	0.132	0.168	0.192	0.207	0.217	0.221	0.223	0.222	0.220	0.216
28	0.072	0.123	0.159	0.184	0.200	0.209	0.214	0.216	0.216	0.214	0.210
29	0.065	0.115	0.151	0.176	0.192	0.202	0.208	0.210	0.210	0.208	0.204
30	0.059	0.107	0.144	0.169	0.185	0.195	0.201	0.204	0.204	0.202	0.198

Table C.29: Probability of a Put Expiring in the Money
as a Function of Time and Volatility
Stock Price = $100
Strike Price = $115
Annual Growth Rate = 15%

Mo	\multicolumn{11}{c}{Volatility}

Mo	0.15	0.20	0.25	0.30	0.35	0.40	0.45	0.50	0.55	0.60	0.65
1	0.997	0.982	0.951	0.914	0.877	0.842	0.810	0.781	0.755	0.732	0.711
2	0.954	0.893	0.835	0.786	0.746	0.712	0.684	0.660	0.638	0.620	0.603
3	0.870	0.795	0.737	0.694	0.660	0.632	0.608	0.589	0.571	0.556	0.542
4	0.777	0.708	0.660	0.624	0.596	0.574	0.555	0.539	0.524	0.511	0.499
5	0.688	0.633	0.596	0.569	0.547	0.529	0.514	0.500	0.488	0.477	0.466
6	0.608	0.570	0.543	0.523	0.507	0.493	0.480	0.469	0.458	0.448	0.439
7	0.537	0.515	0.498	0.484	0.472	0.462	0.452	0.442	0.433	0.424	0.415
8	0.475	0.467	0.459	0.451	0.443	0.435	0.427	0.419	0.411	0.403	0.395
9	0.420	0.425	0.425	0.421	0.417	0.411	0.405	0.398	0.392	0.384	0.377
10	0.372	0.388	0.394	0.395	0.394	0.390	0.385	0.380	0.374	0.368	0.361
11	0.330	0.355	0.367	0.372	0.373	0.371	0.368	0.363	0.358	0.352	0.346
12	0.293	0.326	0.342	0.350	0.354	0.354	0.352	0.348	0.344	0.338	0.332
13	0.261	0.300	0.320	0.331	0.336	0.338	0.337	0.334	0.330	0.325	0.320
14	0.233	0.276	0.300	0.313	0.320	0.323	0.323	0.321	0.318	0.313	0.308
15	0.207	0.254	0.281	0.297	0.305	0.309	0.310	0.309	0.306	0.302	0.297
16	0.185	0.235	0.264	0.282	0.291	0.296	0.298	0.298	0.295	0.292	0.287
17	0.165	0.217	0.249	0.268	0.279	0.285	0.287	0.287	0.285	0.282	0.277
18	0.148	0.201	0.234	0.254	0.267	0.273	0.276	0.277	0.275	0.272	0.268
19	0.132	0.186	0.221	0.242	0.255	0.263	0.266	0.267	0.266	0.263	0.260
20	0.118	0.173	0.208	0.231	0.245	0.253	0.257	0.258	0.257	0.255	0.251
21	0.106	0.160	0.197	0.220	0.235	0.244	0.248	0.250	0.249	0.247	0.244
22	0.095	0.149	0.186	0.210	0.225	0.235	0.240	0.242	0.241	0.239	0.236
23	0.085	0.138	0.176	0.200	0.216	0.226	0.232	0.234	0.234	0.232	0.229
24	0.077	0.129	0.166	0.191	0.208	0.218	0.224	0.227	0.227	0.225	0.222
25	0.069	0.120	0.157	0.183	0.200	0.211	0.217	0.220	0.220	0.219	0.216
26	0.062	0.112	0.149	0.175	0.192	0.203	0.210	0.213	0.214	0.212	0.210
27	0.056	0.104	0.141	0.167	0.185	0.196	0.203	0.206	0.207	0.206	0.204
28	0.050	0.097	0.134	0.160	0.178	0.190	0.197	0.200	0.201	0.200	0.198
29	0.045	0.090	0.127	0.153	0.172	0.183	0.191	0.194	0.196	0.195	0.192
30	0.041	0.084	0.121	0.147	0.165	0.177	0.185	0.189	0.190	0.189	0.187

Table C.30: Probability of a Put Expiring in the Money
as a Function of Time and Volatility
Stock Price = $100
Strike Price = $110
Annual Growth Rate = 15%

Mo	Volatility										
	0.15	0.20	0.25	0.30	0.35	0.40	0.45	0.50	0.55	0.60	0.65
1	0.962	0.906	0.851	0.804	0.764	0.731	0.703	0.680	0.659	0.642	0.626
2	0.830	0.757	0.705	0.667	0.637	0.613	0.593	0.577	0.562	0.549	0.538
3	0.703	0.647	0.610	0.583	0.562	0.545	0.531	0.518	0.507	0.497	0.488
4	0.598	0.564	0.541	0.524	0.510	0.498	0.487	0.477	0.468	0.460	0.452
5	0.513	0.498	0.487	0.477	0.469	0.461	0.453	0.445	0.438	0.431	0.424
6	0.443	0.445	0.443	0.440	0.435	0.430	0.425	0.419	0.413	0.407	0.401
7	0.384	0.400	0.406	0.408	0.407	0.404	0.401	0.397	0.392	0.386	0.381
8	0.335	0.361	0.374	0.380	0.382	0.382	0.380	0.377	0.373	0.368	0.363
9	0.293	0.328	0.346	0.356	0.361	0.362	0.362	0.359	0.356	0.352	0.348
10	0.258	0.299	0.322	0.334	0.341	0.344	0.345	0.344	0.341	0.337	0.333
11	0.227	0.273	0.300	0.315	0.324	0.328	0.330	0.329	0.327	0.324	0.320
12	0.201	0.250	0.280	0.297	0.308	0.313	0.316	0.316	0.314	0.312	0.308
13	0.178	0.230	0.262	0.281	0.293	0.300	0.303	0.304	0.303	0.300	0.297
14	0.157	0.212	0.245	0.266	0.279	0.287	0.291	0.292	0.292	0.289	0.286
15	0.140	0.195	0.230	0.253	0.267	0.275	0.280	0.281	0.281	0.279	0.276
16	0.124	0.180	0.216	0.240	0.255	0.264	0.269	0.271	0.271	0.270	0.267
17	0.111	0.166	0.204	0.228	0.244	0.254	0.259	0.262	0.262	0.261	0.258
18	0.099	0.154	0.192	0.217	0.234	0.244	0.250	0.253	0.254	0.253	0.250
19	0.088	0.143	0.181	0.207	0.224	0.235	0.241	0.245	0.245	0.245	0.242
20	0.079	0.132	0.171	0.197	0.215	0.226	0.233	0.237	0.238	0.237	0.235
21	0.071	0.123	0.161	0.188	0.206	0.218	0.225	0.229	0.230	0.230	0.228
22	0.063	0.114	0.153	0.180	0.198	0.210	0.218	0.222	0.223	0.223	0.221
23	0.057	0.106	0.144	0.172	0.190	0.203	0.211	0.215	0.216	0.216	0.214
24	0.051	0.099	0.137	0.164	0.183	0.196	0.204	0.208	0.210	0.210	0.208
25	0.046	0.092	0.129	0.157	0.176	0.189	0.197	0.202	0.204	0.204	0.202
26	0.041	0.085	0.123	0.150	0.170	0.183	0.191	0.196	0.198	0.198	0.196
27	0.037	0.080	0.116	0.144	0.163	0.177	0.185	0.190	0.192	0.192	0.191
28	0.033	0.074	0.110	0.138	0.157	0.171	0.179	0.184	0.187	0.187	0.186
29	0.030	0.069	0.105	0.132	0.152	0.165	0.174	0.179	0.182	0.182	0.181
30	0.027	0.065	0.099	0.127	0.146	0.160	0.169	0.174	0.176	0.177	0.176

Table C.31: Probability of a Put Expiring in the Money
as a Function of Time and Volatility
Stock Price = $100
Strike Price = $105
Annual Growth Rate = 15%

Mo	Volatility										
	0.15	0.20	0.25	0.30	0.35	0.40	0.45	0.50	0.55	0.60	0.65
1	0.758	0.696	0.654	0.625	0.602	0.584	0.570	0.558	0.547	0.537	0.529
2	0.577	0.551	0.534	0.520	0.510	0.501	0.493	0.486	0.480	0.474	0.468
3	0.465	0.465	0.463	0.460	0.457	0.453	0.449	0.444	0.440	0.436	0.431
4	0.387	0.405	0.413	0.417	0.418	0.418	0.416	0.414	0.411	0.407	0.404
5	0.327	0.358	0.374	0.383	0.388	0.390	0.390	0.389	0.387	0.385	0.381
6	0.280	0.320	0.342	0.355	0.363	0.367	0.369	0.369	0.367	0.365	0.362
7	0.242	0.288	0.315	0.331	0.341	0.347	0.350	0.351	0.350	0.348	0.346
8	0.210	0.261	0.292	0.310	0.322	0.329	0.333	0.335	0.334	0.333	0.331
9	0.184	0.238	0.271	0.292	0.305	0.313	0.318	0.320	0.320	0.320	0.318
10	0.161	0.217	0.252	0.275	0.290	0.299	0.304	0.307	0.308	0.307	0.305
11	0.142	0.199	0.236	0.260	0.275	0.285	0.292	0.295	0.296	0.296	0.294
12	0.125	0.182	0.221	0.246	0.263	0.273	0.280	0.284	0.285	0.285	0.283
13	0.111	0.168	0.207	0.233	0.251	0.262	0.269	0.273	0.275	0.275	0.273
14	0.098	0.155	0.194	0.221	0.239	0.251	0.259	0.263	0.265	0.265	0.264
15	0.087	0.143	0.183	0.210	0.229	0.242	0.249	0.254	0.256	0.257	0.255
16	0.078	0.132	0.172	0.200	0.219	0.232	0.240	0.245	0.248	0.248	0.247
17	0.069	0.122	0.162	0.191	0.210	0.223	0.232	0.237	0.240	0.240	0.239
18	0.062	0.113	0.153	0.182	0.202	0.215	0.224	0.229	0.232	0.233	0.232
19	0.055	0.105	0.145	0.174	0.194	0.207	0.216	0.222	0.225	0.226	0.225
20	0.049	0.098	0.137	0.166	0.186	0.200	0.209	0.215	0.218	0.219	0.218
21	0.044	0.091	0.129	0.158	0.179	0.193	0.202	0.208	0.211	0.212	0.212
22	0.039	0.084	0.123	0.151	0.172	0.186	0.196	0.202	0.205	0.206	0.206
23	0.035	0.078	0.116	0.145	0.165	0.180	0.190	0.196	0.199	0.200	0.200
24	0.032	0.073	0.110	0.138	0.159	0.174	0.184	0.190	0.193	0.194	0.194
25	0.028	0.068	0.104	0.133	0.153	0.168	0.178	0.184	0.188	0.189	0.189
26	0.026	0.063	0.099	0.127	0.148	0.162	0.172	0.179	0.182	0.184	0.183
27	0.023	0.059	0.094	0.122	0.142	0.157	0.167	0.174	0.177	0.179	0.178
28	0.021	0.055	0.089	0.117	0.137	0.152	0.162	0.169	0.172	0.174	0.173
29	0.019	0.051	0.085	0.112	0.132	0.147	0.157	0.164	0.168	0.169	0.169
30	0.017	0.048	0.080	0.107	0.128	0.142	0.153	0.159	0.163	0.164	0.164

Table C.32: Probability of a Put Expiring in the Money
as a Function of Time and Volatility
Stock Price = $100
Strike Price = $100
Annual Growth Rate = 15%

Mo	Volatility										
	0.15	0.20	0.25	0.30	0.35	0.40	0.45	0.50	0.55	0.60	0.65
1	0.335	0.370	0.390	0.403	0.411	0.417	0.421	0.423	0.425	0.426	0.426
2	0.274	0.319	0.347	0.364	0.376	0.384	0.389	0.392	0.394	0.395	0.396
3	0.230	0.283	0.315	0.335	0.349	0.358	0.365	0.369	0.371	0.373	0.373
4	0.197	0.253	0.289	0.312	0.327	0.338	0.345	0.349	0.352	0.354	0.354
5	0.171	0.229	0.267	0.292	0.308	0.320	0.328	0.333	0.336	0.337	0.338
6	0.148	0.208	0.248	0.274	0.292	0.304	0.312	0.318	0.321	0.323	0.323
7	0.130	0.190	0.231	0.258	0.277	0.290	0.299	0.304	0.308	0.310	0.310
8	0.114	0.174	0.215	0.244	0.263	0.277	0.286	0.292	0.296	0.298	0.298
9	0.101	0.160	0.202	0.231	0.251	0.265	0.275	0.281	0.285	0.287	0.287
10	0.089	0.147	0.189	0.219	0.240	0.254	0.264	0.270	0.274	0.276	0.277
11	0.079	0.135	0.178	0.208	0.229	0.244	0.254	0.261	0.265	0.267	0.267
12	0.070	0.125	0.167	0.198	0.219	0.234	0.245	0.251	0.256	0.258	0.258
13	0.062	0.116	0.158	0.188	0.210	0.225	0.236	0.243	0.247	0.249	0.250
14	0.056	0.107	0.149	0.179	0.201	0.217	0.228	0.235	0.239	0.241	0.242
15	0.050	0.099	0.140	0.171	0.193	0.209	0.220	0.227	0.231	0.234	0.234
16	0.044	0.092	0.133	0.163	0.185	0.201	0.212	0.220	0.224	0.226	0.227
17	0.040	0.086	0.125	0.156	0.178	0.194	0.205	0.213	0.217	0.220	0.220
18	0.035	0.079	0.119	0.149	0.171	0.187	0.198	0.206	0.211	0.213	0.214
19	0.032	0.074	0.112	0.142	0.165	0.181	0.192	0.200	0.204	0.207	0.207
20	0.028	0.069	0.106	0.136	0.159	0.175	0.186	0.194	0.198	0.201	0.201
21	0.026	0.064	0.101	0.130	0.153	0.169	0.180	0.188	0.192	0.195	0.196
22	0.023	0.060	0.096	0.125	0.147	0.163	0.174	0.182	0.187	0.189	0.190
23	0.021	0.056	0.091	0.120	0.142	0.158	0.169	0.177	0.182	0.184	0.185
24	0.019	0.052	0.086	0.115	0.137	0.153	0.164	0.172	0.176	0.179	0.180
25	0.017	0.048	0.082	0.110	0.132	0.148	0.159	0.167	0.172	0.174	0.175
26	0.015	0.045	0.078	0.105	0.127	0.143	0.154	0.162	0.167	0.169	0.170
27	0.013	0.042	0.074	0.101	0.123	0.138	0.150	0.157	0.162	0.165	0.165
28	0.012	0.039	0.070	0.097	0.118	0.134	0.145	0.153	0.158	0.160	0.161
29	0.011	0.037	0.067	0.093	0.114	0.130	0.141	0.149	0.154	0.156	0.157
30	0.010	0.035	0.064	0.089	0.110	0.126	0.137	0.145	0.150	0.152	0.153

Table C.33: Probability of a Put Expiring in the Money
as a Function of Time and Volatility
Stock Price = $100
Strike Price = $95
Annual Growth Rate = 15%

Mo	Volatility										
	0.15	0.20	0.25	0.30	0.35	0.40	0.45	0.50	0.55	0.60	0.65
1	0.054	0.111	0.161	0.201	0.232	0.257	0.276	0.292	0.304	0.314	0.323
2	0.075	0.136	0.185	0.222	0.250	0.271	0.287	0.300	0.310	0.317	0.324
3	0.078	0.138	0.186	0.222	0.248	0.268	0.283	0.295	0.303	0.310	0.315
4	0.074	0.134	0.181	0.216	0.242	0.261	0.275	0.286	0.294	0.300	0.305
5	0.069	0.127	0.173	0.208	0.234	0.253	0.267	0.277	0.285	0.290	0.294
6	0.063	0.120	0.165	0.200	0.225	0.244	0.258	0.268	0.275	0.281	0.284
7	0.058	0.112	0.157	0.191	0.217	0.235	0.249	0.259	0.266	0.271	0.275
8	0.052	0.105	0.149	0.183	0.208	0.227	0.241	0.251	0.258	0.263	0.266
9	0.047	0.098	0.142	0.175	0.200	0.219	0.233	0.242	0.249	0.254	0.257
10	0.043	0.092	0.134	0.168	0.193	0.211	0.225	0.235	0.241	0.246	0.249
11	0.038	0.086	0.128	0.160	0.185	0.204	0.217	0.227	0.234	0.238	0.241
12	0.035	0.080	0.121	0.154	0.178	0.197	0.210	0.220	0.227	0.231	0.234
13	0.031	0.074	0.115	0.147	0.172	0.190	0.203	0.213	0.220	0.224	0.227
14	0.028	0.069	0.109	0.141	0.165	0.184	0.197	0.206	0.213	0.217	0.220
15	0.025	0.065	0.103	0.135	0.159	0.177	0.191	0.200	0.207	0.211	0.213
16	0.023	0.061	0.098	0.129	0.153	0.172	0.185	0.194	0.201	0.205	0.207
17	0.021	0.057	0.093	0.124	0.148	0.166	0.179	0.188	0.195	0.199	0.201
18	0.019	0.053	0.089	0.119	0.143	0.160	0.174	0.183	0.189	0.193	0.195
19	0.017	0.049	0.084	0.114	0.137	0.155	0.168	0.178	0.184	0.188	0.190
20	0.015	0.046	0.080	0.109	0.133	0.150	0.163	0.172	0.179	0.183	0.185
21	0.014	0.043	0.076	0.105	0.128	0.145	0.158	0.168	0.174	0.178	0.180
22	0.012	0.040	0.072	0.101	0.124	0.141	0.154	0.163	0.169	0.173	0.175
23	0.011	0.038	0.069	0.097	0.119	0.136	0.149	0.158	0.164	0.168	0.170
24	0.010	0.035	0.066	0.093	0.115	0.132	0.145	0.154	0.160	0.164	0.165
25	0.009	0.033	0.062	0.089	0.111	0.128	0.141	0.150	0.156	0.159	0.161
26	0.008	0.031	0.059	0.086	0.107	0.124	0.137	0.145	0.151	0.155	0.157
27	0.007	0.029	0.057	0.082	0.104	0.120	0.133	0.142	0.147	0.151	0.153
28	0.007	0.027	0.054	0.079	0.100	0.117	0.129	0.138	0.144	0.147	0.149
29	0.006	0.025	0.051	0.076	0.097	0.113	0.125	0.134	0.140	0.143	0.145
30	0.005	0.024	0.049	0.073	0.094	0.110	0.122	0.130	0.136	0.140	0.141

Table C.34: Probability of a Put Expiring in the Money
as a Function of Time and Volatility
Stock Price = $100
Strike Price = $90
Annual Growth Rate = 15%

Mo	Volatility										
	0.15	0.20	0.25	0.30	0.35	0.40	0.45	0.50	0.55	0.60	0.65
1	0.002	0.016	0.041	0.072	0.103	0.131	0.156	0.178	0.197	0.213	0.227
2	0.010	0.039	0.077	0.114	0.146	0.173	0.196	0.215	0.230	0.243	0.254
3	0.016	0.052	0.093	0.130	0.161	0.187	0.208	0.225	0.238	0.249	0.258
4	0.019	0.057	0.099	0.136	0.166	0.191	0.210	0.226	0.239	0.248	0.256
5	0.021	0.060	0.101	0.137	0.167	0.191	0.209	0.224	0.236	0.245	0.252
6	0.021	0.060	0.101	0.136	0.165	0.188	0.206	0.220	0.231	0.239	0.246
7	0.020	0.058	0.099	0.134	0.162	0.184	0.202	0.215	0.226	0.234	0.240
8	0.019	0.057	0.096	0.130	0.158	0.180	0.197	0.210	0.220	0.228	0.233
9	0.018	0.054	0.093	0.127	0.154	0.176	0.192	0.205	0.215	0.222	0.227
10	0.017	0.052	0.090	0.123	0.150	0.171	0.187	0.200	0.209	0.216	0.221
11	0.016	0.049	0.086	0.119	0.145	0.166	0.182	0.194	0.204	0.210	0.215
12	0.015	0.047	0.083	0.115	0.141	0.161	0.177	0.189	0.198	0.205	0.209
13	0.014	0.044	0.079	0.111	0.137	0.157	0.172	0.184	0.193	0.199	0.203
14	0.012	0.042	0.076	0.107	0.132	0.152	0.168	0.179	0.188	0.194	0.198
15	0.011	0.039	0.073	0.103	0.128	0.148	0.163	0.174	0.183	0.188	0.192
16	0.010	0.037	0.070	0.099	0.124	0.143	0.158	0.169	0.178	0.183	0.187
17	0.010	0.035	0.066	0.096	0.120	0.139	0.154	0.165	0.173	0.178	0.182
18	0.009	0.033	0.064	0.092	0.116	0.135	0.150	0.160	0.168	0.174	0.177
19	0.008	0.031	0.061	0.089	0.112	0.131	0.145	0.156	0.164	0.169	0.173
20	0.007	0.029	0.058	0.085	0.109	0.127	0.141	0.152	0.160	0.165	0.168
21	0.007	0.027	0.055	0.082	0.105	0.123	0.137	0.148	0.155	0.160	0.164
22	0.006	0.026	0.053	0.079	0.102	0.120	0.134	0.144	0.151	0.156	0.159
23	0.005	0.024	0.050	0.076	0.098	0.116	0.130	0.140	0.147	0.152	0.155
24	0.005	0.023	0.048	0.073	0.095	0.113	0.126	0.136	0.144	0.148	0.151
25	0.004	0.021	0.046	0.071	0.092	0.110	0.123	0.133	0.140	0.145	0.147
26	0.004	0.020	0.044	0.068	0.089	0.106	0.120	0.129	0.136	0.141	0.144
27	0.004	0.019	0.042	0.066	0.086	0.103	0.116	0.126	0.133	0.137	0.140
28	0.003	0.018	0.040	0.063	0.084	0.100	0.113	0.123	0.129	0.134	0.137
29	0.003	0.017	0.038	0.061	0.081	0.097	0.110	0.120	0.126	0.131	0.133
30	0.003	0.016	0.037	0.059	0.078	0.095	0.107	0.116	0.123	0.127	0.130

Table C.35: Probability of a Put Expiring in the Money
as a Function of Time and Volatility
Stock Price = $100
Strike Price = $85
Annual Growth Rate = 15%

Mo	\multicolumn{11}{c}{Volatility}
	0.15	0.20	0.25	0.30	0.35	0.40	0.45	0.50	0.55	0.60	0.65
1	0.000	0.001	0.006	0.017	0.033	0.053	0.073	0.094	0.113	0.130	0.146
2	0.001	0.007	0.024	0.047	0.073	0.098	0.122	0.142	0.161	0.176	0.190
3	0.002	0.014	0.037	0.066	0.094	0.120	0.143	0.162	0.179	0.193	0.205
4	0.003	0.019	0.046	0.076	0.105	0.131	0.153	0.171	0.186	0.199	0.210
5	0.004	0.023	0.052	0.083	0.111	0.136	0.157	0.175	0.189	0.201	0.210
6	0.005	0.025	0.055	0.086	0.114	0.138	0.159	0.175	0.189	0.200	0.208
7	0.005	0.026	0.056	0.087	0.115	0.139	0.158	0.174	0.187	0.197	0.205
8	0.006	0.027	0.057	0.087	0.115	0.138	0.157	0.172	0.185	0.194	0.202
9	0.006	0.027	0.056	0.087	0.114	0.136	0.155	0.170	0.181	0.191	0.198
10	0.006	0.026	0.056	0.085	0.112	0.134	0.152	0.167	0.178	0.187	0.193
11	0.005	0.026	0.054	0.084	0.110	0.132	0.149	0.163	0.174	0.183	0.189
12	0.005	0.025	0.053	0.082	0.108	0.129	0.146	0.160	0.170	0.179	0.185
13	0.005	0.024	0.052	0.080	0.105	0.126	0.143	0.156	0.167	0.174	0.180
14	0.005	0.023	0.050	0.078	0.103	0.123	0.140	0.153	0.163	0.170	0.176
15	0.004	0.022	0.048	0.076	0.100	0.120	0.136	0.149	0.159	0.166	0.172
16	0.004	0.021	0.047	0.073	0.097	0.117	0.133	0.146	0.155	0.162	0.167
17	0.004	0.020	0.045	0.071	0.095	0.114	0.130	0.142	0.151	0.158	0.163
18	0.004	0.019	0.043	0.069	0.092	0.111	0.127	0.139	0.148	0.155	0.159
19	0.003	0.018	0.042	0.067	0.089	0.108	0.124	0.135	0.144	0.151	0.155
20	0.003	0.017	0.040	0.065	0.087	0.106	0.120	0.132	0.141	0.147	0.151
21	0.003	0.016	0.039	0.063	0.084	0.103	0.117	0.129	0.137	0.144	0.148
22	0.003	0.016	0.037	0.060	0.082	0.100	0.114	0.126	0.134	0.140	0.144
23	0.002	0.015	0.035	0.058	0.080	0.097	0.112	0.123	0.131	0.137	0.141
24	0.002	0.014	0.034	0.056	0.077	0.095	0.109	0.120	0.128	0.133	0.137
25	0.002	0.013	0.033	0.055	0.075	0.092	0.106	0.117	0.124	0.130	0.134
26	0.002	0.012	0.031	0.053	0.073	0.090	0.103	0.114	0.121	0.127	0.131
27	0.002	0.012	0.030	0.051	0.070	0.087	0.101	0.111	0.119	0.124	0.127
28	0.002	0.011	0.029	0.049	0.068	0.085	0.098	0.108	0.116	0.121	0.124
29	0.001	0.010	0.028	0.047	0.066	0.082	0.096	0.106	0.113	0.118	0.121
30	0.001	0.010	0.026	0.046	0.064	0.080	0.093	0.103	0.110	0.115	0.118

Table C.36: Probability of a Put Expiring in the Money
as a Function of Time and Volatility
Stock Price = $100
Strike Price = $80
Annual Growth Rate = 15%

Mo	\multicolumn{11}{c}{Volatility}
	0.15	0.20	0.25	0.30	0.35	0.40	0.45	0.50	0.55	0.60	0.65
1	0.000	0.000	0.000	0.002	0.008	0.016	0.028	0.041	0.055	0.070	0.084
2	0.000	0.001	0.005	0.015	0.030	0.048	0.067	0.086	0.103	0.120	0.134
3	0.000	0.003	0.012	0.028	0.048	0.070	0.091	0.110	0.127	0.143	0.156
4	0.000	0.005	0.018	0.038	0.060	0.083	0.104	0.123	0.140	0.154	0.166
5	0.001	0.007	0.022	0.044	0.068	0.091	0.112	0.131	0.146	0.160	0.171
6	0.001	0.008	0.026	0.049	0.074	0.097	0.117	0.135	0.150	0.162	0.173
7	0.001	0.010	0.028	0.052	0.077	0.100	0.119	0.137	0.151	0.163	0.172
8	0.001	0.011	0.030	0.054	0.079	0.101	0.121	0.137	0.151	0.162	0.171
9	0.001	0.011	0.031	0.055	0.080	0.102	0.121	0.137	0.150	0.161	0.169
10	0.001	0.012	0.032	0.056	0.080	0.102	0.120	0.136	0.148	0.158	0.167
11	0.002	0.012	0.032	0.056	0.080	0.101	0.119	0.134	0.146	0.156	0.164
12	0.002	0.012	0.032	0.055	0.079	0.100	0.117	0.132	0.144	0.153	0.161
13	0.002	0.012	0.031	0.055	0.078	0.098	0.116	0.130	0.142	0.151	0.158
14	0.001	0.011	0.031	0.054	0.077	0.097	0.114	0.128	0.139	0.148	0.154
15	0.001	0.011	0.030	0.053	0.075	0.095	0.112	0.125	0.136	0.145	0.151
16	0.001	0.011	0.030	0.052	0.074	0.093	0.110	0.123	0.134	0.142	0.148
17	0.001	0.011	0.029	0.051	0.072	0.091	0.108	0.121	0.131	0.139	0.145
18	0.001	0.010	0.028	0.050	0.071	0.090	0.105	0.118	0.128	0.136	0.141
19	0.001	0.010	0.027	0.048	0.069	0.088	0.103	0.115	0.125	0.133	0.138
20	0.001	0.009	0.026	0.047	0.068	0.086	0.101	0.113	0.123	0.130	0.135
21	0.001	0.009	0.026	0.046	0.066	0.084	0.099	0.111	0.120	0.127	0.132
22	0.001	0.009	0.025	0.045	0.064	0.082	0.096	0.108	0.117	0.124	0.129
23	0.001	0.008	0.024	0.043	0.063	0.080	0.094	0.106	0.115	0.121	0.126
24	0.001	0.008	0.023	0.042	0.061	0.078	0.092	0.103	0.112	0.119	0.123
25	0.001	0.008	0.022	0.041	0.059	0.076	0.090	0.101	0.110	0.116	0.120
26	0.001	0.007	0.021	0.040	0.058	0.074	0.088	0.099	0.107	0.113	0.118
27	0.001	0.007	0.021	0.038	0.056	0.072	0.086	0.096	0.105	0.111	0.115
28	0.001	0.006	0.020	0.037	0.055	0.070	0.084	0.094	0.102	0.108	0.112
29	0.001	0.006	0.019	0.036	0.053	0.069	0.082	0.092	0.100	0.106	0.110
30	0.001	0.006	0.018	0.035	0.052	0.067	0.080	0.090	0.098	0.103	0.107

Table C.37: Probability of a Put Expiring in the Money
as a Function of Time and Volatility
Stock Price = $100
Strike Price = $120
Annual Growth Rate = 20%

Mo	\multicolumn{11}{c}{Volatility}

Mo	0.15	0.20	0.25	0.30	0.35	0.40	0.45	0.50	0.55	0.60	0.65
1	1.000	0.997	0.986	0.965	0.938	0.909	0.879	0.851	0.824	0.800	0.777
2	0.987	0.952	0.905	0.859	0.816	0.779	0.747	0.719	0.694	0.672	0.652
3	0.937	0.869	0.810	0.760	0.720	0.687	0.659	0.635	0.614	0.595	0.579
4	0.856	0.780	0.723	0.679	0.645	0.617	0.594	0.574	0.557	0.541	0.527
5	0.763	0.694	0.647	0.612	0.585	0.563	0.544	0.527	0.512	0.499	0.487
6	0.670	0.618	0.582	0.556	0.535	0.517	0.502	0.489	0.476	0.465	0.454
7	0.583	0.549	0.526	0.508	0.492	0.479	0.467	0.456	0.445	0.436	0.426
8	0.505	0.489	0.477	0.466	0.456	0.446	0.437	0.428	0.419	0.410	0.402
9	0.435	0.437	0.434	0.429	0.423	0.417	0.410	0.403	0.396	0.388	0.381
10	0.375	0.390	0.396	0.397	0.395	0.391	0.386	0.381	0.375	0.368	0.361
11	0.322	0.349	0.362	0.367	0.369	0.368	0.365	0.361	0.356	0.350	0.344
12	0.277	0.313	0.332	0.341	0.346	0.347	0.345	0.343	0.339	0.334	0.328
13	0.238	0.281	0.304	0.318	0.325	0.328	0.328	0.326	0.323	0.319	0.314
14	0.204	0.252	0.280	0.296	0.305	0.310	0.311	0.311	0.308	0.305	0.300
15	0.175	0.227	0.258	0.277	0.288	0.294	0.296	0.296	0.295	0.292	0.288
16	0.150	0.204	0.238	0.259	0.271	0.279	0.282	0.283	0.282	0.280	0.276
17	0.129	0.184	0.219	0.242	0.256	0.265	0.269	0.271	0.270	0.268	0.265
18	0.111	0.166	0.203	0.227	0.242	0.252	0.257	0.259	0.259	0.258	0.255
19	0.095	0.150	0.188	0.213	0.229	0.240	0.246	0.249	0.249	0.248	0.245
20	0.082	0.135	0.174	0.200	0.217	0.228	0.235	0.238	0.239	0.238	0.236
21	0.070	0.122	0.161	0.188	0.206	0.218	0.225	0.229	0.230	0.230	0.228
22	0.060	0.111	0.149	0.177	0.195	0.208	0.215	0.220	0.221	0.221	0.219
23	0.052	0.100	0.139	0.166	0.186	0.198	0.206	0.211	0.213	0.213	0.212
24	0.045	0.091	0.129	0.157	0.176	0.189	0.198	0.203	0.205	0.205	0.204
25	0.039	0.082	0.120	0.148	0.168	0.181	0.190	0.195	0.198	0.198	0.197
26	0.033	0.075	0.111	0.139	0.159	0.173	0.182	0.188	0.191	0.191	0.190
27	0.029	0.068	0.104	0.131	0.152	0.166	0.175	0.181	0.184	0.185	0.184
28	0.025	0.062	0.096	0.124	0.144	0.159	0.168	0.174	0.177	0.178	0.178
29	0.021	0.056	0.090	0.117	0.137	0.152	0.162	0.168	0.171	0.172	0.172
30	0.018	0.051	0.084	0.111	0.131	0.146	0.156	0.162	0.165	0.167	0.166

Table C.38: Probability of a Put Expiring in the Money
as a Function of Time and Volatility
Stock Price = $100
Strike Price = $115
Annual Growth Rate = 20%

Mo	Volatility										
	0.15	0.20	0.25	0.30	0.35	0.40	0.45	0.50	0.55	0.60	0.65
1	0.997	0.978	0.945	0.907	0.868	0.833	0.801	0.772	0.747	0.724	0.704
2	0.939	0.873	0.814	0.766	0.727	0.695	0.667	0.644	0.624	0.607	0.591
3	0.831	0.757	0.704	0.664	0.633	0.608	0.587	0.569	0.553	0.540	0.527
4	0.716	0.656	0.616	0.587	0.564	0.546	0.530	0.516	0.503	0.492	0.482
5	0.609	0.571	0.545	0.526	0.510	0.497	0.485	0.474	0.465	0.455	0.446
6	0.516	0.499	0.487	0.476	0.466	0.457	0.449	0.441	0.433	0.425	0.417
7	0.436	0.439	0.437	0.434	0.429	0.424	0.418	0.412	0.406	0.399	0.393
8	0.369	0.387	0.395	0.398	0.397	0.395	0.392	0.387	0.382	0.377	0.371
9	0.312	0.343	0.358	0.366	0.369	0.370	0.368	0.365	0.362	0.357	0.352
10	0.264	0.304	0.326	0.338	0.344	0.347	0.347	0.346	0.343	0.339	0.335
11	0.224	0.271	0.298	0.313	0.322	0.327	0.328	0.328	0.326	0.323	0.319
12	0.190	0.242	0.272	0.291	0.302	0.308	0.311	0.312	0.311	0.308	0.305
13	0.162	0.216	0.250	0.271	0.284	0.292	0.296	0.297	0.297	0.295	0.292
14	0.138	0.193	0.229	0.252	0.267	0.276	0.281	0.283	0.284	0.282	0.280
15	0.117	0.174	0.211	0.236	0.252	0.262	0.268	0.271	0.271	0.270	0.268
16	0.100	0.156	0.195	0.221	0.238	0.249	0.255	0.259	0.260	0.259	0.258
17	0.085	0.140	0.180	0.206	0.225	0.236	0.244	0.248	0.249	0.249	0.248
18	0.073	0.126	0.166	0.194	0.212	0.225	0.233	0.237	0.239	0.239	0.238
19	0.062	0.114	0.153	0.182	0.201	0.214	0.223	0.228	0.230	0.230	0.229
20	0.053	0.103	0.142	0.171	0.191	0.204	0.213	0.218	0.221	0.222	0.221
21	0.046	0.093	0.132	0.160	0.181	0.195	0.204	0.210	0.213	0.214	0.213
22	0.039	0.084	0.122	0.151	0.172	0.186	0.196	0.202	0.205	0.206	0.205
23	0.034	0.076	0.113	0.142	0.163	0.178	0.188	0.194	0.197	0.198	0.198
24	0.029	0.069	0.105	0.134	0.155	0.170	0.180	0.186	0.190	0.191	0.191
25	0.025	0.062	0.098	0.126	0.147	0.162	0.173	0.179	0.183	0.185	0.185
26	0.021	0.056	0.091	0.119	0.140	0.155	0.166	0.173	0.177	0.178	0.178
27	0.018	0.051	0.085	0.112	0.133	0.149	0.159	0.166	0.170	0.172	0.173
28	0.016	0.046	0.079	0.106	0.127	0.142	0.153	0.160	0.165	0.167	0.167
29	0.014	0.042	0.073	0.100	0.121	0.136	0.147	0.155	0.159	0.161	0.161
30	0.012	0.038	0.068	0.095	0.115	0.131	0.142	0.149	0.153	0.156	0.156

Table C.39: Probability of a Put Expiring in the Money
as a Function of Time and Volatility
Stock Price = $100
Strike Price = $110
Annual Growth Rate = 20%

Mo	\multicolumn{11}{c}{Volatility}										
	0.15	0.20	0.25	0.30	0.35	0.40	0.45	0.50	0.55	0.60	0.65
1	0.953	0.894	0.838	0.790	0.751	0.719	0.692	0.669	0.650	0.633	0.617
2	0.793	0.724	0.677	0.642	0.615	0.594	0.576	0.561	0.547	0.536	0.525
3	0.643	0.600	0.571	0.551	0.534	0.521	0.509	0.498	0.489	0.480	0.472
4	0.523	0.507	0.495	0.485	0.477	0.469	0.461	0.454	0.448	0.441	0.435
5	0.427	0.434	0.436	0.435	0.432	0.429	0.425	0.420	0.415	0.410	0.405
6	0.352	0.376	0.388	0.394	0.396	0.396	0.394	0.392	0.388	0.384	0.380
7	0.291	0.328	0.348	0.359	0.365	0.368	0.369	0.367	0.365	0.362	0.359
8	0.243	0.288	0.314	0.330	0.339	0.344	0.346	0.346	0.345	0.343	0.340
9	0.203	0.254	0.285	0.304	0.315	0.322	0.326	0.328	0.327	0.326	0.323
10	0.170	0.225	0.259	0.281	0.295	0.303	0.308	0.311	0.311	0.310	0.308
11	0.143	0.200	0.237	0.261	0.276	0.286	0.292	0.295	0.296	0.296	0.294
12	0.120	0.178	0.217	0.242	0.259	0.270	0.277	0.281	0.283	0.283	0.282
13	0.102	0.159	0.199	0.226	0.244	0.256	0.264	0.268	0.270	0.271	0.270
14	0.086	0.142	0.183	0.211	0.230	0.243	0.251	0.256	0.259	0.259	0.259
15	0.073	0.127	0.168	0.197	0.217	0.231	0.239	0.245	0.248	0.249	0.248
16	0.062	0.114	0.155	0.184	0.205	0.219	0.229	0.235	0.238	0.239	0.239
17	0.053	0.103	0.143	0.173	0.194	0.209	0.218	0.225	0.228	0.230	0.230
18	0.045	0.092	0.132	0.162	0.184	0.199	0.209	0.216	0.219	0.221	0.221
19	0.038	0.083	0.122	0.152	0.174	0.189	0.200	0.207	0.211	0.213	0.213
20	0.033	0.075	0.113	0.143	0.165	0.181	0.192	0.199	0.203	0.205	0.205
21	0.028	0.068	0.105	0.135	0.157	0.172	0.184	0.191	0.195	0.198	0.198
22	0.024	0.061	0.098	0.127	0.149	0.165	0.176	0.184	0.188	0.191	0.191
23	0.020	0.055	0.091	0.119	0.141	0.158	0.169	0.177	0.181	0.184	0.185
24	0.018	0.050	0.084	0.113	0.134	0.151	0.162	0.170	0.175	0.178	0.178
25	0.015	0.045	0.078	0.106	0.128	0.144	0.156	0.164	0.169	0.171	0.172
26	0.013	0.041	0.073	0.100	0.122	0.138	0.150	0.158	0.163	0.166	0.167
27	0.011	0.037	0.068	0.095	0.116	0.132	0.144	0.152	0.157	0.160	0.161
28	0.009	0.034	0.063	0.089	0.111	0.127	0.138	0.147	0.152	0.155	0.156
29	0.008	0.031	0.059	0.084	0.105	0.121	0.133	0.141	0.147	0.150	0.151
30	0.007	0.028	0.055	0.080	0.100	0.116	0.128	0.136	0.142	0.145	0.146

Table C.40: Probability of a Put Expiring in the Money
as a Function of Time and Volatility
Stock Price = $100
Strike Price = $105
Annual Growth Rate = 20%

Mo	Volatility										
	0.15	0.20	0.25	0.30	0.35	0.40	0.45	0.50	0.55	0.60	0.65
1	0.727	0.670	0.633	0.606	0.586	0.570	0.557	0.546	0.536	0.528	0.520
2	0.523	0.510	0.501	0.493	0.487	0.481	0.475	0.470	0.465	0.460	0.455
3	0.400	0.416	0.424	0.427	0.429	0.428	0.427	0.425	0.422	0.419	0.416
4	0.315	0.350	0.369	0.380	0.386	0.390	0.391	0.391	0.390	0.389	0.386
5	0.254	0.300	0.326	0.343	0.353	0.360	0.363	0.365	0.365	0.364	0.363
6	0.206	0.259	0.292	0.312	0.326	0.334	0.339	0.342	0.343	0.343	0.342
7	0.170	0.227	0.263	0.287	0.302	0.312	0.319	0.323	0.325	0.325	0.324
8	0.140	0.199	0.238	0.264	0.281	0.293	0.301	0.305	0.308	0.309	0.309
9	0.117	0.176	0.217	0.244	0.263	0.276	0.284	0.290	0.293	0.294	0.294
10	0.098	0.156	0.198	0.227	0.247	0.260	0.270	0.276	0.279	0.281	0.281
11	0.082	0.139	0.181	0.211	0.232	0.246	0.256	0.263	0.267	0.269	0.269
12	0.069	0.124	0.166	0.197	0.218	0.233	0.244	0.251	0.255	0.257	0.258
13	0.058	0.111	0.153	0.184	0.206	0.221	0.232	0.240	0.244	0.247	0.247
14	0.049	0.099	0.141	0.172	0.194	0.210	0.222	0.229	0.234	0.237	0.238
15	0.042	0.089	0.130	0.161	0.184	0.200	0.212	0.220	0.225	0.227	0.229
16	0.035	0.080	0.120	0.151	0.174	0.191	0.202	0.211	0.216	0.219	0.220
17	0.030	0.072	0.111	0.142	0.165	0.182	0.194	0.202	0.207	0.211	0.212
18	0.026	0.065	0.102	0.133	0.156	0.173	0.185	0.194	0.200	0.203	0.204
19	0.022	0.058	0.095	0.125	0.148	0.165	0.178	0.186	0.192	0.195	0.197
20	0.019	0.053	0.088	0.118	0.141	0.158	0.170	0.179	0.185	0.188	0.190
21	0.016	0.048	0.082	0.111	0.134	0.151	0.164	0.172	0.178	0.182	0.183
22	0.014	0.043	0.076	0.104	0.127	0.144	0.157	0.166	0.172	0.175	0.177
23	0.012	0.039	0.071	0.099	0.121	0.138	0.151	0.160	0.166	0.169	0.171
24	0.010	0.035	0.066	0.093	0.115	0.132	0.145	0.154	0.160	0.164	0.165
25	0.009	0.032	0.061	0.088	0.110	0.127	0.139	0.148	0.154	0.158	0.160
26	0.007	0.029	0.057	0.083	0.104	0.121	0.134	0.143	0.149	0.153	0.155
27	0.006	0.026	0.053	0.078	0.100	0.116	0.129	0.138	0.144	0.148	0.150
28	0.005	0.024	0.049	0.074	0.095	0.111	0.124	0.133	0.139	0.143	0.145
29	0.005	0.022	0.046	0.070	0.091	0.107	0.119	0.128	0.134	0.138	0.140
30	0.004	0.020	0.043	0.066	0.086	0.103	0.115	0.124	0.130	0.134	0.136

Table C.41: Probability of a Put Expiring in the Money
as a Function of Time and Volatility
Stock Price = $100
Strike Price = $100
Annual Growth Rate = 20%

Mo	Volatility										
	0.15	0.20	0.25	0.30	0.35	0.40	0.45	0.50	0.55	0.60	0.65
1	0.301	0.343	0.368	0.385	0.396	0.403	0.408	0.412	0.415	0.416	0.417
2	0.230	0.284	0.317	0.339	0.354	0.364	0.372	0.377	0.380	0.382	0.384
3	0.183	0.242	0.280	0.306	0.323	0.335	0.344	0.350	0.354	0.357	0.358
4	0.148	0.209	0.251	0.279	0.298	0.312	0.322	0.328	0.333	0.336	0.338
5	0.122	0.183	0.226	0.256	0.277	0.292	0.302	0.310	0.315	0.318	0.320
6	0.100	0.161	0.205	0.236	0.258	0.274	0.285	0.293	0.299	0.302	0.304
7	0.084	0.142	0.187	0.219	0.242	0.258	0.270	0.278	0.284	0.288	0.290
8	0.070	0.126	0.171	0.203	0.227	0.244	0.256	0.265	0.271	0.275	0.277
9	0.059	0.113	0.156	0.189	0.213	0.231	0.243	0.252	0.259	0.263	0.265
10	0.049	0.101	0.144	0.177	0.201	0.219	0.232	0.241	0.247	0.252	0.254
11	0.042	0.090	0.132	0.165	0.190	0.208	0.221	0.231	0.237	0.241	0.244
12	0.035	0.081	0.122	0.155	0.179	0.198	0.211	0.221	0.227	0.232	0.234
13	0.030	0.073	0.113	0.145	0.170	0.188	0.202	0.211	0.218	0.223	0.225
14	0.025	0.065	0.104	0.136	0.161	0.179	0.193	0.203	0.210	0.214	0.217
15	0.022	0.059	0.096	0.128	0.152	0.171	0.185	0.195	0.202	0.206	0.209
16	0.018	0.053	0.089	0.120	0.145	0.163	0.177	0.187	0.194	0.199	0.201
17	0.016	0.048	0.083	0.113	0.137	0.156	0.170	0.180	0.187	0.191	0.194
18	0.013	0.043	0.077	0.107	0.130	0.149	0.163	0.173	0.180	0.185	0.187
19	0.011	0.039	0.071	0.100	0.124	0.142	0.156	0.166	0.173	0.178	0.181
20	0.010	0.035	0.066	0.095	0.118	0.136	0.150	0.160	0.167	0.172	0.175
21	0.008	0.032	0.062	0.089	0.112	0.130	0.144	0.154	0.161	0.166	0.169
22	0.007	0.029	0.057	0.084	0.107	0.125	0.139	0.149	0.156	0.160	0.163
23	0.006	0.026	0.053	0.080	0.102	0.120	0.133	0.143	0.150	0.155	0.158
24	0.005	0.024	0.050	0.075	0.097	0.115	0.128	0.138	0.145	0.150	0.153
25	0.005	0.022	0.046	0.071	0.093	0.110	0.123	0.133	0.140	0.145	0.148
26	0.004	0.020	0.043	0.067	0.088	0.105	0.119	0.129	0.136	0.140	0.143
27	0.003	0.018	0.040	0.064	0.084	0.101	0.114	0.124	0.131	0.136	0.138
28	0.003	0.016	0.038	0.060	0.080	0.097	0.110	0.120	0.127	0.131	0.134
29	0.002	0.015	0.035	0.057	0.077	0.093	0.106	0.116	0.123	0.127	0.130
30	0.002	0.013	0.033	0.054	0.073	0.089	0.102	0.112	0.119	0.123	0.126

Table C.42: Probability of a Put Expiring in the Money
as a Function of Time and Volatility
Stock Price = $100
Strike Price = $95
Annual Growth Rate = 20%

Mo	Volatility										
	0.15	0.20	0.25	0.30	0.35	0.40	0.45	0.50	0.55	0.60	0.65
1	0.044	0.098	0.148	0.188	0.220	0.245	0.265	0.282	0.295	0.306	0.315
2	0.058	0.115	0.164	0.202	0.232	0.254	0.272	0.286	0.297	0.305	0.312
3	0.056	0.113	0.160	0.198	0.226	0.248	0.265	0.278	0.288	0.295	0.301
4	0.051	0.105	0.152	0.189	0.217	0.238	0.254	0.267	0.277	0.284	0.289
5	0.045	0.097	0.142	0.178	0.206	0.227	0.244	0.256	0.265	0.272	0.278
6	0.039	0.088	0.133	0.168	0.196	0.217	0.233	0.245	0.254	0.261	0.266
7	0.034	0.080	0.123	0.159	0.186	0.207	0.223	0.235	0.244	0.251	0.256
8	0.029	0.073	0.115	0.149	0.176	0.197	0.213	0.225	0.234	0.241	0.246
9	0.025	0.066	0.106	0.141	0.167	0.188	0.204	0.216	0.225	0.232	0.236
10	0.021	0.059	0.099	0.132	0.159	0.180	0.196	0.207	0.216	0.223	0.227
11	0.018	0.054	0.092	0.125	0.151	0.172	0.187	0.199	0.208	0.214	0.219
12	0.016	0.049	0.085	0.117	0.144	0.164	0.180	0.191	0.200	0.206	0.211
13	0.014	0.044	0.079	0.111	0.136	0.157	0.172	0.184	0.193	0.199	0.203
14	0.012	0.040	0.074	0.104	0.130	0.150	0.165	0.177	0.186	0.192	0.196
15	0.010	0.036	0.069	0.099	0.124	0.143	0.159	0.170	0.179	0.185	0.189
16	0.009	0.033	0.064	0.093	0.118	0.137	0.153	0.164	0.173	0.179	0.183
17	0.007	0.030	0.059	0.088	0.112	0.131	0.147	0.158	0.166	0.172	0.176
18	0.006	0.027	0.055	0.083	0.107	0.126	0.141	0.152	0.161	0.167	0.170
19	0.005	0.025	0.052	0.079	0.102	0.121	0.135	0.147	0.155	0.161	0.165
20	0.005	0.022	0.048	0.074	0.097	0.116	0.130	0.142	0.150	0.156	0.159
21	0.004	0.020	0.045	0.070	0.093	0.111	0.125	0.136	0.145	0.150	0.154
22	0.003	0.019	0.042	0.066	0.088	0.106	0.121	0.132	0.140	0.145	0.149
23	0.003	0.017	0.039	0.063	0.084	0.102	0.116	0.127	0.135	0.141	0.144
24	0.003	0.015	0.037	0.060	0.080	0.098	0.112	0.123	0.131	0.136	0.140
25	0.002	0.014	0.034	0.056	0.077	0.094	0.108	0.118	0.126	0.132	0.135
26	0.002	0.013	0.032	0.053	0.073	0.090	0.104	0.114	0.122	0.128	0.131
27	0.002	0.012	0.030	0.051	0.070	0.087	0.100	0.111	0.118	0.124	0.127
28	0.001	0.011	0.028	0.048	0.067	0.083	0.097	0.107	0.114	0.120	0.123
29	0.001	0.010	0.026	0.045	0.064	0.080	0.093	0.103	0.111	0.116	0.119
30	0.001	0.009	0.024	0.043	0.061	0.077	0.090	0.100	0.107	0.112	0.116

Table C.43: Probability of a Put Expiring in the Money
as a Function of Time and Volatility
Stock Price = $100
Strike Price = $90
Annual Growth Rate = 20%

Mo	Volatility										
	0.15	0.20	0.25	0.30	0.35	0.40	0.45	0.50	0.55	0.60	0.65
1	0.002	0.013	0.036	0.066	0.095	0.123	0.149	0.170	0.190	0.206	0.220
2	0.007	0.031	0.066	0.101	0.133	0.161	0.184	0.203	0.219	0.233	0.244
3	0.010	0.040	0.077	0.113	0.144	0.171	0.192	0.210	0.225	0.236	0.246
4	0.012	0.043	0.080	0.116	0.147	0.172	0.192	0.209	0.223	0.233	0.242
5	0.012	0.043	0.080	0.115	0.145	0.169	0.189	0.205	0.218	0.228	0.236
6	0.012	0.041	0.078	0.112	0.141	0.165	0.184	0.200	0.212	0.222	0.229
7	0.011	0.039	0.075	0.108	0.137	0.160	0.179	0.194	0.206	0.215	0.222
8	0.010	0.037	0.071	0.104	0.132	0.155	0.173	0.188	0.199	0.208	0.215
9	0.009	0.034	0.067	0.099	0.127	0.149	0.167	0.181	0.192	0.201	0.208
10	0.008	0.032	0.064	0.095	0.121	0.144	0.161	0.175	0.186	0.194	0.201
11	0.007	0.029	0.060	0.090	0.116	0.138	0.155	0.169	0.180	0.188	0.194
12	0.006	0.027	0.056	0.086	0.111	0.133	0.150	0.163	0.174	0.182	0.188
13	0.005	0.025	0.053	0.081	0.107	0.128	0.144	0.158	0.168	0.176	0.181
14	0.005	0.023	0.050	0.077	0.102	0.123	0.139	0.152	0.162	0.170	0.175
15	0.004	0.021	0.047	0.073	0.098	0.118	0.134	0.147	0.157	0.164	0.170
16	0.004	0.019	0.044	0.070	0.093	0.113	0.129	0.142	0.152	0.159	0.164
17	0.003	0.017	0.041	0.066	0.089	0.109	0.125	0.137	0.147	0.154	0.159
18	0.003	0.016	0.038	0.063	0.085	0.105	0.120	0.132	0.142	0.149	0.154
19	0.002	0.015	0.036	0.060	0.082	0.100	0.116	0.128	0.137	0.144	0.149
20	0.002	0.013	0.034	0.057	0.078	0.097	0.112	0.124	0.133	0.139	0.144
21	0.002	0.012	0.031	0.054	0.075	0.093	0.108	0.119	0.128	0.135	0.140
22	0.002	0.011	0.029	0.051	0.071	0.089	0.104	0.115	0.124	0.131	0.135
23	0.001	0.010	0.028	0.048	0.068	0.086	0.100	0.112	0.120	0.127	0.131
24	0.001	0.009	0.026	0.046	0.065	0.083	0.097	0.108	0.116	0.123	0.127
25	0.001	0.009	0.024	0.044	0.063	0.079	0.093	0.104	0.113	0.119	0.123
26	0.001	0.008	0.023	0.041	0.060	0.076	0.090	0.101	0.109	0.115	0.120
27	0.001	0.007	0.021	0.039	0.057	0.073	0.087	0.098	0.106	0.112	0.116
28	0.001	0.007	0.020	0.037	0.055	0.071	0.084	0.094	0.102	0.108	0.112
29	0.001	0.006	0.019	0.035	0.053	0.068	0.081	0.091	0.099	0.105	0.109
30	0.000	0.005	0.018	0.034	0.050	0.065	0.078	0.088	0.096	0.102	0.106

Table C.44: Probability of a Put Expiring in the Money
as a Function of Time and Volatility
Stock Price = $100
Strike Price = $85
Annual Growth Rate = 20%

Mo	Volatility										
	0.15	0.20	0.25	0.30	0.35	0.40	0.45	0.50	0.55	0.60	0.65
1	0.000	0.001	0.005	0.015	0.031	0.049	0.069	0.089	0.108	0.125	0.141
2	0.000	0.005	0.019	0.041	0.065	0.090	0.113	0.133	0.152	0.168	0.182
3	0.001	0.010	0.030	0.056	0.083	0.108	0.131	0.150	0.167	0.182	0.194
4	0.002	0.013	0.036	0.064	0.091	0.116	0.138	0.157	0.173	0.186	0.197
5	0.002	0.015	0.039	0.067	0.095	0.119	0.141	0.159	0.173	0.186	0.196
6	0.002	0.016	0.041	0.069	0.096	0.120	0.140	0.158	0.172	0.184	0.193
7	0.003	0.016	0.041	0.069	0.095	0.119	0.139	0.155	0.169	0.180	0.189
8	0.003	0.016	0.040	0.068	0.094	0.117	0.136	0.152	0.165	0.176	0.185
9	0.002	0.016	0.039	0.066	0.092	0.114	0.133	0.149	0.161	0.172	0.180
10	0.002	0.015	0.038	0.064	0.089	0.111	0.130	0.145	0.157	0.167	0.175
11	0.002	0.014	0.036	0.062	0.086	0.108	0.126	0.141	0.153	0.162	0.170
12	0.002	0.013	0.035	0.060	0.083	0.104	0.122	0.137	0.148	0.158	0.165
13	0.002	0.013	0.033	0.057	0.081	0.101	0.118	0.133	0.144	0.153	0.160
14	0.002	0.012	0.031	0.055	0.078	0.098	0.115	0.129	0.140	0.148	0.155
15	0.001	0.011	0.030	0.052	0.075	0.094	0.111	0.125	0.136	0.144	0.151
16	0.001	0.010	0.028	0.050	0.072	0.091	0.108	0.121	0.131	0.140	0.146
17	0.001	0.009	0.027	0.048	0.069	0.088	0.104	0.117	0.128	0.136	0.142
18	0.001	0.009	0.025	0.046	0.066	0.085	0.101	0.113	0.124	0.131	0.137
19	0.001	0.008	0.024	0.044	0.064	0.082	0.097	0.110	0.120	0.128	0.133
20	0.001	0.007	0.022	0.042	0.061	0.079	0.094	0.106	0.116	0.124	0.129
21	0.001	0.007	0.021	0.040	0.059	0.076	0.091	0.103	0.113	0.120	0.125
22	0.001	0.006	0.020	0.038	0.056	0.073	0.088	0.100	0.109	0.116	0.122
23	0.001	0.006	0.019	0.036	0.054	0.071	0.085	0.097	0.106	0.113	0.118
24	0.000	0.005	0.018	0.034	0.052	0.068	0.082	0.094	0.103	0.110	0.115
25	0.000	0.005	0.017	0.033	0.050	0.066	0.079	0.091	0.100	0.106	0.111
26	0.000	0.004	0.016	0.031	0.048	0.063	0.077	0.088	0.097	0.103	0.108
27	0.000	0.004	0.015	0.030	0.046	0.061	0.074	0.085	0.094	0.100	0.105
28	0.000	0.004	0.014	0.028	0.044	0.059	0.072	0.082	0.091	0.097	0.102
29	0.000	0.003	0.013	0.027	0.042	0.057	0.069	0.080	0.088	0.094	0.099
30	0.000	0.003	0.012	0.026	0.041	0.055	0.067	0.077	0.085	0.092	0.096

Table C.45: Probability of a Put Expiring in the Money
as a Function of Time and Volatility
Stock Price = $100
Strike Price = $80
Annual Growth Rate = 20%

Mo	\multicolumn{11}{c}{Volatility}										
	0.15	0.20	0.25	0.30	0.35	0.40	0.45	0.50	0.55	0.60	0.65
1	0.000	0.000	0.000	0.002	0.007	0.015	0.026	0.039	0.052	0.067	0.081
2	0.000	0.000	0.004	0.013	0.026	0.043	0.061	0.080	0.097	0.113	0.128
3	0.000	0.002	0.009	0.023	0.041	0.062	0.082	0.101	0.118	0.133	0.147
4	0.000	0.003	0.013	0.030	0.051	0.073	0.093	0.112	0.128	0.143	0.155
5	0.000	0.004	0.016	0.035	0.057	0.079	0.099	0.117	0.133	0.147	0.159
6	0.000	0.005	0.018	0.038	0.060	0.082	0.102	0.120	0.135	0.148	0.159
7	0.000	0.006	0.020	0.040	0.062	0.084	0.103	0.121	0.135	0.148	0.158
8	0.000	0.006	0.020	0.041	0.063	0.084	0.103	0.120	0.134	0.146	0.156
9	0.001	0.006	0.021	0.041	0.063	0.084	0.102	0.119	0.132	0.144	0.153
10	0.001	0.006	0.021	0.041	0.062	0.083	0.101	0.117	0.130	0.141	0.150
11	0.001	0.006	0.020	0.040	0.061	0.081	0.099	0.114	0.127	0.138	0.146
12	0.000	0.006	0.020	0.039	0.060	0.080	0.097	0.112	0.124	0.135	0.143
13	0.000	0.006	0.019	0.038	0.058	0.078	0.095	0.109	0.121	0.131	0.139
14	0.000	0.005	0.019	0.037	0.057	0.076	0.092	0.107	0.118	0.128	0.135
15	0.000	0.005	0.018	0.036	0.055	0.074	0.090	0.104	0.115	0.125	0.132
16	0.000	0.005	0.017	0.035	0.053	0.072	0.087	0.101	0.112	0.121	0.128
17	0.000	0.005	0.016	0.033	0.052	0.069	0.085	0.098	0.109	0.118	0.125
18	0.000	0.004	0.016	0.032	0.050	0.067	0.083	0.096	0.106	0.115	0.121
19	0.000	0.004	0.015	0.031	0.048	0.065	0.080	0.093	0.103	0.112	0.118
20	0.000	0.004	0.014	0.029	0.047	0.063	0.078	0.090	0.100	0.108	0.115
21	0.000	0.004	0.013	0.028	0.045	0.061	0.075	0.088	0.098	0.105	0.111
22	0.000	0.003	0.013	0.027	0.043	0.059	0.073	0.085	0.095	0.102	0.108
23	0.000	0.003	0.012	0.026	0.042	0.057	0.071	0.083	0.092	0.100	0.105
24	0.000	0.003	0.011	0.025	0.040	0.055	0.069	0.080	0.089	0.097	0.102
25	0.000	0.003	0.011	0.024	0.039	0.053	0.067	0.078	0.087	0.094	0.100
26	0.000	0.002	0.010	0.023	0.037	0.052	0.064	0.075	0.084	0.091	0.097
27	0.000	0.002	0.010	0.022	0.036	0.050	0.062	0.073	0.082	0.089	0.094
28	0.000	0.002	0.009	0.021	0.034	0.048	0.060	0.071	0.080	0.086	0.091
29	0.000	0.002	0.009	0.020	0.033	0.046	0.059	0.069	0.077	0.084	0.089
30	0.000	0.002	0.008	0.019	0.032	0.045	0.057	0.067	0.075	0.082	0.086

INDEX